More than Real

More than Real

A History of the Imagination in South India

David Shulman

Harvard University Press
Cambridge, Massachusetts
London, England
2012

Printed in the United States of America

Library of Congress Cataloging-in-Publication Data

Shulman, David Dean, 1949–
More than real : a history of the imagination in south India / David Shulman.
p. cm.
Includes bibliographical references (p.) and index.
ISBN 978-0-674-05991-7 (alk. paper)
1. Imagination—History. 2. Culture diffusion—India—History. I. Title.
BF408.S4518 2012
153.30954—dc23 2011038131

For our grandchildren and gurus,
Nahar, Inbal, Laila, and Matan

Contents

Preface

You don't need to know anything about India to read this book. All the great civilizations, and probably all human societies, have known that human beings are capable of imagining; India merely cultivated this art, or faculty, more boldly than most. The Greeks, the Iranians, and the Chinese had their ways of speaking about this topic, as do we. My goal is to trace whatever is distinctive about the Indian (in particular south Indian) modes of conceptualizing and using the imagination, to see how they have changed over time, and to provide some trenchant and engaging examples. Comparativists may have something to work with; I hope South Asianists will find something unusual in the attempt to thematize imagination as one of the organizing principles, or problems, of the cultures involved; and a general reader, if such a person exists, might find here an introduction to Indian thought from a vantage point privileged over centuries by many South Asians themselves.

Like all other facets of the mind, the imagination must have a history. And like all histories, there are many ways to tell, or to construct, the story. To define, categorize, and analyze the modes of imaginative praxis in South Asian literature, art, and music would require a book the size of the subcontinent. It is, however, possible to say something, in a reasonably concise, essay-like form, about the relations between the theories and the praxis of the imagination in premodern India and about major, though at times implicit, models of mind, or cosmos, or self, in which the imagination plays a central part. I hope some among my students and colleagues will take up the themes where I have left off.

The book has two parts. Although I was trained in the classical languages of south India, especially Tamil and Telugu, the early chapters are devoted to Sanskrit theories and their inflections or reflections in practice, or, more to the point, to imaginative practices of poets and others as theorized discursively by Sanskrit thinkers and scholars. Notwithstanding modern biases and politically driven preconceptions, Sanskrit and the south Indian cultures are intimately interwoven from the beginning of historical time; there is no useful opposition to be drawn here, only a continuous cross-fertilization and a common range of expressive means and modes. There is, however, a specificity about south Indian history as a domain of study, and the main aim of this book is to shed light on a period in that history, roughly from the end of the fifteenth century through the eighteenth century, when new ideas about the imagination came to serve as indices of wider civilizational change—when, that is, the exercise of an active imagination came to be seen as perhaps the defining feature of the human being. Thus after the first, long section on the classical background to and evolution of the theory and praxis of the imagination, the second, more historical section focuses on south India in the centuries just mentioned. A conclusion looks briefly at more modern developments and offers a few comparative comments in the light of Greek, Islamic, and western European theories.

It remains a mystery to me that no one has tried to write a book on this theme before. Many surely would have done it better. My main regret is that for reasons of space I refrained from writing a section on the meaning of imaginative improvisation *(mano-dharma)* in classical Indian music. Perhaps there will be an opportunity to come back to this theme in a volume of essays I am preparing on Carnatic compositions.

Earlier versions of Chapters 4 and 9 were published in the *Journal of Indian Philosophy,* vol. 36 (2008), and *Diacritics,* vol. 38 (2008), respectively. Sections of Chapter 3 first appeared in a volume edited by H. L. Senaviratne, *The Anthropologist and the Native* (Florence: Editrice Fiorentina, 2009). Intimations of Chapter 8 can be found in *World without Walls: Being Human, Being Tamil,* ed. R. Cheran, Dalbir Singh, Chelva Kanaganayakam, and Sudharshan Durayappah (Toronto: TSAR, 2011). The Annamayya poems cited in Chapter 6 are reprinted with permission of Oxford University Press from *God on the Hill: Temple Poems from Tirupati,* trans. Velcheru Narayana Rao and David Shulman (New York, 2005). I am grateful to the editors for permission to reprint. I also thank the late Gwendolyne Lane, fine Sanskritist and a good friend, for permission to cite passages from her elegant translation of Bana's *Kādambarī* (New York: Garland Publishing, 1991).

A few close friends, colleagues, and mentors should be mentioned. Yohanan Grinshpon, expert in Yoga and Advaita, quietly insisted over years that I not give up on this volume, as I was sometimes tempted to do; he also commented incisively on several of the chapters. In January 2009 Jyotirmaya Sharma organized in Hyderabad, with astonishing skill and wisdom, together with the Einstein Forum from Potsdam, an elegant and stimulating conference on the political imagination (our thanks to Dr. Anji Reddi and to Professor Syed E. Hasnain, then Vice-Chancellor of the University of Hyderabad, for making this possible). Yaron Ezrahi's new book on the role of imagination in modern democracy helped shape my perspectives, which were also thoroughly molded and refocused by the seminars Yaron, Don Handelman, and I taught together at the Hebrew University, on Vico, Borges, and Dostoyevsky. Don provided crucial insights at several points as I was writing. Neville Symington responded with fascination and penetrating, magnanimous understanding to the story of Sīmantinī, discussed in Chapter 6. I owe him more than he may realize. Velcheru Narayana Rao, Wendy Doniger, Yigal Bronner, and Gary Tubb all nourished me and bore with me as I took time to write that I might better have spent learning from them. Eviatar Shulman taught me the little I know about Nagarjuna and Candrakirti and suggested a model of their metaphysical world that makes sense to me. T. Sashi Sekhar and K. Ramacandra Reddy created an idyllic space for me in the green and dusty village of Gollela Mamidada, where my mind cleared just enough for me to see how to finish this book. Most patient and generous of all, as usual, was Eileen.

More than Real

— I —

Theorizing Imagination

— 1 —

Mind-Born Worlds

1.1. Pūcalār Builds a Temple in His Mind

This book deals with notions of the imagination, and to some extent with imaginative praxis in literature, visual art, and music, as these developed in major cultures and languages of southern India in the late medieval period—from roughly the twelfth century onward, but with special emphasis on the fifteenth, sixteenth, and seventeenth centuries.[1] In these latter centuries in the south, we can observe a far-reaching thematizing of the imagination as a distinctive, largely autonomous human faculty, one of the defining features of the human as such. I will attempt to trace the evolution of this novel fascination with the imaginative aspect of the mind, to situate a culture-specific concept of imagination within a wider, emergent mental economy, and to outline the features proper to this concept in terms of its cultural and systemic dynamics. Since we have much earlier, indeed very ancient, notions of the imagination in classical Sanskrit sources, and in particular within the mature domain of poetics, we will need to study some of these materials before turning to the late medieval south Indian world. Certain basic issues carry over from classical philosophical formulations into the Tamil, Telugu, Malayalam, and Sanskrit sources that will provide our major focus. I will argue that the appearance of a strong concept of the personal imagination from the fifteenth century on is an index of major civilizational change. If this is so, then south India, on the verge of a "modern" revolution in sensibility, may share something with Renaissance Italy and with the slightly earlier extended moment of creative innovation in Seljuk Anatolia and pre-Timurid Iran.

Surprisingly little has been written about the imagination in South Asia, both ancient and modern.[2] But make no mistake: the topic is one of truly central importance to any understanding of the generative inner worlds of the subcontinent and to their development over time. This is true even before we can speak of a full-fledged articulation of imagination as an independent entity, distinct from other mental activities. Look at the following Tamil story, translated from Cekkiḻār's twelfth-century compendium of traditions about the sixty-three exemplary devotees of the god Śiva, the *Pĕriya Purāṇam:*

> I am about to tell you the story of Pūcalār of Ni<u>nr</u>avūr and his imaginative act [*ni<u>n</u>aivu*]—that same Pūcalār who wanted to raise up a shrine for the god who burned the three cities of his enemies [= Śiva] and, lacking all means, did indeed build a beautiful shrine in his mind [*ma<u>n</u>atti<u>n</u>āl*], knowing that working with his inner feeling [*uṇarvu*] would be best. Ni<u>nr</u>avūr is an ancient village situated in the great, wide Tŏṇṭai country, famous for its righteous way of life—a village where the Vedas radiate their goodness and where the blessings of flawless, upright Brahmins abound. One of them was this great man. All the thoughts flowing through his mind [*cintai tarum uṇarv' ā<u>n</u>av ĕllām*] were focused on the anklets of Lord Śiva. His love was constantly increasing; he nurtured it, and he was ever aware of all the facets and ways of the Veda, the source of all substantial truth. His greatest wish was to do something that would serve the worshipers of the god. Looking for a way to give to them, he had the idea of building a temple where the god with the Ganges in his hair could live. At first he wasn't worried about the fact that he had no wealth. He searched everywhere, painstakingly, for resources—and came up with absolutely nothing. This made him very sad. He didn't know what to do.
>
> Then he realized that he would have to build the shrine in his mind [*ni<u>n</u>aippu*]. He began to collect within his awareness [*cintaiyāl*] all the resources he would need, from the tiniest bits on up. Mentally he sought out carpenters and masons together with their tools and materials. On an auspicious day, he lovingly, attentively [*ātarittu*] laid the foundations according to the Āgamic rules. In his passion, he worked steadily, not even closing his eyes at night. From the upāna moulding above the plinth through the many layers and levels of the structure to the crowning śikhara tower, he gave it shape and precisely measured form in his mind; he worked thus for many days, until the whole edifice was complete as imagined [*niramp' iṭa ni<u>n</u>aivāl cĕytār*]. He put the finial in place and had everything

plastered white; he dug a well and a tank, built the subsidiary shrines and the outer wall and, having seen to all the necessary details, set a day for the ritual consecration of the temple to Śiva.

As that day came near, the king called Kāṭavar Komān was busy putting the finishing touches on the great stone temple he had built in Kacci [= Kāñcipuram] for Śiva, at vast expenditure. On the night before the image of the god (who could not be seen even by Viṣṇu) was to be installed in the new stone shrine, Śiva, adorned with fresh kŏṉṟai blossoms, appeared in the king's dream and said: "I'll be busy tomorrow. I have to enter into the magnificent temple that a certain Pūcal from Niṉṟavūr, a man who loves me, has thoughtfully built over many days. You'll have to postpone your ceremony to some later date."

That's what the god said to the king, so that all his devotees would know. When the mighty ruler woke up, he at once wanted to see the man who had performed this great act of service, and to pay his respects to him. So, deeply moved, he set off for Niṉṟavūr, which is bordered on all sides by verdant groves. When he arrived, he asked the locals where he could find the temple that the devotee Pūcal had put in place. "We know Pūcal, but he's built no temple," they said.

The king summoned all the Brahmins of the village. "Which one of you is Pūcal?" he asked. "He's another Brahmin living in this village," they said. The king, so talented with the spear, didn't want to have him summoned; instead, he went himself to the devotee's home. Seeing him, the king said, "So where is the temple you've built, the one everyone in the world is praising? I came because today is the day you're installing the Lord of the Cosmos there. That's what God himself told me. I came to see you and to worship you."

The Brahmin was utterly bewildered. "If our Lord has been so gracious as to consider me of some consequence, it must be because of the temple that, lacking any other means, I have built for him in my mind," he said. He told the whole story of how he had thought the temple into existence [*cintitt' ĕṭuttav āṟ' ĕṭuttuc cŏṉṉār*]. Hearing the story, the king was amazed. "How great are the devotees whose awareness is without flaw!" he said to himself as he fell to the ground, his fragrant garlands mixing in with the earth. Then, with his army, drums beating, he returned to his capital.

At the auspicious moment, Pūcal installed Śiva in the temple he had built in his mind. For many days he worshiped him there until, at last, he

> merged into the shadow cast by the golden anklets that dance in the Golden Hall [at Cidambaram]. We, too, praise the feet of gold of that Pūcalār who made a temple out of thought [*niṉaippiṉāl*], whose devotion never knew a gap.[3]

We need to look closely at the terms Cekkiḻār uses for Pūcalār's mental activities. In comparison with the lexicon of later, sixteenth-century authors, they look somewhat imprecise. Certainly, the temple comes into being in thought *(niṉaippu)* or, possibly, in an act of projection or visualization or imagination *(niṉaivu)* that is interior to the mind *(maṉam)*. The process involves disciplined and highly detailed *cintai*—"mentation," some act of mental creativity, here somewhat meditative in quality; but also, perhaps, "awareness" in a subtler and deeper sense once removed from what we would call intellection. I suggest this because of the presence of another term, *uṇarvu,* which appears in the very first verse: Pūcal knows that "working with his *uṇarvu* would be best." I have translated this, rather crudely, as "inner feeling." Normally, Tamil contrasts the kind of knowing connected to *uṇarvu*—an intuitive, full, direct, sensed, whole knowledge—with that connected to *aṟivu,* that is, external, object-oriented, discriminatory, discursive knowing. The basic contrast is familiar to us from other Indian languages as well, though the terms may vary (in Sanskrit we have two contrasting and complementary verbs, √*vid* and √*jñā,* with a similar semantic distribution). For Pūcal, *uṇarvu* seems to generate *cintai* ("All the thoughts flowing through his mind were focused on the anklets of Lord Śiva"). It is hard to translate the range delineated by these terms, but we seem to be dealing with thoughts that are textured with profound feeling, that are, as a result, nearly tactile, rich in bodily sensation, and thus conducive to the wider awareness and to the creative work of *cintai.* Let us note that this *cintai* is quite capable of sustaining highly detailed, concrete, focused images and of integrating them into a single complex entity, complete in all its parts. In this sense, Pūcal's *cintai* begins to approach what we would call "imagination."

And there is one more term of great interest in this short passage: Pūcal "lovingly, attentively [*ātarittu*] laid the foundations" of his mental temple. The verb √*ātari,* derived from Sanskrit *ādara,* usually suggests desire, craving, or affection in Tamil; it is also common in contexts of worship. But, as we will see, *ādara* is bound up with the idea of paying attention, and something of this theme survives in the Tamil usage. The devotee creates his mental shrine by acts of attention, motivated by loving desire. Attention apparently has a part to play beside the intuitive acts of knowledge that produce awareness and, with it, a newly created entity, one obviously superior even to the massive external temple of stone that the Pallava king has built.

Indeed, whenever we find in our sources an element of visionary, meditative, or imaginative creativity, we will also encounter the question of reality. Which temple is the more enticing, the more demanding or compelling (for the god), and ultimately the more real? Later tellings of this story distinguish, in a classic Tamil mode, between the king's *puṟakkoyil* or "outer" temple and Pūcalār's *akakkoyil* or "inner" one.[4] The latter is explicitly said to be incomparably better than the former. This conclusion may not always hold, and we should be careful when we formulate a question like the one above, privileging one reality over another, but in the present case there seems to be no doubt about the god's preference for the mental shrine lovingly and carefully erected. The contrast is particularly striking because the king's stone temple is the famous Kailāsanātha shrine in Kāñcipuram, one of the masterpieces of Indian architecture.

Pūcalar's achievement is, in a sense, nothing new. Ancient Vedic literature is replete with examples of ritual performance that takes place on parallel and complementary tracks—one entirely externalized (the domain of articulate speech, *vāc*), the other held silently in the mind.[5] We will return to this distinction. The Brahmin priest in the Vedic sacrifical cult sits silently *thinking* the entire ritual in his mind, also repairing—mentally—anything that might go wrong in it, while other priests are performing the visible, concrete tasks of pouring the oblations, chanting the mantras, and so on. This Brahmin priest is a pivotal and necessary figure in the system, in many ways much more crucial to the success of the ritual than his colleagues who act in the tangible world of "things"; one could also draw a line from the silent, thought-absorbed ritual performer to the first prototypes of the renouncers who have—as we often say—"internalized" the actual performance and thus cut themselves free from the need to enact it in any external, object-oriented way. Unfortunately, we don't usually try to understand what a word such as "internalization" might really mean in this context, that is, what mental operations and linguistic processes are required of such a person, how they relate to one another and to the implicit model of mind that has generated them, and to what effect (or in what domain or domains) they are brought to fruition.

Such issues, never adequately analyzed in the literature on Vedic religion, live on in all South Asian systems of thought, right up to the present day. In classical India, particularly in the philosophical schools focused on grammar, it is speech that bridges the apparent gap between an inner, visionary creativity, such as Pūcalār's, and the object-ridden world outside: imaginative praxis begins in very subtle levels of language. To say anything at all requires the activation of an intralinguistic force—*bhāvanā*—that conduces toward creation, including externalized and objectified realities informed by an imaginative component that gives them shape and texture. In the coming chapters we will study these notions as well as the later hypertrophy of both narrative and discursive works on the imagination that build upon, and transcend, the classical texts. In all cases we will be interested in implicit models of the mind and the cultural intuitions such models always presume.

As we proceed, let us remember Pūcalār's emblematic example: in medieval south India it is clearly possible, axiomatically, to think a monument into existence and even to impart an existential priority to this entirely imagined entity, whose reality and beauty even a god must honor (as, a fortiori, must we). I hope to show how this is possible—how such an eventuality is not only likely but even, in a sense, normative—given certain primary cultural understandings that are amenable to analytical formulation, and I hope to trace the surprising evolution of these intuitions over time. But let us first look at two further examples of mind-born creations, the first taken from the Vedic ritual texts (c. seventh century BC).

1.2. Thirty-six Thousand Fires

> In the beginning, all of this was, as it were, neither unreal nor real. It was in the beginning as if real, yet unreal. What there was, was mind. That is why the Vedic poet has said, "There was nothing unreal in the beginning and, at that time, nothing real" (Ṛgveda 10.129.1). For the mind [*manas*] is neither real nor unreal.
>
> Once this mind was generated, it wanted to become more visible—more articulated, more embodied. It sought a body-self [*ātman*]. It heated itself; it embodied itself. It saw 36,000 Arka fires of its own body-self—made of mind, piled up by the mind. They were kindled by the mind and put in place by the mind. The cups [of offering] were drawn by the mind; they sang praises in the mind and recited in the mind. Indeed, all the

> rituals performed in the sacrifice, all that are linked to the rite, all this was performed in and by the mind, on what was mind-made and mind-gathered, and consisted only of mind.
>
> Whatever these living beings imagine in their minds is performed: they kindle them, they assemble them, they fill the cups in them, they praise in them and recite in them. Such is the power of the mind, such is creation, such is the mind. The 36,000 Arka fires: each one of them is this much, as much as the one before.[6]

A text such as this forces the translator to make hard choices every step of the way. Was the beginning [*agre*] truly a beginning? *Agre* means simply "before." "Real" and "unreal" are possible equivalents to the Vedic *sat* and *asat,* respectively—that is, defined, visible forms, on the one hand, and the potential, still undefined level of being, on the other.[7] Usually these terms are translated, as in most versions of the Vedic hymn cited here, as "existing" and "nonexisting." I don't think my choice requires a long explication, but it is worth noting that the question of reality—as distinguished from truth—comes up naturally whenever the mind, and the imaginative faculty in particular, is discussed. Our text tells us emphatically: "Mind is neither real nor unreal." We will be returning to this theme.

The mind apparently has to be created or "generated" *(sṛṣṭa),* literally "emitted" or "externalized"; the predefined state of its existence was somehow an internal one, if the internal can exist before an external boundary comes into being. The mind has to be created in at least two stages, though in another sense it preexists its own creation. Indeed, creation ex nihilo is almost never an option in Indian metaphysical texts. Thus the mind is waiting, as it were, to be fashioned and formed, or perhaps discovered, such discovery being classed as the second stage of creation—a matter of becoming more clearly articulated *(niruktatara),* literally "spoken out," and also more "embodied" or "substantial" *(mūrtatara).*[8] The latter term is derived from the root √*mūrch,* "to thicken, crystallize, become solid." Mind, like all other generated forces or evolving beings mentioned in this text, arrives with a built-in teleology, a wish to become more solid, visible, defined.

For this purpose it requires an *ātman,* the most elusive and necessary of entities, and the least translatable. Certainly the mind, like Speech, Breath, Eye, Ear, and Action (all appearing in this sequence following the creation of mind and all holding to the same trajectory), needs to be embodied.

And as is the case for all these subsequent entities, substantial embodiment means for the mind a vision of 36,000 fires made up of the substratum of its own body-self. Why 36,000? One for each day in a life lived to the fullest possible extent, an ideal one hundred years. Each day thus has its own distinctive mental production or mental exercise or mode (*manovṛtti,* as the medieval commentator Sāyaṇa tells us). These fires, at work in and upon the great fire altar that is the true subject of the final books of the *Śatapatha Brāhmaṇa,* are mind-born, mind-assembled, entirely made up of mind.

Speech, Breath, and all the rest thus envisage, in turn, 36,000 fires that are consubstantial, so to speak, with the defined being who sees them and who is further defined—thickened, solidified—by this very act of seeing. Speech "speaks" 36,000 speech-made fires, Breath breathes breath-infused fires, and so on. Insofar as the mind is privileged in this series, it is as the first to be mentioned and thus the first in the emanations outward from that preexisting interior space, at once real and unreal. The mind is also the only one in the series to be qualified in terms of its somewhat ambiguous reality-status; as such, it seems to be equated to the initial "this," neither real nor unreal, that is existence itself, or the living cosmos seen as a whole. Such equations of an internal aspect of the person with some external correlate are common enough in the *Brāhmaṇa* sources.[9] Yet the assertion in this passage that mind and cosmos are similarly balanced on a fine, somewhat precarious existential point is far from trivial. The mind is clearly capable of yielding worlds no less tangible and crisply contoured than the one we normally inhabit or the ones we are capable of putting together, in externality, by ourselves.

What sort of worlds are we talking about? First and foremost, the complete, constructed cosmos of the Vedic altar of fire. Anyone who reads the descriptions (or, rather, the operating instructions) will see at once that the altar, painstakingly built up of 10,800 bricks of specified types, is a full-scale model of the cosmos in all its parts and pieces; the text also tells us clearly which layers of the altar are to be equated with which cosmic level, to say nothing of the large set of esoteric equivalences that identify the roles of individual bricks or implements. More specifically, the altar is an attempt to reassemble the fragmented and scattered pieces of Prajāpati, the Creator, and to breathe new life into this reintegrated whole within which the sacrificer himself can live and, if he also manages "to take the altar into himself" (*Śatapatha Brāhmaṇa* 7.4.11), achieve immortality.[10] It seems to me that at no stage in this astonishingly intricate business of world making is the ritualist engaged in what we would call symbolic activity. The completed altar is not symbolic of a cosmos; rather, it models the cosmos concretely and re-creates it in abstracted form, in all its details, as a practical instrument for self-creation, self-definition, and, ultimately, self-transcendence. If the model is to produce the desired result, however, the ritualist must invest it with precise knowledge of the vast grid of correspondences not just between its building blocks and their cosmic counterparts, but also between the outer spheres of existence and the inner plane of mind, breath, and sensory perception.[11] In other words, the ritualist has to think the model into active operation.

For our purposes, the main point lies just here: like Pūcalār and his temple, the Vedic sacrificer can build the monumental altar, brick by brick, solely in his mind. We are told that the bricks themselves are, from a certain perspective, made up of mind. The text also says that "whatever these living beings imagine in their minds is performed" *(tad yat kiṃ cemāni bhūtāni manasā saṅkalpayanti teṣām eva sā kṛtiḥ).* Is "imagination" the right word for the process described here? I have allowed myself some liberty in translating. The verb is *sam-√kalpaya,* which can mean "to conceive, to think, to construct [mentally, in some integrated manner], to intend, to determine." It can also mean "to imagine"—which is to say that imagining is, in some contexts, a process of using the mind to bring something together or to construct something that belongs initially to the world of thought. We will return to this term.[12] It is possible that in this passage the verb indicates little more than the somewhat technical exercise of relating the inner and outer planes on a one-to-one basis—a specialist's knowledge, like that of an engineer assembling a complex machine according to the instructions he has learned. We are, in any case, definitely not talking about flights of creative fancy or about the conjuring up of some hitherto undreamt-of reality. On the other hand, it is quite likely that, like the Vedic ritualist, each day of our lives we are busy imagining ourselves into some kind of mentally appointed reality, one built up of mind-born bricks.

Speech comes fast on the heels of mind in this text. We need to attend to this linkage, one we will encounter many times. Though mind appears first and seems capable, initially, of thinking and desiring before speech has entered into it, we should not take the temporal sequence too literally. Speech, like mind, exists *before* it appears in the cosmogony. Like mind, speech seeks a more articulated, more solid self and achieves this aim by heating itself *(tapas)*. Once heated, speech has the vision of 36,000 speech-driven fires. "All the rituals performed in the sacrifice, all that are linked to the rite, all this was performed in and by Speech on what was speech-made and speech-gathered, and consisted only of Speech." Mind emits Speech, which undergoes precisely the same progression through two stages that we have seen, but the resulting fiery vision coincides with the mental prototype; fire, it seems, is never external to the self-fashioned self, though it may be, as the text says toward its conclusion, more visible *(āviṣṭarāṃ)* than any act *(karman)* that generates it. In any case, in all likelihood these first two emergent entities in the cosmos, Mind and Speech, are in some sense mutually determined, pervading each other from the start, as we see in many other passages.

This intimate intertwining—mind fashioning language and language fashioning mind—is not without a sinister aspect. The cosmogony with which we began (*Śatapatha Brāhmaṇa* 10.5.3) is echoed and resumed in the passage that closes this long discussion of the fire altar (10.6.5); one might say that the metaphysical essay attempted in the passage translated above culminates in a further attempt to make sense of the ritual, including the building of the altar and the fire burning at its heart, before moving on to other topics:

> In the beginning there was nothing here. All this was covered with Death, with hunger—for hunger is Death. He made a mind for himself, thinking "Let me have a self-body." He was luminous with light, and from this radiation water was born. . . .
>
> He felt desire for a second body-self. With his mind he united with Speech—that is, Death united with hunger. The seed of that union became the year, for prior to that there was no year. He carried him and brought him out. No sooner was the child born than he opened his mouth to swallow him, and the child screamed "bhāṇ!"—and that scream became Speech. He thought, "If I kill him, I will have but little food. With that Speech, with that self, he brought forth all this—the Ṛc, the Yajus, the Sāman,[13] the meters and rituals, human beings and animals. And everything that he brought forth, he began to devour.[14]

The subtle ontic balance of real and unreal (neither real nor unreal) we saw earlier has been replaced by a definitive statement: in the beginning there was nothing, a nothing covered with Death, with hunger. How this hunger eventually generates a cosmos is then described step by step; we recognize the driving wish for an embodied self (actually, two such selves in this case). It is the second one that is of interest to us now, the one produced by mind and speech (the latter is a feminine noun in Sanskrit). Mind coupling with speech (that is, Death with hunger) creates time, which did not exist before. Time allows for a real birth—also for the terror of becoming prey to the still-hungry father who has just given life to the child. This terror generates the scream that is the point of origin of all human language and possibly of all language-infused acts of the mind.

In fact, time, born from a mind thinking and feeling through words, *is* the insatiable father continuously devouring, or about to devour, all of us. (In classical Sanskrit, "death" and "time" are denoted by a single word, *kāla*.) Death of the second order, so to speak, as close to us as our own body-selves, has been born, *as time*, out of first-order Death. But have we not, in effect, imagined time into existence by the mind's inevitable, irreversible mating with speech? Yes—hence time is real. On the other hand, an active imagination may well be our only useful defense against this predatory being whom we have fashioned from ourselves. The mind, in short, can imagine a world into being, complete in all its parts; it can also articulate the structure and components of that world in language. In the Vedic ritual system, such imaginings carry the hope of self-transcendence and immortality. But the authors of the *Brāhmaṇa* texts know very well that this movement into articulate thought and concrete image takes place on the very edge of existence and is largely fueled by the terror of nonexistence that inheres in every imagined being.

1.3. Kūṭiyāṭṭam: Thick Space

Now consider the following. A performance is beginning in the classical tradition known as Kūṭiyāṭṭam, the sole surviving form of living Sanskrit drama in India, with a continuous line of transmission of some thousand years (at least) in Kerala, on the south-west coast of the sub-continent. The huge *miḻāvu* drums have already embarked on their solemn rhythms, framing the moment, articulating a boundary. The solo actor enters the stage, dressed in the white pleated skirt and mirror-studded shirt of the Kūṭiyāṭṭam performer, with long, tasseled sash; he wears a heavy headdress, and his face is made up with bright greens and whites and black. A rectangular cloth serves as a minimal curtain, hiding him at first from the audience. He faces the drums, his back to the audience, and salutes them and the drummers *(abhivādyam).* Still hidden by the curtain, his body turned to the drums, he goes through a series of abstract hand and leg movements (*maṟayil kriyā*). No story, no text has yet emerged for enactment. The movements, ritually set, have initiated a process in which a whole world is to be created, peopled, and fixed in place; hence already at this early moment, before the curtain is removed, the actor "ties down" or binds what he has begun to unfold (*kĕṭṭi tiriyuka*) with a series of jumps.

He turns to face the audience, and the curtain disappears *(kaliyam vĕccu tiriyuka).* At first his eyes are covered by his two hands, lest they harm the audience with their power. He lets his hands fall: now we can see him as a whole person, a character about to assume his own nature and story. He recites and slowly enacts with hand gestures *(abhinaya)* the first lines of his text, a classical play. Kūṭiyāṭṭam is uncompromisingly deliberate in each moment of performance; it may take the actor some time to fully enact these few lines, the first taste of the character-to-be. In later nights, this character will present his *nirvahaṇam,* a long retrospective that explains how he arrived at the dramatic moment when we first see him. But tonight, the beginning, the few words of text will suffice. What remains is the set of movements and ritual actions called *nitya-kriyā,* "permanent rites." These will complete the character's "coming out" or emergence—the *puṟappāṭu*—into the reality that he himself must construct for himself, for the temple deity who will watch the performance, and for us.

This *puṟappāṭu,* which includes elements that look like pure dance and geometrically modeled movement, is the first set piece a Kūṭiyāṭṭam student learns and, almost invariably, the first he will be allowed to perform in public. It follows a standard, rather complicated sequence, which I will compress here into a brief and schematic description, concentrating on the main building blocks.[15] The performer enacts a complex series of hand and foot movements, jumping and leaping forward and backward as well as laterally in relation to the quarters of space and the figures or appurtenances that mark them—the drums, the Naṅṅyār female performer who sits to the left and marks time with the cymbals, the oil lamp with the triple wick at the front of the stage, and the "empty" direction to the right. Sometimes the progression through space is clockwise, at other times counterclockwise.[16] At every stage there is tying and binding; without it, it seems, the imagined universe will slip away. Each movement matters; each spatial coordinate has to be fixed in a precise choreography of gesture and rhythm. Five invocation verses *(akkitta)* are sung by the Naṅṅyār and danced by the actor, turning and advancing line by line to encompass all the directions of space. The verses address the gods Śiva and Pārvatī, the cosmic couple; in the middle of the series, the actor literally and painstakingly conjures them into presence by expressive gestures that depict them from head to foot *(keśâdipādam).* Once they are fully present, the divine couple mount the bull Nandin and embark on a tour of the entire cosmos, which has meanwhile come into full existence in the charmed space of the stage, made manifest to the mind's eye by each flexion of fingers or feet and stabilized by the recurrent acts of tying.

The final *akkitta* verses, sung in Śrīkanti rāga, acknowledge each of the eight lords of the cardinal directions—Indra, Agni, Yama, Nirṛti, Varuṇa, Vāyu, Vaiśravaṇa, and Śrīparameśvara [= Īśāna/Śiva]—as well as Brahmā the Creator, Lord Viṣṇu, his wife, Lakṣmī, his eagle, Garuḍa, his conch and discus, and the circle *(maṇḍala)* of minor goddesses *(kalā)* who make up the body of the great goddess. As Śliwczyńska says, "It is the recreation of the whole Universe symbolically represented by the *maṇḍala* with Brahman, the Creator residing in its centre that is the centre of the stage as well."[17] But, to be precise, there is actually nothing symbolic about this universe: it is a real, existentially solid, complete, three-dimensional, fully populated and autonomous world created through the actor's movements, piece by piece, and fixed in place for the benefit of everyone present in the theater. This world will last for the duration of the performance—usually several nights, sometimes as many as forty-one—and will be deconstructed at the end when the performer lifts the burning wicks of the oil lamp at the front of the stage and, after waving them as lustration, casts them onto the stage *(muṭiyakkitta).*

Once it is all in place, the actor dances in worship of the whole of the imaginary cosmos he has created: "the gods, celestial musicians, *yakṣa* spirits, perfected yogis and great sages in the heavenly world; the demons and serpents in the Nether World; the Brahmins, Warriors, Merchants, and Peasants, the domestic animals and wild beasts, the birds and other creatures in our world." He bows to all of them, "from Brahmā the Creator down to the smallest blade of grass and the ants."[18] All are present, and all are necessary. Then, in a final, very moving act of offering, the actor plucks invisible flowers from his mind and throws them into space for all the beings just mentioned. If you haven't seen it with your own eyes, you may find it hard to believe that an act performed in open space, in abstract, regularly patterned, pure dance *(nṛttam),* with a graceful attentiveness to the tiniest detail and without haste, can be endowed with such integrity and can evoke an invisible world of such profound tangibility.

The *puṟappāṭu* ends here, and the actor can exit the stage. If the performance takes place in the dance pavilion *(kūttambalam)* of a temple, he can now go into the shrine and ring the bell to catch the deity's attention (normally only Brahmins are allowed to do this; the Cākyar performer is a non-Brahmin temple servant).[19] A final act of tying *(muṭippu)* onstage, for good measure, closes the ritual sequence. From this point, the play will begin.

A version of the *puṟappāṭu,* structured along the lines described, is enacted each time a new character appears onstage. Each character requires an invisible universe in which he or she can live and act; these universes may be embedded in one another, or they may intersect with one another, or they may all collapse into the same imagined, tightly constructed cosmos (rather like the integral, imagined universes that exist, coexist, and interpenetrate in the ordinary operations of human minds). Sometimes the sequence is telescoped, but its main features—many of them evolved out of very ancient materials recorded in the classic textbook of dramaturgy, the *Nāṭya-śāstra*—are remarkably stable.[20] Moreover, the metaphysics of this imagined cosmos are entirely consonant with the elaborately imagined, hence concrete and convincing reality that the actors will proceed to generate from within their minds over many nights. They like to say that this form of theater rests on *manodharma*—the praxis of an imagination that is fully engaged, inexhaustibly creative, and at the same time perfectly mastered and controlled.

Like the temple erected in the mind, or the fire altar built through disciplined visionary stages, the Sanskrit theater of Kerala is staged in a dimension distinct from the plane of ordinary perception. The texts sometimes refer to the tradition as a *cākṣuṣa-yajña,* a rite aimed at the eye—but what (whose) eye do they mean? Not, I think, the outward-oriented organ that exhausts itself with visible objects. The Kūṭiyāṭṭam stage in performance is nearly bare; for many hours on end, the only prop is a little stool on which the actor sits or stands. The story that holds our attention is performed mostly in thin air, by severely semanticized gestures and, occasionally, with the aid of the verbal, recited text. Yet the ostensibly empty space of the stage teems with living creatures and the thick emotional textures of their experience, which lock into the spectator's imagination and generate—of this we can be sure—epistemic shifts in his or her awareness. We use terms such as "insight," "empathy," or "resonance" or the classical Sanskrit word *rasa,* "taste" (in a very unorthodox sense), to describe what happens to the fully engaged, educated spectator of Kūṭiyāṭṭam. I am not going to explore this matter further here beyond stating, again, the simple facts: the universe imagined into existence by the trained performer is capacious enough to hold spectators, actors, and drummers inside it, and to demand attention and other entirely pragmatic functions, over dozens of hours, for many nights and days, without lapsing into unreality or disjunction or falling into the black hole of something called "illusion." This universe inhabits an unconventional, nonlinear space-time continuum that, once brought into being and then kneaded, chiseled, woven together, and held in place by the movements of the *puṟappāṭu* dancer, survives intact until taken apart. At times it seems to go on expanding, forward and backward, in both space and time; at other moments, it seems to fold inward, creating startling superimpositions and nested internal realities. It is a world not of sharp contours and isolated, stable objects but of deeply interpenetrating and continuously evolving imaginations and their visionary artefacts. I have found from my own experience that in the course of watching a play spread out over more than two weeks, some three to five hours each night, the intervening hours of daytime "normalcy" seemed to exist only by virtue of the far more integral, intensified hours of performance. The latter were, to me, real in a sense quite different from that of my daytime reality. It might be possible to articulate that sense. I suggest we take this perhaps idiosyncratic experience seriously and try to understand it, along with the two case studies already set out, as the classical Indian theorists of mind and awareness tried to understand the imaginative and aesthetic events they had witnessed. Let us begin by following their lead.

1.4. *Bhāvanā:* A Grammar and Logic of Creation

All three of our initial samples offer us trenchant visions of imaginative praxis in relation to what we might call externalized, or objectified, creativity; as we have seen, a division of this sort has antecedents in early strata of the Vedic tradition. We should not, however, rush to conclude that a dichotomy of "inner" and "outer" is basic to all Indian notions of the imagination; it is already clearly the case that any simplistic divide between the "real" and the "imagined" has to be set aside from the outset. To anticipate a later argument: for many of our sources, it is imagination, much more than everyday objects, that is dependably linked to the real. We will attempt to map this linkage in detail in the coming chapters.

It is also important, on principle, to separate implicit, empirical understandings of the imagination as a process transpiring somewhere in the mind from fully worked-out theories of imaginative process within articulated models of an inner economy such as we find in all the major philosophical schools (and among the grammarians). On sound methodological grounds, I think, one could make a good case for privileging the former over the latter: quite possibly, the inductive extrapolation of theory, or metatheory, from living contexts of use will provide us with richer and deeper perspectives than anything the professional metaphysicians, working on the basis of similar shared intuitions, have produced. Nonetheless, we do need to examine some of the basic terms that crop up in the erudite tradition and to situate them within their particular philosophical systems and defined lines of argument. In particular, we will be interested in the prehistory of the crucial term *bhāvanā.* Let us begin with a highly reduced and selective overview of relatively early discussions in Sanskrit about mental processes or faculties that can be associated with what we are calling imaginative process.

Probably the most common terms are derived from the verb √*kḷp*—"to produce, make, effect, shape, fashion, intend, imagine." This root gives us the early term for the science of ritual, *kalpa*—"doing," "generating." We can put this association aside for now, but we have already seen that imagination may have a ritual side. From √*kḷp* classical Sanskrit derives *kalpanā* and *vikalpa;* both words suggest mentation or intellection generally as well as imaginative creation more specifically.[21] *Vikalpa* can thus mean simply "thinking" or "a thought or concept." But images that press themselves upon us while we dream are also *(vi)kalpita,* "thought up," "imagined."[22] Thinking conceptually often involves actual shapes or configurations, *ākṛti.* How real such figures are depends on one's axiological presuppositions. Artists, including musicians, also work through *kalpanā* or *vikalpa,* generating a visible or audible surface. A third derivative of the same root is *saṅkalpa,* "intention, "thought," "determination," "imagination." We will discuss *saṅkalpa* at some length below.[23]

It is not uncommon in Sanskrit philosophical discourse to find both *vikalpa* and *kalpanā* devalued as a form of untrue projection—"mere conceptualization," as in daydreaming—in relation to some deeper truth available through other, perhaps nonintellectual means. Thus in the austere

Advaita of Śaṅkara, *brahman,* ultimate reality, basically a form of intensified aliveness, is devoid of all intellection or imagination *(kalpanā);* we, however, precisely because of *kalpanā,* live with the false notion of a plurality of individual selves, *jīva.*[24] On the other hand, at times, and particularly in poetic or other literary contexts, *vikalpa* as sheer imaginative production tends to be differentiated from error-ridden mental events such as illusion, hallucination, visualization, and dreams, and also from magical tricks or conjuring; as we will have many occasions to observe, imaginative *vikalpa* or *kalpanā,* to some extent like artistic or theatrical productions, is sometimes strongly correlated to notions of true perception, and is by no means simply another instantiation of false or distorted cognition.[25] This point is of critical importance to our discussion, and we will return to it in several contexts. For now, precisely because the √*kḷp*-derived terms are so plentiful and expected, but also because the developmental sequence I want to explore mostly prefers the term *bhāvanā* for imaginative production, I am going to move on.

Bhāvanā is derived from the root √*bhū,* "to come into being," or its causative derivative √*bhāvaya,* "to bring something into being." *Bhāvanā* is, at its most literal, a causing something to be: generation, often in the sense of manifestation or bringing to the surface or configuring (reconfiguring) a form. It is striking that for the Mīmāṃsaka ritualists, the Nyāya-Vaiśeṣika logicians and epistemologists, and the grammarians, this particular kind of generativity transpires in the mind and not, initially, in some external domain. It is not necessarily a mode of imagining—though in later usages that is exactly what *bhāvanā* means—but the mental generation of such things as memory, meaning and, eventually, certain objects does have an imaginative aspect, not always isolated as such. In other words, the trajectory that takes us from the *bhāvanā* of the logicians and the linguists to the *bhāvanā* of the sixteenth-century south Indian poets does make sense. Without going into technical detail, I will say a little more about this crucial term.

For the logicians, *bhāvanā* is an *ātma-guṇa,* an inherent feature of the self, intimately linked with memory, on the one hand, and with particular forms of attention, on the other. One might say that within the model of the mind that the Nyāya logicians developed—by far the most elaborate and subtle of any such model from ancient India—*bhāvanā* functions as the causal ground for vivid perception, including, in particular, perceptions from the past that leave a mark *(saṃskāra)* and are then buried in the mind. For the great medieval logicians such as Śrīdhara, Udayana, and Śrīvallabha,[26] who extended the classical Nyāya system in sometimes radical ways, *bhāvanā* has the uncanny ability to retrieve such earlier perceptions and to make them immediate, so that they fall into the category of *pratyakṣa,* direct seeing—a far more reliable and powerful mode than reconstructed memory.[27] Through *bhāvanā,* we can see the actual, original object again, replete with color, texture, and contours. I cannot go into the subtleties of these discussions here, but what can be said in a general way is that this odd gift of the mind has both an imaginative component, the "bringing into being" of a lost or hidden original, and a crucial element of attentiveness *(ādara)* and/or recognition *(pratyabhijñāna).* Indeed, we might say that attention and imagination are variants of the same mental process, sometimes working in contrastive, at other times in synergetic ways. Or, as Gary Tubb has suggested in relation to the logicians' *bhāvanā,* imagination is really, within the terms of this discussion, a form of focused attention that brings something into being by seeing it, or seeing it as X.[28] We will return to this theme in Chapter 5.

For the grammarians, and to a large extent for the Mīmāṃsaka ritualists whose views are closely linked with the grammarians', *bhāvanā* is an intralinguistic process *(vyāpāra)* critical for all speech (and not only human speech—gods, snakes, and other beings also communicate through a faculty, *bhāvanā* or *pratibhā,* that has an imaginative element, as we will see). This language-based aspect of "generativity" provides the primary semantic coherence without which speech has no intelligible content. "All other word- or morpheme-meanings serve, directly or indirectly, to qualify this element."[29] There are highly penetrating discussions about the precise locus of this *bhāvanā*—in the verbal root (thus the grammarians) or the verbal suffix (thus the ritualists), but what can be said, for our purposes, is that in both these schools language requires the activation of an imaginative faculty in the mind, and that such an activation always has an integrative force.[30] Here is a minimalist and lucid articulation of this position: "Thus the meaning of a verb may be defined as *a conceptually constructed unity of a total action in which subordinate moments of subsidiary actions coming one after another are imaginatively collected together in the constructed totality.*"[31]

Late medieval grammarians such as Kauṇḍa Bhaṭṭa took the analysis of *bhāvanā* much further, focusing on its relation to the various domains of potentiality that infuse any utterance. *Bhāvanā,* they tell us, does the work of bringing the actual verbal object into a coherent relation with its potential for being that object, and it has to bring the agent into relation with his or her agency, thereby turning the potential action inhering in the verb into the act itself. *Bhāvanā* also weaves a dense connectivity between all these separate strands, linking the agent with the object of his or her action and the activity, in the course of its actualization, with both agent and object. More generally, *bhāvanā* could be said to constitute the principle of connectivity itself, especially insofar as it turns potentiality into real performance. We should remind ourselves that we are speaking about a quality or faculty that operates in the mind every time we think a thought or give voice to that thought.

A sentence always brings something into being, perhaps first in the mind and then, if the creative process continues, in other aspects or on other levels of reality as well. But here a question inevitably arises. If we insist that *bhāvanā,* the active, integrative business of creation, resides inside the verb, either in the root or in the final morpheme, are we then describing a linguistic *representation* of creative process or, in some definable sense, the process itself? Although ostensibly the former should be the case, there are good reasons to believe that the latter is more correct. The imaginative integration of potential action into an effective totality is a performative and pragmatic process, not a representational one. Even after Austin, we may find it somehow counterintuitive to claim that what seem to be purely linguistic entities can be so rich with effective causal power, but the Indian grammarians and ritualists had no difficulty imagining that an imaginative act or set of acts unfolding within the sonar, grammaticalized stuff of speech or thought could generate real effects—could bring something into being that had not before been there in that form. Driven by its own internal mechanisms, which are strongly correlated to conceptual processes unfolding within our awareness—not always a conscious awareness, by the way—language habitually generates realities of varying intensities and existential urgency; *bhāvanā* is intrinsic to any such evolution into form. More specifically, the movement from the potential to the actual normally requires an imaginative leap.

The most radical and systematic attempt to theorize the creative capacities of language was that of Bhartṛhari in the fifth century AD; for Bhartṛhari, *śabda,* "sound," that is, language at its most fundamental and comprehensive, is coterminous with the world. This great "non-dualist of sound" *(śabdâdvaita)* had his own way of defining *bhāvanā,* "linguistic generativity," as a necessary, though possibly latent, component of awareness per se.[32] For later "pure" non-dualists such as Sureśvara, *bhāvanā* is equal to the *vāsanā* memory traces located in the internal reflection of awareness, *caitanyâbhāsa,* which generates worlds. Note that once again, but from a different vantage point, imagination and memory are intertwined in the subtle, creative core of awareness itself.[33] But "awareness" is a weighty word, much heavier, I think, than the inner state or process that it is often meant to evoke in both philosophical and pragmatic or everyday ritual contexts. Here a cautionary note, directly relevant to our main theme, may be in order.

By definition, "awareness" is the state of mind of most Hindu gods or goddesses. But the village goddess of south India normally inhabits an internal realm of somewhat sleepy, dreamy consciousness, from which she may temporarily be roused by calls for attention from the outside (from us, who need her). You can sometimes hear people say things like: "Why are you sitting there, lost in yourself, like the goddess?"[34] God or goddess may easily drift into an unfocused, floating attentiveness that is, in my view, akin to the contentless, object-free awareness that the philosophers call *cit:* "[full] consciousness."[35] What is the relation between such states and a discrete imaginative faculty embedded somewhere in the mind? This question provides one promising point of departure for our study. In the indeterminate, unbroken awareness of the deity, we may find, along with the obscure coagulations that ultimately produce knowledge of self and others, a strong vector of imaginative praxis—*bhāvanā,* the mind-born calling of a world, any world, into being.

Here is how we will proceed. Our aim is to understand the mature, radical theories of the imagination as they turn up in the literary and discursive south Indian texts of the fifteenth, sixteenth, and seventeenth centuries, in Telugu, Tamil, Malayalam, and Sanskrit. Every one of these texts carries traces of the whole history of the tradition and, more specifically, of earlier theories of *bhāvanā* and related terms. If we are to see the newness and boldness of the late medieval southern sources, we need to know something of the way Indian poets, poeticians, and metaphysicians thought about the imagination and formulated its primary features in the course of the millennium and a half preceding our period. We thus begin in Chapter 2 with a sample from classical Sanskrit literary texts in which the imagination is deliberately thematized; here we find important ideas that can be isolated and highlighted on the basis of careful reading. Far more systematic statements on the imagination appear, primarily, in two kinds of sources:

the theoretical works on poetics and aesthetics that were composed in Sanskrit, in the discipline known as *alaṅkāra-śāstra,* the "science of ornament"; and what could be described as metaphysical essays, sometimes narrative or liturgical in form, linked in one way or another to the practice and theory of Yoga and meditation and, later, to what we sometimes refer to as Tantric Yoga, with its strong linguistic foundations and its profound links to the feminine and the goddess. Chapters 3 and 4 deal extensively with the first series of texts; Chapter 5 addresses the second. Taken together, they provide, I think, an adequate basis for exploring the later, very rich south Indian materials.

One should not make the common mistake of setting up an opposition between these latter materials, in south Indian languages, and "Sanskrit" as a somehow separate, even alien domain. Let me reiterate what I have said at the outset: in no useful sense can Sanskrit be opposed to a south Indian cultural order defined, in some mythical essentialist way, as "Tamil" or "Telugu" or "Dravidian." The modern political mythologies that have concocted this opposition must be put aside; they bear no relation whatsoever to any historical reality. South Indians, like north Indians, expressed themselves in Sanskrit and in various local languages; the choice, often akin to a choice of register, was always, in itself, a meaningful one and can usually be unpacked or explained in terms of the particular expressive possibilities that each of the languages offered and of the kind of audience the author sought to reach. First-millennium literary and metaphysical materials in Sanskrit are naturally and inherently germane to a second-millennium renaissance, to use a big word, finding its voices in regional languages and, still, in Sanskrit.[36] We will also, of course, be interested in early formulations of imaginative acts by the first-millennium Tamil poets. In short, the following essay aims at an integrative, wide-ranging, and accessible analysis and at a natural historical sequence, in which classical materials, understood in their own terms, underlie and nourish the emergent novelty of the late medieval or early premodern moment of far-reaching systemic change.

— 2 —

Poets, Playwrights, Painters

2.1. Chariots Fashioned in the Mind

Imaginary gardens with real toads in them exist in profusion in the classical poetry of India, and, as we will see shortly, connoisseurs interested in poetic theory accepted the challenge of defining how and why the toads are real. The poets themselves were perhaps less interested in such questions. They knew, from the time of the *Rāmāyaṇa,* the so-called *ādi-kāvya*—the first great work of poetry—that the worlds they were singing into being were at least as real as any externalized and superficially accessible ones. The *Rāmāyaṇa,* and all subsequent works of sustained poetic enterprise, *kāvya,* quite deliberately put in place an intensified, visionary world not subject to the normal constraints of time and space and capable of displacing or replacing our everyday one.[1] Like the Vedic poet, the classical *kavi* author is first and foremost a visionary drawing on resources lying latent in his mind.[2] As such, he enjoys a remarkable freedom, which at times he shares deliberately with the heroes he describes.

Listen, for example, to how Kālidāsa (c. late fourth century) describes King Raghu, who finds himself faced with a practical problem of considerable complexity. He has just given away—quite literally—the entire earth and is left in possession of no more than an earthen pot. He is, as a result, a ruler only in name *(prabhu-śabda-śeṣa),* as the young Brahmin Kautsa, who has come to seek his help, says in polite despair.[3] Kautsa explains to King Raghu that he needs a huge amount of money, and fast; his guru, Varatantu, was so put out by Kautsa's persistent pestering him to name a suitable parting gift *(guru-dakṣiṇā)* at the conclusion of his studies that he said at last: "Fine. What I have taught you is worth 140,000,000 golden coins." On no account can one ignore such a demand from one's teacher.

The penniless student has come to Raghu in the hope that this great king would somehow come up with the cash needed to put the guru's mind at rest.

But where is Raghu going to lay hands on such a sum? His treasury is completely empty. Still, noblesse oblige: "Let no one say that someone who has reached the other shore of learning, who came to beg for money to pay his teacher, got nothing from Raghu and had to resort to some other donor" (5.24). So the king says optimistically to the student: "Wait here for two or three days. I'll try to find a way." His only real recourse is to overpower Kubera, the gods' wealthy banker, so he sets off in his chariot to the northeast, to Mount Kailāsa, where Kubera lives. He parks his chariot and goes to sleep in it for the night, while in his mind he is already imagining Kubera as his subordinate vassal (*sāmanta-sambhāvanayaiva dhīraḥ kailāsa-nātham tarasā jigīṣuḥ,* 5.28). In the morning Raghu is just about to set off for battle with Kubera when the officers in charge of his treasury report that there has been a sudden rain of gold coins straight into his storerooms. Kubera, terrified of the coming battle, has bought off his fierce opponent.

Note the term Kālidāsa has chosen: *sambhāvanā,* the imaginative, intentional act of calling something into existence. Raghu imagines Kubera as already conquered and subdued, and by daybreak this eventuality becomes tangible and real. Perhaps the imaginative act is not the only causal factor operating here—Kubera has his own reasons to be afraid—but neither is it trivial or irrelevant. Remember our skilled imaginer, Pūcalār Nāyaṉār. There are, it seems, certain channels or levels within reality that, when activated successfully in the attuned and focused mind, issue directly into the envisaged result. It may not always work; not every visionary model is actualized in the form and textures in which it is conceived (though most of the examples we find in our sources are tales of success in this active domain). When it does work, the effect is spectacular. Even from this simple example, we can see how eventually a full-fledged Yoga of the imagination might become possible.

Since we are still at an early point in our probing of the classical tradition and its understanding of imaginative praxis, we should probably suspend judgment about the technicalities and practicalities implied in a passage such as the one just cited. Precisely how it works is a question for analysis—and we will get nowhere if we try to explain the question away as wishful thinking, omnipotent fantasizing, and similar modern rationalizations.

Within the axiology of the worlds we are exploring, there is ample room for the notion that mental acts impact in multiple ways on our object-laden world. I'm not even sure that our own modern axiology cannot accommodate some such idea.

Here is another example from this same great work, the *Raghu-vaṃśa*. The exiled hero Rāma has returned to his capital, Ayodhyā, after slaying his enemy Rāvaṇa, the ten-headed demon king of Laṅkā. With Rāma is Rāvaṇa's brother Vibhīṣaṇa, who changed sides in the war and went over to his brother's foe; Vibhīṣaṇa has now been crowned king of Laṅkā. Arriving in Ayodhyā, this friendly demon is lavishly welcomed and soon seated, along with his retainers, in regal chariots that have been exquisitely crafted (by the royal artisans, no doubt) and that are "unequalled even by his [Vibhīṣaṇa's] own chariots that were imagined into existence" (*māyā-vikalpa-racitair api ye tadīyair na syandanais tulita-kṛtrima-bhakti-śobhāḥ,* 13.75). As a magically potent demon, Vibhīṣaṇa could produce elegant chariots—the latest models—simply by thinking of them (they are fashioned from *vikalpa,* thought/imagination). Interestingly, such imagined chariots are here seen as somehow natural, in straightforward opposition to the artificial *(kṛtrima)* vehicles that Ayodhyā's human craftsmen have produced. The artisans have done their work well—so well that their artistic creations excel the perfection of their imagined counterparts. Art can surpass what even a gifted imaginer can imagine. But again we see how swift and direct is the transition from imagination to a concrete reality—at least for beings, such as Vibhīṣaṇa, who are good at doing these things. Demons have a certain affinity with black magic and also, it appears, with mental production or objectification.[4] Perhaps it's a skill that can be cultivated by ordinary mortals as well.

2.2. Harṣadeva: What's in a Picture?

The question of the nature of artistic production and the transition from inner fantasy to living, embodied beings (or from the latter back to the former) figures regularly in classical Sanskrit drama. Indeed, I am tempted to say that it is one of the two or three great themes of the early plays, especially in Kālidāsa and Harṣadeva.[5] It is built into the very existence of the Nāyaka hero, who is invariably prone to an extreme romantic fantasy that is no less invariably punctured, deflated, mismanaged, and brought down to earth by his companion and alter ego, the Vidūṣaka clown. Very often the romantic projection takes the form of a painting, which rapidly takes on a life of its own.[6] Thus Duṣyanta, the amnesiac hero of the *Abhijñāna-śākuntala,* having recovered his memory too late—after failing to recognize his beloved Śakuntalā when she appeared before him—has drawn her picture, only to forget that it is but an image of the absent lover; when a bee approaches the figure's painted lips, the king threatens to punish it with imprisonment.[7] Duṣyanta is explicitly said to be mad, *unmatta;* his failure to distinguish artistic illusion from reality is one clear diagnostic sign.

I want to explore the complex articulation of this same theme in Harṣa's endlessly engaging play *Ratnâvalī* ("The Lady of the Jewel Necklace"—early seventh century). We will look carefully at the second act of this play, which revolves around just such a painted image (or set of images). Here is what you need to know to understand the somewhat intricate plot. King Udayana or Vatsa-rāja is married to Queen Vāsavadattā. In the past, this couple has experienced a passionate and melodramatic romance, replete with danger and adventure, the subject of another well-known play, the *Svapna-vāsavadattā* ("Vāsavadattā and Her Dream," ascribed to Bhāsa). But by now this youthful passion has settled into a less-than-comfortable groove. The king takes pleasure in irritating his queen; in fact, he rather smugly says that he will "make her face purple with anger" when she sees that he has succeeded, with the help of certain mantras taught to him by a wandering Yogi, in making a certain jasmine creeper bloom out of season (2.4). This achievement might sound lacking in significance, and not perhaps a ground for spousal rivalry, but we should note that the king thinks of the newly flowering vine as "quite definitely, another woman, as it were" (*nārīm ivânyāṃ dhruvam;* vines are feminine in Sanskrit). Moreover, for our purposes it is worth stressing that the very act of untimely flowering is itself a triumph of the mind over recalcitrant nature and quite possibly a project of the active imagination.

But the more critical background knowledge is the following. A ravishing young princess has fetched up at Udayana's court after being shipwrecked; her name, or nickname, is, appropriately, "Sea-Borne" (Sāgarikā). In actuality, Sea-Borne is the daughter of the king of Laṅkā, and for political reasons Udayana's minister and advisor, Yaughandharâyaṇa, has been plotting to get the king to marry her. When we first meet her, however, she has become simply another member of the queen's retinue, and while the queen is not aware of her true identity as a possible candidate for marriage to the king, she is still very intent on keeping the girl as far as possible out of sight and away from Udayana. Still, Sea-Borne has caught a glimpse of the king at the spring Festival of Desire and promptly fallen in love with him.

Throughout the second act of the play, which is meant to provide the conditions for the first meeting of the lovers and for Udayana's passionate response to this new romance, there is a phrase that keeps recurring: "Stop imagining things!" (or, at times, "Stop mis-imagining things"—*mânyathā sambhāvaya,* or *anyathā sambhāvini,* also *anyathā-śaṅkhini,* in the vocative). In the leisurely courtly setting, in the first flush of spring, there is ample room for cultivating one's fantasies, with the inevitable misprisions and contretemps that accompany such high-strung indulgence. As the act opens, we see Sea-Borne trying rather desperately to produce a painted likeness of the king on the basis of what she remembers from her fleeting, one-time glimpse of him. To make things worse, she is so distraught and frightened that her hand is totally unsteady. How close a likeness can it be? Still, she says to herself: "Since I have no other way of seeing this person, I'll draw him somehow or other, and then I'll stare at him."

It's quite important that no one—not Sea-Borne herself, any of the later spectators of the painting, the author of the play, nor the audience—is unduly disturbed by the question of verisimilitude. Apparently the painted image is recognizable not so much by virtue of how it is painted but mostly as a prop for projection, with a logical component: who else, after all, as various characters say to themselves when they first see the painting, can this image be? The possibilities are hardly endless. Susaṃgatā, Sea-Borne's friend who steals up on her from behind while the painting is still in progress, makes the natural deduction: "The royal goose will, of course, find delight in a lotus pond and nowhere else." She's quite happy with this match. Unfortunately, Sea-Borne's hope of finding some solace in the painted figure are quickly dashed; her eyes are so full of tears that she can't see it properly. But she does notice her friend's presence and quickly tries to hide the portrait in her sari. This doesn't work.

SUSAṂGATĀ: Whom have you painted here?

SEA-BORNE (embarrassed): It's the God of Love, since his festival has just begun, right?

SUSAṂGATĀ (smiling): Very clever. But this painting looks a little lonely to me. I'd like to draw in the Love God's wife, Rati, with your permission. (Taking the brush, she quickly draws a portrait of Sea-Borne.)

SEA-BORNE (studying the painting, indignant): Wait a minute. It's me you've painted!

SUSAṂGATĀ (laughing): Don't get angry for nothing. My picture of Rati looks at least as good as yours of the Love God. Stop imagining things. And stop fibbing, for that matter. Tell me the whole story.

Either these seventh-century Indian girls are outstanding draftswomen or it doesn't matter all that much whether their paintings match an external model. Each spectator within the play (but also the spectator outside it, in the audience) brings his or her perceptual world, internally structured and molded by context-dependent norms, to bear on each moment of scrutinizing the work of art. Sea-Borne is, however, still eager to keep her infatuation secret, and she swears her friend to silence. Susaṃgatā, for her part, knows it may not be so easy to hide the truth. For example, they have to deal with the particularly intelligent myna bird known as Medhāvinī, "Smart Aleck." Suppose the bird has overheard the two girls' conversation and decides to repeat it at some future, delicate moment. Sea-Borne panics at this new, previously unenvisioned possibility. Susaṃgata, to calm her and cool her down, goes off in search of a few lotus leaves and lotus stalks, the nearest available refrigerants. Left to her own devices, Sea-Borne sings a staccato verse: she can't stand the shame, the loss of control, or this asymmetrical passion; she'd really be better off dead.

We can be sure that the myna bird, once mentioned, will have her opportunity. A monkey escapes from the king's stables and wreaks havoc throughout the palace grounds. Among other things, he opens the myna's cage and lets the bird out. As if that weren't bad enough, the two girls have to rush off to hide from the monkey, leaving the painted portraits behind. Sea-Borne wants to go back to retrieve the canvas, but Susaṃgatā stops her—following the dangerously informed myna takes precedence. Enter the clown, Vasantaka, closely followed by the king.

Both are preoccupied initially with the great event of untimely blossoming and its uses. The king marvels at the "inconceivable" effectiveness of such devices as charmed jewels, herbs, and mantras. He thinks he now has empirical proof that they work; the clown has been sent ahead to check out the jasmine vine and is returning with a positive report. Their excitement at this scientific experiment is, however, interrupted by strange sounds coming from far above them, in the branches of a bakula tree. The clown, cowardly by definition, thinks the tree is haunted by a ghost; Udayana, listening to the gentle tone and the clear enunciation, rightly concludes that there's a talking myna bird in the tree. The clown is on the point of chasing the "bastard bird" away, when the king stops him: "No, you idiot! Let's listen to what the bird has to say." They listen intently, and the clown repeats, word for word, the myna's precise repetition of the conversation cited above, including Sea-Borne's despairing, suicidal verse.

It's not too hard a riddle to unravel; Udayana immediately figures out that somewhere there's a young woman in love who has painted her beloved and pretended that he's the Love God, and that this woman's friend has followed suit by painting her as if she were Rati. The clown is convinced by his friend's interpretation—how could he fail to be?—and is now eager to contribute something of his own to the decipherment of this decontextualized text, but when he hears Sea-Borne's verse, he wrongly concludes that the bird has started reciting verses of the Rig Veda. Indeed, for the utterly unromantic clown, a love poem might sound as arcane as a Vedic passage. But the king corrects him: "It's a song [*gāthā*] sung by a woman in the full bloom of her youth, who has given up on life because she can't attain the man she loves more than anything in the world." The clown responds with one of his (rare) piercing insights: "Why don't you talk straight? It's not just any man, but Your Highness that she wants. Who else could have been portrayed as the Love God himself?" Overjoyed at this deft compliment he has achieved, the clown laughs out loud and waves his arms, with the result that the bird flies away in fright.

One source of information has dried up; another is soon to be discovered. They enter into the pavilion made of banana stalks where Sea-Borne had been painting only minutes before. First they find the myna's cage, its door hanging open. Next they see the painted board or canvas. The clown studies it carefully and, very satisfied with himself, pronounces his judgment: "It's just what I told you. You're the one who's been painted here. Who else could have been portrayed as the Love God himself?" Now the king is excited and wants to see for himself, but the clown won't show him the picture without a little gift in recompense for his efforts; the king removes a golden bracelet from his arm, gives it to him, and eagerly snatches the board. He's not interested in his own portrait but is immediately smitten with the breath-taking beauty of the female image:

> When God created the incomparable
> full moon that is her face, the open lotus he sits on

must have closed its petals, so that he nearly
fell off. (2.10)

Brahmā, the Creator, sits on a lotus growing on a stalk emerging from the navel of Lord Viṣṇu. By poetic convention, lotuses fold their petals at moonrise. A pretty girl's face is like the full moon. Ergo . . .

By now the girls are back, having failed to recapture the errant myna bird. They're about to reclaim the painting in the banana-stalk pavilion when they notice that they're not alone. King and clown are still studying the portraits, and the king, obviously enamored by the charming verse he has just improvised, keeps reciting it over and over. It's clear at once to both girls that the myna has done its worst; now Sea-Borne is hanging between life and death, waiting to her what her beloved will say. Is she beautiful enough for him? Will he like her? It's time for another poem:

KING: It's really hard to say goodbye
to her two thighs; but still, after wandering
for quite a while in the vicinity
of her loins, there's rest to be found
around her waist, a little off balance,
no doubt, because of the three folds of flesh
on her belly. I'm talking, of course,
about my eyes that, still unappeased,
have now climbed up to the summit
of her high breasts, from where they can stare
with longing at *her*
tear-filled eyes. (2.11)

SUSAṂGATĀ, in a whisper: Hear that?

SEA-BORNE (giggling): You're the one who should be listening. It's all because of *your* talent for painting.

CLOWN: Sir, if women like her are so taken with your Royal Highness, you might take a moment to inspect the way she has drawn your royal self.

A good suggestion. The king looks still more closely at the painting and observes the marks left—he's quite certain—by the painter's tears, which make it look as if the painted man were pouring sweat in excitement at her touch. A further episode of forensic deductions and consequent lyrical effusions—the clown discovers the lotus leaves and stalks that Susaṃgatā had brought for Sea-Borne, along with a leaf that must have rested on her breasts—leads even Susaṃgatā to conclude that Udayana is so overpowered by nascent desire that he is losing his mind. She decides it's time for her to intervene, despite Sea-Borne's protests. As if intent on retrieving the painting, she enters the pavilion.

The clown is startled: he recognizes Susaṃgatā as one of the queen's servants and tells his friend to hide the painting at once in his clothes. Susaṃgatā is seated; the king wants to know how she knew where he was. "Your Highness," she answers, "I know not only that but also the whole story, including the painted board. I think I ought to let the queen know, too." This time it's the clown's turn to panic. In an aside to the king, he whispers: "Anything might happen [*sarvaṃ saṃbhāvyate*]. You'd better bribe this chatterbox." The king agrees and offers her an earring. She politely declines, as she doesn't need the earring, but she does have a favor to ask of the king: "My friend Sea-Borne is mad at me for painting her image on this board. Could Your Highness kindly calm her down?" The king rises, very agitated: "Where is she? Where is she?" "This way, sir," says Susaṃgatā, and the clown follows them, taking along the picture just in case it might turn out to be useful.

Sea-Borne, paralyzed by shyness and terror, is introduced to Udayana. The clown is the first to speak: "My guess is that the Creator himself must have been dumbstruck when he saw what he created." Udayana agrees, though he has a somewhat more elegant way of saying it.

> First His eyes grew wide, brighter than the petals
> of the lotus he sits on, then from all four of his mouths[8]
> there were cries of "Eureka!"
> and all four heads shook in amazement
> when the Creator made this woman,
> the most beautiful being in our world. (2.16)

Sea-Borne finds this a bit much and says peevishly to Susaṃgatā, "Nice picture you've retrieved, my friend." Then she stalks off.

The king is familiar with such moods. "Even though you seem to be put out, dear lady, the light in your eyes is not really so harsh. Don't walk too fast. The weight of your remarkable behind just might cause you to stumble." Urged on by Susaṃgatā, he takes her hand—a happy moment for him. But she's still mad, and the clown, in an inspired though inappropriate flash of understanding, speaks the truth: "Looks like Vāsavadattā is back." The queen, as we know, is famous for her bad temper.

But the clown's unwitting statement induces a general alarm. The king drops Sea-Borne's hand in unseemly haste. The two girls rush off to hide in the bushes. The clown clumsily tries to explain that he didn't mean that Vāsavadattā herself had arrived on the scene, but was only establishing a comparison between two somewhat irascible women. The king is furious—he had come so close!—and all of a sudden, in the kind of unsettling synchronicity that Harṣadeva loves, the queen does indeed turn up together with her maid. They're looking for the notorious flowering vine, and whom have they found but the love-stricken king and his clown?

"Hide the picture!" The king is thinking fast; the clown tucks the board under his arm. "So has the vine flowered?" asks Vāsavadattā. "We've been waiting for you, dear," replies the king. She takes a close look at his face, flushed with nervous excitement and arousal—and she knows. "I can see by your face that it has blossomed," she says. "Goodbye."

The clown is so happy at her promise to depart that he starts to dance, waving his arms wildly, with the result, of course, that the picture falls to the ground. The king shakes his finger at the clown; the latter says, "Don't be angry, sir. I'll take care of this." The queen and her maid are meanwhile studying the painting—and they identify the king and Sea-Borne without difficulty. The queen demands to know what's going on.

> CLOWN: Don't start imagining things, my lady. I had remarked to my friend about how difficult it is to draw a self-portrait, so he decided to show me his skill at painting.
>
> KING: That's what happened! Exactly what Vasantaka said.
>
> VĀSAVADATTĀ (pointing to the board): And this young woman who has been painted right next to you—was that Vastantaka showing off his skill?
>
> KING (smiling): Dear, stop imagining things. It's just some girl or other that I imagined in my mind and then painted. I've never seen her before.
>
> CLOWN: It's true, madam. I swear by my Brahmin thread that no one like this has ever been seen before.

The maid chimes in with a soothing remark: "You know, sometimes there really are such remarkable coincidences." The word she chooses, *ghuṇâkṣaram,* literally refers to letters accidentally traced by insects on wood or palm leaf. Such things happen; one doesn't have to posit strong intentionality in every instance. Maybe the picture just *happens* to look like Sea-Borne.

But the queen isn't taken in. "Don't you know," she asks her simple-minded maid *(ṛjuke),* "how Vasantaka always speaks in crooked ways [*vakra-bhaṇita*]?" She wants to go; her pride is very much at stake and, she tells her husband, she's gotten a headache from looking at those paintings. He grabs her sari, trying to hold her back, but she frees herself with determination and leaves him with one parting shot: "Don't get me wrong [*mânyathā sambhāvaya*]. My head is *really* killing me."

She leaves. The clown, intent on his friend's budding romance and perhaps not overly fond of the queen in the first place, is jubilant, but the king knows what lies in store. Vāsavadattā is very angry; he sets off in her wake in the hope of appeasing her. Sea-Borne and Susaṃgatā are mercilessly left behind.

Quite a lot of imagining is going on in this lighthearted, lyrical act. In fact, all the real work takes place in the characters' minds. Neither Sea-Borne nor Udayana knows the other yet; they are in the midst of falling in love with each other, adrift in fantasies that have as yet only the most tenuous link to anything in the concrete reality of their lives. Even the clown, usually the voice of some pointed, deflationary truth, is caught up in the unripe images forming in Udayana's imagination. But were this contrast between projection and retraction all there was to the dramatic action, we would hardly find it compelling. Something far more complex is being said or hinted at. Let us try to make some sense of it in relation to the one object of paramount importance here, the no doubt crudely painted board or canvas.

Let's assume that the images do somehow correspond with the two protagonists. They certainly function as if they do, and we might be prepared to grant the playwright this functional and pragmatic equation. No one seems to have any trouble identifying the painted images, least of all the queen. Shall we then take it as a dramatic convention that a painted portrait in a Sanskrit play will necessarily reflect the visible form it is meant to? That is one way to go. But then why are the principal characters being warned, over and over, to stop mis-imagining things?

Incidentally, it's unlikely that any audience ever saw the painted board. What they would have seen, if we follow the Sanskrit dramaturgical tradition, was an evocation of the painting in space, on the stage, by means of *abhinaya,* the language of hand or eye gestures performed by the actors. It is as if the actor were saying to the spectators with his or her hands, "Imagine now that someone has painted a picture that looks like X." The verses, however they were performed, would have supported and made sense of the grammar of gesture and movement, a sculpting in space that rendered the words of the text literally visible. We might then say that what the audience was called on to do was to imagine, together with the actors, the interactive imaginings of the main characters.[9] The real stage, so to speak, or the screen on which the plot is shown, is situated somewhere in the mind. How many active imaginations were involved at any given moment? At least as many as there were spectators and actors, in addition to those of the main characters. A hall of mirrors is a vastly diminished and impoverished metaphor for the thick theatrical space of a Sanskrit play.

But let us set this outer frame aside (it may, in any case, not be the outermost frame) and return to what the characters themselves have to show us. What about the false identities ascribed by Sea-Borne and Susaṃgatā to the images each has painted? These are ruses *(vyapadeśa),* no doubt about it. Does that make them utterly untrue? I doubt it. Remember that the setting is the spring festival of Manmatha, Desire, God of Desire. Manmatha has every right to be physically present on the stage; indeed, he pervades each moment in the play as a whole. Moreover, axiomatically, the two lovers must embody him and his consort Rati, respectively. There are various ways to state the situation. One could say that Udayana *is* Manmatha for the duration of the festival; or that he is turning into Manmatha; or that he is slowly moving toward a point of unusual self-congruence, the result of which is that he will fully embody Manmatha, at least temporarily;[10] or that Manmatha is superimposed upon him in the mode of the poeticians' figure known as *rūpaka,* a kind of metaphor; or that he is seen as Manmatha in a poetic flight of fancy *(utprekṣā);*[11] or that Udayana and Manmatha overlap in highly dynamic ways that leave areas of incongruence and nonhomologous residues; or that the painting itself, an artistic creation, establishes a nontrivial relation between these two, in spite of the apparent lack of isomorphism between their external forms. Similarly, of course, for Sea-Borne and Rati. Whichever of these options we may select—and more than one might be applicable—we are left with the "fact" that the painting, in some sense, works; that is, it is a true image of Udayana qua Manmatha, or vice versa. It surely represents, to some extent, the character portrayed, but direct representation is perhaps the least important semiotic role that applies.

If we had any residual doubt about the effectual power of imagination here, the queen's response would suffice to remove it. She recognizes Sea-Borne and her husband in the painted images, no question about that.

Precisely because the identification is relatively secure, she has good reason to be afraid of the animating fantasy behind it. It is not Sea-Borne herself whom the queen fears; it is her husband's heated imagination of her (and possibly even her husband's imagination of Sea-Borne's heated imagination of himself), and this whole complex of interweaving projections on the level of imaginative fantasy is exactly what the enacted text of the play reveals to us (or, to use the language of the Sanskrit poeticians, what the play brings into being), the true subject of the entire artistic endeavor. The subtleties of discrete imaginations that have locked into one another, along with the emotional complexities that arise as a result of these interactive fantasies, are what the play is about.

But if that is the case, might not the painted images on the board serve a function no less complex than—indeed analogous to—that of the crafted text of the drama?

We can go still more deeply into the question of what it is one sees in the painted form. Udayana's first proper glimpse of Sea-Borne focuses on the portrait he has stumbled on. He studies it, he is ravished by it, and he bursts into a poem—actually, a series of graceful verses. No one, he says, has ever been so beautiful. God himself must have been utterly shaken the moment he created her. Of course, she was created in certain familiar and patterned ways, with a face just like the full moon, like all other women's faces. But Sea-Borne is still a *unicum*. The king's eyes linger over her thighs, loins, breasts. They're all perfect, possibly better than perfect in the sense that his vision itself intensifies them. He sees not the technical lines of the drawing—they are there, they are no doubt necessary, they might even be true to life—but an infinitely enhanced reality that is processed through his imagination. We see this same enhanced image through his eyes and we hear it (or, once again, see it enacted in gesture) in his poem, another domain designed for this very purpose of deliberate intensification. Note the intentionality that must be part of this perceptual process.

The painting thus tantalizes and teases, but beyond this rudimentary playfulness it also reveals itself to be saturated with volatile mental contents and, even more important, with a particular claim on reality. Is this claim within the play on a par with the claim made by the play itself as a total imaginative production? This is a question we will have to defer for now. That this stage in the love drama should be built around a painting is, however, clearly no random choice. The queen's maid suggests randomness as a possible explanation, or as a possibly mitigating circumstance, for the very threatening emotional reality that has emerged from the mere presence of the painting—but her suggestion is brushed aside. No literate worms are relevant to this painful moment. There is a conscious, intentional aspect to the active imagination in conditions such as those enacted here. We can easily conceive of moments where the imagination is harnessed to apparently random (though at the same time partially patterned and regularly repeating) processes—but not here.[12] A particular range of meanings is evoked by the painted images for each of the characters, those who have produced them as well as those who merely study them. These meanings derive their power, indeed their reality, not from the marks and colors on the board but from the fantasies invested in those marks. They are, in short, real and rich in consequence *because* they are imagined.

Notice that Udayana knows very well that he can concoct an imaginary reality: "It's just some girl or other that I imagined in my mind and then painted." He says this in order to deflate the significance of the picture that has, quite properly, so enraged Vāsavadattā. Here the imagined is, as in our everyday way of speaking, the opposite of the real. The full force of Udayana's statement, however, and the sharp irony that it conveys to the audience derive from the fact that it belies everything that has gone before it—the erotic fantasies of both the protagonists, the props and triggers these fantasies require, the embarrassing revelations of the myna bird, the constant machinations and intrigues, the clown's bumbling but ultimately useful shenanigans, the synergies released by the choreography of the characters' interactions, the crisscrossing linguistic formulations of the only partly conscious contents of their minds, the poetic intervals that punctuate the developing plot. All of these, and more, feed directly into the active interplay of imaginations, including the immediate triangulation of intensely imagining characters, actors, and spectators (with the poet-author, the primary imaginer, hard at work within the triangle, in the fixed text that more and more looks like a rather abstract score for performance).

Other, closely related issues arise from the vantage point I am suggesting—such as the difficulty (stated by the clown) in delineating oneself, probably the imaginative task par excellence. On a certain level, a play such as the *Ratnâvalī* is an extended essay on this more or less impossible challenge, which inspires ongoing attempts by each of the main characters to achieve some relative sense of wholeness in relation to the others. One mechanism adapted to this end is a consistent experimentation with disguise and other externalities. In this respect, the high point is reached in Act 3. The king arrives at a rendezvous with Sea-Bourne, who is, for reasons of discretion, supposed to turn up dressed as the queen, but the queen learns of this plot and comes herself to the meeting. The king, assuming she is Sea-Borne in disguise, sings to her a series of verses of rather mixed quality,[13] until Vāsavadattā reveals herself: "Husband, I really *am* Sea-Borne, since you are so in love with her that you see everyone and everything as Sea-Borne." She once again stalks off in a huff. Meanwhile, Sea-Borne, in an attack of doubt and shame, tries to hang herself; the king and the jester rescue her, thinking they are saving the queen, since Sea-Borne is, after all, wearing the queen's clothes. When they discover the true identity of the would-be suicide, there is general rejoicing at her salvation, until Vāsavadattā, suddenly remorseful at her high-handed response just an hour before, returns and finds the lovers lost in each other. I leave it to the reader to imagine her response.

All of this is vintage Harṣadeva. The external guises—but they are not, perhaps, entirely external—generate a complex series of stratified perceptions, much like the device of the *garbhâṅka* or play within a play (such as Harṣa produces in Act 3 of his *Priya-darśikā*). The play within a play can also continue to exfoliate still more deeply embedded levels. And in the texts of the Sanskrit theater, there is invariably someone present, usually in the audience, who breaks the dramatic illusion by saying, "Don't get so excited—this is *only* a work of art."[14] Such a statement can only confirm the overpowering effect of the dramatic reality; otherwise, there would be no need to remind anyone that a boundary has been crossed. As a general rule of thumb, the deeper the embedding (play within play, dream within dream, guise within guise), the greater the density of being, consequence, or truth.[15] In terms of regimes of the imagination, a similar principle may operate; here is a question for empirical resolution in the materials we are probing. Is the imagination of an imagining a fuller, denser act than a first-order imaginative projection? Related to this principle is a second hypothesis worth testing: to draw oneself requires the coalescence of at least two distinct existential formations—the primary crystallization, which is a set of asymmetrical imaginative projections, and a visible, externalized surface self. But it is likely that a fuller self-presentation would require several further embedded and interwoven levels.

Externalities may also conflate. The *Ratnâvalī* ends with a magical production: a talented magician turns up at the court, and king and courtiers are invited to witness his performance. He generates the illusion of a fire in the palace, and Vāsavadattā, in a panic, calls on the king to save Sea-Borne, whom she has imprisoned in her chambers. This rescue from an illusionary threat provides the context for a wider anagnorisis and reconciliation, and for Udayana's wedding to his new love, with the queen's blessings. *Indra-jāla,* magic, has its instrumental uses. One might be tempted to connect one kind of projection with another; are the magician's games or tricks *(khela)* all that different from what the inner eye sees and projects, imaginatively, into the world? Yes, they are. Indeed, they stand in a relation of almost total inversion, at least in Harṣadeva's play. The magical fire looks real but is entirely false. Figments of the imagination tend to look surreal—they are, for one thing, far more intense and glowing than everyday objects—but they are nearly always ultimately proven to be true, in one way or another. In the present case, a rich braiding of shared fantasies, worked out over the first three acts of the play, culminates, with the technical help of the professional magician's sleight of hand, in the most generative and demanding of all possible eventualities, one clearly envisaged in the minds of both characters and spectators from the start—a wedding.

2.3. Nostalgia and Loneliness: Imagination Therapy

Let me say it again. The notion of a generative, concretizing, and consequential imagination is in no way foreign to the great *kāvya* poets, who also sometimes thematize in varying, context-dependent ways the mental processes involved. Reflexive explorations of artistic production in relation to an implicit mental economy, such as we have just seen in Harṣadeva's work, offer one prominent set of examples. Sometimes the artistic, visually accessible image is explicitly devalued in relation to the internal, entirely imagined one: thus Subandhu's hero Kandarpaketu can "see his beloved as if painted with the paint-brush of his imagination on the canvas of his heart."[16] As Bronner aptly says, "The lovers' impressions of each other are so powerfully and deeply etched in their psyches that they can easily project them outward—perhaps the beginning of the process by which they transform the harsh and external reality of the outside world by means of their inner visions."[17] As we will see, such a trajectory, which depends on privileging the imagined over any possible external counterpart, is almost normative in classical Sanskrit literary texts and in the theories of major Sanskrit poeticians. Subandhu himself is a pivotal figure in the evolution of a model for "fiction" as an ontological category intimately linked to an implicit theory of effectual imagining.[18]

Hyperreflexive poetic works such as Kālidāsa's *Megha-dūta,* the "Cloud-Messenger," and the vast series of messenger poems in Sanskrit and many vernacular languages that later imitated and engaged with this revered masterpiece, also inevitably strive to come to grips with the imagination in its world-creating aspect. An exiled lover sends a cloud to his distant beloved with a message of hope and a promise of future reunion. Who would trust a cloud—a concoction of smoke, light, water, and wind—with a verbal message of critical emotional significance?[19] What does it mean for the desperate lover who initiates the cloud's journey to imagine its progression, step by step, through a landscape enlivened and transformed by intense, detailed, projected scenarios? The entire program envisioned by such a work depends on an explicitly acknowledged and self-conscious act of imagining, repeatedly recalled by subtle markers scattered throughout the long poem. Readers of the *Megha-dūta* are given an exhaustive tour of the protagonist's imagination, including his imagination of his distant lover's imagination—and, of course, of the poet's. One thus finds oneself observing, or actively imagining, one imagination as it imagines another, always in highly concrete terms that might even be called objective, especially if we think of objects as containing, ipso facto, an imaginative component activated by any attempt to perceive them. It is precisely this powerful articulation of staggered, highly interactive levels of the imagination, with differential intensities, working upon a familiar external landscape, that makes the messenger poems as a genre so compelling, both cognitively and affectively. Here the model and the later text that resumes it are always mutually determined, hence mutually dependent, as are the imaginative worlds of the hero and heroine inside the poem, the poet outside it, and the reader or listener positioned in some strangely volatile, intermediary space endowed with its own existential claims. Such a space is always rich in feeling and capable of spinning off further quite tangible realities heavy with the stuff of the imagining mind.[20]

We need to take a moment to explore further the affective aspect of sustained imaginative ventures—and here we need not limit ourselves to metapoetic and deliberately reflexive gestures, although Sanskrit literature is particularly replete with such materials. Consider the following passage from the famous seventh-century prose poem or romance, the *Kādambarī*—

more precisely, from that part of the work supposedly composed by Bhūṣaṇa Bhaṭṭa, the son of the first author, Bāṇa, after the latter's death two-thirds of the way through his story. The heroine Kādambarī is separated from her beloved Candrâpīḍa, who has left her behind in her Himalayan home and returned suddenly to his city in the plains without even saying goodbye. His hasty departure is highly expressive, for Candrâpīḍa, in marked contrast with the standard lovesick male in Sanskrit literature, is more than a little ambivalent about the beautiful Kādambarī; in fact, for much of the book he can't quite make up his mind about how he feels about her. Kādambarī, herself languishing in terminal lovesickness and somehow intuiting the complex emotional state of her now distant lover, sends the eloquent and astute Patralekhā to him with an astonishingly rich, prescient message. We'll examine the earlier parts of the message in a moment, but first let us observe the climax of Patralekhā's personal report, quoting Kādambarī's own words:

> "Because of the Maddener, of Fate, of being separated from a lover, of youth, of passion, of madness, of the heart, or of some other reason, the prince [= Candrâpīḍa] is always with me. Made of fancy he is like a Siddha, and his supernatural powers make him imperceptible to everyone else, even to those standing very near me. This fanciful lover, unlike that real one, has not the cruelty of heart to leave me so abruptly. *He* fears being separated from me. *He* does not concern himself both night and day with the Goddess of Fortune. *He* is not a lord of the earth. *He* does not bow to the Goddess of Speech. *He* does not crave shouting 'Glory!' So I have told you how I see the prince—night and day, whether sitting, rising, wandering about, lying down, waking, dozing, moving, dreaming, on a couch on Beauty Spot, in the palace lotus beds, in the gardens, in the sporting ponds, or in the little rivulets trickling down the Pleasure Hill—that deceiver, whose sole occupation is to mock this foolish person. Enough of this talk of bringing him here!"[21]

Kādambarī has found a way to cope with the terrible exigencies and uncertainties of being in love; at some point in the painful and lonely process, she happened upon a particular possibility already latent in her mind—the production of an imaginary lover, one "made of fancy" *(saṅkalpa-maya),* whom she can control more or less at will. Note the term *saṅkalpa,* which harks back to Upaniṣadic usage for the creative capacity of the mind.[22] Kādambarī has gone beyond the vagaries of Candrâpīḍa's actual behavior;

she's got him permanently at her side, in a mode vastly superior—or so it seems—to the flesh-and-blood lover's utterly inadequate responses. Patralekhā, for her part, instantly recognizes the advantages of this new mental creation:

> "Having listened to her, I thought: 'This is a great support indeed to aid those women separated from their lovers to cling to life, namely, an imaginary lover. It is crucial in the case of high-born ladies, and most of all in that of princesses. For then: love play is free from the awkward times when messengers prostrate themselves; there are a myriad unions at every moment; the amorous meetings are pleasant because they can be had at any time; there is the thrill of capricious encounters; and the virginity of the maiden remains intact. Also, in such love play there are embraces in which breasts do not intervene; there are no embarrassing wounds of tooth and nail marks to be seen; there is no disarray of ornamented tresses; there is no playful seizing of the hair; sex acts are wordless; and the frisky play of biting the lower lip does not produce a shameful rent to be seen by the elders. The imaginary lover is not concealed by a cloak of night, screened by a veil of rain, nor swathed in a blanket of mist.' "[23]

We shouldn't miss the irony (it's not that easy to miss it): Patralekhā's reflection is obviously not meant to be taken at face value. Otherwise she wouldn't have come all the way to Ujjayinī to try to persuade Candrâpīḍa to come back with her to the mountains. For all that, the lover fashioned by the imagination is no empty achievement, nor is he unreal. This passage is thus a relatively early and very powerful articulation of the autonomy and self-sufficiency of the imagination in its generative and, somewhat surprisingly, therapeutic aspects. Kādambarī, in her distress, has made an important scientific discovery. Her words strike a deeper chord than Patralekhā's (the latter are mostly concerned with technicalities of an idealized and always immediately available, though somewhat antiseptic, sexual fantasy). Kādambarī can actually characterize the fantasy lover in very specific ways—he's not obsessed with ego issues; he's not cruel; he's not so good at slick, charming chatter (one of Candrâpīḍa's great gifts)—and, of course, above all, he's dependably there, whole, unchanging. This fantasy lover is the opposite of both male heroes of the book, the "real," rather ambivalent Candrâpīḍa and his friend Puṇḍarīka, who both undergo repeated, radical experiences of amnesiac self-loss and rebirth. Imaginary lovers never forget who they are and whom they love.

More to the point, this delicious stability and continuity are natural and necessary complements to the instability and discontinuity that lurk within Kādambarī's own self-understanding. The two vectors—dependable fantasy and slippery assertions of identity—constitute a single complete set; neither can fully exist without the other. In other words, in this case the workings of the imagination need to be contextualized by an innerness that includes other systemic features. We see this clearly in the earlier part of Patralekhā's report (but please bear in mind that we are still in the second section of the *Kādambarī,* after and adjacent to the break in the work supposedly occasioned by Bāṇa's death). Listen, for example, to the passage that constitutes the expressive core of Patralekhā's message. The messenger is once again quoting the feverish Kādambarī:

> "What can have happened? I am that same Kādambarī who was gazed on by the prince as I reclined upon a flower couch within the Snow House. It was that time of evening when the heartache of separated lovers is reflected in the *cakravāka*'s sad laments intertwined with soft *kolāhala* sounds of swarming bees buzzing honey-drunk; when the ten directions are refreshed by a fragrant wind languid with perfume emanating from blown lotuses. . . . It was into the range of these same eyes, which long to see him ever and again, that the prince came. This is that same wretched heart, so vacant with confusion, into which he entered but in which he could not be held. This is that same body that stayed near him a long time without notice. This is that same hand that, out of a false regard for elders, did not have itself taken in marriage by him. And he is that same Candrāpīḍa who, disregarding another's woe, came here twice, then went away. It is the same Five-arrowed God who is now powerless against others because he has spent his arrows on me and who is the very one made known to me by you."[24]

A telling indexical series: she is pointing at her eyes, her heart, her body, herself, and the formula then extends to the invisible Candrâpīḍa (with an inevitable play on his name: "disregarding another's woe," *an-apekṣita-para-pīḍaḥ*) and the equally unseen Love God. Candrâpīḍa, listening to the message, will shortly echo Kādambarī's statement in a more convoluted syntactic pattern that perfectly embodies his own tortured emotional state: "It is this same heart that is the cause of the princess' monumental suffering and that is the cause of your [Patralekhā's] reproach" *(mūḍha-hṛdayena yad yad evâneka-prakāram . . . bālā balāt kāryate tat tad eva. . . . māṃ grāhayataivam īdṛśasya devyā duḥkhasya tava copâlambhasya hetutāṃ nīto 'smi).*[25]

In this highly charged moment in the text, with the author's own death lurking in the immediate background, the affirmation of sameness and continuous identity has a somewhat unsettling effect. "I am still me; my heart is the same old heart, my eyes the same eyes, my lover the same person he was then." Why do these assertions emerge at this juncture?[26] In a general sense, such assertions of continuity in identity negotiate the gap between one body or birth and another—and this notion is definitely fundamental to the book's metapsychological program. But there is something more specific here. The formula Kādambarī has chosen is itself very old and laden with quite special connotations. We find it, for example, as the mantra meant to be recited by the Vedic *śrauta* sacrificer, the *yajamāna,* at the conclusion of the Darśa-pūrṇa-māsa rite performed on new moon and full moon days. As Heesterman has rightly said, this ritual is "the model of the vegetal sacrifice *(iṣṭi)* which, again, provides the basic paradigm of all *śrauta* sacrifices."[27] As the ritual comes to an end and the *yajamāna* returns from the world of the gods to the everyday world, he says, "I'm still who I am" *(idam aham ya evâsmi so 'smi).*[28] Why should he have to say this? Heesterman insightfully links the formula to the vow *(vrata)* the *yajamāna* has taken at the beginning of the ritual: "Here I am going from untruth to truth" *(idam aham anṛtāt satyam upaimi).* In other words, simplifying considerably, the sacrificer, by embarking on the ritual, has entered into a divine domain that is defined as "truth," *satya;* he has, in effect, become a god or a part-god. Upon the conclusion of the ritual—since we are still at the point where a *śrauta* sacrifice is a two-way process, up to the heavens and then back down to earth—the sacrificer reenters the human domain by proclaiming that he is still, or once again, himself. He has left the divine body *(daivâtman)* that he has been absorbed in creating, by performing the ritual, in storage in the heavenly domain for the day when he will need it.

All this is spelled out for us by the *Śatapatha Brāhmaṇa,* which also somewhat disingenuously recommends the paradoxical statement concluding the rite as being somehow more suitable and "becoming":

> "He who is about to enter on the vow, touches water whilst standing between the Âhavanîya and Gârhapatya fires, with his face turned towards east. Man is impure on account of his speaking untruth. . . .

> Twofold verily is this [universe], there is no third, namely truth and untruth. The Gods are truth and man is untruth. Therefore in saying, 'I now enter from untruth into truth,' he passes from the men to the gods. Let him then only speak what is true; for this vow indeed the gods do keep, that they speak truth. . . . After the completion (of the sacrifice), he divests himself (of the vow) with the text: 'Now I am he who I really am.'[29] For, in entering upon the vow, he becomes, as it were, non-human; and as it would not be becoming for him to say: 'I enter from truth into untruth,' and as, in fact, he now again becomes man, let him therefore divest himself of the vow, with the text: 'Now I am he who I really am.' "[30]

The paradox is glaringly apparent: "I am who I am" actually means something like "I am back in the world where untruth rules," that is, "I am now speaking untruth." Here we have the *yajamāna* as the Cretan liar: if what he says is true, then it must be false.[31] In other words, the Vedic pronouncement on potential disjunctions in continuous identity requires the person in question to "speak himself" as a paradoxical riddle. I think this basic notion extends to Kādambarī's statements, too.

Stated differently, "I am who I am" actually means something like "Though I am somehow continuous with my former self, I am *not* who I was then (or who I used to be)." In Kādambarī's case the suggestion is that her situation is steadily worsening. Her initial meetings with Candrâpīḍa were suffused by ambivalence and hesitation on his part, as we have noted, whereas she had given herself entirely to her love for him. Now he has gone off (to his parents' home) without even stopping by to say goodbye and without sending any communication to the lovesick woman he left behind. "I'm the same person I was then," she says in her message, as if to say, "You left me stuck in the past, in an agony of unfulfilled fantasy, with almost no hope of forward movement"—and also, "Time *seems* to stand still for me, but in fact my strength is waning, and I am losing hope." The paradox of continuous identity echoes the paradox of memory-infused temporality itself, at once frozen in autotelic wholeness and spinning out of control in a devolutionary trajectory. It is possible that *all* identity statements in the *Kādambarī* world, indeed in much classical *kāvya,* have this riddle-like, tensile quality, as if the very notion of personal continuity were vitiated every moment by the experience each person has of himself or herself in a world driven by devolving time.

There is also a rather striking hint of singularity in Kādambarī's message. She is the same, her eyes and heart are the same, her almost-lover is remarkably consistent in behavior and feeling; but Desire, who has wounded her with his arrows, has, she says, depleted his reserve of weapons *(upakṣīṇa-mārgaṇatā)* by shooting over and over at her and her alone (apparently *not* at Candrâpīḍa). As a result, no one else is, at the moment, in danger of falling in love in the extreme way that she has. Her suffering is unique, also uniquely repetitive. Here, too, is a statement that simply cannot be true, like the *yajamāna*'s assertion that he is still the person he was before the ritual began. Were it true in either case, it would constitute an untenable acknowledgment of failure (of the ritual ascent and descent, and of the continuing efficacy of desire in the human realm).

"Sameness," then, really means something like jagged disjunction, possibly even self-deception. Perhaps even Kādambarī has been infected by her lover's hesitancy and doubt, though she doesn't know it. She will eventually be put to a still more severe test. In the meantime, like the nostalgic heroines we know from other Sanskrit sources, she seems almost to be longing for her own former self, when things were, ostensibly at least, a little less complicated. Consider, for example, the following well-known verse from the end of the first chapter of Mammaṭa's textbook on poetics, the *Kāvya-prakāśa:*

yaḥ kaumāra-haraḥ sa eva hi varas tā eva caitra-kṣapās
te conmīlita-mālatī-surabhayaḥ prauḍhāḥ kadambânilāḥ/
sā caivâsmi tathâpi tatra surata-vyāpāra-līlā-vidhau
revā-rodhasi vetasī-taru-tale cetaḥ samutkaṇṭhate//

The man who took my virginity
is now my husband. These are the same
nights of spring, the same wind soaked
with Kadamba and jasmine in full bloom.
And I'm still me, the same woman.
It's just that my heart keeps longing
for the love games we once played
there, on the riverbank,
amidst the reeds.

The reality of the ongoing love relation, with its recalcitrant uncertainties, easily generates such retrospective longing. The speaker says, echoing Vedic statements such as *Bṛhad-āraṇyaka Upaniṣad* 1.4.1, "I'm still me" *(sā caivâsmi)*—as if to state the very opposite, that is, the gnawing sense that her life has changed beyond recognition. Such statements always contain as well an assertion of powerful, essentially atemporal emotional continuity: she knows within herself still-active feelings very much akin to her original experience in the "nights of spring," but these feelings survive in altered physical and existential circumstances.[32] As in the case of Kādambarī, a certain part of the speaker's world is almost timeless, possibly frozen in a remembered or imaginatively reconstructed past moment, while another part looks back at that moment from the altered, and painful, perspective of the present. The interplay of continuous emotional intensity and temporal devolution generates the nostalgic attitude.

We have many other examples in Sanskrit of this volatile, at times truly tragic amalgam. For example:

purâbhūd asmākaṃ prathamam avibhinnā tanur iyam
tato nu tvaṃ preyān vayam api hatâśāḥ priyatamāḥ/
idānīṃ nāthas tvam vayam api kalatraṃ kiṃ aparam
hatānāṃ prāṇānāṃ kuliśa-kaṭhinānāṃ phalam idam//

At first we were a single, unbroken body.
Then you were my lover, and I, to my sorrow, your beloved.
Now you're my husband, and I'm your wife.
What's next?
That's the nature of this goddamned life: hard
as diamond.[33]

Here the vector of devolution has come entirely to dominate the reimagined affective present, and nostalgia takes on an aspect of helplessness and hopelessness.[34]

The theme of nostalgia for a previous self has a wide cachet in the classical sources and occasionally extends even to the successful Yogi-renouncer, poised on the verge of ecstatic extinction.[35] By the same token, however, the very instability of the lovesick self unhappily enmeshed in its own imagined history, along with the disjunction implicit in what it chooses to say about itself, lead, in the instance of the *Kādambarī,* to a remarkable and unexpected move. No sooner has Kādambarī finished telling us (that is, telling the absent Candrâpīḍa by way of Patralekhā and, unknown to either of the latter two, the even more distant Śūdraka, who is listening to the story of his former life) that she is exactly who she always was, than she confesses to having, in effect, solved the problems of fluctuating selfhood and the living lover's enduring capriciousness by the invention of an imaginary lover. By now the wider mental economy should be clear. A compensatory act of imagination, holding things together out of its own autonomous force and self-regulating tendency, is the unexpected response to an elusive, continuously unraveling sense of personal identity, especially in relation to frustrated desire, the common matrix of such identity crises. Imagination, that is, addresses an absence, in a quite "modern" mode strongly linked to an experience of trauma. Note that within such an exposition of the usefulness of imaginative praxis, differential experiences of time—which seem to unfold simultaneously in several disjunctive rhythms—have a natural and central role.

2.4. Summary Ad Hoc

How do the literary materials we have sampled relate to the discursive classical theories with which we began? Let us briefly review. We began with early understandings of *bhāvanā* that predate the late medieval usage of the term to refer to an autonomous mental function akin to what we are calling "imagination." In the views of the grammarians and the logicians, certain elements regularly accompany the process of bringing something—anything—into being. There is, to begin with, a linguistic or, actually, intralinguistic movement. Nothing comes to be without coming to be inside language. A word, far from representing a preexisting object, is properly the early crystallization of the potential object. Even at its most empirical and pragmatic, language never loses this connection to a domain of potential becoming. But it is in no way sufficient simply to speak of the linguistic business of marking and tracing. Emergence, especially of some definable "fruit" implicit in the initial linguistic act of visualizing such a fruit, requires an integrative and, perhaps, causal function operative in normal sentences. This function is definitely situated somewhere in the mind, though it no less definitely impinges on extra-mental reality. Stated in a reductionist way: speech, widely and generously defined so as to include unuttered and/or nonsemanticized sentences (as in music), operates in and upon the mind to make the movement from vision to actualized existence possible. Precisely how this process works in terms of causal process is a matter open to radically different descriptions, in accordance with the different philosophical schools. For the logicians, at least, memory and attention are dependable coefficients or, perhaps, by-products of the initial creative impression, *saṃskāra,* left on the mind. There are circumstances in which the original impression may swallow up its later derivatives—that is, in which perceived forms may dissolve back into the potential state out of which they were generated, or in which the initial impression may naturally reemerge in all its vividness and compelling power.

Distinctive kinds of knowledge thus conduce to what will later be classed as imaginative production. Such modes of knowing are not unfamiliar to the poets. They, too, assume that to formulate thought or feeling in language is to actualize an existence or, to use a concrete image, to fashion a visible and tangible surface. Such a surface is never accidentally textured. For Kālidāsa, who can be shown to be close both historically and conceptually to Bhartṛhari, any such surface—for example, a story or plot—follows the contours of a mark that exists before it in the recesses of language and mind. The mark may settle into the shape of a word or, eventually, of an object encrusted by a story that, in turn, can be said to have "marked" *(lakṣī-kṛ)* its characters, so they find themselves living out that story even as, in another sense, they create it freely moment by moment.[36]

What about more complex modes of generating external realities? Suppose we think of the world as a web of interlacing projections, as the Buddhist philosopher Nāgârjuna sometimes describes it. These projections are mind-based and, again, laden with linguistic traces. They may well be driven by an existential function we could call "imagination."[37] The imaginative origins of these projections in no way preclude their material existence. Harṣadeva's *Ratnâvalī* seems in many ways close to such an implicit metaphysics, as we have seen. Indeed, Harṣa shows us the projective web in the process of constituting and reconstituting itself through the fantasy-driven interactions of his protagonists. At the same time, he is profoundly aware of the integrity and expressivity of artistic production, which both focuses and exceeds the mind-woven tissue of experience. The two lovers move through the artistic media that seek to capture them, including, perhaps, the text that has brought them into being. Such is certainly the case in the performance context, which transcends by far the bare bones of its verbal score.

I have limited myself in this section to texts that more or less explicitly thematize imaginative process. One could easily produce examples going as far back as the Veda, where the first skilled craftsmen, the Ṛbhus, sleep in heaven, in the house of the sun, dreaming time into existence.[38] For now, this sample will have to suffice. A very different perspective emerges when we address the wider range of literary practice—that is, when we ask ourselves not what poets thought about the imagination but how they actually used it, and to what effect. These are the traditional topics of Indian poetics, one of the central domains of Indian science. Let us now allow the professionals to speak.

— 3 —

Singularity, Inexhaustibility, Insight: What Sanskrit Poeticians Think Is Real

Let's say you are a novelist or a poet, composing a rather long text inhabited by characters of your own invention. At some point you get stuck; there seems to be no way to extricate the heroine, Z., from the extraordinary tangle of circumstance and inner conflict that she has gotten herself into—no, sorry, that *you* have imagined for her. (That's the problem with these characters: they very rapidly acquire a surprising autonomy and a certain irreducible integrity vis-à-vis their creator.)[1] Eventually you decide that, for the sake of the novel, maybe even for Z.'s own sake, the best thing is simply to kill her off. In our literary ecology, no one would doubt your sovereign ability to do just that. After all, Z. is only imaginary.

So you concoct a death scene, maybe even a funeral, and everyone inside the novel along with the readers outside it, to say nothing of the author, has somehow to come to terms with the sad loss of Z. Even I can't help feeling a slight twinge, though I hardly knew her.

But what if Z. were suddenly to turn up on the street or in your study and demand attention, protesting loudly that she is still very much alive?

Now let's say that you're a bard specializing in epic stories in Sanskrit; you sing the familiar, inherited tales called *itihāsa* or *purāṇa,* probably to an audience of villagers in some corner of medieval India. Tonight you are describing the melodramatic moment where the young Kṛṣṇa kills his uncle and tormentor, Kaṃsa. Here, too, someone might say about you that tonight you are "killing off" Kaṃsa *(kaṃsaṃ ghātayasi).* As it happens, the famous seventh-century commentary by Jayâditya and Vāmana known as the *Kāśikā,* on Pāṇini's grammar of Sanskrit, makes a provision for precisely this sort of idiomatic usage. The *Kāśikā* is commenting on *sūtra* 3.1.26 of the grammar, *hetumati ca,* which enjoins the use of the suffix *Ṇic* to produce a causative verb. So along with such prevalent and, in India, remarkably useful forms as *odanaṃ pācayati,* "he causes [someone else] to cook the rice," we can also generate sentences such as "he is killing off Kaṃsa" *(kaṃsaṃ ghātayati)* or "he is binding [the demon] Bali in chains" *(baliṃ bandhayati).* That is, the storyteller is narrating these episodes, thereby causing Kaṃsa to be killed or Bali to be bound. In this same passage, a very similar usage is said to be normal for astrologers, who may know, for example, about the conjunction of various planets; we can say that the astrologer literally "joins X to Y" *(puṣyeṇa yojayati/ maghabhir yojayati).*

In a way, the Sanskrit idiom is quite unsurprising. Indeed, we quite naturally use it ourselves. There is, however, a difference between the first and second examples. The novelist who imagined Z. has, we assume, the right to do away with her. The Indian storyteller, however, is repeating some piece of the tradition that (a) everyone knows and (b) is thought to have really happened—possibly even to have happened many times, in each successive, self-repeating cosmic age. So there may after all be a distinctive twist to the *Kāśikā*'s observation about reported speech. I'm not at all sure that the storyteller is not making Kaṃsa die yet again, in some quite factual way, just as a classical drama about the god Rāma may, at certain ritual moments, be seen as an arena in which Rāma does become entirely present and real.[2] Or, to take a somewhat milder position, we could say that the storyteller presents the story in such a powerful way that he makes the death of Kaṃsa palpably real to his audience.[3]

Clearly, there is a problem here, one that can be formulated in various ways. In the Tamil dance-drama called *Hiraṇya-nāṭakam,* the actor playing the god Nara-siṃha, a man-lion, and wearing his enormous orange mask is often said to become possessed by the deity to the point that he breaks the bounds between performance and ritual reality: "Last year the actor was so full of the god that he actually attacked and devoured one of the spectators."[4] On the other hand, classical poeticians such as the great Abhinavagupta (eleventh century) are careful to distinguish what normally happens in the theater from just such ritual modes *(āveśa).* The difference is a matter of principle, not of degree. And yet these same poeticians are fond of telling us that the poetic world with which they are professionally concerned is a kind of ultimate reality, utterly free from the constraints of fate and from the usual unhappy concoction of pleasure and pain that we all recognize as the stuff of everyday experience.[5] What, precisely, do they mean?

Or, stated more simply, what is it that counts as real for these theorists of artistic production and effects, the sober and erudite embodiments of a scientific discipline that is generally hardheaded, empiricist, rigorous, shaped by logical categories of analysis, and often rather skeptical? In India, poetics, the *Alaṅkāra-śāstra,* is one of the central sciences, a natural extension of the great paradigmatic discipline of grammar—not a primary arena for metaphysical speculation about Being in the mode of, let us say, the famous ninth-century Kashmiri text *Yoga-vāsiṣṭha-mahārāmāyaṇa,* where there is nothing that is not imagined (hence both "true" and unreal).[6] For this very reason, because of the care and caution with which it examines a clearly delimited field, poetics constitutes a useful point of departure for forays into the life of the South Asian imagination.

We will proceed as follows, charting a somewhat constricted course through the *śāstra* and its major theoretical texts and paying attention to the way basic notions evolved over roughly a thousand years, from the middle of the first millennium to the seventeenth century. We begin with the figure known as *utprekṣā* ("flight of fancy") that, more than any other, focuses the problem of truth and reality as the poeticians articulated it. We will then look briefly at the theory of suggestion, *dhvani,* and the closely allied notion of *rasa,* "flavor"—the culminating synthesis of thought on poetics in the narrative the tradition tells itself about its history—from the perspective of this problem. Important issues about creativity and inexhaustibility arise organically in the framework of this discussion. We then turn, in the next chapter, to the central concept of *pratibhā,* "inspiration" or "imagination," especially as it was developed by three maverick figures among the great theoreticians—Rājaśekhara, Kuntaka, and Jagannātha. The science of poetics is the most obvious place to look for a full-fledged, nuanced theory of imaginative praxis in classical and medieval India; we should, however, never forget that there is a necessary and enduring lack of congruence between the poeticians' views and the actual praxis of the poets themselves, as in any great literary tradition.

3.1. "Smoke, Light, Water, Wind"

Take a striking example, which I owe to Gary Tubb, who has discussed it together with related instances in two important essays.[7] The great poet Kālidāsa conjures up a vignette in which a dark rain cloud—which has been sent as a love messenger, *dūta,* by an exiled *yakṣa* spirit to his distant wife—is momentarily resting on a mountain peak during the north-bound journey:

channopântaḥ pariṇata-phala-dyotibhiḥ kānanâmrais
tvayy ārūḍhe śikharam acalaḥ snigdha-veṇī-savarṇe/
nūnaṃ yāsyaty amara-mithuna-prekṣaṇīyām avasthāṃ
madhye śyāmaḥ stana iva bhuvaḥ śeṣa-vistāra-pāṇḍuḥ//[8]

Its slopes veiled by groves of ripening mangos,
and with you[9]—black as a glossy braid—on its peak,
the mountain will grab the attention of passionate couples
among the gods, looking down from above,
like a breast of the goddess Earth with a black nipple
at the center and all the rest pale gold.

Imagined as seen from above, the mountain is a visually striking mass of pale golden mangos ripening on the trees (during the monsoon month of Āṣāḍha, always a period of intense erotic emotion in Sanskrit poetry), with the dark rain cloud coiled, like a woman's sleek black braid, around the peak at the center.[10] In short, it is like seeing a breast. But what exactly does "like" (*iva,* in the middle of the final quarter) mean here? Is this a somewhat daring, though appropriately erotic, metaphor? The monsoon season is suffused with passionate longing: the roads have become impassable because of the rains, and lovers who, like the *yakṣa* and his wife, are separated at this season can hardly bear the torment; those lucky couples who are together can give themselves over, undisturbed, to desire. Naturally, then, an amorous pair of gods who steal a moment to look down toward earth will, upon seeing the mountain, think of a breast. But are they projecting or imagining something that we would certainly assume is quite "unreal"? Not necessarily. Vallabhadeva, the earliest commentator on the text (early tenth century?), says tersely, *ataś ca kṛṣṇa-cūcukaḥ samasta-pītaś ca mahī-kuca ivety upamā,* "This is a simile: it is like the breast of the Earth, with its black nipple amidst the rest of its golden flesh." Later commentators, however, such as the great Mallinātha, think the poetic figure is *utprekṣā,* "flight of fancy." Mallinātha, in fact, spells out the implication of his categorization: "You [the cloud] will rest, as it were, on the breast of your beloved, the Earth, like a lover who, exhausted from making love, falls asleep on the breast of his beloved."

At first glance, the difference between the two figures might not seem so very great. It does, however, touch on the question of interest to us. *Utprekṣā,* as we will see in a moment, assumes a certain imaginative leap, something that goes well beyond a mere simile, *upamā.* The latter, moreover, tends to depend on comparing the subject to a familiar, real object. Thus to classify the image in our verse as simile is to imply that the Earth, being a real goddess, does actually have real breasts. This seems to be Vallabha's position. To call the figure *utprekṣā* is to focus on the imaginative reconfiguration of reality that is basic to all examples of this class. We can read the word *iva,* "like," in either way. The poet has not determined our interpretative stance; it is really up to us, as we can see by the commentators' disagreement.[11] In a sense, it all depends on what we think about the whole poetic enterprise in this text, that is, about the somewhat bizarre master trope of asking a cloud to carry a verbal message of love and reassurance to a lovesick wife far away.

Kālidāsa has, in fact, explicitly thematized the issue in one of the opening verses of the *Megha-dūta,* as we have seen.[12] A cloud, he tells us, is just a hodgepodge of smoke, light, water, and wind—not a sentient being (v. 5). How could the *yakṣa* then entrust it with his message? The answer is that lovers tortured by separation will appeal, in their distress, to anything or anybody. So right at the start we have a direct metapoetic statement about the delusional or fictive nature of the primary trope.[13] We know perfectly well that we are in an imagined domain, with its own compelling power. In effect, the entire text is one long *utprekṣā,* continually instantiated in specific figurative expressions. This is not to preclude the possibility that a different kind of reality is somehow brought into play in the course of our entering into the poetic illusion. Perhaps "reality" is too limited a word in such contexts.

3.2. *Utprekṣā* and "Apprehension"

We can now reformulate our question. It is not quite enough to ask, "What did Sanskrit poeticians believe to be real?" We have to add: "Real in what sense?" Or better still: "Real to what effect?" Comparisons with purely philosophical domains, such as Advaita Vedânta, or with the luxurious exploration of the imagination in the *Yoga-vāsiṣṭha,* will not really help. The poeticians must be allowed to speak for themselves. Fortunately, they do address these themes with considerable vigor and with a sensitivity to various competing points of view. They have much to say about the precise nature of the cognition triggered by a work of art, and from the beginning of the tradition they are also fascinated by the logic of perception that operates within each of the major figures. Let us start, then, by taking a close look at some of the attempts to define *utprekṣā* in terms of its reality content.

Utprekṣā, as we have already seen, comprises a flight of fancy in which there is usually some element of comparison, though not a comparison amenable to full analysis in terms of the classical logic of the simile, *upamā.* We have also already intimated the reason behind *upamā*'s insufficiency in this case, that is, the fanciful, imaginary nature of the object of comparison *(upamāna),* be it a substance or a verbal process.[14] When the starting point is an imaginative leap, ontological issues cannot be far away. What interests us is the way such issues are defined.

The early attempts at defining *utprekṣā* speak of a certain "otherness": thus Daṇḍin (early eighth century) says that *utprekṣā* is "imagining something, whether sentient or insentient, as acting in another mode [*vṛtti*] than usual" (*anyathaiva sthitā vṛttiś cetanasyetarasya vā/ anyathotprekṣyate yatra tām utprekṣāṃ vidur;* 2.221).[15] In most cases, what lies behind the notion of something other than usual is the attribution of conscious intention to an insentient object, as the definition itself suggests.[16] Thus the Sun sends its morning rays into the groves and pries open the flowers as if it were searching everywhere for its defeated enemy, now in hiding, Darkness.[17] The subjunctive, "as if" element, which is central to the figure, is explicitly signaled by some verbal token in the verse (like *iva* in our example from Kālidāsa). The fancy is thus largely taken up with imagining an impossible or highly unlikely motivation for what may be a rather ordinary action or event. In the example, *utprekṣā* replaces the literal, naturalistic observation that the flowers in the grove unfold at dawn; now we know why they do so. Note that simile alone cannot explain this verse—not merely because of the complexity and dynamism of the figure, though these deserve attention, but above all because of the poet's imaginative, anthropomorphizing drive.

Later poeticians—Vāmana, Udbhaṭa, and especially Rudraṭa—introduced more powerful, also more subtle, elements into the definition of this figure; we cannot follow their debates in any detail here. But by the time of Ruyyaka (c. 1150, Kashmir), the discourse on *utprekṣā* has shifted into a primarily epistemological mode focusing on the question of what part or aspect of the figure can be seen as "true" or "real." The shift is meaningful and consequential. Even the basic terms have changed: the classical *upameya* (subject of the comparison, that which is compared) and *upamāna* (object of comparison, that to which something is compared) now tend to appear as the *viṣaya,* the "domain" (of the figure, or of the cognitive process active in it), and the *viṣayin,* that which forms, shapes, or molds this domain.[18] What is more, Ruyyaka reclassifies *utprekṣā* as forming a pair with *atiśayokti,* hyperbole, on the basis of a shared cognitive process that he is the first to call *adhyavasāya,* "determination, apprehension."[19] *Adhyavasāya* is what distinguishes the two figures in question from others, such as *rūpaka*—metaphoric identification—based on *āropa,* "superimposition." It is one thing to impose the form of the object on that of the subject of comparison without forgetting that they are not really identical, but quite another to apprehend X as Y while maintaining a clear awareness of what is or is not real in this imaginative vision. Let us see how Ruyyaka explains what happens.

He first offers a definition: "*Utprekṣā* occurs when there is an apprehension [*adhyavasāya*] in which the *process* [*vyāpāra*] is predominant." This elliptical *kārikā* is then expanded in a prose passage of some obscurity:

> When the object of comparison [*viṣayin*] swallows up the subject [*viṣaya*], so that there is the perception of nondifference, that is apprehension. It has two subtypes—in the process of being completed, and completed. The in-process type entails a perception of the object of comparison as unreal. This falseness derives from a perception of some element [*dharma*] belonging to the object, and possible [only] with reference to the object, as being connected to the subject domain. Such an element may take the form of either an attribute or an action. When one considers the question of whether such an element can or cannot come into existence, one may come to the conclusion that the basis for its coming into existence is not truly real, while the other [subject domain] is truly real. When you take something unreal as real, that is an "in-process apprehension." The process itself is the main thing. A "completed apprehension" occurs when the object of comparison, although in fact unreal, is perceived as real. Its reality derives from the absence of any reason to regard it as unreal, unlike the previous case. In this case the end result of the apprehension is predominant. Among these two possibilities, that apprehension in which the process is primary, and the perception is in the process of being

achieved, is what is called imagination, conceit, conjecture, speculation, or *utprekṣā*.[20]

Ruyyaka's understanding of *utprekṣā* could perhaps have been stated more simply. He is interested here, as I have said, both in *utprekṣā* and in *atiśayokti*, hyperbole; the first exemplifies the in-process apprehension, the second the completed apprehension. Thus if one were to say, for example, "Look! Surely the moon, as it were . . ." *(nūnaṃ candra iva)*, that is *utprekṣā*.[21] If one says simply, "Look at the moon" (meaning "look at her face," *candraṃ paśya*), that is *atiśayokti*.[22] In both cases, according to Ruyyaka, an identity is established between subject and object of comparison. But in the first example, the object, *viṣayin*, continues to be recognized as unreal—which means that our heroine's face is not really the moon, and we know it—and we will also usually find some explicit marker of this fact, as in the phrase "surely" *(nūnam)* or "as it were" *(iva)*. The identification, that is, is still in process. In the second case, we have lost all signs of the unreality of the object, and even our awareness of this unreality may have gone; the coincidence is fully achieved, and the unreal object has swallowed up the real subject along with the latter's evident reality.

But it is *utprekṣā* that concerns us. Note the dual awareness that seems to be maintained in the listener's mind: something unreal is being identified, but not in a complete or final way, with something real. You have to be able to maintain the tension between real and unreal to experience the full effect of the figure. The discussion takes a strictly logical turn; there is always some element making the transition from the object domain to the subject domain, and what we want to examine is the existential ground of that element. As the commentator, Vidyācakravartin, says: "What element [*dharma*] are we talking about? And by what logical criterion [*pramāṇa*] can we judge it? The perception of reality or falseness applies to its basis [for coming into being, *āśraya*]. . . . Thus a judgment of truth or falsehood is not without logical criteria. We recognize what is unreal when the ground of its coming into being does not produce an awareness of its ultimate reality."[23]

This amounts to saying that the object of comparison is, in the case of *utprekṣā*, always unreal, unlike the subject of comparison.[24] We could also say that in such a case the fictionality of the figure remains clearly in view. The tension retains a dynamic quality; a certain space opens up in which the imagination can come into play. Another commentator, Samudrabandha (late thirteenth–early fourteenth century, Kerala) makes a slightly different distinction between the in-process and the completed apprehension. In the former, *utprekṣā,* what is swallowed up is the perception or recognition of the subject. In hyperbole, *atiśayokti,* what is swallowed up is the very form or self of the subject.[25] In other words, *utprekṣā* ends up as a kind of "seeing as X"; the everyday perception of the subject is overpowered by the imaginative one. Hyperbole, on the other hand, leaves nothing over of the original subject, as when raw rice is turned into cooked rice.[26] Is hyperbole, then, fiction or fact?

A fiction, no doubt; apparently, one whose fictionality has been suppressed or masked. The figurative reality has swamped any normative, object-driven one. But is this not the aim of poetry—to replace the humdrum world, at least for a moment, with a more powerful and malleable one, infused with an imaginative dimension that makes beauty real? We do indeed find such statements in the Sanskrit *alaṅkāra* texts.[27] But it is striking that the discussion of *utprekṣā,* the most imaginative figure of all, by Ruyyaka and his commentators keeps bringing us back to the cognitive content of an *utprekṣā* moment, and in particular to the struggle such a moment triggers in the listener's mind. Differential truth-claims continue to exist within a figurative process predicated on the notion of fictionality.

Attempts to refine the problem further easily slip into questions of illusion or straightforward error. "Apprehension," says Vidyācakravartin, commenting on the beginning of this same passage in Ruyyaka,

> is definite knowledge. In everyday experience, it has two forms: correct and incorrect [*saṃyag-ātmā mithyā-rūpaś ca*]. Neither has any relation to figuration. If you correctly identify a pearl oyster shell, or if you wrongly perceive it as silver—in neither case is there anything striking [*vicchittiḥ kā-cit*]. What we take for artistic figuration is a projection [*adhyāsa*] distinct from both the above, in which, while knowing [the distinction], we say, "This thing is *in* [or *on*] that thing." The result is an unearthly strikingness. It, too, has two paths. Sometimes the *process* of apprehending is primary, and sometimes it is the subject domain that has been fully apprehended [as the object]. Only the first case is *utprekṣā.*

If Vidyācakravartin is right, what attracts our attention in *utprekṣā* is not the subject and object in their own right but the cognitive business of bringing them into relation to each other. We are, in short, made to see into the workings of our mind when it combines something true or real with something false or unreal. Note that "true" and "real" are not synonymous, nor are "false" and "unreal." And while the ability to distinguish truth from falsehood is clearly relevant to this discussion, the passage seems to have shifted toward an apprehension of what is real. This kind of introspection, which somehow manages to keep the two different truth-values apart even in the course of combining them, generates a characteristic inner mode with its own integrity. The Kashmiri commentator Jayaratha gives this mode a name lifted from Ruyyaka's own list of terms culminating in *utprekṣā: sambhāvanā,* "imagination."[28] Moreover, Jayaratha clearly distinguishes imagination from doubt, *sandeha,* on the one hand, and from *tarka,* logical deduction, on the other. Imagination, he says, occupies an intermediate space between doubt and certainty, like the mythic figure of King Triśaṅku, who forever dangles upside down between heaven and earth.[29]

Jayaratha goes on to offer his own subdivision of apprehension, *adhyavasāya.* Once again we find two types, in this case distinguished by the factor of motivation or intention. Sometimes apprehension of identity—between the subject and object of comparison—happens naturally, without premeditation or purpose. In such a case *(svārasika),* the apprehension is simply a mistake. A separate figure, *bhrāntimat,* is based around such misapprehensions. When the moonlight pouring into a room is so intense that the cat licks at it on the floor, assuming it to be milk, or an exhausted lover tries to wrap herself in it because she thinks it is her nightgown, that is *bhrāntimat.*[30] Notice that in this figure, the listener or reader knows perfectly well what is real and what illusionary; he or she attends to the mistake made by someone else, inside the poem. In other cases, however—we are still following Jayaratha—we can identify a purpose *(prayojana)* behind the apprehension, in which the distinction between true and false is maintained by the poet as well as by the reader. Once again, such a motivated *(utpādita)* apprehension can be either in-process or complete. There is a convergence here with Vidyācakravartin, who also distinguishes unconscious or natural *(svārasika)* error from poetic design; the latter, while issuing from lucid awareness of the distinction in truth-status, has imagination as its inner force *(kalpanâtmā).*[31]

To operate in this figurative domain, imagination requires a high-grade, tensile suspension in which reality and unreality come together in the mind of the listener or spectator without resolving the contradiction between them. "Suspension" may, however, give too static an impression; as we saw, the process itself is primary. *Utprekṣā* could thus be said to be an ongoing negotiation between two perceptions—one seemingly "true," the other "false"—that are made to converge by the very existence of the two structural poles of the figure, the subject and object of imagined comparison.

About a century and a half after Ruyyaka's pathbreaking discussion of *utprekṣā,* another major poetician—Vidyānātha, writing in Warrangal in the Telugu country in the early fourteenth century—slightly revised the terms of Ruyyaka's analysis. Specifically, he made room for the explicit possibility that either the subject or the object of the comparison could be unreal—that is, could be "swallowed up" by the other.[32] He thus effectively spelled out a conclusion implicit in Ruyyaka's way of thinking about the two relevant figures. To conclude this section, we can take a quick look at how Kumārasvāmin, commenting on Vidyānātha's *Pratāparudrīya* in the late fifteenth century, lucidly explicates the processes involved:

> When the poet applies qualities such as sweetness, which belong to the object of comparison, in this case the moon,[33] to its subject, in this case the [beloved's] face, clearly knowing the face *as a face*—saying "Surely this must be, as it were, the moon"—then the moon, being unreal, appears to be swallowed up by the "faceness" of the face, which is perceived as ultimately real. But since the perception of truth and falsehood as being simultaneously identical is impossible, and because words like *nūnam* ["surely"] are capable of conveying a sense of reality even to the object of comparison, we speak of an apprehension that is still *in-process.* It is the ongoing process of apprehending that predominates. But when the word "face" is not uttered and the poet simply says, "This is the moon," then the object of comparison, though unreal, is perceived as real. The absence of the word "face," which is what produces [in the former case, *utprekṣā*] the sense that the moon is unreal, makes this [hyperbole] possible. In this case the subject, though real, is swallowed up and concealed, thus appearing unreal. Here what predominates is what has been [finally] apprehended.[34]

Thus there are linguistic triggers, slight residual markers—evidentials—that generate a sense of reality; the absence of such a trigger may be enough to make the real appear unreal, though probably not enough to do away entirely with the base awareness that we are within the magnetic field of figuration. A trained listener will recognize hyperbole when he or she hears it and will not crudely literalize its message. Still, the whole description of these figures is saturated with the terminology of real and unreal, as if there were a danger, lurking in the back of the theoretician's mind, that the unreal could indeed "realize" itself, at least in consciousness, at least momentarily. What is more, it is the interplay of these two ontic categories that gives the relevant figures their effective punch.

What have we learned so far? A central poetic trope, *utprekṣā,* is defined, on the one hand, in terms of the relative reality-content of its members and, on the other hand, in terms of an ongoing, unfinished cognitive process that may in itself demand most of the reader's attention. Such a trope is not susceptible to classification as valid or invalid, true or false; more precisely, the knowledge that lies at its core cannot be classified in these terms. Some different sort of knowledge is involved, apparently sparked by the unresolved tension between real and unreal *within* the figure. This other knowledge is linked to imagination, a generative principle or faculty that has its own claim to truth.

3.3. "A Little Extra": On *Rasa, Bhāvanā,* and Resonance

Sanskrit poeticians have tried to say something about this other kind of knowledge. In fact, we find ourselves close to the heart of their discussions about aesthetic experience, its epistemic and ontic status, and its true purpose. Some of the materials are very well known, in particular those relating to the theory of *rasa* or aesthetic "flavor" as crystallized in the magisterial synthesis of Abhinavagupta (c. 1000, Kashmir). I want to look briefly at a few selected moments in the centuries-long debate about what happens in the mind of a spectator at a play, a debate recorded for us by Abhinavagupta himself in his commentaries on the *Bhārata-nāṭya-śāstra* and on Ānandavardhana's *Dhvanyāloka.*[35]

Perhaps the clearest statement about what the spectator's knowledge is *not* comes from a mid-ninth-century poetician known as Śrī Śaṅkuka, whose theories are known to us through Abhinavagupta's (clearly somewhat programmatic) summaries.[36] Śrī Śaṅkuka offers a mimetic theory of art built around the intertwined notions of imitation, *anukaraṇa,* and inference, *anumāna.* He thinks the delight that affects the spectator results from a rather complicated set of inferences about the actor and what he or she represents onstage—in particular, about what the represented character is feeling (i.e., *rasa*).[37] The poetic-dramatic text is, as the spectator knows, a fiction sustained by all the artificial *(kṛtrima)* factors and devices used to unfold the illusion—although the spectator tends not to realize this at the time.[38] Both the actors and the spectators have to work hard, the first in order to generate the illusionary world of the drama, the latter at logical or inferential thinking. All of this produces in the audience an awareness that cannot be defined as doubt *(sandeha),* truth *(tattva),* or error *(viparyaya)*—just as we saw in the case of figuration. Rather, the logical status of the spectator's cognition can be stated as "This is that" *(asav ayam),* a statement that is distinct from "This is *really* that" *(asāv evâyam).*[39] Moreover, this cognition, lacking as it does any perceptions that might contradict it *(viruddha-buddhy-asambhedāt),* and rooted in direct experience, cannot be invalid. It is also quite capable of being causally effectual (as false cognitions can sometimes be).

Śrī Śaṅkuka spells all of this out by excluding a whole set of possible cognitive positions from the spectator's response. The spectator is *not* thinking, "This actor is happy,"[40] or "This actor is really Rāma," or "This actor is unhappy," or "This actor might or might not be Rāma," or "This actor is similar to Rāma." Rather, the cognition takes the form "That Rāma who is happy—this man [the actor] is he." The twelfth-century poetician Mammaṭa restates Śrī Śaṅkuka's logical map a little more clearly:

> The perception [of the spectator] is quite distinct from cognitions that are true, false, dubious, or based on similarity, *e.g.*, (1) "He [the actor] is Rāma and Rāma is he," (2) "He is Rāma"—but no, a later cognition rules out the first and shows us that he is not Rāma, (3) "He might or might not be Rāma," and (4) "He is similar to Rāma." Rather, it is like looking at a painting of a horse.[41]

These four possibilities are, as the commentator Vidyācakravartin tells us, the four main cognitive options in everyday experience *(tatra tāval laukikī pratītiś catur-vidhā).* What happens in the mind of the spectator at a dramatic performance is something altogether different. When one admires a painting of a horse *(citra-turage hi kautuka-daśāyām),* the question of its particular reality or unreality does not arise; one sees a generalized or universal horse in a perception that is "dense with wonder" *(camatkāraika-ghana).*[42] For the Sanskrit poeticians, this notion of wonder, *camatkāra,* is one of the keys to any understanding of artistic experience; in the context of logical cognitive process, wonder is clearly of another order than everyday perceptions.[43] It apparently defies standard analysis in terms of truth-claims.

Although Śrī Śaṅkuka's views were ruthlessly rejected by his successors, including Abhinavagupta— in the eyes of the major theoreticians, mimesis is simply not an adequate basis for artistic experience—he does point to something important that should not be obscured by the direction the theory later took. It is as if Śrī Śaṅkuka were saying to us: You cannot ask a poem (or a painting) if it is true. The moment we phrase the question, we have utterly vitiated the reality. Poetic reality is real, but we cannot know it to be real in the way we know other things. We know the poem or the painting is generated through "artifice" and is, in a trivial sense, fictive, but this knowledge does not change the fact that we know the poem or painting to be real in its own terms, whatever they may be (also in terms of what it does to us).

The stumbling block for Śrī Śaṅkuka, as Abhinavagupta shows, lies in his insistence on inference. By his own account, Śrī Śaṅkuka shows that any normal truth-claim presented onstage must be invalid—for the simple reason that Śrī Śaṅkuka thinks an imitation is going on.[44] In other words, Śrī Śaṅkuka, rather like the tradition of Aristotelian poetics in the West, is stuck in a representational mode, whereas Abhinavagupta (and his brilliant precursor Bhaṭṭa Nāyaka) were convinced that there is nothing truly representational about dramatic or poetic art. This is a critical point. To think of our painted horse as representing something is to make the same old mistake of asking whether it is or is not real. There is another way. Similarly, if the poor spectator is expected to engage in a lengthy process of logical deduction or inference, then all we really have is a theory that explains what fails in artistic production. Normally, Abhinavagupta will show us, there are far more important things for the spectator to do; also more important things for him to know.

So what does happen in the theater? Again we find ourselves faced with the generative and integral role of the imagination, which, however, is meant to work along certain regular, predetermined lines. Abhinava's predecessor Bhaṭṭa Nāyaka made the decisive breakthrough by introducing into poetics the notion of *bhāvanā*—generating, bringing into being, "production."[45] We encountered this term at the very outset of our study, where we explored its links with memory (for the Nyāya logicians) and linguistic expressivity per se (for both the grammarians and the Mīmāṃsaka ritualists).[46] Sentences, we should recall, are driven by the urge to bring something into being—something real, we might add, by virtue of the driving forces of expression *(vivakṣā)* and conceptualization *(vikalpa, kalpanā)* in and of themselves. But a literary work also brings something into being—something unusually powerful, even overwhelming, if all goes well—and it does so, at least according to Bhaṭṭa Nāyaka, by a process of *bhāvanā* or *bhāvakatva* that is analogous in certain ways to the way linguistic statements in the Veda generate ritual action in the ritual performer.

Bhaṭṭa Nāyaka's major contribution lay in harnessing the Mīmāṃsā theory of *bhāvanā* to explain what happens in a spectator's mind when he or she is moved by a dramatic or literary performance. For the Mīmāṃsakas, *bhāvanā* is a "teleological" process that ultimately produces the promised fruit of a ritual by moving the ritualist to enact a Vedic injunction and (no less crucially) by amplifying the original injunction with the various procedural details necessary for the performance.[47] In short, language—we are speaking about authoritative, Vedic language, but the Vedic paradigm operates on other linguistic levels as well—is effectual and contains within itself all that is required to induce an action and its consequences. Something very similar happens in the theater, another language-informed domain, albeit one using a distinctive kind of language, rich in tropes, phonic and syntactic textures, and other features proper to literature. This particular kind of poetic language fulfills itself in the listener's or spectator's experience of intense pleasure, the "output," so to speak, of the *bhāvanā* generative system. This insistence on pleasure is highly nontrivial; it deliberately marginalizes other potential aims of a literary work, for example, moralistic and didactic goals. But it is not just any kind of pleasure. Bhaṭṭa Nāyaka—and Abhinavagupta in his wake—were eager to characterize specifically the emotional state induced by art.

Bhaṭṭa Nāyaka coined a word for it: *bhogī-kṛttva,* "pleasuring" or "experientialization" (in Pollock's neatly corresponding neologism). The experience in question has extraordinary *(alaukika)* qualities such as self-absorption, the "coming to rest" in oneself *(viśrānti)* or turning inward *(antar-mukhatva),* a forgetfulness of the outer world, and, above all, a "tasting" *(āsvāda)* of the *rasa* in all its fullness. The sense of satisfaction this tasting produces is akin to what great Yogis feel.[48] Bhaṭṭa Nāyaka seems to have thought that this altered state of consciousness could be further defined in relation to four distinct "mental planes" *(citta-bhūmi),* depending upon the major *rasas* involved (the erotic, the heroic, the gruesome, and the furious).[49] Abhinavagupta reformulated the primary features of this total aesthetic experience as fluidity (deobjectification, *druti*), expansion *(vistara),* and illumination *(vikāsa)*—a set that became canonical. According to Abhinavagupta, ultimate consciousness *(saṃvid)* should naturally have these aspects, but it is usually blocked by constriction and confusion; what the poem or the play achieves is simply the removal of these latter forces, so that consciousness can happily rest in itself, in its innate goodness, brilliance, and joyfulness.

It is quite possible, however, that Bhaṭṭa Nāyaka conceived of this goal in a more nuanced manner; Pollock pointedly calls it a "complex kind of living-through, or disengaged engagement with, the various emotions."[50] The disengagement may well remind us of the floating, unfocused awareness of the village goddess, an inner mode that I have tried to connect to the elusive metaphysical ideal of the Advaita.[51] In any case—and here we come back to *bhāvanā* or *bhāvakatva*—the basic move that makes this "pleasuring" possible is, according Bhaṭṭa Nāyaka's highly original insight, a "universalization" *(sādhāraṇī-karaṇa)* that does away with the particularity of the characters on the stage, at the same time completely removing any egoistic investment on the part of the spectator in the emotions they are triggering.[52] In other words, the Rāma we see on the stage is not the historical figure and epic hero but a stylized abstraction that is meant solely to provide a basis for a transient internal reorganization of the spectator's emotional reality. The stable emotion *(sthāyi-bhāva)* that the character *should* be feeling actually overtakes the spectator from within through a mode of empathic identification that lacks all personal, egoistic features; the happy result is an oddly depersonalized pleasure defined as savoring the *rasa*. It is almost as if the taste were there—fully accessible, free of blockage or constraint, and entirely real—without the taster. Universalization, along the lines just described, transports the spectator beyond his or her normal, everyday awareness into a state of delicious self-forgetfulness and rapturous absorption, free from anxiety, doubt, and the usual background noise of consciousness. Abhinavagupta insists that such a state is, in fact, our true, radiant nature, the very ground of our being, though it is obscured by quotidian experience. It is the great merit of the aesthetic media of poetry, drama, and music that they can restore us to "ourselves," at least momentarily, by inducing the radical self-forgetfulness that is defined as a flood of *rasa*, the fullness of liquid, pure, impersonal feeling.

There is no denying the tremendous explanatory power of this theory, which utterly transformed the terms of discourse within the tradition of Indian poetics; but at the same time we cannot help but notice how odd it is. We'll come back to the question of the spectator's mental state in just a moment, but notice first how "universalization" does away, in a single, sweeping movement, with everything that makes any given character in a drama distinct from others of his or her type. It almost makes no difference whether we are looking at Rāma or Udayana, at Śakuntalā or Sītā or Vāsavadattā; the particularities of plot, too, become quite secondary to the business of *rasa* production by means of typologized abstraction. So radical is this way of understanding artistic endeavor that it cannot possibly be true for any classical Sanskrit play, although it took the discursive-theoretical tradition several centuries to recover from the rampant universalizing impulse. For our purposes, however, and in order to address again the problem of what counts as real, this kind of *bhāvanā* requires one further level of analysis.

Where, we might ask ourselves, is imagination in all this? The answer, though insufficiently theorized by the orthodox Kashmiri poeticians (unless, of course, it was fully worked out in Bhaṭṭa Nāyaka's lost masterpiece), is that the internal mechanism of *bhāvanā/bhāvakatva* depends primarily on acts of imagination on the part of the spectator or listener. We find clear statements to this effect in summaries of Bhaṭṭa Nāyaka's view by somewhat later theorists such as Dhanika and Siṃhabhūpāla.[53] One way to state what happens is as follows: Within the heightened linguistic world of the theater, and given the basic receptivity of the spectator to the expressive process that is being enacted, universalization of the emotion is what enables the spectator's imagination to establish a personal link to what he or she is seeing. The spectator now sees the emotional reality of the character, denuded of its particularity, as linked to something that exists in the spectator's own mind. Once Rāma ceases to be the historical Rāma and becomes only an embodiment of noble (or passionate, or heroic, or tragic) feeling, suitably enhanced by the whole set of auxiliary factors built into the performance, then the spectator is free to identify himself or herself with that character and, very immediately, with the character's emotional reality. It is the imagination, and only the imagination, whatever we might want to call it—*utprekṣā, vibhāvanā, bhāvanā, pratibhā,* et cetera—that can forge this empathic linkage. Imagination alone can bridge the gap between character and spectator, perhaps because of its capacity for resonance and high-velocity communication between discrete minds. *Bhāvanā,* in the poeticians' usage, thus transcends its roots in grammar and syntax and even, for that matter, its unique association with the theory of ritual acts—for, confronted with the particular challenge of poetry, *bhāvanā* necessarily puts into play its innermost mechanism, a capacity to imagine and thereby reappropriate an emotional reality that was hitherto largely veiled, buried, or occluded. Once imagination effectively kicks in, overcoming the entropic resistance that is inherent to mental life, the full-bodied tasting of pleasure can begin.

But this statement by no means exhausts the operation of the imaginative faculty in the context of aesthetic experience. There are at least two other related domains in which imagination is decisively present. First, the language of poetry—which Bhaṭṭa Nāyaka refers to by a general term, *abhidhā* (distinct from the semanticists' usage of the term to mean "denotation" alone)[54]—works by means of the integrating capacity of imaginative insight. No other part of the mental apparatus is capable of enabling the illuminating understanding without which figuration, to name but one crucial element, remains lifeless and ineffective. Second, imagination suffuses and makes possible what the poeticians call "resonance," *saṃvāda,* with reference to a specific set of cognitive activities.[55] We will return to *saṃvāda* later.

Note that imagination, in the sense relevant to this discussion, is not about discovering or inventing something new, except perhaps in the sense that a mathematician might discover a hitherto unanticipated, preexisting formal linkage among discrete realities. The spectator at the drama does not have to invent the stable emotion underlying his experience of savoring. It exists a priori within his or her mind and in the world outside his or her mind. What does have to happen is the recognition that *that* emotion, sparked by words, gestures, and music, is actually *this (my)* emotion, accessible to my experience now in the special circumstances of the aesthetic setting. Such a discovery may well feel intoxicating, and it always includes an imaginative leap.

Thus according to the Kashmiri theorists, at the height of the aesthetic process we imagine not some delimited and particular object but a generalized, nonindividualized reality. Anything overly specific, especially insofar as it attracts some form of egoistic involvement on the part of the spectator, can never unblock a consciousness that suffers precisely from being exiled in the constricted domain of the concrete. Moreover, there is something to be said for the shared, collective work of the depersonalized imagination, which seems to be active in the theater.

What about knowledge, the particular cognitions present in artistic enjoyment? They are, we are happy to discover—following Abhinavagupta's radical extension of Bhaṭṭa Nāyaka's theory—still very much part of the whole process. The spectator does know something, though what he knows is not a reality normally accessible to direct perception *(sākṣātkārāyamāṇa-tva)*. In fact—shades of Śrī Śaṅkuka—it is not an ordinary perception, nor is it false *(mithyā)*, ineffable *(anirvācya)*, similar to something familiar *(laukika-tulya)*, or a superimposition *(tad-āropâdi-rūpa)*. It is something you can taste *(rasanīya)*, and as such, it is free from the constraints of the particular *(viśeṣântarânupahitatvāt)*. One way to describe it is as a kind of intensification of reality *(upacayâvasthā)*.[56] Anyway, being a taste, it has an integrity and a reality resistant to ontological questioning of the type that has plagued many modern discussions of this issue.[57] In our (obviously anachronistic) terms, a taste is not susceptible to falsification.

Without lingering over the point, we might at least take notice of Abhinavagupta's two somewhat surprising analogies relating to the spectator's cognitive state. Having defined the *rasa* experience as a direct perception in the spectator's heart, one free from the obstacles that usually clutter our awareness, he mentions the universalizing factor *(sādhāraṇya)*; it is something not delimited *(parimita)* but rather expanded *(vitata)*, as when one realizes the universal concomitance of smoke with fire *(vyāptigraha iva dhūmâgnyor)* or of trembling with fear. Have we returned to the logic-driven cognitions of Śaṅkuka? Not quite. The thrill that comes from establishing concomitance is expansive, since it moves away from any individual fire and smoke toward a level of abstract, universal law. There is sheer wonder, *camatkāra*, in this discovery, as there is when a theatrical performance works its magic on the audience. The spectators achieve the necessary depersonalized, universalized awareness, *sādhāraṇī-bhāva*, because the two sets of constraining perceptual or experiential factors—time, space, a perceiving observer, and so on, one set belonging to our everyday world, the other to the fictive world of the play—simply cancel each other out *(niyama-hetūnām anyonya-pratibandha-balād atyantam apasaraṇe)*. Notice how, once again, a certain tension between true and false, real and unreal, held in suspension, seems to spark the transition in awareness that poetry can achieve.

What is seen on the stage is not an object *(siddha)*, nor is it fully knowable through the usual criteria of knowledge *(aprameya)*. Yet our cognitive processes are still intact as we watch the play: the spectator, says Abhinavagupta, has *not* simply disappeared *(atyanta-tiraskṛta)*, nor has he or she survived as a full-fledged, "polished" or "crafted" individual consciousness *(ullikhita)*.[58] Again and again we are told that this special awareness generated by poetry is something out of the ordinary, and that it is really a savoring or tasting set free from anything that could, in normal life, block it. And there are still other ways to characterize this awareness—for example, as dense and continuous *(ekaghana),* also as somehow restless, insatiable, and dynamic.[59] But there is also a linguistic component to all this, one naturally central to the question of cognition. Just as in a Vedic ritual context, certain injunctions, technically couched in the past tense, have to be interpreted by the ritualist in an imperative mode by a semantic transfer *(saṅkramaṇa)* away from the literal meaning, a person qualified for aesthetic experience *(adhikārin)* reaches toward a perception that has "a little extra" *(adhikâsti pratipattiḥ)*—something beyond a literal semantics.[60] Poetic *bhāvanā,* the very heart of the entire enterprise, is the production of this enhanced, intensified, nonliteral, nonindividualized, linguistically motivated, densely continuous consciousness.

Linguistically speaking, there is another term for it—*dhvanana,* "reverberation," or *dhvani,* the "reverberating" or "resonant" sound that is the core "self" of poetry, according to Ānandavardhana's masterwork of poetic science, the *Dhvanyāloka.*[61] When we go beyond the literal, and also beyond logically extended, transferred usage *(lakṣaṇā),* we find ourselves in the echo chamber of *dhvani* or *vyañjanā,* both normally translated as "suggestion." But we should not lose sight of the original meaning of *dhvanana/dhvani,* which goes back to the early grammarians' distinction between any individual's particular articulation of a syllable *(vaikṛta-dhvani)* and the abstract sequence of phonemes underlying each such articulation (*prākṛta-dhvani,* to use Bhartṛhari's terminology). If we go still further back, not historically but philosophically, to the creation of linguistic expressivity as such out of something more akin to music, we will encounter the *sphoṭa,* the unitary, potential syllable or word waiting to "burst open" into articulated meaning. The world is alive with the phonic energies analyzed in these categorical levels—the same energies utilized by the poet who deliteralizes language and thereby makes the underlying reverberation audible.[62] That, in fact, is what we listen for in a poem, along with the whole range of meaning-laden playfulness and the necessary "twist" *(vakratā)* built into most poetic speech. If we are lucky, we can hear sound emerging from a presemanticized, potential level to one saturated with all kinds of specific resonances and meanings, a compelling process not far removed from what happens in musical performance, according to the musicological texts.[63] What is real to our perception is just this deep reverberation, the extra, intensified piece of knowing—which, however, is not knowing X, or even knowing or seeing X as Y (as in *utprekṣā*). The content of what is known to the mind of the listener—content that, as we saw, is not amenable to the naive question "Is it real?"—reflects the always astonishing movement, via indirection, from a latent, generative order of sound to the specific echoes that can become "real" in the ordinary sense of the term. This is how poetry brings something into being *(bhāvayati)*—in effect, by amplifying a preexisting echo. In such a world, poets can easily let ordinary objects—these somewhat crude crystallizations, almost the recalcitrant residues, of intralinguistic process—fend for themselves.

3.4. Inexhaustibility

There remains, for our present purposes, one crucial notion, a somewhat surprising outgrowth of the set of premises and intuitions embodied in Abhinavagupta's great synthesis of poetic theory. We have to return briefly, from another vantage point, to the question of the general and the specific.

As we have seen, the Kashmiri poeticians, unlike Descartes, insist upon generalization, *sādhāraṇī-karaṇa*—a movement away from the particular to a nonspecific, almost abstract perception—as the key to all successful imaginative or artistic experience.[64]

> *Rasa* in Sanskrit poetics is not an emotion. It is rather the idea of an emotion, depersonalized through the process of conventional observations. . . . The aesthetics of court poetry are aesthetics of distance and ideation, rather than immediacy and feeling. The personal experiences of the poet, if there are any, are dissolved in the sea of faceless abstractions through meticulously controlled and ordered literary elements in strict adherence to accepted conventions.[65]

Aesthetic moments, then, are "real" only insofar as they are imagined or brought into being in a highly patterned and generalized way. No one is interested, in this context, in the particular smoke and fire that burned down a particular, historical village.

Here the problem of verisimilitude comes into play. Abhinavagupta lists a failure of verisimilitude, or general improbability, as the first obstacle to the release of *rasa* through watching a play.[66] The dramatic reality must have a minimal consistency and integrity. Elsewhere, however, the issue is examined in another light. The relevant passage is strategically placed at the very end of the *Dhvanyāloka,* in the fourth and final chapter, which deals with the question of creative originality and its inexhaustibility in principle. After a long and nuanced discussion of particularity versus generalization, in which Ānandavardhana concedes that poets can and should depict subjects in their individual character, "as they really are," he brings up the subject of *saṃvāda*—the shared or coincident perceptions that, he says, are common among highly intelligent people (such as gifted poets).[67] In other words, we will often find poets treating similar subjects in similar ways. Here Ānanda anticipates one of the more common modern complaints about Sanskrit poetry—all this, however, in the context of an attempt to prove that good poetry will always be fresh and new.[68]

Saṃvāda, he goes on to tell us, is "similarity of one thing to another." It may take several distinct forms, just as it does in the case of living people—a reflection in a mirror, a painted picture, or a body that just happens to look like someone else's. Now comes the unexpected recommendation: the poet should shun the first type (mirroring), since it has no real "self" of its own *(ananyâtma),*[69] and also the second type (the painted portrait), which has a worthless or empty self *(tucchâtma),* but he need not avoid the third type (similarity in bodily form), since it has a definite self. "You cannot say that a person is the same because he happens to resemble another person."[70]

Take a moment to consider what Ānandavardhana is saying. Ostensibly he is exploring what it means when one poet reproduces an idea or phrase used by another, but Ānanda's statement extends beyond the notion of technical imitation to a more general theory of poetic production. Perfect verisimilitude, as in a reflection, is valueless in art; it is no more than a dead, mechanical reproduction. Beautifully crafted paintings are no better than mirror images. They are utterly meaningless for artistic purposes. Poetry is simply not mimetic. It is probably not even representational in any significant sense. But what about the physical likeness of one living person to another?

The analogy is of considerable consequence. In ninth-century Kashmir, no less than in twenty-first-century Jerusalem or Berlin, individuals, although they may resemble one another, are understood to be unique. Resemblance, in itself, is an impoverished heuristic principle. Still, we know there are certain given "facts" or, if you like, conventions with which the poet begins his work: "A subject, if it has a truly distinct self, even if it conforms to a configuration used before, glows like the face of a pretty girl, which poets compare to the moon."[71] Women's faces are, by definition, like the moon—as we saw in the context of *utprekṣā* (where, however, the moon is not quite real). So what? In itself, this fact of life is rather trivial. The real question is what the poet does with his inheritance. Ānandavardhana explains in the prose *vṛtti* following this verse: "A subject that takes up the shadow [or: reflection, beauty, *chāyā*] of something ancient and lovely will attain ultimate beauty, just like a body. And there is no fear of redundancy or repetition, any more than in the case of a pretty girl's face that is like the moon." Abhinavagupta, commenting on this passage, adds that when Ānanda uses the word "self" (*ātman;* see above) he means the true element *(tattva)* that is the inner essence *(sāra-bhūta)* of the subject.

At the very beginning of his book, Ānanda has told us what constitutes the "self" of poetry, its inner life (as opposed to various external, structural and formal elements); only *rasa-dhvani,* the echo that generates "taste," can fill this role. Clearly, it is this same self that is meant here, at the end of the treatise. Thus a poet can, indeed should, reuse the materials available to him from centuries of poetic production; so long as *dhvani* is brought to bear upon them, he will have no reason to fear that he will be accused of boring repetition. The next verse states this clearly, borrowing the language of Śaiva metaphysics: whatever subject bursts upon the poet's mind, charged with light and movement *(sphuritam),* even if it follows some earlier form of beauty, is a good subject for a poem. What is more, good poets who are reluctant to compose on a topic previously used by others can rely on Sarasvatī, the goddess of poetry herself, to supply them with what they need.[72]

This final resort to the goddess is fascinating in its own right. I think it points in a direction that is almost never articulated explicitly in Kashmiri poetics, one much closer to poetic praxis as understood in medieval south India, for example. A rather different understanding of the imagination and its generative mechanisms is hinted at here.[73] But even if we stay within the terms of Ānanda's preceding discussion, we can see something that most discussions of Sanskrit poetry tend to neglect.

The overriding principle of *rasa,* driven by "suggestion"—the indirection that opens up a reverberation in a good poem—has the ability to make even hackneyed topics appear new, "like trees in spring" (*kārikā* 4.4, from this same chapter). So far so good. As Abhinavagupta says (on this verse), poetry occupies the place of springtime *(kāvyaṃ madhu-māsa-sthānīyam),* the mysterious natural force that brings new buds out on barren branches. In this context, Daniel Ingalls has noted, following Abhinavagupta, that

> the variety of suggestiveness is placed outside the human mind; it is the cause, not the result of poetic imagination. It is as though our authors thought of the objects of the world as existing in a pattern which rendered them amenable to mutual suggestions when viewed by a great poet. The poet's imagination, in this view, would be the medium, not the primary cause, of the creation of new worlds. The worlds would be already there through the magic which underlies *dhvani.*[74]

The poet's task is thus to reveal, through an imaginative series of connections, the particular freshness that *always* emerges from a vision of such relations. However, it is possible, and perhaps more likely, that the poet's vision and the underlying set of hidden interrelationships are mutually determined, each side to the creative transaction shaping and, in a sense, discovering the other; we will return to this point. But the truly remarkable implication of this entire discussion is that such a revelation depends upon, and brings into focus, the singularity of each such poetic perception. Generality, which is more or less taken for granted, and which informs and patterns the presentation of a pretty face as the moon, is no more than the occasion for a singular experience. Singularity means, in terms of this discussion, a particular aliveness animating external form. It is this irreducible aliveness, made accessible by *dhvani,* that forms the true subject matter of any poem and that alone counts as real.

There is no dearth of hackneyed poetry. But neither is there any lack of radical new perceptions that take us beyond the conventional and the mechanical. The potential for such freshness is literally infinite *(ananta),* as Ānanda says again and again. What Bhaṭṭa Nāyaka called *bhāvanā,* this poetic "bringing into existence" through imagination, now seems to depend upon a sensitivity to the singular embodiment, to the lively inner being encased in external form. Every pretty girl's face is like the moon *in a uniquely personal way.* That is what imagination means in this period, and that is why its products are so real. Fictionality, whether operating within figuration (as for Ruyyaka and Vidyācakravartin) or within the dramatic reality onstage (as for Bhaṭṭa Nāyaka and Abhinavagupta), is no more than a pale, though necessary, precondition for releasing this unrepeatable living awareness. Even the process of abstraction and generalization, the heart of Bhaṭṭa Nāyaka's insight about the way imagination works in drama, turns out to be intimately tied, not without tension, to an earlier but enduring notion of singularity. The tensile combination of the real and the unreal is joined to a perceptual process in which general, nonspecific, or conventional traits are viewed through the lens of singularity. Or we could say that the visionary poet stands somewhere between the reality of endless, generative potentiality, which is nonparticular and abstract, and its repeated, indirect instantiations. Hence his power to work upon the world of objects—but that is another story.

3.5. The New Critics: A Seventeenth-Century Perspective on *Bhāvanā*

Before we conclude this initial exploration of the *śāstra*, we should take a moment to review developments in the seventeenth century, when the concept of imagination—including the poet's practice of *bhāvanā*—underwent remarkable revision. We can see something of this in Jagannātha's compendium of poetics, the *Rasa-gaṅgādhara*, composed at the Mughal court in the seventeenth century. Jagannātha is often seen as the last of the great Sanskrit poeticians. He, too, begins his work with a long chapter on *rasa*, but in the course of this discussion, in which Abhinavagupta's canonical view is prominently stated, he offers a surprising twist on the issues we have been studying.

Jagannātha summarizes and analyzes eleven distinct views on the meaning of the term *rasa* in a poetic context, beginning with Abhinavagupta, and without committing himself to any of them. In itself, this encyclopedic review is suggestive of a new, critical stance toward the whole history of the tradition.[75] For our purposes, views 2 and 3, devoted to Bhaṭṭa Nāyaka and to an unspecificed group of "new critics" *(navyāḥ)*, respectively, are of special relevance.

Bhaṭṭa Nāyaka, we recall, was the first to speak of *bhāvanā* as the distinguishing feature of the spectator's experience in the theater. Jagannātha is interested in characterizing the operation of this *bhāvanā* more carefully (in general, throughout his book he strives to define arguments very precisely, mostly in terms of the "new logic," *navya-nyāya*). So he begins with the statement that a person who is neutral, that is, uninvolved in the dramatic proceedings *(taṭastha)*, will not be able to taste *rasa*. But what is going on in the mind of a spectator who *is* involved? Something rather complex. For one thing, he (Jagannātha and Bhaṭṭa Nāyaka are only concerned here with a male spectator, as will become clear) has to forget something important, that is, the fact that the heroine Śakuntalā, for example, is not actually available to him *(agamyā)*—she is, after all, married to the hero, King Duṣyanta.[76] The spectator is supposed to be feeling a generalized desire, *rati,* but for this desire to focus on Śakuntalā, something in his mind must at least momentarily block the knowledge that she is strictly off-limits. We might think that this problem is taken care of by the spectator's projected identification with the hero of the play, Duṣyanta (for whom Śakuntalā is an altogether appropriate lover). But no—the spectator knows very well how different he is from Duṣyanta, who is noble and fearless and, moreover, belongs to another era; the spectator is a modern man and has to admit to being rather cowardly. In short, the spectator's awareness is marked by certain necessary blockages, on the one hand, and by an unbridgeable inner distance from the actor and his role, on the other. Even at the theater, we are who we are.

So what *does* happen? *Bhāvanā,* an imaginative universalization, takes over. The first stage is sparked by the direct meaning of words *(abhidhā)*—not by indirection, as we may be accustomed to thinking—which sets in motion a generative process *(bhāvakatva-vyāpāra)* that highlights a sense of Śakuntalā's desirability *(kāntatva),* conducive to *rasa,* at the same time blocking the knowledge that she is totally inaccessible *(agamyatvâdi-rasa-virodhi-jñāna-pratibandha-dvāra).* Now, when Duṣyanta, Śakuntalā, and the coordinates of time, space, and circumstance have been universalized, and the generative process has more or less exhausted itself (literally, become crippled, *paṅgau pūrva-vyāpāra-mahimani*), and when all that is impure[77] has disappeared through an innate faculty of "enjoyment" *(bhogakṛttva-vyāpāra),* the spectator can relax into a direct experience, universal in essence, brought about thanks to *bhāvanā,* that takes the form of coming to rest in his own consciousness.[78] This is *rasa.* It is an experience quite distinct from prior, ordinary ones, and also from memory; it is neither purely verbal *(śābdī)* nor mental *(mānasī),* but rather something sui generis, approximating the ecstasy that comes from "tasting" ultimate reality *(brahmâsvāda-savidha-varti).*

Apparently, what *bhāvanā* actually does, in this perspective, is to recycle the stuff of the dramatic context as the various supports, triggers, and concomitants *(vibhāva, anubhāva, vyabhicāri-bhāva)* of *rasa.* A new world is fashioned, with the help of poetic language, before our eyes. Two new elements in this description should be stressed. First, the generative, imaginative process *(bhāvakatva)* clearly involves a kind of distancing, leaving the spectator with an awareness of his own distinct status even as he gives himself to the spell of the play. Second, this distancing effect has to finish its operation before the true goal—"enjoyment"—can be achieved. There is a clear progression through three stages—articulation, generation, enjoyment—and an evident intensification of the spectator's inner experience through this process. The complex, internally divided awareness that exists in the early stages, including the necessary element of blockage or forgetting, gives way to a restful, apparently integral consciousness, which is really an experience of consciousness itself in its own true nature.

But it is with the "new critics" that Jagannātha reaches an entirely unfamiliar, no-nonsense perspective, one in which the cognitive content of the spectator's experience is, once again, the center of interest. *Bhāvanā* is still the basic mechanism at work in producing *rasa*. But this imaginative force is now classed explicitly as a *doṣa,* a false or defective cognition.[79] The spectator himself produces or projects this fictive, imagined reality in which Duṣyanta feels desire for Śakuntalā; moreover, the spectator's own self, *svâtman,* is temporarily veiled by the imagined Duṣyanta identity that has taken over and which is, by definition, a kind of ignorance, *ajñāna*—as in the classical analogy of a person who mistakenly sees a piece of shell as silver.[80] Without the cognitive error, it wouldn't happen, and when the error is recognized, the experience is over. In other words, the "mistake" is willfully, deliberately projected by the active spectator, who feels, as he does so, a special pleasure that cannot easily be distinguished from the "ultimate" pleasure that comes next. His own self makes the fictive reality visible *(sâkṣibhāsya);* crucially, this reality is not amenable to articulation *(anirvacanīya),* which is to say, in classic Vedântic fashion, that it cannot be reduced to the status of being either true or false.[81] The precise reality-content of the spectator's self-identification as Duṣyanta is also resistant to articulation *(avacchadakaṃ duṣyantatvam apy anirvacanīyam).* It as if the spectator were saying to himself, "I, for the duration of this play, am a fictive Duṣyanta who feels desire for Śakuntalā." This desire—nourished, no doubt, by unconscious karmic memories in the spectator—merges with Duṣyanta's rather ordinary desire as portrayed by the actor. In this sense, given that the spectator knows very well that he is not "really" Duṣyanta, poetic suggestion, *vyañjanā,* can be said to operate by creating an in-between space where desire, or any other poetically intensified emotion, is neither real nor unreal.

What about universalization or generalization *(sādhāraṇya)* à la Bhaṭṭa Nāyaka? It is impossible, says Jagannātha (in the name of the new critics), without this special kind of fabrication *(doṣa-viśeṣa-kalpanā)* that produces a sense of Śakuntalā, for example, by repeatedly invoking her name. Once we allow for the conscious, fictive identification with Duṣyanta, the rest follows naturally. The result will be the peculiar tasting that poetry generates and which is utterly different from any other cognitive experience *(vilakṣaṇo hi kamanīyaḥ kāvya-vyāpāra-ja āsvādaḥ pramāṇântara-jād anubhavāt).*

In effect, the whole notion of universalization has been jettisoned. The new critics think they have a more economical explanation of artistic experience. Again there are stages—the linguistic trigger sparks the false cognition, enhanced by all the other factors operating in the dramatic space, that produces pleasure. *Bhāvanā* is no longer about generalizing experience and consequent loss of ego awareness but rather about maintaining the tensile fiction that is neither true nor false. The spectator who gives himself willingly to the feeling seems to hold the tension of true and false within him, to invest in it in the interest of generating the distinctive joy that depends entirely upon this very tension. He remains aware throughout, in a layered, complex cognitive state. And while his knowledge of himself as Duṣyanta is, in the technical language of the logicians, "adventitious" *(āhārya)*—non-intrinsic—his experience in the theater cannot be false, for its effects are wholly real. It cannot, however, be based on valid or correct perception.

We have come back to the problem posed by *utprekṣā* and its processual merging of what is false with what is real, in Ruyyaka's analysis. For the third time in this chapter we have run up against an insistence that what is most powerful, and probably most true, in a poetic moment is the balancing or suspension of real and unreal, or their compacted intertwining, in a mode that allows some sort of breakthrough (cognitive, emotional, existential). According to Ruyyaka, Abhinavagupta, and Jagannātha, each in his own way, the cognitive aspect of poetic experience requires an intermediate kind of knowing, not reducible to a question such as "Is what I am seeing or hearing real?" Any answer to such a question cannot but be wrong. But in all three instances, there is a crucial leap: either one sees something unreal as real and studies the process of their interpenetration, thereby reaching toward an imaginative reality with its own integrity, or one somehow moves through a posited fictive reality to some hyperreal, intensified internal state, still laden with conscious cognitive elements. Still, it is important to note in Jagannātha's discussion the fresh spirit of the seventeenth century; his new critics have, in effect, debunked the canonical vision of Abhinavagupta.[82] Epistemic concerns have overruled an ontic enigma, even if these concerns still allow for—in fact require—a readiness on the part of the aficionado to contain the unresolved tension in his mind. For the new critics, too, this combination of irreconcilable truth-values, utterly immune to ontic determination and rooted in an inner perceptual act on the part of the observer, is the key to imaginative experience and its effects. In essence, it now defines imaginative activity per se. But this is only part of a much wider conceptual revolution, which we examine in detail in Part II.

— 4 —

Poetics 2: Illumination

4.1. Introducing *Pratibhā*

Bhāvanā—the production of powerful aesthetic effects through imaginative acts and other processes unfolding within the mind—is one way the Sanskrit experts on poetry talk about the imagination. When all is said and done, it's a somewhat limited way. The poets themselves are far more daring: they are not afraid to make room, almost nonchalantly, for objects created entirely by thought, imagined into existence by skilled sorcerers of the pregnant word. In the medieval south Indian traditions, such objective effects are quite normative; poets unable to achieve them lack a crucial qualification for practicing their trade. But if we linger a little longer with the poeticians, we will find wider applications of the notion of imaginative practice and new domains where we might seek it. No one doubts that real poets have access to a penetrating vision and that this gift of theirs is, finally, a critical component of their poetry. But how are we to understand the mechanics of poetic seeing? Where does the vision come from? Is it a matter of something like divine inspiration, or can it be cultivated by hard work and unrelenting self-discipline? And just what is it that poets see—some natural but latent facet of the world they are describing, or a possible creative and innovative intensification of certain aspects of that world, or a restructuring of the elements and forces that somehow cohere in given objects, or a grid of subtle relations among pieces of reality that only the artist can integrate and describe? For that matter, is the poet really the author of his or her poem? Or does the poem have an autonomous existence outside the poet's mind, thus predating his or her awareness of it? Finally, if the means available to the poet are largely figurative and oblique, is it possible to read the imagination itself as a peculiar figure, or metafigure, in its own right? We examine in this chapter the theoreticians' attempts to deal with these questions. Although some of their discussions may seem burdened with technical language and arcane arguments, and the larger questions are sometimes posed indirectly, in muted terms, the answers that emerge (particularly in the later Ālaṅkārikas, from Ruyyaka on) are bold, engaging, and important for any understanding of the fully mature models of the imagination that await us.

So let us start again, with another term often used by poeticians for the workings of the imagination: *pratibhā*, "illumination" or, more literally, "counterradiance"—a visionary, luminous mode. If one were intent upon tracing the lineaments of a Sanskrit theory of creativity, the notion of *pratibhā* would be a natural point of departure. Sanskrit poeticians regularly claimed that this mental faculty or propensity was a sine qua non of poetic creativity and somehow close to the elusive impulse, possibly divine in origin, that drives the poet; however, definitions vary widely, as do modern glosses on the term. Some scholars feel that *pratibhā* is as close as we can get to an equivalent of our notion of "imagination."[1] In any case, the domain of *pratibhā* is not coterminous with that of *bhāvanā*, studied in the previous chapter. We need to explore the distinction in the light of contrasting models of the mind, particularly in the works of three unconventional masters: Rājaśekhara (tenth century, Kanauj), Kuntaka (late tenth century, Kashmir), and, once again, Jagannātha (mid-seventeenth century, Delhi, the Mughal court).

First, a quick look at the older sources. The radiance involved may be concrete and physical, an actual flashing in the mind and, as such, something accessible to introspective meditation. Bhartṛhari (mid-fifth century) uses the term to explain the way we understand an utterance (or sentence, *vākya*)—in a single, unitary "flash" that goes far beyond any analytical or logical concern with the individual building blocks of syllables and words (which are anyway seen as largely fictive entities) and their interrelations. The words trigger the flash that *is* the meaning[2] and that is, interestingly, utterly resistant to paraphrase, the result of the individual listener's own experience *(praty-ātma-vṛtti-siddhā)*, and not really consciously known or capable of being described by this listener.[3] Note the stress on the irreducible singularity of *any* utterance, seen as an intelligible whole and emerging from nonrepeatable experience that may in itself resist articulation.

Direct auditory perception is a staple element in Bhartṛhari's *pratibhā*, as is the linguistic potentiality that he calls *bhāvanā:* the "bringing into being," through memory and other processes internal to the mind, of whatever meaning is meant to effect.[4] It is striking that, for Bhartṛhari, *pratibhā* is by no means limited to human beings or to the rational mind: it is this same innate, effortless faculty that moves the male cuckoo to sing in the spring and other birds and animals to make nests or homes, just as it moves them to eat, love, hate, and hop or leap.[5] The stress is on a faculty or principle that is integrative, active, activating, unconscious, and instantaneous in operation. But there is nothing "mystical" about it—it is a natural, definable feature of linguistic reality, like the softness that goes with the full ripening *(paripāka)* of fruit or other things (hearts/minds?).[6] Nor does it seem to involve an imaginative act or process in any way.

Things change when we enter the poeticians' thematic-semantic world. Here, as already stated, *pratibhā* has a particular salience, though often more in relation to what we might call "inspiration" than to the imagination proper. Nonetheless, the visionary capacity of the poet's mind is clearly involved in these discussions. Ānandavardhana tells us in an early *kārikā* verse (1.6) that the goddess of speech, Sarasvatī, reveals—by pouring out particularly sweet meaning-matter *(artha-vastu)* that belongs to great poets—a special, shimmering illumination that is not part of everyday worldly experience *(aloka-sāmānyam . . . pratisphurantam pratibhā-viśeṣam).* This illumination or "genius," as Ingalls, Masson, and Patwardhan translate, is defined by Abhinavagupta in his commentary on this passage as *apūrva-vastu-nirmāṇa-kṣamā prajñā,* "an intuitive understanding capable of creating something unprecedented."[7] Abhinavagupta rounds out his definition by adding that "the special feature of this [*pratibhā*] is its ability to generate poetry of great beauty and clarity because of its being infused with *rasa.*" So *pratibhā* enables creativity, specifically the creation of poetry that is fresh and original; the goddess of speech herself has responsibility for this gift of the true poet, a gift that is literally divine, supermundane in its working, possibly transempirical in consequence. It involves a certain kind of light that the goddess shows—if we only have the readiness to see it—to be operating in the poet's mind (for Abhinavagupta, this light also seems to have taste, *rasa*). In Filliozat's felicitous paraphrase: "La pratibhā (litt. illumination) est la production d'une connaissance par la mise en lumière intérieure d'objets intérieures."[8]

4.2. Rājaśekhara: Creative Listening

Other poeticians provide us with similar statements that have been ably collected by Sreekantaiya.[9] Possibly the most extensive and surprising formulations are by Rājaśekhara in early tenth-century Kanauj—a moment of major innovation in the Sanskrit literary world, one in which a new image of the ideal poet as a professional craftsman, who can be trained to excel at his craft as opposed to "merely" inspired by divine powers, has emerged and come to dominate other, earlier images. Rājaśekhara's *Kāvya-mīmāṃsā* is, in effect, a handbook for the aspiring poet who may also be interested in the theory, and the theoretical controversies, underlying the rules of his guild. It adopts the severe style of scholastic argumentation—laconic, seemingly obsessed with classification, with frequent ellipses and occasional flashes of personal insight. At an early point in this fascinating work (Chapter 4), immediately after a long pseudomythical account of the First Poet *(kāvya-puruṣa),* the author embarks on a detailed, categorical discussion of *pratibhā* as a necessary feature of any really accomplished poet.[10]

He begins, however, with other preconditions for producing poetry. First comes *buddhi,* a basic intelligence (divided into two main types, "natural" and "adventitious," that is, acquired through practice). He then quotes a certain Śyāmadeva, who thinks that profound meditation, *samādhi,* is the key to producing good poetry. *Samādhi* is a deep secret of the goddess, a focusing of the mind that knows whatever can or should be known *(vidita-vedya-vidhi).* So this kind of well-integrated meditation clearly allows for a special kind of knowing; it also identifies the poet as primarily a visionary or seer, with a direct link to the divine. Another theorist, however, named Maṅgala, thinks that "practice" *(abhyāsa)* is what counts. Never mind waiting for, or working toward, inspiration: practice, if continuous, imparts an extraordinary skillfulness. This tension between some kind of supramundane revelation, on the one hand, and the rewards of assiduous practice, on the other, survives in theoretical discussions of the *śāstra* for centuries. As usual in this text, Rājaśekhara, after quoting his predecessors, proceeds to set forth his own, rather commonsensical view. Both these elements, he says, are useful: meditation is an internal effort, practice an external one. Both make "talent"—*śakti*—shine forth. And it is talent that is the primary source of good poetry.

But talent, the real bedrock of poetic endeavor, has its own further aspects and roles. First and foremost, it is talent that activates or motivates the two intertwined processes of *pratibhā*, "inspiration," and *vyutpatti*, "training, *Bildung*." Rājaśekhara has devoted part of Chapter 5 to the latter; the rest of Chapter 4 is given over to exploring and ordering our topic of *pratibhā*. What exactly is it, and how are we to understand it? And just what does the poet see in the flashing light of his mind? *Pratibhā*, Rājaśekhara says, is the feature or faculty that, operating in the heart, illuminates the whole mass of words, the "caravan" of meanings, the figures, and the modes of speech. Even a poet born blind can see—if he has *pratibhā*. How do we know this? Because great poets describe for us things they can't possibly have known from their own experience, such as foreign landscapes, or what goes on inside the protagonist of their poem, or various other matters. Rājaśekhara gives examples of all these categories; let us look briefly at the last one ("miscellaneous"), illustrated by *Raghuvaṃśa* 6.82:

tathāgatāyāṃ parihāsa-pūrvaṃ sakhyāṃ sakhī vetra-bhṛd ābabhāṣe/
ārye vrajāmo 'nyata ity athaināṃ vadhūr asūyā-kuṭilaṃ dadarśa//

The companion smiled, cane in hand.
She could see what was going on inside
her friend. So she said, "Dear lady,
let's move on to someone
else." The bride threw her a look
crooked with indignation.

The setting is the *svayaṃvara* or bridegroom-choice of the lovely princess Indumatī. She has been led by her companion Sunandā through a long line of hopeful suitors and has finally reached Aja, the hero of this part of the poem. Sunandā runs through Aja's resumé, emphasizing his distinguished lineage, but Indumatī is already in love with this candidate—though she is too shy to admit it openly. But then there is not really any need for verbal statements: Indumatī's hairs are standing on end and she is thrilling with desire, and her friend obviously sees this. That's why Sunandā smiles.

She teases Indumatī: "Let's move on." As if there were anywhere to go. The bride-to-be throws her a crooked look. The moment is critical; a silent decision has been made and communicated. The two women understand each other—and this empathic, almost wordless interchange is no doubt part of what interests Rājaśekhara. It is something poets know about, possibly even the main basis for their work. But there is more. Indumatī feels *asūyā*—indignation, anger, impatience, even perhaps a twinge of envy of her friend (for this princess is about to undergo a radical change in her life, and she may have some residual longing for the innocence of childhood that she must soon relinquish). All this is compressed in a single adverbial compound *(asūyā-kuṭilam),* "crooked with indignation." And this is where the poet's *pratibhā* comes in. Kālidāsa has seen, envisaged, or imagined all manner of countries, continents, people, human situations; he also knows, with certain, intuitive knowledge, what is going on in Indumatī's mind. How does he know? There is that luminosity of inner vision, the gift of a real poet. Still, how does this vision operate? Take this as a central question for our analysis. It will haunt us throughout the rest of this book, as it seems to have haunted Rājaśekhara. There is a kind of knowing from inside that does not require what we might describe as the standard, expectable procedure—a movement, say, from the inside of one mind outward through the exterior of the body, then through the external body of the other person and into her mind. That is not how the poet knows what he knows.

But the example may take us a little further into Rājaśekhara's metapoetic world. He quotes this verse to some purpose. That crooked look speaks not only to the heroine's emotional state but also to the poet's discipline and creativity. *Pratibhā* is his major tool, one that requires the slight twist of indirection, the crooked or jagged movement of the mind that allows the poet to speak truth. In other words, empathic understanding and insight nearly always require a certain imaginative leap, normally expressed by implication or other indirect, twisted, and nonliteral linguistic means. A charming "crookedness" is of the essence, and the verse, as Rājaśekhara reads it, actually points to this elementary, necessary aspect of the poetic life.

In short, the professional poet must have the confidence to tell us what is going on in his character's heart, but the usual perceptual or inductive ways of knowing are of little use in such a process. It is something the poet can see.

But it is also something that can be cultivated. This is a crucial point for Rājaśekhara, one that is linked to no less crucial notions of taste and that marks a profound shift in the way the artist's role is understood. We will have to take a moment to unravel the convoluted exposition he offers in order to make this point; please be patient. There is an advantage to following Rājaśekhara's own chosen mode of explanation. *Pratibhā,* he says, can be either active, *kārayitrī,* or receptive (critical, creative), *bhāvayitrī.* The latter category is perhaps the more interesting one for our purposes; we will come back to it shortly, but first we need to observe the three ways of being active in poetic production. Active *pratibhā* can be congenital, adventitious, or learned *(sahajā, āhārya, aupadeśikī)*. We discover that one can be born with the talent for visualization, the result of processes of polishing or refinement that took place in some other life *(janmântara-saṃskāra)*; it can develop or be developed by refinement that one achieves in one's current life; or it can simply be taught, in perhaps rather technical ways, on the basis of existing texts *(mantra-tantra)*. The result of this tripartition is, not surprisingly, yet another set of three: there are poets who are divinely gifted *(sārasvata)*, naturally intelligent *(buddhimān)*, endowed with a refinement rooted in experience in their earlier lives; others can achieve greatness by practice in this existence *(ābhyāsika)*, while the residual type includes those unfortunates who are naturally unintelligent but who can yet be shown the power of language *(vāg-vibhava)* by a capable teacher.

A certain recursivity and mutual determination are built into Rāja-śekhara's scheme, taken as a whole: thus talent motivates inspiration and practice and is itself illuminated, perhaps activated, by them in turn. But the apparent hierarchy of types is rather unstable. The third, relatively debased category—the poet lacking understanding who depends wholly on skilled instruction—turns out, in the end, to be no less "divine" *(sārasvata)* than the first type, if only he can persuade or coerce the goddess Sarasvatī, by rituals of a Tantric cast *(tantra-mantra-prayoga)*, to take him for her vehicle.[11] It's possible that much of the best poetry is produced by forcing the hand of the goddess in just such ways.

This recursive logic is perhaps why Rājaśekhara rejects the attempts of authoritative teachers *(ācāryāḥ)* to rank the three types of poet in a simple progression from top to bottom. "Grapes, being naturally sweet, don't need to be sweetened by sugar-cane juice"—thus the teachers. No, says Rāja-śekhara: double causation doubles the effect. This apparently means that congenital talent can be amplified and further refined by education and further practice. In any case—we have now reached our author's straight-forward conclusion—what really matters is excellence *(utkarṣa)*, however it is achieved.

He concedes, citing a verse, that it isn't often that one finds in a single poet the marvelous combination of intelligence, mastery of the sciences, and the mysterious talent *(upaniṣac-cakti)* that, together, conduce to the best poetry. Just at this point Rājaśekhara quotes another poem that aims at an empirical ranking of the relative merits of various poets:

ekasya tiṣṭhati kaver gṛha eva kāvyam
anyasya gacchati suhṛd-bhavanāni yāvat/
nyasyad vidagdha-vadaneṣu padāni śaśvat
kasyâpi sañcarati viśva-kutūhalīva//

Some poems sit in the poet's house,
others make it to a friend's door.
A good poem travels the world
on the lips of brilliant people,
as if it had an endless wanderlust.[12]

Another triplet: excellence apparently has its vindication in the reader's experience. Some poems—the ones that have a built-in restlessness—break through the limits of space and, perhaps, of time. They travel the world. This achievement is not, it seems, a matter of mere distribution, the number of copies sold or learned by heart, but rather a function of a visionary, empathic, and cultivated talent that unpredictably carves out a space for poetry in the minds of those capable of responding to it. As Mandelstam said, a millennium after Rājaśekhara: it is not faith but taste that moves mountains.

So much for active *pratibhā*. We can see how it quite naturally drifts into the mode of reception. The poet does not create the poem by himself. There has to be a capable listener, whom Rājaśekhara calls a *bhāvaka,* a "producer," that is, someone gifted with a "receptive inspiration," *bhāvayitrī pratibhā*. Both terms are interesting. They express the notion of bringing something into being. "The receptive *pratibhā* brings the poet's effort and intention into existence" *(sā hi kaveḥ śramam abhiprāyaṃ ca bhāvayati)*. Or, more picturesquely: "The tree of composing poetry bears fruit through this receptive *pratibhā*. Otherwise it would be barren *(avakeśī)*." But the ancient teachers again object: What difference is there, really, between these two kinds of inspiration? Is not the poet someone who brings things into being *(bhāvayati)*, and is not the bringer-into-being *(bhāvaka)* a poet?

It's a good question. The visionary empathy that our author has been describing may, after all, be a single faculty, shared by the poet and his or her listener. On the other hand, Kālidāsa is quoted as saying that such is not the case: The two are definitely distinct. One knows how to compose, the other how to listen. It's like the difference between gold and the touchstone that tests its quality. Both abilities, however, seem to be necessary (also mutually dependent). Rājaśekhara leaves this controversy unresolved. The discussion veers off into another categorical division, this time within the ranks of the *bhāvakas:* resuming a passage in Vāmana,[13] the author distinguishes between the exotic categories of "those lacking appetite" *(arocakinaḥ)* and "those who consume everything, down to straws / blades of grass" *(sa-tṛṇâbhyavahāriṇaḥ)*—in other words, something like prissy pedants, who find fault with nearly everything they hear, as opposed to enthusiasts who are unable to discriminate at all.[14] We can take leave of the discussion at this point, noting only that Rājaśekhara can't resist adding yet two more categories—the envious *(matsariṇaḥ)* and those immersed in truth *(tattvâbhiniveśinaḥ).* The envious are universally encountered; not even an immensely gifted *bhāvaka,* who can truly distinguish faults from merits, is likely to be free of envy. As for those with access to truth, *tattva,* we have no doubt that they are Rājaśekhara's favorites along with the naturally intelligent apprentice, similarly endowed, with which he began.

What have we learned about the notion of poetic imagination after this long discussion? Compared to the later Ālaṅkārikas, such as Ruyyaka and Vidyānātha, Rājaśekhara seems never to break through into a full thematization of imagination as such.[15] His *pratibhā* wavers somewhere between a divine gift of vision, mostly internally focused, and a certain talent for empathic understanding that can and probably should be honed, intensified, and refined by an aspiring poet. This visionary faculty does, however, function as a particular mode or imaginative project common to the poet and his audience. The interdependence of these two figures is of the essence: a poet can probably find a master, a friend, an advisor, a disciple, a teacher—but it's always a miracle *(citra)* if he finds a *bhāvaka,* that is, someone who will understand him and thereby bring his poem into full reality.[16] Such a person, if he or she exists, will be endowed with the good taste that depends on real discrimination and insight *(viveka, vivecana).* If we step back from the proliferating categorical series, with all the types and subtypes mostly ordered in triplicate, we are left with just three, or possibly four, primary and overlapping concepts. Poetry requires talent, *śakti,* whatever its source; good taste, which can be taught; and the flash of tangible insight, *pratibhā,* that comes alive only through the sympathetic act of the person who can make it do so, the *bhāvaka* specializing in precisely this active and creative project. The stress on the *bhāvaka*'s role and its existential potential is important in terms of the subsequent history of the tradition—both for the theoretical debates among the poeticians on the nature of poetic process and for the implicit theories of the poets who embody their understanding in praxis. When we arrive, in the sixteenth and seventeenth centuries, at a more extensive application of imagination as a central element in aesthetic experience and, beyond the field of art, in human life in general, it is again a kind of "bringing into being," *bhāvanā*, that defines the concept. Like the *bhāvaka* of Rājaśekhara, the imaginatively gifted practitioner of *bhāvanā* (the fourth basic concept) becomes the real guarantor of the poem's truthfulness and ultimately, beyond even truthfulness, of its *reality*. Rājaśekhara is not yet there, though he clearly adumbrates this line of development. And we should not forget that, for all his investment in a serious regimen of training for poets and in the abstract conceptual series that rationalizes such a regimen, he leaves room at the end for the mysterious and unpredictable action of the goddess Sarasvatī, who is apparently capable of short-circuiting the entire process and pushing even the illiterate country bumpkin over the brink into inspired poetry. She may even be amenable to manipulation to that end by someone drunk on *kāvya* and prepared to pursue his passion to the end.

4.3. Kuntaka: On Intensification

Kuntaka (late tenth-century Kashmir) often cites Rājaśekhara; perhaps, nonconformist that he was, he felt some affinity with this utterly unconventional predecessor, relatively close to him in time. Indeed, if we think of Rājaśekhara as providing something of a model sensibility for Kuntaka, despite the latter's far more pressing theoretical and philosophical concerns, then Kuntaka's splendid isolation within the Alaṅkāra tradition—his strikingly "flexible and . . . open ended" analysis, which "departs from the conventional understanding of the purpose of poetry and the purpose of Alaṅkāraśāstra as well"—may be slightly tempered.[17] Kuntaka is also, of course, interested in the origin of the poetic impulse and in issues of originality, and he thus mentions *pratibhā* repeatedly in the course of his long essay, the *Vakrokti-jīvita* or "Life of Poetic Utterance"; as with other key terms that turn up there, he seems to use this concept somewhat idiosyncratically.[18] Perhaps his most trenchant discussion of *pratibhā* comes near the beginning of the third chapter, in which he graduates from the analysis of the charming "twist" *(vakratā)* in language, and in cognition, that imparts beauty on the level of the individual word to an exploration of this twist as it operates within a full-fledged utterance or sentence *(vākya)*. Somewhat surprisingly, the discussion opens with a question, not entirely explicit, about ornamentation *(alaṅkāra)* in a wider sense—more specifically, about whether ornamentation is to be understood as intrinsic or extrinsic to the subject matter of a good poem. We have the recognized figure of *svabhāvokti,* "naturalistic description": is this or is it not a true *alaṅkāra?*[19]

There are, says Kuntaka, certain kinds of poetic perception that are inimical to conventional means of ornamentation. When something naturally very beautiful is concerned, the poet's propensity for figuration is likely to exact a high cost; even a simple simile may serve to distract our attention and to obscure what really needs to be seen. This idea is a familiar topos in the works of Sanskrit poets; Kuntaka cites Kālidāsa:

tāṃ prāṅ-mukhīṃ tatra niveśya tanvīṃ
kṣaṇaṃ vyalambanta puro niṣaṇṇāḥ/
bhūtârtha-śobhâhriyamāṇa-netrāḥ
prasādhane saṃnihite 'pi nāryaḥ//

They sat her down facing east,
and then they lingered there, sitting
around her with the makeup
ready to go. They couldn't help staring
at a beauty that was
what it was.

This is *Kumāra-sambhava* 7.13—the prelude to Pārvatī's wedding to Śiva, the moment when the bride is to be dressed and decorated. All the poet wanted to do, says Kuntaka, was to bring out the innately ravishing, extraordinarily delicate or subtle beauty of this woman. Like the women charged with getting her ready for the ceremony, the poet, too, fears that the act of further adornment *(alaṇkaraṇa-kalāpa-kalana)* will only spoil this perfect, natural *(sahaja)* beauty. Best to leave well enough alone. Let the poet focus on seeing, and helping us to see, what is already there.

But only on one condition—that his subject is endowed with some extraordinary feature, some heightened intensity or excess, to begin with. This critical point is deeply linked to Kuntaka's understanding of *pratibhā,* as we will see. He has only contempt for the notion that a poet might start out with any old thing, a general or common perception of an object *(sāmānya-vastu-mātram)* that would serve as the basis for his act of ornamentation. To attempt to adorn an object devoid of that necessary "extra value" or "excess" is to fail, at the outset, at the poet's primary task of creating delight in the mind of the connoisseur; such a poem, empty at its core, can no more give delight than could a hungry demon.[20] Note the force of the simile. No doubt there are always such hungry, empty, predatory poems lurking in ambush for the hapless reader.

In fact, Kuntaka's observation goes still deeper. Poetry is not a matter of desperation, an occupation of last resort. Nobody is forcing you to compose poems.[21] But if you *are* going to write poetry, you had better take seriously your obligation to please, and this means you have to find a subject that has its own intrinsic power or interest, some outstanding feature *(utkṛṣṭa-dharma)* that deserves attention and, perhaps, further enhancement without going beyond what is appropriate in the given context. If you opt for a subject lacking this basic quality of intensity, it will be like painting a polished picture on some utterly unworthy surface, say some poor piece of a wall.

Again and again, we hear the language of excess *(atiśaya, atyanta-ramaṇīyatā, mahiman).* Poetry is not about the ordinary; the poet's primary task is both to notice the extraordinary and to create or re-create it in language. In the very first, defining *kārikā* of this chapter, Kuntaka tells us that poetic beauty *(vakratā)* is the description of something in terms of its own extraordinary, throbbing loveliness *(udāra-sva-parispanda-sundaratvena varṇanam)* falling within the scope of extraordinary linguistic means. He then glosses each of these terms. *Udāra* means "eminent and all-surpassing" *(sotkarṣaḥ sarvâtiśāyī). Parispanda* means *svabhāva-mahimā,* "endowed with intrinsic greatness." *Sundaratva* means *saukumāryâtiśayaḥ,* a "superabundance of subtlety"—in other words, being linked to an intrinsic quality of surpassing loveliness, since in Kuntaka's world subtlety, delicacy, and refinement are all practically synonymous with true beauty, or the truth of beauty. And when an intensely interesting object of description is naturally radiant, as we have seen, further embellishments are positively dangerous. This is not to say that the poet, faced with such an object, has to abstain from figuration entirely. Rather, the examples Kuntaka cites are sparsely configured, as we see from the following ironic *utprekṣā* taken from Rājaśekhara's *Viddha-śālabhañjikā* 1.13, an intimation of springtime:

garbha-granthiṣu vīrudhāṃ sumanaso madhye 'ṅkuraṃ pallavā
vāñchā-mātra-parigrahaḥ pika-vadhū-kaṇṭhodare pañcamaḥ/
kiṃ ca trīṇi jaganti jiṣṇu divasair dvi-trair mano-janmano
devasyâpy cirojjhitaṃ yadi bhaved abhyāsa-vaśyaṃ dhanuḥ//

Fresh flowers are unfolding
between the joints of the vines, and you can see
the first frail shoots emerging
from the buds. The cuckoo sings
when the mood strikes. Give us
another two-three days, and the Love God
could conquer the whole world
with his bow, long put aside—if only he'd resume
his target practice.

We have seen Rājaśekhara's concern for practice, *abhyāsa,* in the apparently analogous domain of writing poetry. Here the figure serves the opening naturalistic description, which Kuntaka clearly sees as the main thrust of the poem. Is it an intimation that the speaker, drunk on the beauty of spring, is eager to fall in love, hoping somewhat restlessly that this will happen within a day or two?

Kuntaka's great opponent in this discussion of *svabhāvokti* or "naturalistic description" was his younger contemporary, Mahima Bhaṭṭa, who distinguished ordinary *(sāmānya)* perception of objects, a perception informed by and translated into everyday language, from the poet's ability to perceive the true distinctiveness of an object and to make it present to us through *pratibhā.* This *pratibhā* is a certain kind of awareness *(prajñā)* arising from a momentary, direct touch that reaches the essence or deep reality of the object *(kṣaṇam svarūpa-sparśotthā);* in this, it is like the god's third eye, a creative, penetrating instrument of vision. This second, poetic sort of perception is, according to Mahima Bhaṭṭa, a figure *(svabhāvokti);* the first kind of perception, generalized and ordinary, is something "waiting to be adorned" *(alaṅkārya).* We should note that for Mahima Bhaṭṭa *pratibhā* has features of directness, of dynamism, and above all of singularity, the foregrounding of the distinctive *(viśiṣṭa)* and intrinsic *(svabhāva)* feature of the object.[22] We know that Kuntaka, too, would never accept an ordinary, *sāmānya* perception as the basis for a poet's visionary task. Thus in the end the difference between the two theoreticians may not be as stark as it seems. Both of them think of a true poet as someone endowed with extraordinary faculties of seeing and articulating; for Kuntaka, this gift precludes the choice of a dreary topic in the first place—though he does grudgingly acknowledge that if a poet is describing some object endowed with the excess or intensity that he demands, one that for this very reason cannot bear the weight of any additional ornamentation, this might count as an example of *alaṅkāra* after all. We would thus be left with a kind of back-door *svabhāvokti,* a figure that reflects, minimally, the poet's defining quality of trading in excess.[23]

For our purposes, the existence or nonexistence of this touchstone-like figure is less important than the opening up of a space in which *pratibhā* can be reexamined and, perhaps, redefined. Kuntaka attempts this in his second *kārikā:*

aparā sahajâhārya-kavi-kauśala-śālinī
nirmitir nūtanollekha-lokâtikrānta-gocarā//

"Another kind of creativity[24] marked by the poet's skillfulness, whether innate or adventitious, has a scope transcending ordinary experience and a fresh, unprecedented polish."

Kuntaka is following Rājaśekhara, who also distinguishes between the inborn *(sahaja)* and the adventitious or acquired *(āhārya)* when it comes to talent *(śakti),* as we have seen. But now, characteristically, Kuntaka shifts the discussion to another level and integrates it into his own aesthetic cosmology. First he tells us that the transcendent scope of this kind of creativity is, as we might have guessed from his earlier stance, a matter of all-surpassing excess *(sarvâtiśāyī gocaro viṣayo yasyāḥ).* Then he restates the problem in terms of his understanding of poetic process *tout court:* "It is not that poets impart existence to nonexistent entities whose nature they describe. Rather, they apply a certain intensity to entities that are vibrant with mere 'being,' so that they achieve a loveliness that ravishes the hearts of connoisseurs."[25]

The poet does not create ex nihilo; he does not invent or imagine phenomena into existence. However, by virtue of an intensification of simple being *(sattā-mātra)*[26] and a further aesthetic crafting or polishing *(ullekha),* the object of description begins to glow in its true brilliance, which completely overrides or hides its previous, unilluminated state *(vāstavasthiti).* All this comes from an extraordinary *(alaukika)* excess of beauty *(śobhâtiśaya),* and the result is an appearance of newness, as if we were seeing something unprecedented—as the *sūtra* has already intimated. In this sense, Kuntaka says, citing a well-known verse, the poet is like God:

apāre kāvya-saṃsāre kavir eva prajāpatiḥ

In the infinite cosmos that is poetry,
the poet is God the Creator.[27]

Thus the poet works with preexisting materials. His business is to enhance them, to release the brilliance that is theirs—a radiance that only he can see initially—and thus, in a sense, to re-create them. The process depends directly on his craftsmanship, and this means primarily his mastery of figuration, *alaṅkāra.* The particular strikingness, *vicchitti,* that a poem should have is, in Kuntaka's view as stated in this context, entirely a matter of figuration. Somewhat surprisingly, we now see that the question of what is "natural" and what is "adventitious" has been transferred from the domain of the poet and his powers to that of the object described and the particular forms of beauty made present in it; such beauty, *vakratā,* may be either innate or acquired (through poetry). Kuntaka brings a famous verse from Kālidāsa[28] to illustrate this point; after a fine explication of the verse, he concludes that the great master has managed, because of that extra something *(atiśaya)* that he has brought to bear on his subject, or brought out of it, to create in his listeners the sense that they are witnessing something never seen before. The principle of singularity surfaces once more.

By now the major features of his theory should be clear. Intensity, or intensification, is the name of the game. That's why a poet needs his luminous *pratibhā.* By first seeing with his mental eye and then configuring (or polishing or otherwise enhancing) what he has seen, the poet presents us with a fresh reality constructed out of the earlier, mundane stuff of experience—though even there, the poet needs to pick a promising subject, potentially extraordinary in its own right, before he goes to work. But where in all this is the imagination? Is that what *pratibhā* really means? Kuntaka twice cites a remarkable proof text that hints at a mode of poetic creativity by no means exhausted or, for that matter, even roughly defined by his discussion so far:

līnaṃ vastuni yena sūkṣma-subhagaṃ tattvaṃ girā kṛṣyate
nirmātuṃ prabhaven manoharam idaṃ vācaiva yo vā bahiḥ/
vande dvāv api tāv aham kavi-varau vandetarām taṃ punar
yo vijñāta-pariśramo 'yam anayor bhārâvatāra-kṣamaḥ//

One kind of poet can tease out the subtle truth
hidden in a thing, and put it
into words. Another kind
can use words to create outside
his mind this thing that charms
others' minds. I honor them both.

Even more would I praise
the one who knows how hard
they work, who can lighten
their load. (2.107)

So we have the visionary who articulates the hidden essence of some already existing object and the innovative creator who externalizes some apparently imagined entity. Both deserve respect. Yet Kuntaka knows something about a third type of poet who, it seems, has a gift of a different order entirely—a certain lightness of touch, and perhaps (we can only speculate) the naturally charged, high-voltage perception, sensitivity, and linguistic facility that allow novelty to emerge. It is striking that Kuntaka cites this verse, for the second time, at exactly the point in his discussion where the issue of creativity is formulated analytically, that is, right before the verse on the poet as God the Creator (cited earlier).

Clearly, there is a hint of an inventiveness somewhat more radical than anything Kuntaka has mentioned so far. What would such invention imply in terms of the dynamics of poetic composition? Kuntaka tells us that this particular, novel form of excess derives from scrambling or reshuffling the interrelations among items or components of a complex utterance *(vākyârtha)*.[29] Once again, there is no question of creation ex nihilo; rather, we have a systemic, almost structuralist understanding of the utterance as a whole whose parts are potentially in movement, changing position vis-à-vis one another to very far-reaching cognitive or emotional effect. Such reconfigurations give the sense of real creativity *(nirmiti)*—and here, at last, the *pratibhā* that conditions such internal and systemic reorganization is, indeed, an imaginative act par excellence. Kuntaka gives us an example, which he then glosses in terms of this understanding of the poet's task:

kas tvaṃ bho divi māliko 'ham iha kiṃ puṣpârtham abhyāgataḥ
kiṃ tenâstu mahān krayo yadi mahac-citram tad ākarṇyatām/
saṅgrāmeṣv alabhâbhidhāna-nṛpatau divyâṅganābhiḥ srajaḥ
projjhantībhir avidyamāna-kusumaṃ yasmāt kṛtaṃ nandanam//

"Who are you?"
"I'm the gardener of the gods."
"So why are you here?"
"I came to get flowers."
"What for?"

"It's a big order, and the price
is right."
"How strange!"
"Let me explain: There's a king
called Alabha, gone to war.
The goddesses welcomed him with garlands
when he died. Now you can't find
a single flower anywhere
in heaven."

It is common knowledge that goddesses bring flowers to welcome dying heroes into heaven. One might, then, imagine a situation where the arrival of a particularly heroic character would create a severe shortage of fresh flowers, so the relevant celestial official would have to look for a new supply elsewhere—say, on earth. Here is a rather elegant and charming way to praise a king recently slain in battle (perhaps the father of a newly crowned successor and patron). There's a question about the figure: Kuntaka speaks of *utprekṣā,* "poetic fancy," combined with *aprastuta-praśaṃsā,* "displacement." But *utprekṣā,* as we have seen, is intimately linked with the kind of excess that we call *atiśayokti,* "hyperbole" (Kuntaka quotes Bhāmaha here).[30] It all comes down to *atiśaya,* the added value that makes the poem and that is part and parcel of the fanciful vision at play in the reshuffling of familiar materials. The point is that in the present, rather slight example the delight generated by the poem cannot be produced by logical inference based on direct perception or other criteria, nor can it derive from the observation of some naturally existing entity. Rather, it depends entirely on the polished ornamentation or reconfiguration that *pratibhā* allows a sophisticated poet to achieve.[31] What is more, poetic *pratibhā,* at work in figures such as "poetic fancy," makes quite incredible things seem perfectly acceptable, even logical, though they would hardly be so normally or naturally *(svātantryeṇa).*

We might note in passing that "suggestion," the principle of first resort for Ānandavardhana a hundred years earlier (and for Kuntaka's contemporary Abhinavagupta), is apparently irrelevant to Kuntaka's discussion here. He is focused on the experience of creative novelty as reflecting an intensely playful imaginative process acting upon the systemic features of a richly appointed poetic world. By rearranging conventional themes and ideas and thereby extending their cognitive and emotional impact, a skilled poet can produce something unique, indeed personal, a creative artifact that reflects more than simple "inspiration" or a happy moment of hitting upon some charming new combination. A poem that is truly novel, even unprecedented, requires a leap in the mind, a visionary act transcending both empirical and standard logical procedures—something akin, it would seem, to the third mode, of scintillating lightness, that Kuntaka has outlined somewhat enigmatically in the verse quoted above. This mode now seems intimately linked to a particular kind of imagination that can play creatively with whatever materials lie close to hand.

One last point. Once Kuntaka has come this far, he cannot resist mentioning the infinity or inexhaustibility of this poetic universe. In his discussion of *kārikās* 3 and 4, he quotes the *Gauḍavaho* (87):

> Day after day,
> from the beginning of time,
> good poets draw from the treasury of words,
> and still its lock
> remains unbroken.

Poetry can never be emptied out; despite daily withdrawals from the account, the reserves of poetic language are untouched, whole, and truly limitless. How is this possible? Not surprisingly, it is a matter of *pratibhā*. Kuntaka rightly sees the verse as implying a kind of boast. The gifted poet thinks: "No one before me has understood the truth *(tattva)* or taken anything at all out of the treasury of poetry, but my *pratibhā* has opened the way to ultimate reality; the lock is about to be broken." Kuntaka obviously knew his poets. (He also knew Rājaśekhara's somewhat cynical remarks about the envy inevitably found among poets as well as among their listeners and critics.) Putting aside the astute psychological insight, we can conclude that in the ongoing debate among Kashmiri poeticians about originality, also singularity, as a value in its own right, Kuntaka opted for *pratibhā* as the one guarantee of this critical potentiality. At least at this point, he seems to think of it as a matter of imaginative intensification *(vijṛmbhaṇa)* or excess.[32]

To sum up: For Kuntaka, *pratibhā* is a critical link in the generation of poetic beauty, *vakratā*, with its inherent obliquity or indirection. *Pratibhā* underlies the gift of transfiguration: an observable object, inherently interesting, even extraordinary if seen in the right light, is presented to our awareness by a process of linguistic intensification, with or without ornament and figuration; or else the systemic relations operating among known, perhaps conventional components of the poet's world will be jumbled and reconstituted, thus changing the terms of their internal composition. In both cases, there is an enhanced or intensified seeing, a seeing of X as more than X or as something else, perhaps in the context of a wider set that includes Y and Z. A real poet will have this gift of visionary transfiguration either congenitally or through some process of study and training. The knowledge involved is intuitive and creative, not really amenable to or exhausted by logical analysis; it has what can only be called an imaginative component, at its height involving the tangible imaging of something both deeper and lighter than either enhanced empirical description or linguistic externalization per se can achieve. We may be tempted to say, from our own external perspective, that the kind of imaginative excess Kuntaka has in mind is utterly remote from representation, just as it cannot be subsumed under the *rasa-dhvani* ethos that structured the discourse of Kashmiri poetics at this period. To understand it more clearly, we may need to go back to the Bhartṛharian notions of irreducible, unparaphrasable, effortless, and integrated insight with which we began.

4.4. Jagannātha: Narrowing Down *Pratibhā*

The question of the true source or cause of poetry retained its hold over the poeticians right up to modern times, with the same tensions and varying emphases that we have seen in Rājaśekhara and Kuntaka. Mammaṭa (twelfth century) offers us a typically inclusive, textbook-like conclusion: poetry has three causes that must operate concomitantly, and these are inspired talent *(śakti)*, cultivation *(vyutpatti)*, and practice *(abhyāsa)*.[33] The commentators tend to identify *śakti* with *pratibhā*, so the two terms have become synonyms—a marked departure from Rājaśekhara's conception of a distinctive mutual determination. We find a similar conflation in Kumārasvāmin's gloss on the benedictory verse of Vidyānātha's *Pratāpa-rudrīya* (Kumārasvāmin lived in the mid-fifteenth century): worshiping the feet of Sarasvatī is, according to Vidyānātha's blessing, a way of sowing the seed of literary creativity *(sārasvata-prakriyā-bīja-nyāsa)*, and Kumārasvāmin explains that the seed in question is *śakti-pratibhâdy-apara-paryāyaḥ saṃskāra-viśeṣaḥ*, a mental function called variably *śakti*, *pratibhā*, and so on.[34] This seeming unexceptional orthodoxy was attacked by later, more "modern" poeticians including the last great polymath working within the discipline, Jagannātha Paṇḍita, in the opening passage of his seventeenth-century masterpiece, the *Rasa-gaṅgādhara*.[35] As we saw in the previous section, Jagannātha shows the impact of the new conceptual order that was crystallizing in his time both in the south of India and at the Mughal court where he lived and worked. He is eager to redefine poetry itself—as "language producing a charming sense" *(ramaṇīyârtha-pratipādakaḥ śabdaḥ kāvyam)*—and then, using the honed tools of the New Logicians, to redefine the components of his own definition and, that accomplished, to address the causal issue. It is easy to miss the true import of this opening cri de coeur, or to dismiss it as a somewhat barren juggling of logical terms. Logic, in Jagannātha's hands, serves to rationalize a theory of poetic production as based entirely on autonomous, self-contained, self-referencing aesthetic values that also entail an explicit cognitive aspect, of a type and content quite new to the discourse of Sanskrit poetics.[36] Within this novel aesthetic economy, there is a role to be played by a reconceptualized faculty of imagination, and the term *pratibhā* is recycled and extended to express something of the new imaginative domain.

Before we see how Jagannātha works with *pratibhā,* almost at the start of his long book, we need to look briefly at his explication of the opening statement about "charm," *ramaṇīyatā.* What exactly is meant by "charm"? It is "the property of being the object of a cognition that produces extraordinary pleasure."[37] Cognition is of the essence: the charmed listener or reader knows something (new) as a result of hearing or reading a poem. But what is the meaning of "extraordinary" here? It is something synonymous with *camatkāratva,* the state of wonder, a certain "amazingness." Second-order abstraction haunts this opening discussion, imparting a rarefied tone of severe intellection; not "wonder" alone, *camatkāra,* but wonder abstracted and generalized as a logical category underlies the charm of poetry. It is important that we think clearly and prevent any slippage in our language, especially when dealing with matters of truly extraordinary import. Thus "extraordinariness," *lokottaratvam,* is itself a genus *(jāti-viśeṣa)* whose existence is attested, or proved, by "experience" *(anubhava-sākṣika).* Whatever cognition is involved in listening to a poem, it has an empirical basis capable of articulation by the theoretically inclined listener.

Now comes the first causal statement: this extraordinariness, a category in its own right, integral to poetic charm, rooted in real experience, is the result of a certain kind of *bhāvanā* that consists in the repeated act of attentiveness *(anusandhāna)* to that which has just been defined as falling within range of the cognition that produces this kind of pleasure. If we suppress the irritation we might feel at this convoluted way of saying things, we are left with something rather important. Whatever it is that is amazing about poetry requires *bhāvanā,* the mental act or series of acts that brings something into being by imagining it, or by calling it up from memory, or by paying attention to it. True to his Nyāya antecedents, Jagannātha draws from a model of mind in which imagination and attention are, in effect, mutually determined, but this model now serves to explain the peculiarly intensified awareness that comes into being under the specific circumstances that concern poets and poeticians.[38] We are breathing the fresh air of the seventeenth century, in which the cultivated listener attunes himself to something utterly unusual that is transpiring within the mind—something that he knows, or that he knows he knows, and that he can mull over with the help of a sensitized imagination.[39] This is what poetry is all about. It is, says Jagannātha, driving the point home, quite different from what happens to us when someone gives us good news such as "I'm giving you a lot of money" or "It's a boy!" Such statements may make us happy, but they lack the intensified, out-of-the-usual charm of a good poem.[40]

So what generates a good poem? There is, for Jagannātha, only one real cause, and that is *pratibhā,* defined technically and almost tautologically as "being in the presence of words and meanings conducive to the composition of poetry" *(kāvya-ghaṭanânukūla-śabdârthopasthitiḥ).*[41] In other words, *pratibhā* is a mental state suffused with verbal materials, both aural and semantic, that under unspecified conditions can generate a poem. We will try to see something of what this might mean, but in any case it is clear that *pratibhā* alone drives the creative process. Any attempt to spread out the causal network so as to include other factors is rejected out of hand. It all comes down to *pratibhā,* a self-contained genus *(jāti-viśeṣa).*[42] And where does *pratibhā* itself come from? Sometimes it's a matter of good luck *(adṛṣṭa)* flowing, for example, from a god or some other eminent personage who shows a graceful kindness, *prasāda.* Sometimes unusual training and cultivation *(vilakṣaṇa-vyutpatti)* or practice *(abhyāsa)*—the old categories—may feed into *pratibhā.* You certainly don't need all three, *pace* Mammaṭa. Even young children, utterly lacking in training and practice, can produce good poetry through the blessing of someone great. There follows a slightly fussy discussion, following Rājaśekhara and other earlier voices in the tradition, as to whether some young poet devoid of proper education should or should not be presumed to have enjoyed such *Bildung* in a former life.[43] A principle of parsimony is invoked: why insist on such karmic predetermination, which complicates matters unnecessarily, as it can never be proved, and anyway may be quite foreign to what actually moves the budding poet to compose? One should, says Jagannātha, resort to such highly speculative explanations only when some exception to the rule cannot be handled by the normal criteria of knowledge *(vyabhicārasya vāraṇāya)*. This is clearly not the case we are discussing here.

We need to attend to the remarkable inversion that has taken place. As we have seen, Daṇḍin, Mammaṭa, and many others argued for the canonical claim that poetry arises from the combination of *pratibhā* (or *śakti*), training, and practice. Jagannātha turns the tripartite causal sequence around. Now *vyutpatti*. training, and *abhyāsa*, practice, together with an unpredictable unseen factor *(adṛṣṭa)*, are potential causes *(hetu)* for *pratibhā*. The old debate, amply documented in Rājaśekhara (6) and the *Dhvanyāloka* (3.6), as to the relative importance of *pratibhā* and *vyutpatti* is resolved by the final subordination of the latter to the former. Only *pratibhā* counts as a source of poetry, and *vyutpatti* is only one of the causal factors of *pratibhā*. Moreover, the entire causal sequence has been rendered linear and unidirectional, unlike the complex recursive dynamic of interdependence that we saw in Rājaśekhara, or Kuntaka's nuanced exploration of the distinct modal variations of *pratibhhā*. Once again, Jagannātha's straightforward understanding of this sequence is by no means a matter of logical precision alone. A different sensibility has emerged. The very nature of the poetic endeavor as well as its goals and textures have undergone a major shift.

So *pratibhā* has three possible sources. It can't always be a matter of good luck: one sees poets who suffer from writer's block, a clear failure of inspiration, who nevertheless are able to go back to writing poetry after being trained to do so and then practicing the art. For them, *pratibhā* does reemerge: "inspiration"—this now seems to be what Jagannātha means by the term—is sometimes a matter of discipline.

But if we accept luck—an unseen *(adṛṣṭa)* factor operating autonomously—as a possible conditioning factor for a poet's doing good work, we have to admit that it may well predate any degree of cultivation and practice. And if luck is so dependable an element in this business of being a poet, then maybe we should posit bad luck, or bad *karma*, as an explanation for a poet's failure to write. Bad luck, in other words, can perhaps block *pratibhā*. Forget about cultivated taste and all that. No, says Jagannātha. Once again we are slipping into a clumsy lack of parsimony. Rather than posit these two unseen forces—good luck and bad luck—as determining the fate of poetry, we would do better to think about what we are now calling discipline or the lack thereof. It is always *pratibhā* that makes for differences in poetic quality, and *pratibhā* can come from luck *or* from discipline. But then what about the would-be poet who has had the best possible training but who nonetheless fails to produce good poems? Is this a violation of the basic notions of causality? It is not. Cultivation and discipline are perhaps helpful, capable of generating inspiration, but they are not *necessarily* sufficient. Maybe the training was not quite what the individual poet needed. People are different. *Pratibhā,* too, is different from one person to the next.[44]

Note this conclusion. You can't write poetry without inspiration—including its imaginative component, no doubt—but you also can't determine with certainty what will inspire the individual artist. There is, it seems, something irreducibly personal in all of this as well as a high degree of sensitivity to context. Some people are galvanized into song by a lucky coincidence, the auspicious gaze of a god or goddess, the blessing offered by one's guru, or other unpredictable factors. Others sit down at their desks at 8:15 every morning and work away at it until the poem—crafted, polished, and intensified—happens to emerge. It's true that one can always assume the "absence of obstacles" *(pratibandhâbhāva)* as a necessary condition. Things can always get in the way. By now Jagannātha's severe tone has taken on a humane note. Everyone knows of writers, even great writers of many books, who get stuck for a while, for one reason or another—perhaps a spell cast by an enemy, or some other "paralysis of the voice" *(vāk-stambha).* Such problems, says Jagannātha reassuringly, usually pass by themselves after a few days.

It is difficult to brush aside the impression that the *pratibhā* Jagannātha is describing reflects a further professionalization and autonomization of the practicing poet, far beyond what Rājaśekhara conceived of half a millennium earlier. The gifted poet, if his mind is working well, if sounds and words are flowing, if he is receptive, and if he is not blocked by some transient impediment, will probably be able to produce poetry that will fulfill the condition of charming the cultivated mind or heart. Moreover, the whole business has been radically deontologized. Poets should please and entertain. Profound metaphysical experiences have other genealogies. Not that poetic experience is in any sense shallow—quite the contrary. It engages the whole person, including his self-conscious, wide-awake mind (remember that Jagannātha, as we saw earlier, demands just this kind of wakefulness from the attuned spectator at a play). Precisely to this purpose, the poet needs training, practice, and good luck—so that he will have the inspiration, and perhaps the active imagination, to perform his task. But why has

Jagannātha, like the other New Critics *(navyāḥ),* made everything so dependent on *pratibhā,* at the same time demoting the components of training and erudition? Pollock has suggested that we see here a reflex of vernacular, *bhakti*-oriented poetics, a devotional stance in which we often find overt skepticism about, indeed hostility to, the inherited norms of Sanskrit poetry.[45] Direct experience and divine inspiration are what sustain the *bhakti* poet's self-image, not technical mastery of the poet's craft and the knowledge that it demands. But we need to remember that all such statements and the narratives that sometimes go with them have a mise-en-scène very remote from the world of courtly Ālaṅkārikas such as Jagannātha.[46] In any case, as the medieval vernacular sources themselves recognized, and as Pollock also notes, we are dealing essentially with a disingenuous pose. Vernacular *bhakti* poety is no less crafted, and often no less learned, than the great *kāvya* masterpieces. What is more, vernacularization produced self-conscious, highly complex, and elevated *kāvya* in the *vyutpatti*-based style in all of the emergent regional literatures. In Tamil and Telugu, to take but two examples, such elevated, Sanskrit-like works stand at the very origin of the literary tradition.

We may thus have to widen our search for an explanation of the hypertrophied role of *pratibhā* in sixteenth- and seventeenth-century poetic theory in Sanskrit. One possible hint comes from the passage in Jagannātha that we have summarized. For this theorist, *pratibhā* has a natural, well-articulated link to *bhāvanā,* the true source of the "extraordinariness" that guarantees the presence of true poetry. If *pratibhā* denotes the "cause" or the impulse to write, *bhāvanā* is the deeper force of creative attentiveness that allows a poem to come alive and to do its work. The term itself, whose prehistory we have traced in the previous sections, has undergone a revolution in meaning. By the seventeenth century, *bhāvanā,* rooted in Bhartṛharian discourse and in the Nyāya models of the mind, has come to indicate the volatile blend of attention and imagination that motivates creative activity wherever we find it. Moreover, this new *bhāvanā* has a marked personal and individual quality: each of us imagines his or her own world into being, not ex nihilo, of course, but on the basis of a particular subjective experience.[47]

By now we are standing on new ground. When Jagannātha speaks of both *pratibhā* and *bhāvanā,* and of their interaction, he is effectively pointing to a far-reaching and newly crystallized theory of the imagination in practice. Something fundamental has changed as part of a general cultural or civilizational shift, which we examine in detail in Part II. Suddenly the imagination has been upgraded to the point where it defines the thinking, feeling, and above all creative human being as such. It is striking that this theme cuts through linguistic, geographic, and literary-cultural borders; we find it no less prominent in the Indo-Persian literature of the seventeenth century, the so-called *sabk-i hindī,* with its astonishing stress on the creative imagination at work generating new meanings and fresh perceptions as the very stuff of the poetic enterprise. One has only to read the work of Jagannātha's junior contemporary, Bedil, for example, to sense an affinity between Indo-Persian metapoetic speculation and the refurbished notion of *bhāvanā-cum-pratibhā* formulated at the Mughal court:

> Word is what owns the high note as also the low.
> Not just the weeping, it owns the silence too.
> When one speaks with the imagination
> One chooses a manner from poetry's manners,
> And if silence has its hints and gestures
> So has speech its own texts too.[48]

4.5. Interim Summary: What Does the Poet See?

So is *pratibhā* a word for the imagination? It seems that even for Jagannātha Paṇḍita, the original connotations of vision—a particular kind of vision—have survived into the discussion of the necessary conditions for writing poetry. Without such vision, there will be no poetry. Interestingly, however, one can be trained to see with the poet's eye. It's all very well to receive this gift as a blessing from a third party, divine or human, but in the absence of such unpredictable blessings, poetic vision can still be acquired by education and long practice. Such vision has several analytical components. It is, for one thing, linked to a certain mode of knowing things. Seeing means knowing. More to the point, in a way, is the relation to attention. The poet sees something that, by being seen or being attended to *(ādara),* comes into being. Such attentiveness has an imaginative element as well: *bhāvanā,* in the full-fledged, rather individualized seventeenth-century use of the word.

More generally, by the time we reach this period in both south and north India, we find a richly exfoliated typology of seeing. We have the older notion, attested in the early poeticians, that the poet sees things as they truly are—*yathârtha*. On a more popular level, this idea translates into the belief that the true poet simply knows without having to see directly, as many of the stories of the *Bhoja-prabandha* and other *cāṭu*-related materials clearly demonstrate. Poetic vision does not even require eyesight: Rājaśekhara recalls the names of blind poets, such as Bhaṭṭi, famous in the tradition, and similar statements about the penetrating insight of the blind turn up regularly in the regional literatures.[49] In short, the poet's vision, at work in the inner eye, is of a different order than ours.

Then we have the remarkable intuition, lucidly articulated by Kuntaka, that the professional poet enhances or intensifies whatever he sees. Here the creative operation of an imaginative faculty is clearly crucial. By heightening or deepening the vision, by repositioning the vantage point and altering perspective, and by attending to details that normally elude notice, the poet generates an intensified and largely autonomous poetic world. Once again, it is a matter not of seeing in some technical sense but of a much more powerful visionary mode, with an inbuilt perspectivism that imparts complexity and depth. One aspect of this mode, and an index of originality, is the poet's gift of seeing latent connections, that is, of rearranging the internal relations of the set of subjects he is describing, or of reframing them with reference to far wider levels of existence or experience, thus undoing linear framing and subverting the illusionary flatness of the apparent surface. The poet sees the world through a wider, stronger lens, which tends to bend or fold the surface into far more supple, interconnected, and above all dynamic shapes; language, especially indirect or "crooked" language, supplies the lens.

In the praxis of the sixteenth- and seventeenth-century poets, as we shall see, we can observe yet another mode: both the poet and his or her protagonists (and with their help, the reader/listener) have the useful ability to *see through* the visible surface. Thus vision itself may have a haptic quality, a tangible texture accessible both to eye and to touch, synesthetically transcending normal visual experience.[50] This haptic "seeing through" is, perhaps, the imaginative act par excellence;[51] it is no wonder that it is soon theorized and connected to a metaphysical order in which a category such as "literary fiction" can emerge. On another level, no less synesthetic, effective poetry comes to mean the translation of sound into vision and of vision into sound; for example, consequential sounds, such as the Vedic *mantras* or Tantric condensations of divine presence, can, indeed must, be *seen* in order to become present and fully real.[52] We will be returning to these themes.

Finally, we have the logician-poetician's notion, only partly articulated in the austere language of the *Navya Nyāya,* that poetic vision at its best operates through the combined force of imagination and attention, and that each visionary moment has its peculiar integrity. It is clearly not enough simply to open one's eyes to the world. In a way—though Jagannātha does not, of course, formulate the matter explicitly in these terms—one sees what one imagines, and if one keeps looking and contemplating, patiently and repeatedly, what one knows to be imagined is also, in the end, what one takes to be real. Seeing is a rather personal way of knowing, including knowledge of one's own imaginative investment in what is seen and known. Such an epistemic state is truly inspired or, in Jagannātha's words, open to amazement. The deeper reaches of such a state require the active, shaping presence of *pratibhā,* by now truly close to the domain defined, in an early modern European mental economy, by imagination (for example, in Montaigne).[53] What we imagine is suffused with light, which also illumines the act of imagining, or of illumining, itself.

Clearly, the great masters of Sanskrit poetic theory saw imagination, in its various names and forms, as a universal property of the mind, a property particularly productive in poets, whose talent it defines. We have followed their discussions and highlighted certain key, recurrent notions: illumination, intensification, refining, polishing, superimposition, determination, attention. The set itself is remarkably stable, although each of the major poeticians offers a unique configuration; even more to the point, the relations between these basic notions and actual poetic practice are at best always oblique. It would, in principle, be possible to outline a rough typology of the classical poets' primary expressive modes, one that would cut straight through the standard categorization by figures as well as the metaphysical analyses of the *rasa-dhvani* school.[54] For the record, let me say again that, however compelling intellectually Abhinavagupta's summation of aesthetic experience may be (and even more so, his predecessor Bhaṭṭa Nāyaka's revolutionary theory), most extant Sanskrit poetry has nothing to do with *rasa* and its alleged effects upon awareness.[55] Such a statement will sound perverse to orthodox ears, even though several of the most insightful of the great Sanskrit poeticians—including Kuntaka and Jagannātha, as we have seen—represent, in effect, and each in his own way, dissenting views when it comes to the orthodox Kashmiri theories of art. Moreover, the standard *Dhvanyāloka* typology of suggestion, *dhvani,* also fails to include the more conspicuous and, I think, interesting kinds of poetic suggestion that we find in profusion in our texts. This is not, however, the place to substantiate this claim.

Before we leave the domain of poetic theory, we should at least note that there is one more figure directly and specifically identified with the life of the imagination. This figure—*bhāvika,* "the imaginative"—takes the imagination itself as a trope, one among other tropes but, unlike others, endowed with a general applicability to a work of art *taken as a whole.* A great poetic work can be characterized by *bhāvika* if it is uniformly pervaded by a sustained texture of extraordinary, and lucidly formulated, insight.[56] Since I have dealt with *bhāvika* at length elsewhere, let me simply note that discussions of this figure confirm much of what we have learned from our study of *pratibhā* (and, to a large extent, what we have learned about the poeticians' *bhāvanā* and the truth-claims of poetic art).[57] Here is a simple, spare summary, which can also serve as a précis of our last two chapters and as a bridge to the next.

The poet builds a world in a detailed, crafted, and visionary way. This world has certain dependable features: it is extraordinarily vivid—far more so than ordinary worlds—and establishes its own temporality, drawing matter freely from past and future, which are made visible in an intensified present. Each such world has its own integrity and singularity as well as a quasi-objective, or possibly hyperobjective, mode of existence; it moves readily from one mind to another in accordance with the mutual resonance of poet and listener, or the reflection of the former's thought in the mirror of the latter's inner eye. To see such images one needs a certain receptivity, and one needs one's own awake, thinking self, in good working order. Such a world may impinge in various ways on other active worlds, notably that of the everyday objects that surround us, since the communicative, resonant, and interactive medium of the imagination continually brings things into being *(bhāvanā).* There is an affinity—not, however, an identity—between imagined reality and precise, naturalistic description of everyday objects, seen each in its special or particular way, poetically described, and thus intensified and understood anew. In general, *penetrating naturalistic perception has an imaginative component.*[58] Imagined reality, however, in the sense of an internal, visionary perception, claims a status superseding ordinary experience and may well be more enduring and more causally effective than the latter, as it is also more beautiful and (hence) more real. On the other hand, the later poeticians' analysis of major figures asserts that a tensile, unresolved bond between real and unreal underlies the particular truth-claim of a poem.

There is no doubt that we have here the lineaments of an articulated theory, or rather of a set of theoretical perspectives, defining the work of the imagination as a basic, possibly the most basic, component of fine poetry. To my taste, the most penetrating formulations of imaginative process in action, indeed of the problem of the imagination as a whole, come from the later poeticians such as Ruyyaka and Jagannātha, who reconceived the science of poetics after it was, in a sense, hijacked by the Kashmiri *rasa* theorists. Even so, there seems to be something missing in the implicit model of the mind that informs this domain. In the last analysis, the critical question of how images move from one mind to another—of just what the reader or listener has to do to allow this to happen—remains unclear. I suppose that if one thinks of the world as an infinite field of sonic (that is, mostly musical) expressivity, resonating through each of us, then it is not impossible for such echoes to strike sympathetic chords in many receptive minds, even if they are generations removed from one another. It is, perhaps, mostly a question of ardent listening—and here the poeticians are undoubtedly right that, insofar as the music is endowed with meaning, indirection and suggestion are intrinsic to all such listening, as they amplify the resonance. Still, for a more detailed template of interactive, objective imagining, its modes and meanings and its place within the mental world of the imaginer as a whole, we will have to look elsewhere—to the meditative worlds of Yoga, Tantra, and temple worship, with their entirely practical goals and their special existential burdens.

— 5 —

Toward a Yoga of the Imagination

5.1. Three Non-Boys

It's time we moved away from the realm of technical discussions to more practical domains, if one can use such a term for forms of practice that mostly undermine the concrete givenness of the world and the discrete existence of its visible objects and effects. Consider the following unsettling story, supposed to have been told by a nanny to amuse an innocent child and recorded in the great Kashmiri classic of metaphysical narrative, the *Yoga-vāsiṣṭha-mahā-rāmāyaṇa* (ninth century):

> Somewhere or other, in a city that was totally nonexistent—a wide and empty city, like stars reflected in water—there were three handsome and courageous princes. Two of them were never born, and the third never even entered the womb. As it happened, they lost all their families; so, grieving at heart, their faces grim, they left that empty city in search of some fine reward, like when Mercury, Venus, and Saturn come together in the sky. Their bodies, however, were extremely delicate, soft as the *śirīṣa* flower, and the sun burned their backs as they walked on the path over glowing sand; they were like fresh buds wilted by summer's heat, or like deer lost to the herd. Sharp *darbha* grass pricked the soles of their feet; their joints were inflamed; in torment, they kept calling out to their absent fathers. After they had walked a long way, their bodies gray with dust, they happened upon three trees in full bloom, with fruits hanging from their branches, home to many animals and birds. Two of those trees had never been born, and there was never even a seed for the third.
>
> They rested there, as Indra, the Wind, and Yama rest in the shade of the wishing trees in heaven. They feasted on the delicious fruit, drank

their juices, and covered themselves with garlands made from the flowers. Then they set off again. It was high noon when they arrived at three rivers, their waves murmuring and shimmering. One of the rivers was totally dry, and there was no trace of water in the other two, as there is no vision in blind eyes. Being utterly exhausted because of the heat, they were all too happy to bathe in these rivers, like Brahmā, Viṣṇu, and Śiva bathing in the Ganges. They played in the water and drank their fill; then, refreshed, they moved on. Toward evening, as the sun began to set, they came to a vast city that was about to be built. It was filled with banners and lotus ponds, with water blue as the blue sky, and you could hear even from a great distance the buzz and hum of its inhabitants.

In the city they happened upon three marvelous palaces made of gold and precious stones, tall as mountain peaks. Two of these palaces were not yet built, and the third had no walls. They entered that third one, explored it, sat down, and found three golden bowls, two of them broken into pieces, the third ground to dust. In the bowl that was ground to dust they cooked ninety-nine minus one hundred measures of rice and invited three Brahmins for a meal—two without a body, one without a mouth. The one without a mouth ate all hundred measures of rice, and the three princes ate up whatever was left. They were completely satisfied. Those princes are still living happily in that city that will one day be built; mostly they spend their time hunting. Isn't this a nice story that I've told you, little boy? If you take it to heart, you'll grow up to be wise.[1]

Is this a nursery tale, of a type known in many literatures? A bedtime story, not free of aggression, meant to tease the listener into sleep and dreaming? Somewhat unusually for Sanskrit narrative genres, the young listener is not allowed to respond, to ask for more information or clarification, or to check the earnestness of the narrator. What would the child have said? "Don't be silly! How can someone go into a city that is not yet built?" And probably, after a while, with a groan or a smile: "Not again!" But perhaps the child would enter into the game, which can surely be extended indefinitely. Always there will be 2 + 1, a complete set of nonexistent entities, the third even more outrageous in its nonbeing than the first two. You can read the story in linear sequence, as it is told, but you can also read it as a deepening progression through a series of nested layers: in the experience, or the minds, of the unborn boys there are three dry rivers flowing not far from a nonexistent city, in which there are unbuilt houses with broken pots in which a negative quantity of rice can be cooked—to everyone's utter satisfaction. Each subsequent stage of nonexistence inheres in the prior one and is generated out of the prior one[2]—if nonexistence is something that can inhere (this is a classical theme in Indian logic). There is no lower limit to these encapsulations except for the concluding experience—the story must, after all, have an end—of universal satisfaction, which I take to be real.

At the bottom of a progression that has no bottom lies the satisfaction proper to a subtle internal space empty of objects, hence utterly full. This same space is the locus of imagination, as the text proceeds to explain.

Before we listen to it further, we should render the spatial topology more precise. A vertical linearity is unlikely to be any more accurate than a horizontal one. In all probability—though this is only a guess—this little story, like so many others in this profoundly unnerving book, speaks to a notion of simultaneous mutual embedding and mirroring. A is in B insofar as B is in A (the overlap may, however, be incomplete; there may be gaps and discontinuities). Where, exactly, does this interweaving take place? Possibly among the minds of the three non-boys; possibly somewhere between the minds of narrator and listener, to which we have to add the mind of the reader (*our* mind); probably all such minds and players are active at any given moment.

Why insist on the role of the mind? Because the narrator explains his story, at least up to a point:

> Like this story about the boys, this universe, which looks so solid, is in reality entirely a tissue of mentation [*vikalpa-jālikā*] and the stuff of reflections *(pratibhāsâtmikā);* like the story, it, too, is constructed from fierce, tough acts of imagination [*ugraiḥ saṅkalpair dṛḍha-kalpitaiḥ*]. Nothing whatsoever exists apart from the imagination. Whatever is there by force of the imagination is not really a "something," or it might be a "little something." Just like the boys, the rivers, and the city-to-be, the existence of the world is an imaginary production, tremulous, shimmering all around us. (32–37)

Before we rush to characterize this passage, or indeed the whole of the *Yoga-vāsiṣṭha,* as "idealist" in the Western European sense, we would do well to examine the terms of its explanation more closely. The two key words are *vikalpa* and *saṅkalpa,* which we have already encountered.[3]

Both come from the root √*kḷp,* the verb of making, fashioning, determining, performing. In the *Yoga-vāsiṣṭha,* the former term tends to mean something like "conceptualization" or "thinking" generally; it is not uncommon for the narrator to tell his listener (Rāma, according to the framing story) that thinking generates the stuff of experience. *Saṅkalpa,* on the other hand, while it can also mean just "thought," especially a thought heavy with intention or resolution or determination, commonly serves in this text for an imaginative act, as I have translated. Not thinking alone but thought crystallizing into active and vivid images that look and feel real is what *saṅkalpa* conveys in these stories. In the explication the storyteller offers for the story just cited, *saṅkalpa* has a "fierce, tough" quality. These adjectives are eloquent testimony to the substantial, even recalcitrant nature of imaginative production and present a lucid contrast with our modern, Western notions of fantasy as somehow ethereal and lacking in existential power.

Saṅkalpa is explored and discursively defined, often with subtle distinctions, in many passages in the *Yoga-vāsiṣṭha,* which could well be renamed "The Yoga of the Imagination at Work." Take another explanatory example, from the most baffling and complex of all narratives in this book, the quasi-allegorical romance "The Woman in the Stone":

> An effect must proceed from a cause, as the shoot emerges from a seed. If there is no seed, there will be no shoot. Has anyone ever seen a tree standing free in the empty sky? What is seen in empty space—let us say a tree—is apparent because of the imagination [*saṅkalpa*]. There is no object that is unimagined.[4]

This does not mean that there are no objects. Once imagined, objects exist, though not perhaps in the stubborn, rigidly contoured way we tend to think of them. In the *Yoga-vāsiṣṭha,* imagined objects have a tendency to merge with one another, to fill up, by an extraordinary expansiveness and restless inter-existence, the originally empty but creative space of the cosmos. In this cosmos, nothing unimagined has any real ontic claim except, possibly, the truly unimaginable openness that continuously generates these shifting forms. The real contrast here lies not between what is imagined and what is experienced as real but between imaginative mentation, on the one hand, and "awareness" or "consciousness" in itself, as the deeper repository of existential reality-making, on the other. Such awareness has the density and simultaneity of rock:

> Tender, luminous, soft to the touch, very expansive, continuous, always without gaps—somewhere or other, there is a great rock like this. Inside it, as if inside a lake, there are very many flowering lotuses, lovely and limitless. Their leaves are tangled together; some are separated from one another, others are growing on top of one another, some hidden, others visible. Some have roots in the sky, others have roots down below, some lack roots of any kind. Nearby are hundreds of thousands of conch-shells and masses of wheels, folded into themselves like lotuses.[5] . . . What I am describing to you is an awareness-rock, in which the whole universe abides. For awareness is indeed a rock—because it is condensed and entirely self-contained. A vast array of worlds exists inside that rock, even though it is so solidly condensed and utterly without gaps, like the wild wind blowing in the sky.[6]

Such rock-like awareness has, among other properties, a propensity to generate imaginative worlds inside itself. "Awareness" is the more comprehensive state, we can be sure. But unlike the Advaita system, for example, which seeks to awaken us from the illusion that we take for normal reality, the *Yoga-vāsiṣṭha,* as Gary Tubb has shown in an important essay, seeks to wake the reader *into* the illusion that the mind creates.[7] In much the same vein, the famous Buddhist philosopher Nāgârjuna and his successor Vasubandhu seem to want us to internalize a reality that is continuously reimagined and thus neither empty nor full (to use their language) but rather a beginningless and endless series of what might be called "true illusions."[8]

In what sense can an illusion be true? For both the *Yoga-vāsiṣṭha* and the Mahāyāna Buddhists, there are at least three primary options for making sense of such a paradox. First, we have a pragmatic and intersubjective consideration. The shared illusions we call reality actually "work"; indeed, by virtue of the continuous interweaving of our projections, the images we see constantly corroborate our perceptions of them and normally act in the ways we expect them to (sometimes, however, they don't). Second, these projections are profoundly rooted in consequential acts of linguistic creativity, like all other forms of the imaginative life considered in this book. Finally, and most interesting, an operative distinction emerges between what is real and what is true (with a slight preference for insight committed to the latter term). In the *Yoga-vāsiṣṭha,* such insight occasionally intensifies the apparent paradox by asserting that *only* such real illusions can be true—that is, what we are calling illusion is the proper stuff of a reality defined, ab initio, as the imagination in action, even if the base state of open-ended awareness is in theory, as I have said, a still more profound repository of existential experimentation. (One does well, in such a system, to avoid linear notions of "ultimacy" altogether.) But this conclusion is not the only possible trajectory branching off from the crossroads we have reached; in Part II we will trace the further history of this critical distinction in medieval south Indian materials, which, as we will see, for their own reasons tend to privilege the "real" over the "true."

We could also restate the whole problem in a more moderate and general, but perhaps rather routine, way with wide application throughout the South Asian schools, both Hindu and Buddhist. Underlying the notion of true illusions is an appreciation of the creative capacity of the mind and, above all, of the imaginative faculty, which constitutes the core of the experiential domain we inhabit, however this core is characterized. What would a nontrivial articulation of this hypothesis look like? It is probably time to move away from the attempt to ascribe differential degrees of reality-content to mind-generated projections. Only a very narrow reading of the story of the three Brahmins would follow this familiar path. Those who were never born or even conceived live a remarkably rich and happy life, apparently undisturbed by metaphysical niceties; they rest peacefully in nonexistent shade and consume to their satisfaction the nonexistent rice, as, it seems, do we. On the other hand, the nonexistent heroes are quite capable of feeling grief and physical pain (as do we). How is this possible? We might posit a world of such dense, organic interconnectivity that it makes no sense at all to separate out the mind as an alien spectator or actor from some point outside the frame of perception. Of course, words such as "mind" and "language" define aspects of the reality brocade that have their proper pragmatic functions; but just as language is largely coterminous and isomorphic with the phenomena it names (thereby also generating them, certainly not simply representing them), similarly the mind observes and projects from within the compacted—rock-like, simultaneous, restless—space of awareness. Language is the medium we breathe in and think in, mind its close analogue or derivate. In such a world, "nonexistence" is not an absence or a lack. It is an integral part of the brocade, internal to it, woof to its warp. In what sense, then, can a profound perception of "nonexistence" free the perceiving person from suffering—as the *Yoga-vāsiṣṭha* repeatedly tells us it can? It allows for, or perhaps reestablishes, a capacity for further connection, which is akin to the capacity for movement in any direction. Such a capacity, which we could even call "objective,"[9] frees the individual for unencumbered, though still patterned and rule-bound, imagining.

Such a cosmos, set in motion and driven forward from within, is also held together from within. *Saṅkalpa*, in the sense of imaginative projection, may well be its primary motor and bonding agent. What *saṅkalpa* generates, however, is in general unlikely to be entirely new, though it may well be singular. We will come back to this point. Also, *saṅkalpa*, like *bhāvanā*, must have a history. Jumping ahead, we can foresee a moment when, with the hypertrophy of the imagination as a personal and specifically human faculty, the extreme organicity of the cosmos will be shattered, the homology between human minds and the rest of existence attenuated and disturbed. When that happens, the role of a Yoga of the imagination will also have to be reconceived.

Let us return for a moment to *saṅkalpa* and its historical antecedents. The word appears in several well-known passages from the Upaniṣads, at times with the connotation of intentionality or a more general mode of intellection, sometimes accompanied by very concrete internal images.[10] *Chāndogya Upaniṣad* 8.2.1–10 fills out the semantic range of the term. The text has just told us that a person who has come to know *(anuvidya)* the self and its true desires *(satyān kāmān)* will be able to move at will throughout all worlds (7.1.6). How so? Such a person, "if he wants the world of the fathers, by his *saṅkalpa* alone the fathers will arise, and the world of the fathers will be his."[11] Similarly with the worlds of mothers, brothers, sisters, friends, perfumes and garlands, food and drink, singing and instrumental music, and women: by *saṅkalpa* alone, they will be his. Whatever object he desires, *saṅkalpa* will produce it for him (verse 10). "Intention"[12] fails, I think, to capture the mental process at work here, as does "thought" in a general sense. The point is that the self-possessed person conceives a definite image of whatever he or she would like; by virtue of having come to know the inner self—the vast space hidden in the heart (8.1.2)—this newly configured person can achieve immediate access to that image and all that it contains, proceeding as it does from out of that creative space. The mental image allows an accelerated movement into the particular world constituted, or so it would seem, by that very image. I don't think we should hesitate to translate *saṅkalpa* here as "imagination"; both the plasticity and the concrete vision implicit in acts of imagination are present, as is the sense of radical freedom intimated above.

In classical Sanskrit and, even more strikingly, in the regional literatures, a linguistic specification has taken place very much in harmony with the direction just outlined. We saw how Kādambarī, Bāṇa's heroine, created an "imaginary lover" *(saṅkalpa-mayaḥ kumāraḥ)* who is always with her, a steady and dependable person far superior to any flesh-and-blood suitor.[13] When Nala, entirely invisible thanks to the gods' magic, enters Damayantī's harem, he is hallucinating, seeing everywhere around him images of his beloved, so palpable that to some extent they blind him to the flesh-and-blood women before his eyes. These images are, Śriharṣa tells us, *vikalpopahṛta* "conjured up by his mind."[14] How was Nala able to produce such images, since he has never actually seen the woman in question? Well, he might have seen her in some former life, or maybe it was because he saw her painted portrait; perhaps it was just some magic trick *(śāmbarī-śilpa)* of the Love God.[15] When Śrīnātha, in the late fourteenth century, translates this passage into Telugu, he presents us with a slightly expanded list of possibilities:

> Maybe he had met her in the endless chain of lives he had lived through.
> Maybe it was a repeated projection that came from staring at her ravishing portrait painted on a board.
> Maybe it was the creamy, delectable, indeed addictive description presented in words by the goose.[16]
> Maybe it was the Love God's masterful art of conjuring that drives the whole world astray.
> Maybe he was possessed by his own many-faceted imagination.
> Whatever the reason, he saw her image, soft as a flower, gleaming like a flash of lightning when the rains begin, filling all space.[17]

We are interested in the final item in the list: *vividha-saṅkalpa-kalpanâveśamunano,* "possessed by his own many-faceted imagination." The imagination, *saṅkalpa,*[18] is so powerful, so capable of producing vivid and credible images, that it is assimilated to demonic possession, *āveśa,* when the self is occupied by another will or persona or profoundly locked into itself. Not by chance does this hypothesis come last; it is, we may assume, by far the most likely explanation for what is going on in Nala's mind, and one the Telugu poet has himself added to the list he inherited from his Sanskrit source, in conformance with the newly emergent late medieval south Indian model of the mind.

Once we find ourselves in the charmed world of Nala and Damayantī, we should not neglect the Malayalam version of the *Naiṣadhīya* by Maḻamaṅgalam Kavi (sixteenth century?). The two lovers are, as usual, obsessed with their imaginings of each other, so much so that they can't fall asleep. There's a playful explanation of this not entirely unhappy state. Sleep, *nidrā*, is a female noun in Sanskrit, hence she must be a woman or a goddess:

> Sleep came to them over and over,
> but each time she thought to herself,
> "*I*'m not about to create an obstacle
> to the intense joy they're feeling
> by making love in their imagination"—
> so each time she went away,
> as a tactful friend should.[19]

This wise goddess won't disturb the *saṅkalpa-saṅgama,* the lovemaking that happens in the imagination, perhaps the most satisfying of all; *saṅkalpa* has by now achieved a definite and delimited meaning, not quite synonymous with medieval *bhāvanā* (a somewhat wider and more supple term), but clearly referring to the same generative function of the mind.[20]

5.2. Making a Goddess

We now need to revisit *bhāvanā* in a new set of pragmatic contexts, all rooted in the south, reaching their most radical expression in the twelfth to thirteenth century in fully crystallized Tantric meditational practices. We have studied *bhāvanā* in the domains of grammar, logic, and, especially, classical poetics; we saw how the poeticians, beginning with Bhaṭṭa Nāyaka, extended the scope of the term (and the closely allied *bhāvakatva,* "generativity") so that it eventually came to include full-fledged productions of the imagination, whether unrolling in the minds of the characters onstage, in the highly energized mental processes of the spectator-reader, or in some intermediate and interactive space. But by the middle of the first millennium AD, *bhāvanā* was also a common word for meditative or contemplative practices; this is how we tend to find it in Buddhist sources, as we do in a striking range of Hindu devotional and ritual texts, particularly in the worship of the god Śiva and of the goddess who goes by many names, but whom we will call here Tripura-sundarī, "Most Beautiful in the Triple Cosmos." In general, we are talking about focused meditation with a strong component of visualization; not by chance, such practices are also intimately linked to the attempts to bring the deity into substantial forms of presence or being, as the root *bhāvayati*—"to make be"—would suggest.

Thus the early Tamil Śaiva poet Tiruñāṉacampantar (seventh century?) says:

Oh you who live in Tĕḷicceri, where the gods
come with flowers three times every day
to worship your golden anklets:
it is in your nature, it appears,
to stand here, to be imagined
as a Hunter chasing the boar
with the goddess beside you acting
the same part.[21]

Pāvakam = *bhāvaka,* a visible form brought into being—perhaps by the god Śiva himself, perhaps by the poet who is singing to him, perhaps by every pilgrim to the Tĕḷicceri temple. The particular form in question is that of Śiva as the Kirāta hunter who revealed himself to Arjuna and entered into a contest with this hero. The modern commentator glosses the term *pāvakam* as "unreal" *(mĕyallāmai),* meaning, I suppose, an image that is generated by the mind and presented to the eye, either inner or outer, in all its ravishing tangibility. One can call up this image by worshiping at this shrine, among others, and once the vision is in place, various emotional and transformative experiences inevitably follow: those who can sing the ten verses of this poem, the poet says in his final verse, will come to exist *inside the words,* surrounded by the whole assembly of gods *(iruppavar cŏllile).* As Norman Cutler showed in a subtle and powerful study, such Tamil *bhakti* poems regularly move the listener toward actual identification with the deity and incorporation into the mythic or ritual scene that only appears, initially, to be situated somewhere outside.[22] In the present instance, the poem claims to have generated an autonomous universe, with the god at its core, where the listener or singer can find refuge. This universe exists in the sung words themselves, as do the gods and the various visualized forms of Śiva and his consort. But such a domain is not a datum, preexistent in some factual mode; it is brought into being—*bhāvita*—by the act of singing and, we can be certain, of imagining the deity who comes alive precisely through such imaginative and poetic means. He seems to stand there, "to be imagined." He is susceptible to, and possibly even dependent upon, just such far-reaching creative moves. One could also say that he is there only insofar as he is imagined—a bold ontic assertion, not at all beyond the axiology of Tamil *bhakti* works. Note the immense self-confidence of the poet, who knows how effective his words and his music truly are.

The modern gloss is thus, in a way, misleading unless you know how to read it against the pragmatics of Tamil Śaivism. Śiva assumed (in the past) and assumes again (whenever one performs this meditation) the guise of a tribal hunter. The guise in no way exhausts the existential richness of the deity, but neither is it some adventitious and external accretion. Indeed, it far surpasses in sheer ontic terms the entropic guises of the everyday world—although, once again, we don't really need to haggle over the precise reality-quotient of such statements as *Tevāram* 2.3.1. It's more than enough if we recognize that the business of bringing the Hunter into being, *bhāvaka,* is not an as-if, fictive endeavor but rather is grounded in what is seen as empirical observation and experience (quite capable, incidentally, of being reproduced under analogous laboratory conditions, though the Tamil poets wouldn't have put the matter in these terms). Where would we find such a laboratory? We don't have far to look. As Cutler has said, *all* the personae and poetic voices that turn up in the Tamil *bhakti* corpus are essential aspects of the poet's self and thus of the selves of the devotees who identify with the poet and, through him or her, with the god waiting to be imagined.[23]

Thus it is very natural for Cuntaramūrttināyaṉār, another of the *Tevāram* poets, a century or more after Tiruñāṉacampantar, to identify Śiva (at Tiruvārūr) as "honey flowing through the minds of those who imagine him" *(pāvippār maṉatt' ūṟum at-teṉai).*[24] *Bhāvanā,* the generative imagination, is where the god exists—a sweet, delicious existence, internal to the practitioners, whose inner space must thus somehow be similarly structured in each case. Can we say something more about this inner space? Many have tried. One common way to talk about it, encountered in varying degrees in all the Tamil *bhakti* poets, is as a fragmented, often conflictual zone where the god hides himself, almost as if to taunt his tormented lover by the very fact of inaccessibility. The language used to describe such states is one of brittleness, heaviness, solidity: "I am," says Māṇikkavācakar, "a puppet made of iron."[25] Given the human propensity for such states of being or awareness, the role of the imagination becomes crucial; it is the mechanism most readily available for deobjectifying, desolidifying the rough, opaque surfaces of the self and allowing for renewed movement, a honeyed flow. But this process is only one of several that occur normally, and repeatedly, within consciousness; each system, indeed each major poetic voice and each ritual-meditative complex, has its own way of mapping and understanding the possibilities for blockage, veiling, and release.

One of the most popular and widespread systems in the south is the Tantric worship of the goddess Most Beautiful in the Triple Cosmos, the focus of the beloved text known as the *Wave of Beauty, Saundarya-laharī,* which we now assign to the twelfth or thirteenth century despite its traditional attribution to the philosopher Śaṅkarâcārya. The *Wave of Beauty* was certainly composed in the south, and it even refers, it seems, to our *Tevāram* poet Tiruñāṉacampantar (whom it calls a "Tamil boy," *draviḍa-śiśu,* verse 75). A later tradition claims that this Tamil boy composed the text and inscribed it on Mount Kailāsa, where Śaṅkara saw it and managed to memorize the first forty-one verses even as the goddess herself, concerned about her privacy, was trying to erase them.[26] Within the medieval tradition that has grown up around this text, verses 1–41 are seen as a separate unit, the so-called *Wave of Joy, Ānanda-laharī,* while the remaining verses, 42–100, or the combined text, are the *Wave of Beauty* proper. The division makes sense. The first forty-one verses build up a mantric universe, condensed into the famous *Śrī-cakra* diagram or *yantra,* in which the goddess dwells; here we find practical exercises in visualization and the use of encoded mantras to bring her into an active presence, along with descriptions of a Yogic physiology that is correlated to cosmological and epistemic registers. If you follow the rules laid out here, albeit rather cryptically, you can awaken the Kuṇḍalinī female principle coiled at the base of the spine and, as a result, enter into ecstatic states of utter fullness and power.[27] The remaining segment of the text gives us a lyrical depiction of Tripura-sundarī, inch by inch and limb by limb a blueprint for visualization. Many people in south India recite the entire text each day in order to bring the goddess alive in their heart or home.

The *Wave of Beauty,* rooted historically in the Tantric ritual and metaphysical complex of the *Śrī-vidyā,* explicates with unusual clarity a classical premodern south Indian theory of the pragmatic imagination.[28] The method it describes is *bhāvanā,* and the relevant verb is, again, *bhāvayati,* "to bring into being." It is hardly alone in highlighting these terms; we have, for example, the *Bhāvanā Upaniṣad,* also focused on this goddess and her *yantra,* with technical instructions for her worship and stage-by-stage meditation given in detail by the great eighteenth-century commentator Bhāskara-rāya.[29] We cannot follow each step in the program of loving visualization these works assume and in the immense corpus of commentary they have generated; instead, we will look closely at three important verses of the *Wave of Beauty*, seen through the prism of a practical metapsychology of direct relevance to our theme.

First, a verse (22) from the applied segment of the text:

bhavāni tvam dāse mayi vitara dṛṣṭiṃ sakaruṇām
iti stotum vāñchan kathayati bhavāni tvam iti yaḥ/
tadaiva tvam tasmai diśasi nija-sāyujya-padavīṃ
mukunda-brahmendra-sphuṭa-makuṭa-nīrājita-padām//

I started to praise you in my song by saying,
"Goddess, I would be your
slave, look kindly at me"—
but no sooner did I say the words "Goddess, I would be you . . ."
—*bhavāni tvam*—
than *you* made me over as yourself.
I got what the great gods long for when they illumine your feet
with the light from their crowns.

I've tried to preserve the double entendre that lies at the heart of this verse. In Sanskrit, *bhavāni* is a homonym meaning either "O Goddess, you . . ."—a vocative—or a first-person imperative, from the root *bhū*—to be, to become. So *bhavāni tvam* can mean "I must become you" or "I would become you." Adepts of the *Śrī-vidyā* do want to make themselves, quite literally, into the goddess, so the first-person imperative is by no means an outlandish statement in this context. Actually, though, what the speaker thought he wanted to say was only "Goddess [in the vocative], look kindly at me." But because of the second, unconscious layer—homonymy in Sanskrit, at least in domains such as this, is rarely accidental—the speaking "I" at once became, truly, a "you." The syllables worked automatically and immediately; no sooner were they uttered than the speaker had truly turned into Tripura-sundarī. Note that the speaker's intention is quite irrelevant to the pragmatic result. We will later see another example of this basic linguistic fact.[30] Insofar as intentionality of any kind is operating here, we would have to assume that when the goddess hears the phrase in question, given her compassionate nature, she enacts it along the lines of extreme existential transformation, even if the poet meant something quite different by it. Another possibility is that the unconscious homonymy expresses the poet's deeper intention, beyond his surface consciousness, and explains his choice of that particular vocative.

Bhavāni is the first-person simplex imperative form corresponding to the causative *bhāvayāni,* "I would make [myself] X," "I would imagine X." We can assume the wish nested within the overt vocative is an active one and that it is accompanied—like all other first-person statements in this text—by an ongoing process of strong internal imaging. So here, rather like the *Tevāram* passage studied earlier but in the framework of a quite different ritual and axiological orientation, we have another example of an imaginative gesture classed as a linguistic act. We have to keep in mind the fact that this root, √*bhū,* gives us *bhāvanā:* thus "Let me become," articulated clearly, or perhaps even silently in the mind, makes "becoming" happen (always in a particular vector) when the supreme Subject of the cosmos, the goddess who is, by definition, the prime cause of all existence, assumes her active causal role in any given case or moment, perhaps in response to an appeal, conscious or not, of one of her worshipers. Under ideal conditions, the correct but unwitting connection of syllables will thus suffice to produce the imagined result.

But we might also suggest, as the medieval commentator Rāmakavi comes close to doing, that the Tantric goddess whom the text wants to materialize imagines the speaker as herself—very possibly in conjunction with his own latent imagination of himself as her.[31] Surely, some interactive movement is taking place within a structured field of identities, with imagination as the engine for a very complex series of internal shifts. Try not to think of this series as some "magical" force in the common, rather degraded use of this quasi-analytic term. It is, rather, a patterned, nonrandom, highly interactive, language-based negotiation that has the effect of deconstructing—or, better, deobjectifying—the speaker/author and then refashioning him (or her?) into a new, fully subjectified being. The goddess, though entirely real, cannot be an object in the usual sense of the word.

The metaphysical end result is called *sāyujya,* literally "complete connectedness." One being has fused with another. The great gods, Viṣṇu, Brahmā, and Indra, seek this state by bowing, their crowns glowing, at the feet of the goddess. The implication, however, is that the poet's Freudian slip is more effective, and certainly quicker to achieve its end, than such long-standing acts of worship by these deities. You can rely upon language, which is not given to caprice, more than you can on the gods. What we don't know yet, on the basis of this one verse, is what the flow of awareness between the conjoined beings has by way of contents, apart from the mutual joyful "quivering" that the Ḍiṇḍima mentions. We'll get to this question shortly.

You might have some doubts about my way of reading the verse; in particular, the link to the imagination is not quite explicit there. So let us move on to another verse from near the end of this same text, where this problem is specifically addressed:

sva-dehotbhūtābhir gṛṇibhir aṇimâdyābhir abhito
niṣevye nitye tvām aham iti sadā bhāvayati yaḥ/
kim āścaryaṃ tasya trinayana-samṛddhiṃ tṛṇayato
mahā-saṃvartâgnir viracayati nīrājana-vidhim// (96)

Anyone who says: "You are me!" imagining you [the goddess]
into being, you who are eternal, worthy of worship,
in the midst of the light pouring from his own body,
disdains all of God's riches, and no wonder:
the fire that burns the world at the end of time
is no more than a lamp waved to light up his face.

It isn't as simple as it sounds. For this metamorphosis to happen, one has to complete the rigorous process of visualization and mantric reconstitution of the goddess as spelled out in nearly one hundred previous verses of the text. But at the end of the process, so we are promised, it is indeed possible to "imagine the goddess into being"—*bhāvayati*—in the form of one's own true self. If you reach this point—and notice that the choice is yours, a voluntary act or series of acts, each step along the way requiring another willing choice—you will not be tempted to reverse the direction and reimagine the goddess as the former, empirical "you." That you is gone, replaced by a more compact,[32] full, liquid, enhanced, and—if we are to believe the poet—incomparably delightful female self that must have been there all along in some potential, latent dimension. There is nothing subjunctive about the change that takes place; rather, the dependent, contingent self that began the process has truly changed from within, thereby instigating a chain reaction without. It happens through *bhāvanā,* a disciplined imaginative progression. Once achieved, the reconstituted identity is resistant to time and death, even to the destruction of the entire created universe at doomsday. One no longer has to worry about such paltry things.

Why not? Because the self has now filled up to the limit of imaginable fullness, a totality equal to the plenitude that defines existence itself when that definition follows the contours, and the rhythms, of the goddess who is Most Beautiful. The totality—a specific embodiment, with discrete features—never dies. I think that the immortal aspect of the fullness requires an epistemic act, that is, indubitable knowledge that one has become this goddess and can now speak and act only *as* her and *through* her.

Let me restate the elements I have mentioned. We have (1) an act or process of imaging that is (2) highly patterned, determined, and probably irreversible, a process that (3) reflects a true but latent identity that is (4) made manifest largely by linguistic means. Such images are what reality is about. So (5) the end result is entirely real, just as the goddess is now fully real and alive—but only (6) insofar as one imagines her as such, interactively. A mutual determination works itself out in this manner. Stated negatively, and extrapolating slightly on the basis of the textual evidence, the goddess is not there until you imagine her to be there, and you will not become this goddess unless her imagination locks into yours.

Lest the conclusion we have arrived at appear too neat, too watertight, impervious to further contemplation, we should look at one of the final statements of this text (in the Vulgate), which adds another, critical element—a somewhat skeptical one—to our story of radical self-reinvention.

samudbhūta-sthūla-stana-bharam uraś cāru-hasitaṃ
kaṭâkse kandarpaḥ kusumita-kadamba-dyuti-vapuḥ/
harasya tvad-bhrāntiṃ manasi janayām āsa madano
bhavatyā ye bhaktāḥ pariṇatir amīṣām iyam ume// (102)

Full, heavy breasts,
flirtatious smile,
all of desire condensed into a glance
from the corner of the eye,
skin luminous as a flowering *kadamba* tree:
Those who serve you, Goddess,
ripen into this beguiling image
generated by Love
in God's mind.

The medieval commentators (e.g., the *Ḍiṇḍima-bhāṣya* once again) link this verse directly to the former one. Imagination moves—actually grows, develops, "ripens"—in a definite direction. The language of ripening is not accidental. A seed, planted, nourished, watered, is free to grow—but only into a certain tree. *Bhāvanā* directed at the goddess produces an identification *with* or *as* that goddess—as the Ḍiṇḍima commentator remarks, it is like the beetle that is so terrified of being stung by a bee that, through constant anxiety about and concentration on this enemy, it actually *becomes* a bee *(bhramara-kīṭa-nyāya)*. The mind shapes the physical body—one's own or another's. Perhaps I should add that "ripening" in India is always connected to notions of softening, melting, liquefying—the therapeutic response to terminal objectification. So once again, imagination, harnessed here to a meditative program, is the most effective tool we have to melt congealed surfaces, internal or external, and thus to mature, to surpass our limits, to be free.

But the surprising, even shocking part of this process comes through in the second half of the verse, one of the boldest statements I have seen about the workings of the imagination. A person, male or female, can turn himself or herself into a goddess. In itself, this result is quite unexceptional. Creative meditation can produce it, if pursued in a disciplined, serious way. Proper use of the mantras—that is, of language at its most powerful and compressed—will also do it. The result is a normal part of the psycho-physical universe, an achievement consequential for the practitioner but in no way exceeding the cognitive map the culture has produced. We are, all of us, this goddess, though we may have forgotten this identity. It's conceivable, as in the case of the pretty girl's face and the moon, that each of us is the goddess in a quite personal, even singular way.[33] What may get lost in the far-reaching patterning of this meditative praxis, with its precise focus on the particular goddess and the disciplined progression that makes one over into her, is the distinctiveness and freshness of the individual result. The impulse itself is undoubtedly a personal one, and the transformation, however predictable, is no less specific to the individual practitioner. And yet it is precisely this theme of the individual processing of the imagination that is not worked through in our Tantric text. Poet and goddess could be said freely to create each other; their respective existence (vis-à-vis each other) is, it appears, the only practical constraint on the forms their far-reaching fusion will assume. So far so good. However, the sixteenth-century south Indian sources will take another, decisive step.

Let us, then, assume that some of us, many of us, have managed to turn ourselves truly into the ravishing goddess described in the first half of the verse—with full breasts and that seductive glance from the corner of the eye. The change demands attention—please note again this stable link between imagination and attention—on the part of God (Hara-Śiva) himself, who immediately falls in love (he is, says the commentator of the *Ānanda-laharī-ṭīkā*, beside himself, helpless in his passion, *kāma-vaśa*). Imaginative self-generation is irresistible. In the poet's way of saying this, we, who have fully ripened, become an image, or a beguiling, misleading idea—*bhrānti*—in God's mind. So now we have to imagine a world in which God is receptive enough, pliant enough, impressionable enough to be overwhelmed by the work of *our* persistent self-imaginings. This statement could possibly serve as one definition of the Tantric "God." One might say that God is the plasticity of potential emergence into being that is continuously operated upon, in definable ways, by imaginative process (ours, yours, mine, the poet's, His). God is thus a certain susceptibility to playful, imaginative enticement. But the images he holds in his mind, while true experientially for us, are actually classed as a kind of error or misperception; that is what *bhrānti* means.

One of the commentators on this verse, Kaivalyâśrama, sees here the well-known figure of *bhrāntimat*, "confused perception," in which the listeners outside the poem enjoy the spectacle of misperception on the part of an actor within it. For example:

> The cat licks at the white flood in its bowl.
> The elephant sees it shattered by the branches of the trees
> and reaches for it, certain that it's delicious lotus-fiber.
> My lover, after our loving, sees it lying on the bed
> and tries to put it on like a nightgown.
> The moon, drunk on its own brilliance,
> drives the world mad.[34]

If our verse falls into this class, the confusion belongs to God. That God sees us as a goddess is, for us, the final act of maturation, a necessary outcome of the interdependence and mutual determination of the goddess and her worshipers: this, says Kaivalyâśrama, is the astonishing fruit *(phala-mahiman)* of *bhāvanā*. But surely we must then conclude that God sees what he sees as a consequence of the impingement of our imagination upon his mind, and that in the present instance, utterly delightful as it is said to be, he has made a mistake, as any Naiyāyika logician could have pointed out to him. We cannot extricate ourselves from this rather awkward conclusion by positing some sort of artificial hierarchy in being, let us say by subsuming Śiva within the wider or deeper principle of the goddess, thus allowing him to err from time to time—for how could the concrete image of Most Beautiful be an error? And to go in the opposite direction, turning desire into a second-order disturbance within the mind of a transcendent, mostly unruffled God, militates against the primary thrust of the *Wave of Beauty* as a programmatic work. Neither possibility will do. There must, then, be a universe in which God is confused on a matter of utmost existential urgency, and a universe in which the mingled imaginations of devotee and goddess constitute the highest imaginable soteriological goal. Apparently we are speaking of a single, sometimes incongruous universe.

In any case, the principle is worth restating: rigorous contemplation—a Yoga of the imagination—acts directly upon the cosmos and at the same time infiltrates the widest possible angle or vantage point on this cosmos. God must be susceptible, perhaps infinitely susceptible, to our ways of imagining him or her. His or her own imagination has no existence independent of ours. There is room for mistakes. And though I used the adjective "indubitable" just a few paragraphs back to characterize the knowledge that comes with "engoddessing" oneself, it appears that a skeptical undercurrent may survive in the framing of such knowledge. Here is one way to address the contents of the conjoint quiver that concerns us.

5.3. *Bhāvanā* and *Pūjā:* How Meditation Works

This slightly skeptical conclusion takes us back, surprisingly, to the Advaita world of severe philosophical nondualism, with its reluctance to grant full reality-status to any imaginative projection of the mind.[35] A strong yet permeable boundary divides the Advaita philosopher from the Tantric practitioner. For Śaṅkara—*not* for the author of the *Wave of Beauty*—knowledge that counts, that is, the knowledge that the self *(ātman)* is identical with *brahman,* with metaphysical ultimacy, must be free from anything that smacks of figurative language. The identification of *ātman* and *brahman* is a fact, not a *façon de parler.* Śaṅkara gives a series of negative examples—how *not* to understand this crucial fact. It is not what is called *sampad,* a correspondence or identification, apparently on the basis of some shared attribute, between some internal and some external entity, such as we see in the Upaniṣadic verse "The mind is infinite, and the All-Gods are infinite, and infinite are the worlds he [the Brahman priest] wins by this [mind]."[36] Nor is metaphysical truth a matter of pure projection *(adhyāsa),* as when one says, "Worship the mind as *brahman*"[37]—an "as-if" statement with pragmatic uses, not to be taken literally. Nor can we take the identification as explaining or rationalizing some form of ritual activity *(viśiṣṭa-kriyā-yoga-nimitta),* or as an adjunct to such activity, as when the sacrificer's wife purifies the butter offering by looking at it. It is not as if one who deeply knows himself or herself to be *brahman* had to purify the self, pure by definition, by seeing "it" in a certain way. Were one to read the great statements of identity—*tat tvam asi,* "You are that,"[38] or "I am *brahman*"—as a kind of *sampad,* or any of the other nonliteral, projective modes just mentioned, then, says Śaṅkara, primary linguistic operations *(pada-samanvaya)* would be vitiated. What is more, the effective goal of such statements—that is, the dissolution of ignorance—will no longer be achievable.[39]

We should listen carefully to such pronouncements. When it comes to truth embodied in words, backed up by Vedic authority, any attempt to diminish, in any way, the full force of the utterance will endanger the normal workings of language itself. Syntax, reference, primary semanticity, pragmatics—all these will be impaired *(pīḍyeta)* if we allow the slightest slippage from the identity equation X = Y, which actually means X = X. Such statements are *not* props for meditation or window dressing for some extraneous (ritual) act. You cannot explain them away, allegorize them, or claim that, merely by being subject to articulation, they are only inadequate expressions or approximations of something better conveyed by silence. Taken as true statements, they are capable of doing a specific, necessary kind of work. We have hit a point where the philosopher must take a stand if he wants to preserve as meaningful any piece of his own rather wordy commentaries, to say nothing of the acute, life-changing words of the Scriptures, embedded and explicated in the former. Within language, there are what might be termed sites of ultimacy, where truth resides; such sites guarantee a minimal workable efficacy for Vedic speech, first of all, and then, by extension, for speech in general.

Yet to say that these "great statements" *(mahā-vākya)* are *literally* true, as implied above, is a little too simple. The whole post-Śaṅkara tradition of Advaita struggled with this problem. Sureśvara, supposedly Śaṅkara's direct disciple, several times suggests that "You are that"—a statement that, he says, cannot be true in ordinary ways—might have to be heard and properly interpreted as *lakṣaṇā,* "indirect" or metaphoric modes of speech.[40]

Such statements generate transformative experience not by direct denotation, and not even at moments where the listener thinks he or she understands them rationally, but by virtue of particular, context-dependent, usually transient states of receptivity on the listener's part—basically, a kind of attention. We'll return to this point shortly. Moreover, even Śaṅkara acknowledges that *sampad* and other inner devices and modes of awareness prevalent in Vedic texts, including modes we would call figurative or projective, have their uses. He recommends structured meditation as a path to release, and he takes pains to ensure that such meditation is not seen as inherent to the ritual activity with which the texts tend to associate it;[41] rather, it is an autonomous mental process conducive to the overriding soteriological goal. He knows very well that one can create a fire altar, complete with all its thousands of bricks, layers, fires, and ritual implements, entirely in the mind *(manasā)*, as the Veda recommends. He cites the *Brāhmaṇa* passage about the 36,000 mental modes *(mano-vṛtti)*, one for each day of a human life that lasts a hundred years, which are correlated to the mind-generated bricks of the altar.[42] Such meditative acts establish an efficacious mental connection to the ritual activity, and this connection is, says Śaṅkara, the result of *sampad*, a linkage wrought by and in the mind. Imagination, to use our term, in the form of focused mental acts of disciplined and precisely specified vision, has found a back-door entrance to the Advaita system at its most exacting.

Thus even if God, for the Śaṅkara Advaita, must be devoid of an imagination, those who want to realize their divine identity, not as an objectified cognitive act but as a true experience, may well have need of precisely this faculty, whatever one wants to call it. By the time we reach the devotional and Tantric worlds sampled above, meditative visualization, suffused by imaginative processes, has become a primary form of praxis *(sādhana)*, the key to nearly all other prescribed activities. Temple worship itself, the main venue for Hindu metaphysical experimentation in the south, is completely structured around just such mental acts, codified in the rich literature of the Āgamas and Tantras. For a typical example, we can turn to G. C. Tripathi's detailed description of daily worship, *pūjā*, by the Brahmin priest or *arcaka* at the famous temple of Jagannātha in Orissa:[43]

> The worshipper, first of all, dissolves his mundane body in meditation in order to create a new, ritualistically pure, divine body which is endowed with the character and the nature of the deity herself. Thus assuming the

nature of the deity, the worshipper meditates upon the Mantra of the deity with which he can realize the deity in his heart.[44]

This process involves imagining one's body as a *yantra* diagram housing the goddess, then mentally extracting her brilliance *(tejas)* from one's heart by means of the breath *(prāṇa)* and implanting that brilliance in the external image to be worshiped. Such an "external sacrifice" *(bahir-yāga)* is followed by rites of mentally welcoming the enlivened image as an honored guest who must be greeted, seated, bathed, clothed, fed, and so on. Some of these rites are enacted upon the visible, concrete image; others remain within the supple confines of the mind and the subtle, abstract images it generates. Verses uttered during acts of external worship explicitly proclaim the "as-if" nature of the concretized deity who, the worshiper says, properly exists within awareness alone, the ritual attention to the visible image being no more than a pragmatic convention *(loka-pravṛtti-mātra).*[45] This point is interesting: if one has to decide which is more real, the internal thought-image or the tangible, external object, there is no doubt whatsoever that the former will come out ahead.

Every stage in the lengthy process is accompanied by precise acts of mind that utterly transform the worshiper's body and link it, in turn, to the various building blocks of the cosmos, including, above all, the subtle sounds *(mātṛkās)* that precede and inform audible syllables and thus generate all of language, itself a divine medium. It is as if the very being or self of the practitioner had become a resonant, musical, mantric instrument, as such identical to the no less resonant deity. Transitions between inner and outer domains are regular and frequent: at the height of the transfiguration, there is a quadripartite *bhāvanā* meditation in which the meditator uses his breath to bring the glowing goddess onto his fingertips and then touches his own body, in the process of self-divinization, with this fiery presence. The *mātṛka* syllables are then applied to the icon, which eventually opens up to receive the full, living being of the goddess via flowers transferred from the forehead of the meditator—like a lamp lit from another lamp *(dīpād dīpântaraṃ yathā).* Mental production of fully autonomous worlds, peopled by various divine beings, proceeds apace until the godly glow is transferred back from the live image to the priest's heart, from which it originally emerged (this is *udvāsana,* "retraction"). If we find this continuous interweaving of outer and inner worlds somewhat baffling—and by now we may well be wondering if we are using the terms correctly or meaningfully, given the mind-based locus for the *pūjā* as a totality—then what will we make of such acts as the preliminary bathing of the gods' images not in water but, in the form of their *reflections,* in a space internal to mirrors set up before them?

It is critical to understand that none of these activities transpiring within awareness, with its external correlates, is "symbolic" in any of the senses of the word familiar to us. I would be prepared to argue that symbolism as such is relatively rare in South Asia, and I recommend avoiding the word altogether for contexts such as those discussed here. When the practitioner burns up the black Pāpa-puruṣa, the "man of sin," lurking in the lower left part of his belly, first drying him up with the *mantra* of wind and then igniting him with the *mantra* of fire, a part of the psychophysical self is truly destroyed. This part will have to be burnt again tomorrow, as it was yesterday, given the entropic processes inherent to existence and, no less crucially, to normal mentation. But if the deity is to take up residence in one's body, transformed into a suitable receptacle for him or her, then the mind—the finest tool available for this purpose—will have to be harnessed to the business of generation, *bhāvanā,* just as *bhāvanā* is prescribed for the height of the advanced sexual ritual that Abhinavagupta outlines in his *Tantrâloka.*[46] God, that is, exists *for* us, *in* us, or *as* us if we bring him or her to be through acts of guided and controlled awareness, including concrete imaging informed by mantric syllables and their specific energetic contents and trajectories.

Is such imaging akin to the imaginative acts we have studied in other contexts? Yes, insofar as we are dealing with vivid internal perceptions crystallized as mental images amenable to definition in words, and also insofar as the *bhāvanā*-production at work in *pūjā* presents us with very powerful, and by now familiar, reality-claims. However, this pragmatic, ritual *bhāvanā* is distinctive in certain aspects. Let us begin by attempting to distinguish it from other forms we have seen. First, it is *not* a product of visionary poetic inspiration, *pratibhā,* such as we see operating in works of *belles lettres.* That is, Yogic *bhāvanā* is not an expression of open-ended inventiveness within a highly structured field, a creative exploration of unforeseen relations among objects or images or ideas normally kept apart. Such explorations are for poets. But neither does it fit the Mīmāṃsā paradigm of language as a set of injunctions, a domain of teleological imperatives. Nor is it really capable of being classed as the removal of veils and mental obstacles to true perception, with the consequent release of liquid *rasa,* as in Abhinavagupta's poetics, although it is certainly possible to establish linkages between the latter and the intricate meditations of the Puri priests. Most important, the various stages in the ritual enacted each day by these priests do *not* constitute a descriptive progression of any kind—they are more a series of embodiments and interlacings of personae—and at the same time, the identity statements that underlie them are *not* simple denotative truths. They have a poetic quality infused with imaginative projection, with the truth-claims proper to such work, very much as we saw with the verses from the *Wave of Beauty*. Yogic *bhāvanā* is also not a good example of the Nāgârjunan vision of reality in its entirety as a web of crisscrossing imaginations, nor does it suit the metaphysics of the *Yoga-vāsiṣṭha*, examined above. The deity so elaborately constructed out of the worshipers' awareness is far too alive and concrete to be in any sense illusory, dream-like, or only tenuously existent, even if the tangible image in which he or she resides is demoted, verbally at any rate, to a lesser form of active being.

All these negatives lead me to suggest that *bhāvanā* of the type we are discussing must have its own distinctive truth-value, one quite resistant to the standard criteria of proof and validity.[47] In this sense, it does share a common epistemic foundation with the poeticians' understanding of poetry as true in its own terms, indeed unfalsifiable, given the special status of the "twist" in language, *vakrokti*, that is everywhere in evidence. Can we, however, characterize Yogic *bhāvanā* and its linguistic components in more positive terms? I think we can. First of all, it is encoded, in more than one sense. It operates through a system of mantric speech of profound semiotic complexity, though capable of being deciphered.[48] The mantras quite literally generate the deity—*bhāvanā* at work. But there is another layer or order of sonar activity governing the process of generation, one derived from the science of syllabic combinations: both in Kashmir and in south India, sounds are, at base, not neutral, random, or arbitrary vibrations. They are effectual building blocks of transformative experience, capable of blessing, reviving the dead, killing an enemy, making someone fall in or out of love, and a host of other useful projects.[49] Above all, correctly combined in rule-bound sequences, they can produce a goddess and a penumbra of auspicious energies surrounding her. Second, this kind of *bhāvanā* is fully controlled, concentrated, and precise, with an end result that is always specifically contoured and known. It requires training and concentration, though it makes use of the mathematical and musical resources of mantric language, which can work without the intervention of conscious intention. Third, it transpires within a consciousness seeking to discover something, or someone, axiomatically preexisting within itself; the fire transferred from the worshiper's heart to the icon of the deity was always there in the heart, though it has to be fanned into flame by the mind. In any case, the process of creation moves, somewhat oddly, toward producing what is already existent, though hitherto inactive or unknown.[50] This process is not one of creation ex nihilo, any more than is any other form of imaginative praxis we have discussed.

But in what shape do these latent entities exist in the mind? We might posit that there are always, so to speak, lumps of awareness congealing somewhere out of sight, emerging and melting away in the multitextured space of free-floating attention. These lumps can be retrieved and refined. The general principle involved is twofold, ubiquitous in ritual domains as well as in Indian models of the mind: the subtle and invisible always generates (devolves into) the crude and the visible, and what is initially externalized or objectified in imperfect form can, indeed must, be reworked through mental, mantric, and/or ritual processes to become whole *(saṃskṛta)* and serviceable. On one level, the two component vectors of this principle might seem to be at odds with each other, one mapping the direction of devolution, the other working upon its unhappy products. But seen in a wider perspective, these are two complementary movements of a single continuous process of mind-driven acts of working upon any given reality, fashioning and refashioning it with the available tools of concentrated thought, word, and inner image.

Again and again the texts speak of mind (*manas*—usually not *buddhi*), though they mean something like "awareness." The goddess grows out of a practiced, trained awareness—her proper matrix—that is subject to the internal movements of the mind as a finely honed instrument. When it works at its best capacity, the mind acts, it seems, as a kind of mirror, the kind in which you can wash reflections of the gods' images or generate more such images out of an unstructured depth. Mirroring, then, in a mind striving to bring life and breath to a deity who lives there, is primarily a mode of receptivity and sensitivity. In effect, the practitioner sensitizes himself to the potential existence within himself of a deity who can be projected outward into the world in interactive process. As this happens—as the lump of awareness assumes far more tangible and refined features—we could say that image becomes imagination, a creative, efficacious faculty of the focused mind impinging directly on the world of experience.

5.4. Summary: Attributes of Meditative Imagination, with a Note on Attention

By the time of the great southern Vaiṣṇava philosopher Vedânta Deśika (1268–1368), the Yogic devotional praxis of *bhāvanā,* along the lines we have traced, had become routine, a prevalent, recognized, and regularized way of making contact with a deity and, at the same time, of effecting change in the self. Consider the following verse from this poet's *Haṃsa-sandeśa,* in which Rāma sends a goose as a messenger to his wife, Sītā, imprisoned helplessly in Rāvaṇa's capital in Laṅkā. How will the goose recognize Sītā when he sees her? Rāma gives him detailed instructions, which include the following:

ceto-vṛttiṃ śamayati bahiḥ sārvabhaume nirodhe
mayy ekasmin praṇihita-dhiyaṃ mānmathenâgamena/
abhyasyantīm an-itara-juṣo bhāvanāyāḥ prakarṣāt
svântenântar-vilaya-mṛdunā nirvikalpaṃ samādhim//

And I'm sure she's practising Yoga—
calming the mind by blocking everything external,
focusing her awareness entirely on one thing:
me. The text she follows
is the Scripture of Love. In the vast power
of her imagination, which has no other
object, her heart melting,
she's dissolving into
the deepest place.[51]

With not much else to do, Sītā must—this is Rāma's logical deduction—be keeping herself busy in Yogic exercises of a meditative nature, and the obvious object of her meditation/visualization can only be her absent and beloved husband himself (that is, for Vedânta Deśika, God, the natural focus of Yogic contemplation). Her meditation, as is only right, follows scriptural authority—the Scripture of Love. No random, floating consciousness here. The technique involved, as we should expect, is *bhāvanā*—imagination, with all its vast power *(prakarṣa)*. Note the expression "focusing her awareness" *(praṇihita-dhī)*, which we will meet again in a moment. By this focusing, a form of attentiveness, in the context of imaginative creation or generation of the visualized object, Sītā, like any good practitioner, has "dissolved" into the "deepest place" *(nirvikalpa-samādhi)*, an internal state in which all normal mentation is suspended. Such is *bhāvanā* of the standard Yogic variety: image-bound, transformative, attentive, patterned, and pragmatic.

Very similar is a passage from this same poet's famous *Century on Compassion (Dayā-śataka)*, in which compassion is pictured as a living goddess, consort of Lord Viṣṇu-Veṅkaṭeśvara at the great pilgrimage site of Tirupati (Bull Hill):

praṇihita-dhiyāṃ tvat-saṃpṛkte vṛṣâdri-śikhāmaṇau
prasṛmara-sudhā-dhārâkārā prasīdati bhāvanā/
dṛḍham iti daye dattâsvâdaṃ vimukti-valāhakaṃ
nibhṛta-garuto nidhyāyanti sthirâśaya-cātakāḥ//

When we fix our mind on that Jewel
of Bull Hill, set in you, Compassion,
a certain vision becomes clear, limpid
as a steady stream. We're like the birds
who live on raindrops, not moving
a feather, our whole being turned toward
the cloud that surely tastes
of release.[52]

The vision in question is again *bhāvanā*, an imaging that, by the steady fixing of the mind (again *praṇihita-dhī*) has become effective imagining, a mode of Yoga that is single-minded and compelling, like the state of those *cātaka* birds that are nourished only by raindrops and wait, their whole being thirsting and anxious, for the rain cloud. We need to think for a moment about the poet's characterization of this *bhāvanā* as "clear, limpid as a steady stream." The normative *bhāvanā* of these high medieval southern texts is precise in its chosen object and, as a result, limpid and serene. The verb here is *prasīdati*, literally, "to settle," as when mud or other impurities settle to the bottom of a pool or river, leaving the water perfectly clear.[53] Such transparent, lucid states, when applied to the mind, always have an added resonance of gentle gracefulness, *prasāda*, a primary attribute of god.

Bhāvanā, in this case, is not an active production or generation of the deity so much as a clairvoyant, clearly focused, and peaceful image of him or her as filling the inner space or the inner eye. The interactive and mutual aspect of *bhāvanā* that we saw in the *Wave of Beauty* is muted now; the decisive qualities are clarity and steadiness, the total engagement of one's psychophysical being with the object of meditation.[54] In a way, this visionary moment is *bhāvanā* by default, with little left of the creative impetus we have seen elsewhere, although overtones of scientific control, technical knowledge, and metaphysical mirroring, in the sense just described, remain present. Such *bhāvanā* does still have a "vast power"—especially when it comes to changing the parameters of one's internal epistemic apparatus—and, once again, a truth-claim that must be sui generis, different from any other claims, whether empirical, logical, or experiential.

All of the features just mentioned, including the new element of spectacular clarity and precision, will recur in the more elaborate theories of imagination from sixteenth-century south India, to which we are about to turn. Let me state the historical linkage more simply, adumbrating what lies ahead. Yogic, meditative *bhāvanā* is a necessary precursor to the individualized forms of the imaginative faculty that, together with other mental functions, make up the new metapsychological matrix of late medieval Telugu, Tamil, and Malayalam sources. The *bhāvanā* of the grammarians, the logicians, and the poeticians, though also feeding into this matrix, will not suffice to make sense of the later developments; we will need the personal, strongly transformative aspect of the Yoga of the imagination, and something of the intersubjective quality that we saw in texts such as the *Wave of Bliss,* to understand the nature of the conceptual evolution that took place. And there is one more important piece of the puzzle.

Let us stay another moment with Vedânta Deśika. You will remember the goddess Compassion at Tirupati. Her relations with the god on the mountain, Veṅkaṭeśvara, are manifold and often conflictual; she is, on the one hand, his deepest, most characteristic self—God in his innermost being—but on the other hand, she often has to fight for space and for attention from him. Look at verse 27:

ati-laṅghita-śāsaneṣv abhīkṣṇaṃ
vṛṣa-śailâdhipatir vijṛmbhitoṣmā/
punar eva daye kṣamā-nidānaiḥ
bhavatīm ādriyate bhavaty-adhīnaiḥ//

Time and again we break the rules
and the God of Bull Hill boils with rage.
But then you marshal the reasons
for having patience, Compassion,
and make him mindful, once more,
of you.[55]

The god on the mountain is capable of violent, fiery rage, which is particularly in evidence when human beings let him down, as is often the case. At such moments Compassion, an active, female component of his nature, rushes in to cool him down (literally). This alternation in state is standard and recurrent. What is striking, however, is that the poet classes it as a struggle between inattention and attentiveness or mindfulness. The god is often inattentive, not only in phases of anger but also when he is lost in the deeper, stony recesses of his consciousness. Compassion, by way of contrast, is effortlessly and continuously attentive, and as such, she forces the god to pay attention to her (that is, his) generous and forgiving impulses. She makes him mindful, not in the familiar Buddhist sense of the term as a kind of insightful awareness but in a simpler, straightforward mode of paying attention, allowing the mind to focus or refocus—*ādara* (appearing in this verse as the verb *ādriyate*).[56]

We have encountered *ādara* as a major factor in the logicians' model of the mind, a subcategory of *bhāvanā* linked to the particular freshness of perception or the ability to see something new—a certain kind of attentiveness.[57] By now we have seen repeated instances of this link between *bhāvanā* and *ādara* (or, moving away from the strict Nyāya model, between imagination and attention). There is thus nothing very surprising about the conjunction of the two notions in Vedânta Deśika's text: *bhāvanā* is the "clear, limpid" vision that the pilgrim-practitioner cultivates, *ādara* the response he or she hopes for from the deity in either or both divine personae, male and female. When *ādara* seems to be lacking, the poet complains in his own voice, simultaneously allowing himself to boast of his attainments and express his desperation:

prāye daye tvad-anubhāva-mahâmbu-rāśau
prācetasa-prabhṛtayo 'pi paraṃ taṭa-sthāḥ/
tatrâvatīrṇam atala-spṛśam āplutaṃ māṃ
padmā-pateḥ prahasanocitam ādriyethāḥ//

Take all those classical poets—from Vālmīki on.
They came all the way up
to a vast ocean of experience,
the experience that is you,
but they never even dipped their toes.
Compassion: shouldn't you pay me
some attention? *I* jumped in,
I can't touch bottom,
I'm drowning, and God
sits there smiling.[58]

Even Compassion has her lapses. Ironically, perhaps, they are unforgivable to the poet who plunged, without thinking of the consequences, into the ocean of forgiveness and gentleness that is anyone's experience of this goddess. He's taken the risk; God, in his male guise, seems to mock him, or to be indifferent; and Compassion has lost her concentration, her *ādara*. When *she* is inattentive, survival itself may be jeopardized.

But even verses such as this one, though dialogic in tone and structure, mostly bear witness to ongoing internal psychodramas. The attention that is lacking is an intimate quality of the speaker who, like the god himself, has Compassion as a profound, central, and active piece of his self—a piece not always accessible. Just as visualization is a practical option for the meditator, so attentiveness is a possible and, indeed, highly recommended mode of choice. As in Nyāya epistemology, these two faculties go hand in hand, complementing each other. In very general terms, one sees in the mind's eye what one attends to, and one attends to what captivates the inner or outer eye. But the two terms are by no means synonymous. Thus a comprehensive theory of *bhāvanā* in its imaginative aspect will require a certain attention to attentiveness in its relevant forms. A systematic study of attention in classical Indian sources has never been attempted; here we can only outline a few characteristic usages in the context of our particular concerns.

Sanskrit has many words, subtly differentiated, for attention: *śraddhā, ādara, āsthā, kutūhala, avadhāna, upâsīnatā,*[59] and *īkṣaṇa,*[60] among others. Probably the most common term—also in the south Indian vernaculars—is *śraddhā*, very often translated, in both Hindu and Buddhist contexts, as "faith." Minoru Hara, in an exhaustive study of the Sanskrit evidence, concluded that "*śraddhā* expresses a state of mind or activity directed toward impersonal objects" and that "the nature of *śraddhā* is more intellectual than emotional."[61] One way to make sense of this conclusion is to stress the context of attentiveness: *śraddhā* is a mental function that tends to involve focusing and seeing clearly, which is to say, paying attention. "Faith" or "belief" may well be secondary developments from this primary meaning.[62] Thus when the *Bhagavad-gītā* tells us that "the person endowed with *śraddhā* achieves wisdom" (*śraddhāvāṃl labhate jñānam,* 4.39), I would be tempted to translate: "Whoever is attentive becomes wise." Similarly, in *Bhagavad-gītā* 17.3: *yo yac-chraddhaḥ sa eva saḥ,* "You are what you pay attention to." Here is a bold insight into the workings of the mind and the nature of the self, an insight we can easily link to the related mental function of bringing something into being, *bhāvanā.* We have, in fact, already seen this linkage to be operative, in various ways, in the Yoga of imagination.

In general, without attempting at this point a fine-grained analysis of the different kinds of attention implied by the various terms just mentioned, we can broadly distinguish in our sources two kinds of attentiveness relevant to the mental processes of imagining. One is really a kind of absorption or intense concentration, akin in many ways to the orthodox Kashmiri theory of aesthetic fascination;[63] the other is a receptive, cognitively engaged, less focused mode of attention, not far removed from what we might call "noticing" or "taking notice,"[64] but with a special twist or charge to it capable of effecting real change in the attentive observer or in the objects he or she observes. Each of these two kinds of attention has its correlated antithesis: acute metaphysical distraction (our normal state) for the first, and a less dramatic but perhaps no less consequential failure to attend for the second. Let me illustrate.

Bhāravi, in the sixth century, gives us a splendid vignette of absorption (as noticed by Arjuna as he is walking through fields and forest on his way to the Himalaya):

> *kṛtâvadhānaṃ jita-barhiṇa-dhvanau surakta-gopī-jana-gīta-niḥsvane/*
> *idaṃ jighatsām apahāya bhūyasīṃ na sasyam abhyeti*
> *mṛgī-kadambakam//*[65]

> A herd of deer, absorbed in the sweet songs
> of girls herding their cows—
> sweeter by far than the peacock's call—
> lost all interest in eating and stayed away
> from the ripening crop.

"Absorbed" *(kṛtâvadhānam)* is glossed by Mallinātha as *ekâgra-cittam*—a term familiar from descriptions of Yogic concentration. The deer are focused, "one-pointed" (in the current calque on the Sanskrit), oblivious of their surroundings and of bodily hunger. Aesthetic production, as we know—and as the poeticians insisted—regularly generates this state of charmed self-forgetfulness, which seems, on the whole, to be somewhat passive, not an active paying attention but a filling up of the mind with whatever has charmed it into absorption. Such intense concentration can also take lesser, somewhat diluted forms capable of impacting upon other modes of attentiveness. Consider the following verse by Bhaṭṭi, Bhāravi's near contemporary:

dattâvadhānaṃ madhu-lehi-gītau praśānta-ceṣṭaṃ hariṇaṃ jighāṃsuḥ/
ākarṇayann utsuka-haṃsa-nādān lakṣye samādhiṃ na dadhe mṛgāvit//[66]

He was intending to kill a deer that was
utterly still, absorbed
in the music of the bees,
but the calls of the homesick geese
distracted the hunter, and he failed to focus
on his target.

Once again, there is absorption—the deer riveted by the melodic humming of the bees—but we also see how attention wanes or is disturbed; the hunter, perhaps identifying with the geese, perhaps lonesome for his own distant beloved, cannot focus his aim (*samādhi*—that bringing together of all psychic capacities that Yoga sees as the final goal of meditative praxis).[67] The contrast emerges out of a rather charming similarity: as Oliver Fallon says, "There is a neat parallel here between the innocent and unsuspecting deer absorbed in the beauties of nature listening to the bee and the cruel hunter hearing the geese and becoming similarly harmless."[68] Distraction can thus, in itself, be a form of attention. Both this verse and Bhāravi's clearly share the vocabulary as well as the conceptual template of intensified, highly focused Yogic praxis; in this sense, the mode of total absorption they evoke has much in common with *bhāvanā* in its meditative form, not only in classical Yoga but also in Tantric ritual, as we have seen, and in Buddhism. One can certainly be absorbed in the mutual imaginative creation of, say, goddess and self, along the complex and highly disciplined lines we have sketched above; and it is also eminently possible to be wholly absorbed in the contemplation of the ravishing goddess in all her parts ensconced in the no less radiant *maṇḍala* cosmos that enfolds her. This is one major form of attention, in which imaginative *bhāvanā* can play a part; such absorbed attention can even provide the necessary condition for the successful working of the imagination, although we should bear in mind that the forms of Tantric *bhāvanā* we have studied above require disciplined cognitive efforts alongside or within the attentive immersion or focusing that the sources label *avadhāna* or *ekâgratā,* among other terms.

Such "one-pointed" absorption is actually the enemy of the second major mode of effective attention. I am not speaking of the common, pragmatic sense of paying attention in a task-oriented, nonintrospective,[69] and selective manner, as when we focus our attention on X at the expense of other mental contents, with the host of integrative, second-order processes that modern cognitive psychologists have linked to such acts. Illustrations of these everyday forms of attentiveness naturally abound in our sources, and there is little to be gained from exploring them here. (Examples of clearly differentiated modes of inattention are another matter.) Far closer to our primary theme is a relatively unfocused, even floating, receptive attentiveness, neither inward- nor outward-directed, perhaps analogous on one level to the default awareness of a south Indian deity.[70] Such states are conducive to sudden moments of unpredictable insight or "realization."[71] Both trivial and highly consequential perceptions or understandings may emerge from this form of receptive consciousness, particularly favored by Advaita philosophers such as Sureśvara:[72] thus a person might hear a metaphysical statement such as *tat tvam asi,* "You are [like] that," many times over, might even rehearse the phrase to himself or herself for weeks or months or years, might focus his or her mind on it in the absorptive manner described above—all to no effect whatsoever; but then there comes a moment, no doubt contextually determined, dependent upon all sorts of factors (one's physical state, one's mood, one's relation to the speaker or the text, the time of day or night or the season of the year, the activation of buried memories from the present or from a former birth, and so on), when the words are suddenly, nonvolitionally heard or recognized as true and instantly change the person's life. Even ghouls and demons are capable of such transporting moments *(piśācakavat).*[73] The great Telugu poet Kṛṣṇa-deva-rāya offers an especially trenchant and moving example, one among many.[74] One suddenly, quite accidentally, pays attention to something perhaps already quite familiar but never properly attended to. Absorption precludes such attentiveness, which always has a personal, cognitive component. There is no question of self-loss or self-forgetting, though it is, of course, possible that chance perceptions can be powerful enough to block out other thoughts or feelings at least temporarily, as in the case of Bhaṭṭi's hunter, who, entranced by the lugubrious calls of the geese, seems to become aware of his own deep loneliness. There may even be moments when the two kinds of attention we have articulated in a contrastive manner might converge—when sudden insight triggers absorption, or when absorption acquires the light, free-floating quality of receptive awareness.[75] In general, however, both the experiential texture of attention and its relations with other mental processes differ strikingly in these two modes.

It is the latter aspect that matters to us here. If absorption is linked to meditative *bhāvanā,* receptive attention—possibly the more widespread and generative of the two varieties—connects to effective imaginative praxis in a range of intrinsic and causal ways. For example, in a Bhartṛharian linguistic metaphysics, the ordinary operations of speech—above all, the transition from a level of pure sound to intelligible, meaningful words and sentences *(artha)*—transpires in the receptive, unfocused mind governed by the potentiality he calls *bhāvanā.*[76] In the latter case, attention to meaning plays a part in the continuous process of objectification; more generally, attention is often a defining, objectifying move, as we have seen. By paying attention, we shape, even create, the object of that attention. But the attentiveness that comes out of unfocused receptivity, a kind of baseline aliveness, is much more likely to deobjectify a congested or frozen state, whether internal (mental) or external, as in Sureśvara's example quoted above. Such attentiveness, that is, readily issues into imaginative and playful perception that restores movement to insentient, existentially heavy objects *(jaḍa).* Attention and imagination, in this context, are still far from identical, but they assist each other in a single teleology of perception. The Indian theorists who addressed this point are close to White's careful statement, from another vantage point entirely, in which the particular form of attentiveness that produces "realization" is contrasted with the imaginative act of "seeing as" in terms of limits and constraints: "There will be external criteria as to what something has been realized to be but no limits except imagination to what something may be seen as."[77] In our sources, too, imagination has the wider scope and a more fundamental power, but attentiveness *(ādara),* as the logicians argued, has its own creative potential, which has to be classed with *bhāvanā.*

The Yoga of the imagination addresses therapeutically our normative lack of focus, our continuous distraction and the consequent siphoning off of our deeper powers. Nothing more need be said here about the latter empirical observation, elevated to an axiom in most of the Hindu systems. Inattention of a more specific type, however, deserves at least one or two examples. Consider the following verse by Kālidāsa, describing King Dilīpa, who has taken a vow to follow and watch over a certain cow as she wanders through the wilderness:

sā duṣpradharṣā manasâpi hiṃsrair ity adri-śobhā-prahitekṣaṇena/
alakṣitâbhyutpatano nṛpeṇa prasahya siṃhaḥ kila tāṃ cakarṣa//[78]

He was certain that no wild beast would have the temerity
to assault her, so his attention wandered
to the mountain landscape, and thus he failed
to notice when a lion suddenly
pounced and dragged her off.

The king, like the hunter we met earlier, is entranced or distracted by something in the external setting; his attention *(īkṣaṇa)* wanders, and he is thus inattentive to the critical moment of action. He is in a state precisely opposite to the positive one in which unexpected perception or insight may strike. Absorption is, again, the false friend of attention. Like our reliable, indeed foundational state of distraction, such moments of milder inattention are a matter of constant, everyday experience. Śrīharṣa describes them as a kind of sleepiness, *an-avabodha-nidrā:* Damayantī tells the goose messenger to Nala to pay attention to the latter's mental state and to hold back on delivering her message if Nala is preoccupied with other matters—since the "sleepiness that precludes lucid understanding" often takes the form of contempt.[79] Inattention, in short, is a soporific loss of awareness—the very awareness that a fully alive person would do well to cultivate in order to be receptive to those unpredictable moments of life-changing insight. As we will see, attentiveness of this order fits easily into the new models of mind and, above all, of the imagination that begin to crystallize in the fifteenth and sixteenth centuries in the far south.

— II —

The Sixteenth-Century Revolution

— 6 —

Early Modern *Bhāvanā*

Sometimes it's easy to recognize a new voice, even, or especially, when five hundred years have passed since it first spoke. The freshness and immediacy never really age. When we listen to the short Telugu *padam* poems by Annamayya, or Annamâcārya, from the mid-fifteenth century at the major temple site of Tirupati, there is no mistaking the distinctive, indeed unprecedented tone:

> Seeing is one thing,
> looking is another.
> If both come together,
> that is god.
>
> If you look for an elephant,
> he comes as an elephant.
> If you look for a tree,
> he's a tree.
> If you look for a mountain,
> he'll be a mountain.
> God is what you have in your mind.
>
> If you look for empty space,
> he appears as space.
> If you look for an ocean,
> he'll be an ocean.
> If you look for a city,
> he will come as a city.
> God is what you have in your mind.

If you think of the god on the hill,
married to the goddess,
that's who you'll see.
What you look for
is the god in you.
What you see
is the god out there.
God is what you have in your mind.[1]

The poem ripples and flows—light, disarming in its simple diction, intimate in tone, devastating in its message. It is couched as a meditation ostensibly aimed at Veṅkaṭeśvara, the god Viṣṇu at Tirupati, and is thus a so-called *adhyātma* or "metaphysical" poem, though, as argued elsewhere, the tag "introspective" would certainly suit it better.[2] At most, the god on the hill eavesdrops on the poet's restless internal conversation. That conversation reveals, in *padam* after *padam,* a highly personal, unsteady, mood-driven, and doubt-filled awareness, rather like what most of us probably know from our own experience of ourselves. The poems tend to be reflexive: what is being described is not so much something that can be seen, a contoured object in space, as the business of seeing itself and the consequences of that continuous process of projection. Seeing is not the same as looking; the latter requires an attentiveness to the mark or sign *(sūṭiguṟi)* that actively defines what one sees. Looking attentively is perhaps a formative seeing that impacts upon the visible surface.[3] What is god, *daivamu,* combines seeing and seeing oneself seeing.

But the poem is not only about seeing and projecting. It is very clearly about the mind, *manas*—not the rather low-grade, devolved sensory organ of the classical Sanskrit sources, regulating the constant flow inward of sensual impressions, but a far more creative perceptual and intellectual organ, something much closer to what we mean when we speak of "mind" in English. The old philosophical vocabulary has been retained and at the same time radically resemanticized; we will observe examples of this process again and again in the following pages. So god is *mano-gocaruḍu,* something within the purview of the *manas,* a mental production said repeatedly to emerge or to become visible—*pŏḍacūpu*—in accordance with an image the mind contains a priori. Such a god is pliable, sensitive to (mental) context, adaptive: you get whatever you see, and you see whatever you imagine. One could hardly conceive of a more unsettling theology.

So is god real? Unquestionably so, though perhaps the meaning of a word such as "real" has also changed in relation to the sources studied in the previous chapter. "What you look for is the god in you": *bhāvame jīvâtma.* The fully alive part of the self, internal to the self, is *bhāva,* an existential, cognitive, or emotive state that *bhāvanā*—imaginative process—is supposed to generate, as we know. On the other hand, "what you see is the god out there": *pratyakṣamu paramâtma,* that is, a form of ultimacy that is also completely evident to the eye. In both cases, we are apparently speaking of something conjured up by the mind. God is real but not, perhaps, factual. *Daivamu,* "god," is an interactive creation of the moment, and apparently in constant movement (recall the interactive meditative process that generates a goddess or makes oneself over into a goddess, in the *Wave of Beauty*).[4] A perspectivist standpoint is inherent in such a god's very existence.

One gets a sense from even so slight a poem that *manas,* the newfangled mind of the fifteenth century, is somehow bounded and systemic, a functioning organ rich in thought and image and quite capable of generating from within itself external percepts that can also be called objects. But the poet is not about to insist on the finer details of this epistemic chain: he is singing to us, not lecturing, and we would do well to avoid imposing a false earnestness on the surprising propositions he articulates. Perhaps it is all no more than a passing whim, the kind of thought or feeling we sometimes have when we step back from whatever we are doing or seeing and say something like: "Wait a minute. Am I imagining all this? Maybe I've made it all up, or twisted it to fit my needs and wishes. Maybe my mind has played a trick on me." We all know such fleeting feelings, which we usually hasten to suppress. What is striking about the present poem is the poet's gentle reassurance that even in such a case—that is, in all moments of perception—the god will inevitably become present. A deep humaneness colors these verses; we think and feel and imagine, and these very acts, however arbitrary or random they might seem, however idiosyncratic and even solipsistic, have a godly aspect. They are, above all, human acts, hence classed as divine. However, it is a good thing to pay attention to the ways and patterns in which they occur.

All of this exegesis is a bit too heavy, at odds with the whispered tone of the poem. Long sentences will kill the poetry. Explanations distract and distort. So I offer no commentary whatsoever on the following daring *padam:*

Imagine that I wasn't here. What would you do with your kindness?
You get a good name because of me.

I'm number one among idiots. A huge mountain of ego.
Rich in weakness, in giving in to my senses.
You're lucky you found me. Try not to lose me.
Imagine that I wasn't here.

I'm the Emperor of Confusion, of life and death.
Listed in the book of bad karma.
I wallow in births, womb after womb.
Even if you try, could you find another like me?
Imagine that I wasn't here.

Think it over. By saving someone so low,
you win praise all over the world.
You get merit from me, and I get life
out of you. We're right for each other,
god on the hill.
Imagine that I wasn't here.[5]

I guess there is one thing that does have to be said: Annamayya is interested in the imagination. Sometimes he thematizes it fully, as in the following poem, so close to our central concerns that it does deserve a brief explication:

You're just about as much as one imagines you to be.
As they say, the more dough, the more bread.

People who follow Viṣṇu love you as Viṣṇu.
Philosophers speak of you as the ultimate.
Those who go with Śiva think of you as Śiva.
Those who carry skulls see a skull in your hand.
You are as one imagines.

People who serve the goddess think you are their goddess.
Different schools of thought measure you by their thoughts.
Small people think of you to get rich, and for them you become small.
Thoughtful minds contemplate your depths, and for them you are deep,
as deep as one imagines.

There's nothing missing in you.
The lotus spreads to the limits of the lake.
There's water in the Ganges, also in wells on the shore.

You're the god on the hill,
the one who's taken hold of me.
For me, you are real,
as real as I imagine.[6]

Here "to imagine" is mostly *talacu,* which also means simply "to think." In the Telugu of the fifteenth century, thinking can readily slip over into imagining (similarly with Telugu *ūhiñcu,* Tamil *ni<u>n</u>ai,* Sanskrit *smṛ,* and so on), as we will see. We will be pursuing such semantic specializations in the late medieval sources; in the present verse, there is no doubt that the mental processes involved are those of perceiving or thinking of X as X and then truly finding this X as previously conceived, very much as in the first poem we looked at. But there's also a slight variation worth attending to: "small people" *(alpa-buddhi dalacinavāriki),* that is, those who think small (focusing on material wealth), will end up with a god who is as small as their minds, whereas god has depth for those who think deeply *(ghanam' ani talacina ghana-buddhulaku).* An attribute of the thinking or imagining person has attached itself to the object of thought. One gets exactly what one imagines. Even more striking is the crescendo that culminates in the final assertion of god as an irreducible reality *(para-tattvamu)*—a typical conclusion to statements about the works of the imagination in sources from this period, where, in general, what is real is real *because* it is imagined. It is also of interest that the imagined object of meditation, the Tirupati god, is complete in himself, with "nothing missing" *(kŏrate ledu)*—another attribute of mentally constructed beings. The fullness or completeness spills over into the next lines of this final verse: lotus blossoms pervade the lake to its edge, and water fills the Ganges and the wells on the shore. Such wholeness, a product of the mind—as the refrain pointedly tells us—has "taken hold" of the speaker, filling him up from inside as only something entirely real can do.

What has made it possible for statements such as these to emerge with such clarity in south India of the fifteenth and immediately following centuries? Something profound has changed within the culture as a whole. We see the change in many areas: in social and economic life, in the nature of the state systems that crystallized at this time, in the structure and self-perception of erudite domains, in notions of self and of gender, in the new theories of the mind and the forces that drive and shape it, in perceptions of the natural world, in the conceptualization of time and history, and in all the major expressive media (verbal and nonverbal, the latter including painting, sculpture, and music) that reconfigured inherited aesthetic traditions and their modes of operation. I have argued elsewhere, together with Velcheru Narayana Rao and Sanjay Subrahmanyam, that, in part, this civilizational shift reflects the rise of a new elite, drawn largely from the so-called left-hand castes of warrior-merchants and other nonlanded groups that sought to profit from an increasingly cash-oriented economy with its new opportunities for self-made men, free from ascriptive determination.[7] Such self-made entrepreneurs, many from the margins of the social and geopolitical world, founded small-scale kingdoms—which we call Nāyaka, after the warriors who comprised their institutional backbone—in the Tamil, Telugu, and Kannada realms. In Kerala, something rather similar took place from the fifteenth century on in the so-called Zamorin state of Calicut, the first modern state on the Kerala coast and the arena for the first strong articulations of a distinctive, self-conscious Malayalam cultural identity. Powerful thematic continuities bind together the Nāyaka states of the south and east and the emergent state system of Malabar, with its innovative poets and scholars; indeed, throughout south India, we discern in this period the lineaments of a fresh anthropology and the sometimes implicit, sometimes explicit redefinition of what counts as human.

The line we draw from political and socioeconomic developments to conceptual and cultural phenomena is always a tenuous one, and I hesitate to make any simple causal argument linking these domains. But neither would I want to deny the relevance or reduce the complexity of the historical contexts within which the new, protomodern sensibility took root. I refer the reader to the extensive studies of these contexts just cited and to my work in progress on early modern Calicut.

We are interested here in one central aspect of the radically refashioned sensibility of the sixteenth century—the role of imagination as a defining feature of the new human being whom we meet everywhere in our sources. Suddenly we find that the notion of a personal, generative, image-driven faculty of the mind—usually referred to as *bhāvanā* (Tamil *pāvaṉai*)—is powerfully and consistently thematized in both literary and discursive-erudite materials from this period, as we have seen it to be, in a preliminary way, in Annamayya's *padams*. We will be concentrating on the former category of sources, and our sample is necessarily far from exhaustive—though the richness of the theme and the regularity of the conceptual patterning should quickly become clear. We begin with two case studies from mid-sixteenth-century Tenkasi in the southern Tamil country, where a Renaissance-like moment produced Tamil works of astonishing brilliance under the aegis of the Tenkasi Pāṇṭiya dynasty and the somewhat eccentric polity they consolidated. We then move north to Vijayanagara at the height of its imperial power in the early sixteenth century and to the great Telugu *prabandha* texts that were composed there and, a little later, in the royal courts of southern Andhra. We will conclude with a major Sanskrit allegory on the imagination written in this same period at Senji in the northern Tamil plains. The classical theories of *bhāvanā,* studied in the first part of this book, remain relevant at every step; by the end of our brief tour, structured around a few major texts studied in some depth, we should be ready for some comparative observations.

About the salience of the theme itself there need be no doubt. Its importance was noted and commented on, sometimes in reflexive and even parodic ways, by voices from within the literary culture of this period, such as we can hear in the following popular story (probably retrojected into a sixteenth-century setting from a somewhat later, perhaps seventeenth-century, scholastic attempt to order and make sense of the high-Vijayanagara-period canon):

> King Kṛṣṇadevarāya had a lovely pavilion built and invited a renowned painter to cover its walls with pictures. When the master painter was finished, he invited the king and his courtiers to admire his work. Tĕnāli Rāma, the king's close companion and court jester, staring at a figure drawn in profile, asked innocently, "Where are the other parts of this one's body?" The king laughed and replied, "Do you not know that you must *imagine* them because of the painter's use of perspective?" "Now I understand," said Tĕnāli Rāma.
>
> After some months, the jester came to the king and said, "I have been practicing the art of painting for months; I would like you to see my skill." "Fine," said the king; "you can wipe away the faded paintings in the pavilion and cover the walls with *your* work." Tĕnāli Rāma erased the master's paintings and produced his own: he drew a fingernail here, a lone finger somewhere else, two disconnected hands in another spot, an isolated toe, an eye, a kneecap. When the walls were filled with these disjointed elements, he called the king to see his work. "What is this?"

> cried Kṛṣṇadevarāya at the sight of his new palace murals. Said the jester: "Have you forgotten about the imagination [*bhāvanā*] necessary to appreciate art?"[8]

Here is a king, together with his refined courtiers, who is clearly fascinated by *bhāvanā*. But does he really understand it? On one hand, straightforward artistic convention—the language of representation and verisimilitude—is pointedly mocked. The jester exposes his king's rather rudimentary conception of what "imagination" might ordinarily mean (the minor adjustments appropriate to realistic portraiture, which, incidentally, is profusely documented from the sixteenth century on). On the other hand, Tĕnāli Rāma reveals, by concrete example, an imaginative world that far exceeds normative courtly etiquette or restraint, in the direction of a quite modern, abstractly expressive reality. There are other ways to tell the story. Sometimes they say that the jester painted murals consisting of scattered daubs of mud in an otherwise empty space, and he told the king that he had painted a beautiful likeness of a horse. When the king and his courtiers saw the paintings, they asked where the horse was. "He ran away when he saw all these people," said Tĕnāli Rāma; "look at the mud left behind by his hooves."[9] Mere abstraction is hardly adequate to the jester's iconoclastic aesthetic; stable notions of time must also be subverted, the painting reduced to a residue left behind by its living subject, who necessarily eludes the eager spectators. Such a vision is riddled with imaginative force that, for all the evident parody, retains a stubborn integrity and a sense of newness. So did the jester *really* paint a horse? Perhaps he did. Once the imagination has cut loose from representation—if, indeed, it was ever really bound up with the latter in south India—then further radical experiments will naturally unfold, and no less radical truth-claims may become commonplace. Tĕnāli Rāma, universally admired in the Tamil and Telugu countries for his perspicacity and wit and for speaking, or enacting, the truth he knows, may unwittingly adumbrate the very modern thesis elegantly argued by Gabriel Motzkin: "*What we imagine* may actually be closer to the nature of physical reality than *what we perceive*."[10] To fine-tune such a statement for sixteenth-century south India, we need only attempt to put aside the implied distinction between two kinds of reality, ranked in terms of ontic priority (a physical and external one and an imagined, visionary one). The new theory of *bhāvanā*, a process producing effects unquestionably real for both the poets and their audiences, is not concerned with approximating any external world.

— 7 —

Sīmantinī: Irrevocable Imaginings

7.1. Tenkasi and Montaigne

They say you get release from the endless cycle of births by dying in Varanasi, on the banks of the Ganges; but they also say you achieve the same result just by being born in Tenkasi, or by living there (if necessary, you can also do it by dying there). Today Tenkasi is a small, sparkling Tamil town clinging to the eastern side of the Western Ghats, some twenty kilometers northwest of Tirunĕlveli. From anywhere in town, you can see purple-blue mountains spilling down into the paddy fields. The god Viśvanātha inhabits the core urban space; immense monolithic carvings of royal warriors and fierce gods, all sixteenth-century creations, watch you as you go inside. Just outside the town is the mountain resort of Tirukkuṟṟālam, with its waterfall, beloved of Tamil films, and another fine temple to Lord Śiva of Kuṟṟālam and the Goddess Whose Voice Sings Like a Flute. No less musical is the crisp Tamil of the southern Pāṇṭiya region that you hear in these parts. The crumbling remains of the old royal palace, once the site of vibrant cultural production, can still be seen, mostly engulfed by the fields. But if you ask someone on the street about Ativīrarāma Pāṇṭiyaṉ, the king-poet who lived and ruled in Tenkasi in the second half of the sixteenth century, or about his elder brother Varatuṅkarāmaṉ, who ruled from his capital, Karuvai, in the last decades of that century, you can't be sure the names will ring a bell.

There is something odd about this. It is as if the names of Petrarch and Dante had been forgotten in Florence and Padua. For these two brothers, together with a third, the eldest, known as Varakuṇarāmaṉ, largely reinvented the world of Tamil letters in a moment of far-reaching structural innovation.[1] These prince-poets, clearly aware of the experimental, protonovelistic *mahākāvyas* emerging in Telugu in the early sixteenth century, composed a series of large-scale, well-integrated discursive works, very different in tone and intent from the much shorter, often abstruse poetic texts—known as *ciṟṟ'ilakkiyam* or *prabandham*—that dominated literary production in Tamil from the mid-fourteenth century on. The very existence of these major narrative poems in Tamil by the three Rāma brothers is today mostly ignored, although a mere century ago these works, and in particular Ativīrarāmaṉ's *Naiṭatam,* constituted the foundation of a standard Tamil education. Seen as parts of a single, highly intertextual, contemplative corpus, these books have the same boldness, energy, and sense of brilliant innovation that one sees in the great carvings ushering pilgrims into the Viśvanātha temple. What is more, we have no more trenchant expression in late medieval or early modern Tamil of the primary themes that occupied the minds of the literati, first among them being a fascination with the workings of the imagination within a reformulated mental economy.

We thus begin in Tenkasi, first with Varatuṅkarāmaṉ, then with Ativīrarāmaṉ. Varatuṅkaṉ has given us a lyrical Tamil version of one of the most popular of all medieval Sanskrit texts from south India, the *Brahmottara-khaṇḍa* (in Tamil: *Piramottara-kāṇṭam*), originally the localized *purāṇa* of Gokarṇam on the western coast.[2] Versions of this beloved work exist in all the languages of the south (some six in Telugu alone, of which only two have been published). The centerpiece of the *Brahmottara-khaṇḍa* is the well-known story of Queen Sīmantinī, which we could define as a focused essay on the pragmatic imagination, in some ways surprisingly akin to the essay on this topic by Varatuṅkaṉ's exact contemporary Montaigne. A mysterious metaphysical linkage, skeptical and contemplative, links Tenkasi and Aquitaine at the dawn of the modern era. The two texts really should be read side by side.

The Sanskrit original of the Sīmantinī story, which antedates the first regional-language versions by some two centuries at least, has its own interest, but we will concentrate here on the way the story was presented in mid-sixteenth-century Tenkasi. I offer a slightly streamlined prose translation of the poet's fast-paced verses:

> In Vidarbha there were two Brahmin boys—Sumedhā, son of Vedamitra, and Sāmavān, son of Sārasvata. When they had achieved deep knowledge of Veda and the traditional arts and sciences, their Brahmin parents said to them: "Go to the king and win his heart with your great

learning. With the wealth he will happily give you, you can marry and set up house."

The boys did as told, and the king was indeed suitably impressed and asked them what they desired. The boys said: "Great king, to tell you the truth, we came here to win enough wealth to marry." The king laughed, showing his white teeth. "Sīmantinī, the wife of the Niṣadha king, worships Śiva every Monday, to the great astonishment of the gods. Each time she invites Vedic sages to come with their wives, and when they arrive she imagines them to be Moon-crested Śiva and his wife Umā—and she then worships them joyfully in her mind [*ĕṇṇip puntiyā<u>n</u> maki<u>l</u>nt' arcca<u>n</u>ai va<u>l</u>ipaṭal puriyā,* 10]. Then she lavishes jewels and gold on them. You two should go there: one of you as a man, the other adorned and guised as a woman. Under this ruse you will make off with much of her wealth, which you can spend on your weddings. If you turn down this idea, I'll have you punished."

The boys were rather disturbed at this plan. "Alas and alack! Is this a good idea for us? If we, who came to your palace seeking help, assume this phony guise [*veṭam*], our mothers and fathers and, indeed, both our families will perish. We'll be condemned to hell not just in this lifetime and the next but for seven subsequent rebirths. If you would only think of some proper scheme, we would happily adopt it."

The king's eyes turned red with rage, and he exploded in words. "If a preceptor [*tecikar* = *deśika*] or a mighty king says something and worthless people refuse to listen, then it is only right to punish them so that they shudder in terror. If you won't listen to my order, I'll have you punished as if you were Untouchables, not Brahmins."

Standing there before him, the Brahmin lads were afraid. "Don't be angry, O king," they said. "We'll go to Niṣadha, where the rivers shake the coconut and areca trees with their waves." So, at the king's command, women expert in the arts of adornment came to make Sāmavān up as if he were a woman. They made him breasts, plastered him with saffron and sandalwood paste, hung a pearl necklace around his neck, and fashioned a long braid so black it put night to shame. His eyes they shaded with kohl; they stuck earrings in his ears; they made the Śaiva *puṇṭaram* marks on his milky forehead and draped him in a sari that was worth at least as much as the entire world.

In short, by the time they were finished he looked positively ravishing. They showed him to the king, who approved and gave them leave to depart. So they joined the large crowd of Brahmins going to Niṣadha with their wives.

When they arrived at the palace of Sīmantinī, she welcomed them and invited them to sit down together with all the other Brahmins. While she was ministering to these guests, she took a good look at the faces of the two boys and realized at once that they were both males. She was a rather compassionate person, but still she frowned.

Then she hid her face. She always thought of whoever came to her, in whatever guise or mode [*ĕttiṟattāṉum*], as Śiva and the goddess Umā. So now, too, she worshiped in devotion and fed them all a rich meal of milk, fruit, honey, sweet drinks, rice and snacks, served on golden plates. Then she presented them with fragrant garlands, sandalwood paste, flawless clothes and jewels, white camphor, and areca nut. Praising all the Brahmins as Śiva and Umā, she gave them leave to depart.

On the way back, the incomparable Sāmavān turned into a woman—exactly like the guise he had worn—all because of Sīmantinī, who had imagined them as Umā and Śiva. "He" totally forgot that he used to be a man. What is more, he now turned to his companion, Sumedhā, with the idea of making love, like a woman. "Husband," said Sāmavān, "stop walking forward. Find some sheltered place in this thick forest where you can caress my firm breasts with your bejeweled hands, kiss my mouth, red as coral, and make love to me. If you refuse, I'll simply die. When sharp-eyed women are filled with desire, it is not right for a man to reject them."

She was begging him, aflame with desire. Sumedhā, marching along the path, was sure his good friend and companion was teasing him. So he gave no answer and kept on walking. But the woman with eyes dark as the nymphea addressed him again: "Embrace me. Now. Right here."

The Brahmin lad, still not realizing how fully his inseparable friend had become feminine, turned, a little scornful, to study "his" face. Not an iota of the masculine was left in it. Amazed, he saw that everything about his friend had melted into a lithe, vine-like grace. Her luminous, budding breasts, smeared with sandalwood paste; her long, thick curls, black as night; her face radiant as the full moon and—like fish darting through the moon—the long eyes shooting lethal looks; the red glow of her body, like an unfolding bud; her bangled wrists, delicate fingers, bejeweled belt, the perfection of her loins . . . He didn't know what to praise first, but it was clear to him that, apart from the goddess Lakṣmī on her lotus, no other woman in any world could compete with this beauty. With all this on his mind, he spoke to her: "Lady, I came to this forest together with my good friend. Now I don't see him anywhere. I'm astonished to find you here, so close. Who are you? How did you get here? Tell me."

She smiled and said, "My dear husband! Listen. I used to be your friend Sāmavān. Now I'm a woman named Sāmavatī. In fact, I'm your wife. Desire to make love to you drove me to speak. Embrace me, so that the golden pallor of my breasts will be healed. I'm weak with passion." She was begging him, and the young Brahmin replied: "You wicked woman—you're a bad one, and what you say is also bad. You've forgotten your noble descent from Sārasvata, your pure family, the greatness of your discipline. You're speaking like some seductive courtesan, words remote indeed from the rules of the Veda."

She replied, "In this world, what all women want is to make love—isn't it? My dear Brahmin lover, put aside the doubt in your mind. Have a good look with your own eyes. I am a woman. I am *not* a man." With this, she revealed her whole body to her lord.

He took a good look. He saw, to his astonishment, that no other woman in the whole wide world had such a beautiful body as this courtesan. He realized that all this had happened because of the power of imagination exercised by Sīmantinī in her heart on Monday, Śiva's day. He was losing his grip, even quite forgot how to speak.

"Handsome Brahmin," she continued, "you have seen me in all my parts. You have cut through any doubt. I'm begging you to end the pain of my longing by embracing me. *Now.*" He heard her, his mind troubled.

"Listen to me, young lady," he said. "I have studied the Veda and all other authoritative books, as well as all the minor arts. What we have done is wrong—a strike against caste and *dharma.* We didn't inform our fathers when the king suggested this deceitful trick. We just went along with it. We went to that woman. Though she saw through the trick, she still worshiped us, without any doubt, as if we were Śiva and Umā. That, my girl, is how we got into this mess. When someone cheats another person without stopping to think about what will happen if he lies, the disgrace always rebounds on him. Therefore, we must rid ourselves of this sorrow by following a strong ascetic regime. If it doesn't work, then I definitely will make love to you."

She didn't accept this line of reasoning.

He tried again. "Do you think it's right for our caste to adopt the *gandharva* type of marriage through mutual consent? That's for kings who own big elephants."

But by now she was severely disturbed by Love's arrows and far beyond thinking about what was or wasn't right. She took his wrist and raped him, then and there, to her great satisfaction.

He, on the other hand, felt no pleasure. In fact, he was deeply distressed. "Come with me," he said, "to tell our fathers all about this unhappy sequence of events." So they traversed the vast empty space of the wilderness and arrived home in their city, where the young Brahmin boy tearfully reported everything to his father—how they had dressed up in accordance with the orders of the poisonous Vidarbha king, how the gentle Sīmantinī had seen it all but still worshiped them, and how, as a result, his friend had become a woman. The boy's father rushed to tell the "girl's" noble father, who heard him through—and exploded in anger. Burning with rage, he rushed to the king and told him the whole story.

"King," he said, "you should either give people what they ask for or tell them honestly that you have nothing to give them. To bring them to grief out of your own avarice and deceit is not right. Look what you did, without any qualms, to my flawless son, learned in the Veda! You wrought havoc, like any low-down rogue. Shame on you! Other kings will laugh at you. I was sure we would achieve ultimate good through our fine son—the good place that those without sons can never reach. Instead, you've imprisoned me in hell. The eyes that should have rejoiced in seeing him as a bridegroom now have to look at him in *this* form. It must be *karma* from an earlier birth." His mind was whirling, and he was howling with pain. Then he said:

"Neither I nor my wife will be able to bear seeing our son like this. We will give up the life in our bodies right here, in front of you; and the whole world will blame you." The words burned right through the king's ears. He didn't know what to say. Trembling, he fell to the ground, like a tiger riddled with porcupine quills.

When he got up—the words still twisting in his heart like a heated spear—he turned to his Brahmin advisors and asked them: "That this boy became a woman because he was imagined in this way by that highly disciplined lady, Sīmantinī—is that really my fault? Is there anything else you could say? I would do any kind of penance to ameliorate the disaster that has overtaken this young Brahmin student; just tell me what to do."

One of them, Bhāradvaja, heard him and said: "No matter who you are or what you may have done, if you worship the coral-red feet of Śiva's wife, you will be on the right way; anything bad will disappear, as darkness dissipates at sunrise. So put aside any crookedness in your mind, now so full of sorrow, and seek out the Lady of the fragrant hair. Hold her in your thought [*karuttin̲ vaittu*]. Recite her *mantra* at midnight, night after night." And he taught the king Umā's *mantra* and sent him off to the temple of the goddess.

There he changed the operation of his five senses and all his perceptions. His mind rooted in the right path, he served the goddess unswervingly for three full nights. On the third night, the goddess showed her body to him—like many millions of luminous moons—and emerged from her shrine. He bowed to her, thinking that his pain had come to an end, and said: "Jewel that gives all desires, please take my suffering away."

"Don't worry," she said. "Just tell me what would give joy to your heart." The king said, "Let the young son of the stricken Brahmin regain his former guise [*veṭam*]."

"Can't do it," she said. "Even if someone disciplines himself for millions of eons, no one, not even God himself, can take away something that my devotees imagine [*ĕnat' an̲par nin̲ainta pān̲maiy ŏruvarkkum ĕmm īcar tamakkum ŏḻikkal āmo,* 68]. Ask for something else."

"Good Lady," he pleaded, "at least put one more son in the womb of that Brahmin's wife, so that they don't have to suffer the misery of sonlessness." Even before the king got these words out of his mouth, the goddess said, "Done!" She went on, "See to it that the lovely Sāmavatī is married to her Brahmin friend in the Vedic way." Then Umā retired into her shrine.

The king was entirely amazed. He bestowed the girl on the Brahmin student. He himself lived a householder's life with his black-haired wife. The father who had suffered so deeply got another lucid and learned son and lived on, without further sorrow, for a long, long time. The king was happy, too. Somewhat worn out by all of this, he went on ruling the earth, honorably, for ages without end.

Those who praise the feet of Śiva, the god of ultimate knowledge—is there anything they can't have?[3]

7.2. Doing Things with Mental Images

Clearly, we have a compelling story, economically told, which raises some basic questions about the imagination. A young man becomes a passionate young woman simply by the force of *bhāvanā* (Tamil: *pāvaṉai*)—not, it seems, a conventionally structured meditation or Yogic exercise, as we might expect from the earlier materials we have studied, but rather a full-fledged, rapidly executed imaginative act of focused visualization that produces irrevocable results. Why should they be irrevocable? If things are so fluid in the internal economy of awareness, should we not be able to reverse or replay one set of transformations at will? How free is the imagining agent? Is Queen Sīmantinī, for example, free to use her imagination as she likes?[4] Or does it have to follow a preconceived course, with its necessary, far-reaching consequences? Simplest of all, and most tantalizing, is the question of why, or how, it works.

The latent logic is, I think, capable of formulation. We need to pay close attention to the shift in the meaning of the crucial term, *bhāvanā,* and its synonyms, analogues, and paraphrases (such as *niṉaitta pāṉmai,* literally "mode of mentation," used by the goddess toward the end of our text). But perhaps we should begin with a quick comparative glance at Montaigne.

Montaigne's essay "Of the Force of the Imagination" beautifully complements and contrasts with the Sīmantinī story in its Tenkasi retelling. Like the latter, Montaigne is concerned, above all, with the efficacy of imaginative visualization. His motto is *Fortis imaginatio generat casum,* "A strong imagination begets the event itself," and he cites a range of empirical examples—many of them with a predominant sexual aspect. A pregnant woman gives birth to a child in the very form of the images she has carried in her mind. Fantasies of being a man are quite capable of rendering a woman male, and not in superficial or metaphoric ways: Pliny reports an embarrassing case of such a transition on the very day of the young woman's wedding, and "Pontanus and others report the like metamorphosis to have happened in these latter days in Italy." Note, however, the direction of the sex change, the opposite of Sāmavān's. This link between imagination and gender transformation is a stable one in much early modern European literature (as it is in contemporaneous south Indian sources; we will shortly turn to one more example).

The other element that seems most to preoccupy Montaigne in this context is a profound anxiety about impotence. Too much imagination, he says, tends to produce this result. I won't explore the rationale for this conjunction, which surely reflects a European axiology; only let us note that it is completely absent from our Tamil story. More generally, however, for Montaigne imagination is a capacious term, by no means limited to the production of mental images; it includes, for example, anxiety, dread, earnest wishes, grief, and horror as well as sensually driven mentation. Most often it is a negative aspect of the self, akin to infection; such is especially the case "when the imagination works not only upon one's own particular body, but upon that of others also." It can contaminate another's body with disease, and it can kill. It works in "brute beasts" as well as in human beings, though most of Montaigne's examples are supplied by the latter. "Vulgar and more easy souls" are more vulnerable to its operations, which make them "think they see what they do not see."

There is a reason for this constant danger—the "close affinity and relation betwixt the soul and the body intercommunicating their fortunes." An elementary dualism fuels Montaigne's suspicion of the imagination, as is commonly the case in early modern European views on this subject.[5] Sturdy intellection and pervasive skepticism are possible antidotes, though at the outset Montaigne admits to being particularly susceptible to the tricks his imagination plays on him. In short: imagination, broadly understood, produces very real effects, crosses the boundaries between one person and another or one body and another, regularly clouds perception, destabilizes a person's internal balance, and is particularly dangerous when it comes to sexuality and gender identity. Imaginers beware.

What, then, can we say about Sīmantinī and the two Brahmin boys?

1. In contrast to our own, mostly Romantic ideas, but in some ways similar to Montaigne's, imagination in the south Indian tale is transitive, nonsubjective, and interpersonal. In this sense, an imaginative act is very much a "fact" (though not quite an object). We can start with the surprising observation that Sāmavān's transformation into the beautiful lady Sāmavatī comes not from his own private self-imagining but from an external observer or actor, the pious queen. *She* is the one who embarks upon the journey of *bhāvanā,* even though she knows perfectly well what her perceptive eyes have told her, namely, that there are two males in this couple. She nonetheless proceeds to relate to them as a male and female couple, a human model of a familiar divine paradigm. Sīmantinī makes a conscious, explicit decision to see these two as the god Śiva and his wife, Umā. That does the trick. Her vision, with its mental concomitants, is what

counts. The boy's own volition seems, at first glance, irrelevant. *Bhāvanā* can operate independently of the transforming subject's wishes. It is an active, transitive force existing somewhere, in someone's mind (often, the mind of a necessary other). In this sense, it is very close to a dream, which is also frequently seen, in this cultural world, as a factual, nonsubjective, often impersonal existent. That is why two or more people can have the same dream, or can participate actively in the mutual shaping of a dream, exactly as if it were a waking conversation.[6] In other words, *bhāvanā,* in the sense of imaginative production within an active, generative, and attentive consciousness, must truly give rise to something that can only be seen as real and that will, as a result, have real effects.

But this very factuality of the imaginative process allows the intersubjective dimension to come into play. So now we should ask ourselves if there is some sense in which Queen Sīmantinī and the Brahmin boy Sāmavān are acting together to effect the change, even if this interaction is only partly conscious.

2. What the text tells us is that Sāmavān, now Sāmavatī, *forgets* that he was ever a male.[7] Later, in conversation with his startled friend, he/she remembers that he used to be a man; but the identity conversion is still complete and, apparently, non-negotiable. We began our study of the imagination by looking at the classical Nyāya model of the mind, in which memory *(smṛti)* and recognition *(pratyabhijñā)* are intimately associated with *bhāvanā* as the force of causal connectivity underlying true perception.[8] That is, our ability to identify anything at all, or to remember anything—even who we are—is entirely a matter of *bhāvanā,* a creative capacity situated at the core of the mind *(ātma-guṇa).* We might think we are remembering objective experiences that are part of our cumulative repertoire of self-knowledge—but in fact we are re-creating them, or perhaps reimagining them. *Bhāvanā* brings the initial sensory mark or impression back to the surface, thus allowing for an immediate, nondubious perception. Such a view may explain something of what the Brahmin boy-turned-woman is experiencing, and something of what Queen Sīmantinī is perceiving, although sixteenth-century *bhāvanā* is not by any means limited to the Nyāya model, as we will see. Forgetting, incidentally, will have to be classed in this new mental economy as a particularly powerful form of remembering.

Sāmavān seems to be involved, not wholly passively, in the transformation that Sīmantinī's imagination works upon him. Look at the active presence of desire once the change is complete. The whole passage leaves us with the impression that something interactive has taken place. But in that case, we might have to posit the existence of a somewhat deeper reality operating within Sāmavān from the start. Was he—perhaps like other males—a volatile amalgam of superficial masculinity and female core self (assuming that this south Indian self can have a core)? The words of the goddess, at the very end of the story, may tend in this direction: "Even if someone disciplines himself for millions of eons, no one, not even God himself, can take away something that my devotees imagine." On the face of it, this looks like a very far-reaching proclamation of the autonomy of the imagination. Perhaps that is in fact what it means. But *what* one imagines also matters. The cultural universe we are investigating is profoundly patterned and, in general, nonrandom in its operation, though any particular configuration may still be relatively indeterminate. So at the very least we could say that when Sīmantinī unleashes her *bhāvanā* on the two Brahmins, the result reflects a real, if normally invisible, level of experience that is not foreign to them. In that sense, her *bhāvanā* is uncovering or activating a preexisting force within the boy. Otherwise, it wouldn't work. Transformation always depends upon some such structured field, as we see, for example, in the way curses or blessings regularly change the world.

Note—not for the first time in these pages—how far we are from phrases, endemic in modern Western discourse, such as "magical thinking" or "magical effects." Here is a temptation to be resisted. As intimated earlier, "magic" is a weak, impoverished word that speaks mostly to an impoverished sensibility. There is nothing magical, in the literal sense of the word, about what happens to Sāmavān. It seems, rather, that his own, quite personal imagination locks into Sīmantinī's willed imagination of him. Look at the way the two texts, the Sanskrit parent version and the Tamil reworking, articulate the progression. The Sanskrit poet says: "Seeing these two Brahmin boys, an artificial couple, she [Sīmantinī] realized something and smiled. Then she thought of them as Śiva and Gaurī. Then she invoked Sadāśiva, god of gods, into all the Brahmin males [who had come to the Monday feast], and she invoked the goddess, mother of the world, into all their wives."[9]

The "invoking" is a technical, ritually oriented term: *ā-vāhaya* is literally "to carry" or "to transfer"—usually a divinity of some kind—into someone or something, thus filling up a receptive vessel with the existential force of the god or goddess, as in the template of worship at Puri discussed in the previous chapter.[10] A mental act of imaging involving the projection of the images across physical boundaries and a suspension or abrogation of the inner-outer distinction has the consequences we have seen. The process is classed here as "thinking" *(mene)*. When we move into the Tamil version, the language of thinking is retained (*ĕṇṇi,* 10; *matittu,* 23), but imaging is now a more radical and definitive imagining, *pāvaṉai* < *bhāvanā,* and a discursive description is supplied: "Each time she [Sīmantinī] invites Vedic sages to come with their wives, and when they arrive she imagines them to be Moon-crested Śiva and his wife Umā—and she then worships them joyfully in her mind [*ĕṇṇip puntiyāṉ makiḻnt' arccaṉai vaḻipaṭal puriyā,* 10]."

A little later, during the unsettling conversation in the forest, the surviving male in this couple correctly concludes that the transformation has happened or appeared *(viḷaintav āṟu)* because of the *bhāvanā* operating upon Sīmantinī's innerness (*akam,* 36). That is, an intrapsychic, personal move leads to acts of joyful worship that, in turn, because of their imaginative content, effect the change in Sāmavān's nature, in exact accordance with the guise or form *(kolam)* that he had donned (26). That this guise has an intrinsic relation to some aspect of the boy's nature becomes clear from the direct, passionate statements of Sāmavatī, who does eventually recall her prehistory as a Brahmin boy. She has a story to tell about her evolution into the complete woman she now feels herself to be.

3. Can we define the kind of causality operating here? The imaginative act is, let me repeat, transitive, intersubjective, and patterned in nonrandom yet not entirely determinate ways. It causes irreversible change. A personal quality colors it at every crucial step. But it is not, I think, adequate to describe the process as the impingement from without of one awareness upon another, as if Sīmantinī were intervening, in some simple way, in the workings of Sāmavān's mind. The extent of her impingement depends entirely upon her attentiveness, as we might expect from our earlier discussion of this theme. The factuality and consequentiality of the imaginative act derive largely from the seriousness with which it focuses attention. Sīmantinī notices something in the disguised, pseudofeminine boy, something that does away with the "pseudo-" prefix. Her attentiveness constitutes a moment of recognition, which could also be classed as understanding. As Neville Symington has said in an important essay addressing the Sīmantinī text: "Understanding comes when something within the personality has received attention, a focused attention."[11] No doubt

there are many kinds of understanding, but here we have a particularly powerful and moving kind where the pure cognitive content appears, first and foremost, as an intuition, or perhaps an emotion, or even a tactile sensation. As such, it generates change. It does not need to penetrate the external contours of the body in order to touch the mind, though it does affect those contours from within. In part it is able to do this by virtue of a resonant receptivity in the person who is being attended to.

We can say something more about the cognitive component of Sāmavān's trajectory, with a glance at themes that have already come up in relation to the content of an imaginative act. Insightful understanding creates, by virtue of attunement, something that already exists. It issues from an interactive or intersubjective domain, such as we find in operation at the very heart of our Tamil text. Here is Symington again, commenting on the Sīmantinī story: "The idea that something can be created in another is foreign to our thinking. . . . We are also so tied to a causality based on the notion that one thing is the result of another that we cannot conceptualize that something can come entirely from me and yet be a creation issuing from another."[12] Let us put aside the apparent paradox—more apparent than real—and limit ourselves to the principle animating the entire Sīmantinī narrative: "It is what is most deeply me that has to be created."[13] Clearly, as in nearly all imaginative productions discussed in this book, we are talking not about creation ex nihilo but about the shaping, articulating, and reorganizing of preexisting aspects or parts of the self that, by virtue of these very processes, become newly central or dominant. The language of discovery and surprise, that is, of a profound experience of newness, is also appropriate, as comes through clearly in this text. Such creation can take the form of a definition in human language of something previously only dimly perceived or even entirely unknown. It can also, the story suggests, take the form of an undeniable, prelinguistic physical sensation that reaches into, or emerges from, the recesses of self-awareness. Once created in this way, in the context of active attention from the perceptive other, reality becomes fact. External attention triggers such factual knowledge, but Sāmavatī clearly now knows what she knows from within—hence the indubitable character of such understanding. "Creations of the imagination are facts. They are the only certain facts, the only facts that can be known. I only truly know that which I have created."[14] Sāmavatī's self-perception, following the dramatic change in his/her nature, is no less an imaginative act than that of the queen who sparks this change by *her* imaginative vision of the boy. Varatuṅkarāmaṉ, writing in Karuvai and Tenkasi with the Sanskrit *Brahmottara-khaṇḍa* before him, has anticipated Vico by more than a century. We can allow ourselves to remark on the boldly modern character of the Tenkasi vision of the mind.

4. Once we have reached this point, we become sensitive to other features of the Tamil telling. No less "modern" in character is the skeptical undercurrent that runs through the entire story (again, shades of Montaigne). Mostly this skepticism is voiced by Sumedhā—the victim of his friend's transformation—but I think that Sumedhā is also speaking for the author and for us, his readers. Indeed, skepticism and a bold theory of the effective imagination go hand in hand. What, can mental acts really do what they are said to have done to Sāmavān? In a commonsense view, it seems unlikely. Fierce doubt and profound ambivalence fuel Sumedhā's side of the conversation in the forest. He has been, to say the least, surprised, and he is not alone in this: look at what happens to the king when he finds out what the deception he planned, without thinking, has produced. Deceit is worked into the whole imaginative sequence, even if the guise, *veṣam,* adopted by the boy ends up subsuming "his" entire being—as it is the nature of such a guise to do. Think of it as something pressing and real emerging onto the surface, with concomitant features of amazement, disbelief, and ambivalence. The latter are often present when imagination is invoked. Another way to state the matter is to highlight the inevitable tension of the concrete. Objectification, even if it follows the logic of the cosmos, contains the seeds of its own restless self-dissolution, which we experience as doubt. Even in this rather daring conceptual system, one cannot turn a man into a woman and leave things at that. Definition of any sort, and especially rigorous self-definition, almost never releases the defined from anxiety; rather, it exacerbates the tension internal to any contoured word or thing.

5. *Bhāvanā* thus brings something into being by binding the tension of being into the contours of a name. It is a subtle act, initially internal to the mind, although "internal" and "external" are, at best, approximations of the field of force within which consequential imagining happens.[15] Indeed, the inner/outer division can happen only through *bhāvanā* itself, as the Sanskrit grammarians recognized.[16] The bound state generated by imagination would itself be "intralinguistic"—like everything else—in a Bhartṛharian universe; or, since semanticity itself is a problem on this level of very delicate sensations, we could propose that imagination is a specialized mode of listening to the still undefined vibrations that underlie all phenomena.

Such inchoate, almost inaudible sounds may well include such matters as gender identity and the self-awareness that goes with it; thus Sīmantinī would be capable of hearing something below the threshold of Sāmavān's own range of aural attention. *Someone* has to hear it and, hearing it, give it shape and consistency if the subject is to know, that is, to reimagine, himself or herself. In any case, one quite unsurprising fact remains—that of the singularity of the imagined being. Sāmavatī, newly imagined into femininity, is clearly distinct from all other females. Her friend Sumedhā explicitly tells us so. "She" also belongs to a historical moment in which imagination has individuated itself as never before in south India. Sāmavatī's novel sexual identity is perhaps only the beginning of a much wider and more complex personal trajectory, the untold sequel to our story. Still, as with Montaigne, a fascination with the theme of transition in gender is one clear sign of an incipient conceptual revolution.

7.3. Sarpavaram: *Bhāva* Reexamined

The primary themes of the Sīmantinī story are played out, with interesting variation, in the structures of a well-known, living temple in the Godāvarī delta. The Bhāva-nārāyaṇa Svāmi temple at Sarpavaram, on the outskirts of Kākināḍa, predates the sixteenth century, as a twelfth-century pillar inscription in Tamil shows, but the crystallization of the local *purāṇa* and its narratives seems to have happened much later, almost certainly during the Rĕḍḍi period (fifteenth century), at the time many of the architectural features we see today were put in place.[17] Thus there may well be a historical matrix underlying the themes of imaginative gender transformation and its cognitive consequences that we find in both sites, Tenkasi and Sarpavaram. Sight, insight, conscious reflection, and above all imaginative projection—such are the instruments and modes of malleable personal identity in late medieval or early modern Tamil and Telugu. We find them beautifully articulated as such if we read the temple itself as a text, no less eloquent in its own right than the narrative we have just considered.

Here is the story Sarpavaram tells of its origins and its god, Lord of Feeling and Being *(bhāva)*—this elusive and persistent term for affective-cognitive states replete with effective imaginative force:

> First there was the eponymous snake, *sarpa*. His personal name was Ananta, "Endless" (also Śeṣa, "the Remnant"), and he was the last survivor

of the entire genus of snakes. The ancient sage Kāśyapa had two wives, Kadrū and Vinatā, sisters who were caught up in fierce, undying rivalry. Kadrū produced a thousand eggs, whereas Vinatā bore only two; all were kept in jars for 500 years, after which Kadrū's eggs hatched into a thousand serpents (Vinatā's two eggs had a very different fate). The two sisters made a bet about the color of the tail on the pure white horse, Uccaiḥśravas; whoever lost the bet would become the slave of the other. Vinatā said the tail was white, like the rest of the horse's body, but Kadrū claimed it was black—and ordered her dark sons to hide in the hairs of the tail so she could win the wager. But her sons, unhappy at this act of deception, refused to do so, so she cursed them to die in a sacrificial fire.

All this we know well from the first book of the *Mahābhārata;* Sarpavaram has appropriated the story as a useful frame for what happened next. That sacrifice, masterminded by King Janamejaya, took place at this temple.[18] Now you know: the ophidian heroes of the epic were rooted in the soil of deltaic Andhra. Luckily, one snake—our Ananta/Śeṣa—was spared. He meditated on Lord Viṣṇu at this site, and the god appeared in accordance with the internal vision, *bhāva,* that the snake had nurtured in his mind. Some say that Ananta, subject like his 999 brothers to the mother's curse, was able only to choose the manner of his dying; he prayed to die *into* Lord Viṣṇu.[19] This bold request, probably the best any of us can do, produced immediate results. When Viṣṇu manifested himself to Ananta, the snake asked to be allowed to stay forever with the god; so Viṣṇu made him into his own shadow, *chāyā*—and also into the mattress on which he reclines. Hence the name of the shrine, Snake City *(sarpa-pura),* in Sanskrit.

If one thinks steadily of the deity in a focused way, with a vivid inner image always visible to the mind, then there is a chance of graduating to the existential state of a shadow or reflection (*chāyā* can mean either of these). There are clear advantages to being a reflection: normally, it emerges from a great depth and retains something of the wholeness and creative potential of that depth, as we will soon see in other contexts. Something of this idea comes through in the physical structure of the Sarpavaram temple: the god has split himself into two parts, a buried, underground self (lying asleep on Ananta) in a basement chamber and an upright, illuminated self situated, with his consort Rājyalakṣmī, in the upper story of the shrine. A huge mirror occupies the whole wall to the right of this upper-level god, its generative, reflective surface compensating for the depth lacking in daylight existence.

The mirror offers one familiar kind of reflection—by no means exhausting the genre. Other options are explored by the central segment of the local *purāṇa*. For this purpose, we need a classical figure capable of undergoing extreme existential experiment.

Once the sage-musician Nārada, a man of greatly attenuated awareness and the false pride that regularly accompanies this state, declared himself to be immune to the workings of Viṣṇu's beguiling delusion, *māyā*, which continuously afflicts all of us. Happening upon our temple site, Nārada encountered an ascetic, Kapaṭa Muni, "the Cheat"—Viṣṇu himself, who had assumed this form for pedagogic purposes—and boasted again of his mental firmness. Kapaṭa Muni inspired him to bathe in the local pond, known today as Mukti Kuṇḍam, the "Pool of Freedom." When Nārada emerged from the pool, he had been transformed into an amnesiac but very beautiful woman named Sudatī. "Being then a lady, she was looking for a mate."[20] Nakunda, the prince of Pīṭhāpuram (one of the largest royal courts in this area), saw her while out hunting; the two fell in love and married, and over time Sudatī gave birth to sixty sons, each named for one of the years in the sixty-year Telugu calendar. The princess, unconsciously androgynous, was thus, in effect, the womb of time itself.

But one day an enemy king, Ripuñjaya, invaded Nakunda's kingdom. In the battle that ensued, Nakunda and all sixty sons were slain. Sudatī lost her mind in grief. After some days, however, she became intensely hungry; she saw a fruit growing on a tree in the wilderness, too high for her to reach it. She dragged the corpses of her sons to that spot, piled them on one another, and climbed up toward the fruit. The urge to go on living at any cost is stronger than any other inner power: such is the working of Viṣṇu's *māyā*.

The god reappeared at this crucial moment in the form of an aged Brahmin and advised the widow to bathe in the pond, but to hold one hand high and out of the water—only thus, he said, could the fruit be attained. Upon entering the pond, the famished and grief-stricken Sudatī was transformed back to her former male self, as Nārada, except for the hand that remained dry and feminine. With the reversion to maleness, Nārada also regained his memory. Now he understood the overriding force of *māyā*—something far more powerful than a dream, or simple mental confusion, or a magical illusion *(indrajālika)*.[21] The old Brahmin had meanwhile disappeared, but Nārada, even more desperate than before, prayed to Lord Viṣṇu, who came rushing to the world of human beings with such speed that he went right through the surface of the earth and landed in the netherworld. Hence the god at Sarpavaram is known as Pātāla Bhāva-Nārāyaṇa Svāmi, Lord of Feeling and Being in the World Below. That is how we see him today in the underground chamber just mentioned.

Some say that after this final revelation, Nārada dipped his feminine hand in the Pool of Freedom, and it, too, became male again.[22] What is certain is that Nārada, after this lesson in the intricacies of the mind, installed the god here and named him Bhāva-Nārāyaṇa. The name and the idea behind it are popular in the Telugu-speaking country; Sarpavaram is one of a set of five Bhāva-Nārāyaṇas (the others are at Paṭṭisīma on an island in the Godāvarī near Rajahmundry, Bhāvadevarapalli in Krishna District, Ponūru in Guntur, and Bāpaṭla near Cirāla). A strong tradition at Sarpavaram links the site with the great Tamil Śrīvaiṣṇava teacher, Maṇavāḷamāmuni, at the turn of the fifteenth century—another suggestion that the temple assumed its present form during the Rĕḍḍi time.

The story of Nārada's mind-bending transformation into a woman is very well known;[23] Sarpavaram has localized it and linked it creatively to other materials, such as the *Mahābhārata*'s opening account of the tragic history of the snakes. This process was in no way simple or mechanical. It evolved in a historical moment, the fifteenth century, and within a defined thematic spectrum that sheds light on what exactly is felt to be at stake in this site. The elements are familiar enough; it is their combination and reconfiguration that give a particular meaning. Thus we have the serpents, the mother's curse, the lone survivor and his meditation, the wish to die into a god who is bifurcated into upper and lower forms or registers, the mirroring and shadowing, the emphasis on the god's relation to the domain of feeling and imagining, and—perhaps most striking of all—the linkage between the latter domain and the notion of gender transformation, as with Sīmantinī. As in other texts,[24] we have a strong example of the cost of failing to imagine; this is precisely Nārada's punishable offense, it seems. He thinks at first that he has a grip on reality, and he mistakes surface for depth, probably the most common and potentially lethal of all mental errors in the south Indian cosmos.

As with Sīmantinī and Sāmavān, we can ask what makes Nārada's transformation possible, or, better—since to turn a man into a woman is, as we have seen, not really such a problem, given the notion of a residual, goddess-oriented female self lurking inside the male—what it is that governs the incomplete reversion from female to male and its concomitants on the level of awareness. Here it seems that the ability to imagine, a state that is the very opposite of the mental torpor and occlusion that constitute *māyā,* has healing properties and, for that very reason, has been fully articulated in the god's name and form.[25] *Bhāva,* a meditative mode of being, including a rich and varied emotional texture as well as imaginative insight, is concretely linked in this shrine both with the remote depths of the netherworld, home to snakes and various demonic creatures, and with the visible world of human experience; indeed, it may be the most precious feature of the latter, though it normally exists in some less accessible subterranean or subconscious form. God's role at Sarpavaram is to activate *bhāva,* the mental process that moves Nārada from illusion to a fuller and more total (also less arrogant and egoistic) awareness. The trajectory proceeds via an imagined, richly populated world that has its own profound integrity, though it eventually self-destructs.

One could go further. It is possible that "god" refers here, as its primary meaning, to the faculty of creative working of one mind upon another or to the arena in which such communicative, interactive, and transformative processes can occur.[26] "God is what you have in your mind." The resonance with Sīmantinī's story is even greater than might appear at first sight. Bhāva-Nārāyaṇa himself fulfils Sīmantinī's role as the attentive transformer/imaginer, attuned to the wider spectrum of true personae inhering in the obtuse and arrogant Nārada. But here, perhaps because a male deity is involved, the transition in state is not irreversible. Observe the hand that is held high above the water and that, as a result, remains feminine when the rest of the body reverts to being a masculine entity. This hand, disjunctive and anachronistic, shows us something about how Nārada's memory works. The external sign preserves an element of the world this man-woman has lost. In standard retrospection, something important is always left behind.

The story stresses physical transformation—its tangibility, its felt reality—very much as in the case of Sāmavān. Once again, we should beware of thinking that the physical change is somehow automatic, a function of a dip in the pond and nothing more. It is, in fact, anything but a technical achievement. Rather, like Sīmantinī, the god *thinks* Nārada into the female form that is waiting for him and that, presumably, already exists somewhere in the darker spaces of his self, like the dark shadow of the ophidian

Remnant that has come to stay forever in this shrine. That is why the bath in the pond works so well. Nārada, a naive literalist, unskilled at imagining, cut off from this essential property of the mind, is condemned to live out an imagined sequence full of terror, an expression of his own rather stymied nature. The god is forced to think first *for* him, then *with* or *as* him; eventually, an imaginary clarity, informed by memory, is attained, though possibly not for long. Five shrines celebrate the imaginative prowess of this deity, his aliveness within the world of human feeling and knowing, his subversion of his own continually projected illusion.

The shadow self, foundational for this shrine—embodied in the identity of the great serpent who marks the moment of origin—is arguably more stable, suffused with greater existential power, and hence more real than the primitive self of ordinary awareness. Thus, as with Sāmavān, the business of "feeling and being," *bhāva,* includes for Nārada a test driven by decisive imaginative effort, interactive, teleological, and effectual. Without this imaginative component, the story would be a relatively routine statement about illusion and how to transcend it, as it is in the *purāṇic* sources that Sarpavaram has drawn upon. *With* the imagination, the story is about the way the human mind works and, above all, about the way a god, however we define the word, can change us—interactively—by means of empathic imagining. True to its genre, reduced largely to the bare narrative contours, the *Sarpapura-kṣetra-māhātmya* lacks the rich, discursive emotionality of the Tenkasi telling of Sīmantinī's story, but it shares with the temple that provides its spatial and tangible correlates the Tenkasi focus on the creative powers of the mind and their particular modes of operation. As I have said, this focus seems to be a fifteenth- and sixteenth-century obsession, replete with novel empirical and metapsychological observations. We turn now to a more elaborate and explicit set of examples from Tenkasi at the height of its creative phase.

— 8 —

Nala in Tenkasi and the New Economy of Mind

8.1. Introducing the *Naiṭatam*

The centerpiece of the Tenkasi "renaissance" is the monumental work composed by Varatuṅkarāmaṉ's younger brother, Ativīrarāmaṉ, and known as *Naiṭatam*—a Tamil version of the Sanskrit poet Śrīharṣa's great *Naiṣadhīya-carita.* The sheer scope of this book, with its 1,173 intricate verses, its metapoetic and metaphysical proclivities, and its sustained delineation of character, makes it a primary source for the newly emergent vision of the human being and, in particular, the human mind. The *Naiṭatam* also shows us with great clarity the semantic shifts that key terms for the mind and its workings have undergone in relation to earlier, classical usage. In addition to such matters of immediate relevance to our concerns, I would like to stress the compelling beauty of the text both on the level of individual verses and, even more to the point, as a unified, seminovelistic whole. To reveal the power of this book as a single, well-integrated statement would require a much longer exposition than I can offer here; I hope that the verses we examine will suggest something of that wider vision. I use the word "novelistic" advisedly; the *Naiṭatam,* in my view, is a work of self-conscious literary fiction and hence very close to the Telugu masterpieces to be studied in the next chapter.

The *Naiṭatam,* like its prototype, tells the well-known story of two lovers, Nala and Damayantī. Specifically, it gives a very elaborate account of the early stages of their romance, including Nala's incognito mission to his beloved Damayantī as an emissary of the great gods of space (Indra, Agni, Varuṇa, and Yama), who are also in love with her, followed by Damayantī's *svayaṃvara* or bridegroom-choice in a public arena—a particularly excruciating ceremony in this case, since the four gods just mentioned assume

Nala's form and appear as suitors alongside him. Damayantī's problem is thus to distinguish the real, human Nala, with whom she is in love, from this series of precise doubles; Ativīrarāma<u>n</u> presents a somewhat unusual reading of this famous moment, as we will see. The Tamil *Naiṭatam* departs from Śrīharṣa's parent text in offering a concise version of the rest of the story, from Nala's possession by the jealous Kali (the degenerate deity embodying the present, unhappy era) to the lovers' tormenting exile and the climactic moment of exorcism and reuniting.

It is also important to note that the Tamil text does not follow the chapter divisions of the *Naiṣadhīya*. Ativīrarāma<u>n</u> has restructured the entire book, creating what are, in effect, more logical and coherent units than we find in the Sanskrit text. Discrete segments of the Sanskrit *mahākāvya* have been combined to create a strong sense of continuous experience; the evolution of the major characters in the light of their own self-understanding emerges naturally from this course of development and is conveyed to us in their own words. Not only does this restructuring depart from Śrīharṣa's vision of his characters and their story, but it is also without parallel in the earlier Tamil literary tradition, which always preferred somewhat shorter narrative segments of more or less similar length within an overarching narrative frame.

Clearly, this reorganization of a unitary work, meant to be read as such—perhaps over a period of several consecutive weeks—is a matter of some consequence.[1] The sense of innovation, not merely in structure but even more in style and tone, is very strong. Hence, not surprisingly, we find a set of eloquent oral narratives about the *Naiṭatam* as a sustained, highly complex, and demanding literary work. The late medieval literary tradition tells us that Ativīrarāma<u>n</u> wanted to get the approval of his elder brother Varatuṅkarāma<u>n</u> for the first 940 verses of the *Naiṭatam*—up to his description of the young couple's water games after the wedding. He sent Varatuṅkarāma<u>n</u> the manuscript, but the brother reacted negatively to the whole project, which he classed under the pejorative rubric of *nara-stuti*, the praise of a mere human being: "My younger brother has sung about a king, someone like us [and not about the god with the Ganges in his hair]."[2] This response so dispirited Ativīrarāma<u>n</u> that he finished off the rest of the narrative in a mere 233 verses, in marked contrast to the leisurely pace and baroque description that characterize the earlier segment.

In fact, the oral reframing of the *Naiṭatam* is still more complex. The two brothers have, as it were, divided between them the two distinct roles of courtly poet and *bhakti* poet (Varatuṅkarāmaṉ is, as we saw, the author of both the Tamil *Brahmottara-khaṇḍa* and a set of three devotional works, *antâtis,* to the god of Tirukkaruvai, the site of his royal residence; he also composed the most popular work of erotics in Tamil, the *Kŏkkokam.*)[3] Some say that Ativīrarāmaṉ went on a pilgrimage to Kāśī to atone for his sin of *nara-stuti,* praising a mortal, and that he composed the Tamil *Kācikaṇṭam* as part of this same repentant move.[4] But there is also a story claiming that Ativīrarāmaṉ was so incensed by his elder brother's disdainful response to the *Naiṭatam* that he went to war against him, besieging him in Colainakar, and that he lifted the siege only after Varatuṅkarāmaṉ sent him a Tamil verse urging him to take Rāma's brother Bharata—rather than Sugrīva, Rāvaṇa, or Arjuna—as his role model. All of these narratives may well point to the deeply ambivalent relationship of a highly innovative poet to the Sanskrit "elder-brother" text on which he bases his own work. But there is more. In some desperation, Ativīrarāmaṉ sent his completed *Naiṭatam* to his elder brother's wife, who was also a poetess.[5] Alas, she too was harsh in her criticism, focused precisely on the question of the uneven pace of the narration. She sent word to her brother-in-law that his book had the quality of a hunting dog that sets off for the chase in a fury, barking loudly and continuously, until it suddenly gets tired and comes to a halt *(itu nāy veṭṭaikku viraintu oṭic cĕṉṟu iraikka iraikka iḷaittu niṉṟāṟ poṉṟa taṉmai uṭaiyatu).*[6]

Clearly, the late medieval tradition was very sensitive to the disparity between the first nineteen cantos of the *Naiṭatam* and the last nine, certainly composed with another aim in mind, possibly even by a different hand. But the sister-in-law's attack goes a little further. It is as if she, or the oral literary-critical perspective speaking through her, were somewhat skeptical about the intrinsic power of the heavily encrusted, hypotactic lyricism of the first 940 poems, here reduced to the noisy barking of a dog. By the same token, this implicit judgment attests to the real originality of the work and to the implicit demand that it engage a new kind of reader, preferably one familiar with the Sanskrit *Naiṣadhīya* as well as with earlier erudite works in Tamil and Sanskrit and, at the same time, capable of a rich personal response to the complexities of the verses.

The *Naiṭatam,* once taught to children at an early stage in their schooling—the principle being that once the child had mastered this difficult book, he or she would be able to read anything—was one of the first Tamil works to be published with extensive commentary by the nineteenth-century poets-turned-pandits of whom Sascha Ebeling has written.[7] The *editio princeps* was, we think, in 1842 (Madras), and the pandit-commentator who left his mark on most subsequent editions right up to modern times was Tiruttaṇikai Caravaṇappĕrumāḷaiyar (though his commentary ended with the fifth canto, *Kaikkiḷaippaṭalam,* and was completed by other scholars such as Kāñcipuram Kantacuvāmi Aiyar). Many later editions based themselves on Caravaṇappĕrumāḷaiyar's exegesis of the text, though they often touched up his careful formulations and added further material. My own copy, which lacks a title page (it turned up miraculously in the now vanished Moore Market of Madras in 1984), seems to have been published in the early years of the twentieth century, and can be shown to have recycled, with some changes, the original Caravaṇappĕrumāḷaiyar commentary.[8] The commentary reveals impressive thematic continuity with the fresh emphases of the sixteenth century, including a clear interest in the imagination in its various modes.

8.2. *Uyir* and *Uḷḷam:* The Core of a Living Person

One way to begin exploring this text is to attend to its varied and sometimes confusing vocabulary for the forces active within the inner space of a human being. Most of the terms are familiar from earlier Tamil works. Thus we have *uyir,* the life-breath or life-force; *nĕñcam,* the feeling organ, situated in the breast, probably the site of *uṇarvu,* that is, deep understanding or intuitive perception; *āvi,* a near synonym for *uyir,* but occasionally endowed with sentience in contexts of life-or-death decisions; *ma<u>n</u>am,* "mind," the somewhat limited faculty of derived intellection and perceptual processing (but also the usual source or site of desire); *cintai* or *karuttu,* "awareness" or "thought," both of them apparently marked by strong cognitive elements; the metaphysical term *ātma(n),* "self," relatively rare in Tamil literary texts; and a more general, very common word, *uḷḷam,* the "inside" or "interiority," which also quite often seems to be linked to some kind of thinking/intellection (as with the related verb *uḷku,* "to think, ponder"). There are also subcategories of *uḷḷam,* such as *uṭpula<u>n</u>,* the inner eye, sometimes identified with the *itayam,* "heart" (Skt. *hṛdaya.*)[9] Note that Ativīrarāma<u>n</u> has *not* invented a new word for "person" or "self." He happily recycles all these earlier terms, often extending their range in specific ways.

Take *uyir,* for example. I would suggest that in classical Tamil sources, right through the end of the Chola period, we find an implicit metapsychologycum-anthropology organized around the core concept of breath, the life-force that is always in movement, in and out of the body, and which is always, by definition, a unitary force.[10] *Uyir* flows through bodies that seem to contain it but are really only precarious vessels for it. Moment by moment, the person breathes the entire cosmos in and out, and the cosmos itself, infused with *uyir* and moving with its rhythm, is also breathing in and out—so there will be both a transient, internal *uyir* on the level of the individual and an external, transpersonal one. The latter is sometimes said to be creative in the out-breath and absorptive in the in-breath; this may also be true, on a lesser scale, of the internal *uyir.* God breathes out the world into some form of existence and then reinternalizes it, deobjectifying it or melting it down. Breathing is, however, much more than breath alone. In a way, it is about differential intensities of living and feeling (not thinking) and about the particular rhythmic cycles of such processes, which are sometimes given special names (thus the god Tyāgarāja at Tiruvārūr continually dances the rhythm of breathing called *ajapā* or *acapai,* the "unuttered").[11]

The world, with its profusion of sense and texture and color, continually goes in and out, opening and closing space within the person; there is also a profoundly interactive or interpersonal aspect to this unending rhythm. Loving, for example, is at least partly about the merging of breath. Look, for example, at what happens to Rāma and Sītā when they first catch sight of each other in Mithilā, according to Kampa<u>n</u>'s twelfth-century *Irāmâvatāram* (1.10.592–93):

They bound and tugged at each other's insides *(uḷḷam)*
with the noose of that first hungry look,
and thus the lord of the tightly bound bow
and the girl with eyes deadly as swords
entered, by turns,
each other's heart [*itayam*].

The breath [*uyir*] in two bodies—that of the girl
with no waist and that of the boy
without flaw—merged back into one.
When the two lovers, once joined
on their bed in the dark sea and then
torn apart, came together again—
was there need for words?

We have three pieces of a person's inner world: the *uḷḷam,* capable of being captured by a look from another person's eyes and thus dragged outside; the *itayam,* which can be penetrated by another person, through strong feeling and sudden desire; and the *uyir,* which clearly dwarfs its bodily containers and seeks to fuse with itself, a single, rather impersonal force, the rhythmic breath of life itself. This *uyir,* we might note, tends also (like *nĕñcam*) to be intimately linked to *uṇarvu,* intuitive knowledge or understanding, or to a kind of insight not usually derived from intellection.[12]

Ativīrarāmaṉ also knows about the *uyir;* for him it is an internal, alive part of the person, and a rather vulnerable part at that, easily susceptible to destabilization and to death.[13] Obviously, no one can manage without it. Somewhat surprisingly, however, *uḷḷam* now seems to be the wider, more elastic and comprehensive term. *Uḷḷam* mostly overrides the *uyir* and usually contains and rules it. Quite often this new *uḷḷam* seems to mean something akin to our notion of "mind."

Look, for example, at *Naiṭatam* 4.29:

karum puyaṉ maṟaikku' mati katir veṭṭal kairava malar pĕṟātatu pol
arump' iḷa muṟuval iḷa mulaip pokam aiya nīy ĕytutaṟk' aritāl
virumpiṉar ākiy amararum iruntār viṇṇavar iṭatt' avaḷ ārvam
purint' iṭāt' uṉatu per ĕḻil ava' ṭan uḷatt'iṭaip pŏṟippal kāṇutiyāl

As the night lily can't enjoy the light of her lover,
the moon, on a night of dark clouds,
it won't be so easy for you, sir,
to taste the breasts of that woman
whose smile unfolds like a bud.
Also, I have to tell you that the gods
want her, too. To block any passion
for them, I'll paint your great beauty
in the middle of her mind [*uḷḷam*]—
just watch!

This is the matchmaker goose speaking to Nala before flying off to negotiate with Damayantī. He chooses his image carefully: the *kairavam* flower is uniquely suited to the Moon, as, by implication, Damayantī is to Nala; but sometimes there are cloudy nights or other impediments. To ward them off, the goose will paint *(pŏṟippal)* a verbal image of Nala in Damayantī's *uḷḷam*—not her interior in a general way, and probably not even her "heart" *(itayam, maṉam)*, but some part of her mental economy where she can see, visualize, imagine, fantasize, feel desire, deliberate, and make a choice: in short, her mind.[14]

Is it possible to offer a list of the *uḷḷam*'s functions in the new anthropology and to show how the latter differ from earlier, much less precise descriptions of the *uḷḷam* and from the typical modes of the *uyir?* I think it is. Here is a tentative set of features extrapolated synoptically from the *Naiṭatam:*

1. First, the *uḷḷam* knows how to think, in marked contrast with the *uyir.* This is not a trivial matter. There are different modes of thinking and of knowing, some more complex and far-reaching than others. If we compare the Tenkasi *uḷḷam* with the inner world of the *bhakti* poet (say, Māṇikkavācakar, or Cuntaramūrttināyaṉār, or Nammāḻvār), then the latter consistently offers self-images of fragmentation and diffusion in which the mind plays, for the most part, an invidious role; by contrast, Nala frequently scans his awareness and seems to use his mind to hold the sometimes dissonant pieces of himself together.
2. Second, the *uḷḷam* has an inside, which is to say that it has some sort of external border, however tenuous or porous. It is a bounded entity, full of generative content, welling up continuously, and at the same time apparently, in its deeper reaches, unconstricted and spacious. We will want to explore this space further.
3. Third, it has parts, some more prominent than others. I believe there is a particular privileging of the imagination, as I will try to demonstrate in a moment. A possible hierarchy of components emerges, with *karuttu* and *maṉam,* for example, like *uyir,* subsumed within *uḷḷam,* the wider principle. Moreover, certain of these parts provide the mechanism for the connectivity of one *uḷḷam* to another and for the possibility that one *uḷḷam* can create novelty in another, as we saw so dramatically in the case of Sīmantinī.
4. Fourth, *uḷḷam* has a pronounced, rather modern tendency to doubt itself. It easily moves into the ironic. It knows itself, not in the split-off way that the *bhakti* persona naturally chooses, but in some reflexive mode that allows for an intrapsychic awareness of mistakes, illusions, fantasies, hallucinations, and madness, all understood—if not always, at least at times—as less than wholly true (the *uḷḷam* can

also distinguish different *degrees* of delusion). All these may in some sense constitute the dynamic core of personhood, with the *uḷḷam* there to provide an enveloping membrane. I stress again: these extreme states, the very stuff of a love story such as that of Nala and Damayanti, are now perceived as wholly internal to the "self" (that word again). Even possession, a particularly powerful displacement particularly relevant to Nala's personal trajectory, is primarily endogenous, not an invasion from outside. The *uḷḷam* is thus capable of observing its own self-generating fantasies in action, as we will see.

5. Fifth, the *uḷḷam,* where perception mostly happens and is processed, makes judgments about what is and is not real. It is the major site for existential debate, again internal to the person.
6. Sixth, the *uḷḷam* is a locus for mood, as distinct from emotion/feeling. "Mood" is a discovery. It implies the existence of a minimally integrated, irreplaceable person. It also implies a certain instability of internal states, a rapid and more or less continuous transition among nuanced feelings that can be introspectively articulated in complex fusions or combinations.[15] Such transitions are everywhere in evidence in Ativīrarāma<u>n</u>'s Nala and Damayantī and sometimes elicit expressions of wonder. Mood also links up empirically with doubt and introspection (point 4).
7. Finally, the *uḷḷam,* unlike the classical *uyir* that we met in Kampa<u>n</u>, is not synchronized with extrapersonal, cosmic rhythms and functions. I will clarify this point with an example in the next section of this chapter.

First, let us try to get a feel for the kind of doubt and inner conflict that so regularly afflict our heroes' *uḷḷam.* Both Nala and Damayantī have acquired an introspective, even meditative quality. Consider the following moment. On his way to the *svayaṃvara* ceremony in which Damayantī will choose her husband, Nala is stopped by Indra and three other gods, who cruelly request that Nala argue *their* case before the woman whom he loves.

> Other than you, who have conquered Love,
> for all his power, by your own
> beauty, who is there to heal
> the suffering spread by *his*
> honeyed arrows?[16] (11.26)

Indra's demand is much worse, the poet proceeds to tell us, than asking Nala to give up his life, *uyir*. Nala at once loses his ability to think, *karuttu;* he forgets who he is *(taṉṉaiyu' maṟakkum)*. He cannot say no to the gods, cannot lie to them—though suddenly "lying" seems to him to lose its terror, and "truth" to expand its register. Uncertainty washes over him:

> Is it her eyes (think of her bangles, think of her waist,
> studded with jewels), is it the arrow of hostile
> Desire, is it this dharmic business of lying
> being classed as "bad"?
> Something is eating at my life [*uyir*]
> when I'm at my weakest, most vulnerable,
> like a sword twisted in my heart.[17] (11.29)

Tamil poets are fond of such inner states, but Ativīrarāmaṉ has pushed the analysis farther than usual—far beyond anything in the parent text of Śrīharṣa. He seems to see directly into Nala's mind and to listen carefully to the words that this mind produces in an emergency. Nala wavers, protests, debates with himself, briefly turns against conventional morality and its hollow categories, hesitates again, makes silly pronouncements, and ends up, like most of us, complying with external constraints. Doubt colors this difficult moment, which ends in an acknowledged cognitive failure: something—Nala doesn't know what it is—is eating at his life, his *uyir*. This something is experienced in his *marumam,* his most vulnerable inner place, his guts. Do we not recognize the type? Is he so different from ourselves? Note that this Tenkasi Nala is endowed with freedom of choice and undoubted agency, clearly in evidence in the very richness of his inner monologue and in his doubt.

Such moments, keyed to the character whose internal monologue we overhear, are far from rare in the *Naiṭatam*. But there are many other kinds of doubt, often worked into the figurative mechanisms that shape the verses. Here is one more example, from the inspired description of Damayantī by the prescient and calculating goose who wants Nala, his interlocutor, to fall in love with this girl:

> *kumiḻ micai maṟintu kuḻaiy ĕtir naṭantu kŏlaittŏḻin maṟaliyaip payiṟṟiy*
> *amiḻtiṉiṉ viḷartt' u'ṇañciṉiṟ karukiy aiyari citaṟi mai toyntu*
> *kamala' mĕṉ malarai vaṉam pukuttiya veṟ kaṇṇ iṇai māṉ maru'ṇokkan*
> *tamat' ĕṉak kavarntu kŏṇṭavo maṭa māṉ ṟaṭaṅ kaṇiṉ cĕyal*
> *kavarntaṉavo* (4.13)

Blocked by the *kumiḻ* flower (that is her nose)
but pushing on toward the leaf in her ear
after teaching Death how to kill,

whiter than ambrosia at the edges
but blacker than poison in the middle,
streaked with delicate lines
and soaked in kohl

are her two eyes, sharp
as spears. By the way,
they've exiled the gentle lotus
to forest and pond. But suddenly I'm
unsure: did they steal the maddening
glance of the deer and make it
their own, or was it the deer's eyes
that learned from hers how to quiver
and stare?

This corresponds to *Naiṣadhīya* 2.21:

sva-dṛśor janayanti sāntvanāṃ khura-kaṇḍūyana-kaitavān mṛgāḥ/
jitayor udayat-pramīlayos tad-akharvekṣaṇa-śobhayā bhayāt//

The deer are, it seems, doing their best to comfort
their drooping eyes, scared and defeated
by the great beauty of Damayantī's
not-so-very-small ones, by rubbing them
as if to heal their itching
with their hooves.

You can decide for yourselves which of the two verses is the more beautiful—Śrīharṣa's deft, compact, and rather heart-rending image, couched in his usual arcane diction, or Ativīrarāmaṉ's surrealistic confabulation of second- and third-order figures, some of them deliberately at odds with one another, ending in a disingenuous, pseudointimate statement of doubt by the goose (who can't be sure who stole what from whom). Perhaps the Tamil poet is no less disingenuously uncertain as to who thought up the primary trope—Śrīharṣa or himself. (As Borges says, the original is unfaithful to its translation.) At base there is the familiar simile comparing a woman's eyes to the soft ("maddening") eyes of the deer. But both the Tamil and the Sanskrit verses squeeze a lot more from the comparison. Śrīharṣa imagines that the deer's eyes have lost in some unspoken contest with Damayantī's; defeated by the astonishing beauty of the latter, they are, as it were, being comforted by the deer themselves, who rub them with their hooves, "just as a person tries to comfort someone who has been defeated and is frightened—by gently patting him with his hands."[18] The primary figure of *utprekṣā,* poetic fancy, which attributes intentionality to the deer,[19] moves toward *vyatireka,* "surpassing"—since the subject of the comparison, Damayantī's eyes, has clearly overpowered (defeated) the object of the comparison, the deer's eyes.[20]

Ativīrarāmaṉ has turned the contest into a cognitive doubt, *sandeha:* who was the original owner of that gentle, intoxicating glance? On top of, or preceding, this conclusion to the verse, we find a cascading series of ornaments[21] that, as the nineteenth-century commentator remarks, amounts to a multilayered *cervaiyaṇi=saṅkara,* "mixture." But the precise definition of the figures and their complex interrelations may not much matter. The point is that the goose has produced a marvelously intense, if slightly baffling and dissonant, concatenation of attributes that truly impart a sense that Damayantī's eyes are very special, indeed unique, and he has done this (with the help of the poet) in an ever-so-slightly ironic or self-mocking tone implicit in the mere cumulation of these overdetermined ornaments and explicit in the final admission that the goose can't be sure about the final comparison, conventional as it obviously must be.

Better still, we could observe how Śrīharṣa's playful image of deep and gentle eyes has become in the Tamil verse almost a battleground, with gentleness perhaps last on the list of pertinent attributes. Those eyes of Damayantī's are no doubt also gentle, but they seem mostly occupied with rather violent activities: killing, spearing, exiling . . . The poem is an oxymoron before all else. If you read it over a few times, the incongruity and dissonance become more and more pressing, and also more and more beautiful. "Irony" is too loose a term to characterize the resulting cognitive effect. We might think in terms of a radical reframing, slightly mordant and more than a little skeptical, and what that means for our emerging sense of the pair of doubtful and all-too-modern lovers who configure the entire story. Incidentally, the fact that these Tamil verses repay repeated reading—that they take time, sometimes quite a lot of time, to sink in and work their magic—also tells us something about the aesthetic that has generated them and the new protocol of reading, perhaps silently, by a connoisseur.

8.3. The Mind Sees and the Person Knows

Where does the imaginative faculty come into play in all this? Look first at the following example from the end of this same passage. Once the goose has finished his exhaustive description of Damayantī, Nala, who has listened intently, can respond. He knows about Damayantī, has heard many reports about her, has even more or less fallen in love with her on the basis of these verbal testimonies. But listening to the goose has changed something in his way of thinking *(karuttu)*:

vĕṇṇakait tuvar vāy aṇaṅkĕḻil palarum viḷampiṉar niṉ mŏḻi yavaḷ ĕṉ
kaṇṇ ĕtirppaṭṭāḷ polu' mĕyt tuṇaiyāṟ karuttiṉāṟ kāṇṭale kāṇṭa'
naṇṇi muṟ ṟoṉṟum pŏruḷu' nuṇṇiya'te' ṉāṭutaṟk 'ariyalā mukattiṟ
paṇṇiya nokka' nokkunarkk' aḻaku payappatai yaṉṟi veṟ' uḷato

Many have spoken of her white smile, her mouth
red as coral, her overpowering
beauty, but your words have almost placed her
before my very eyes. Seeing through
the mind of a true friend is really
seeing. Eyes that barely see
what's right in front of them,
especially something very fine,
are only there to touch up
the seer's face. (4.32)

As so often, the Tamil closely reproduces Śrīharṣa's thought, but with a telling difference:

akhilaṃ viduṣām an-āvilaṃ suhṛdā ca sva-hṛdā ca paśyatām/
savidhe 'pi na-sūkṣma-sākṣiṇī vadanâlaṅkṛti-mātram akṣiṇī// (2.55)

Everything is lucidly perceived
by those who see through the heart
or through the heart's true friend.[22]
The two eyes that sit on our face,
that can't detect anything fine
no matter how close it comes,
are merely there
for ornament.

Nala, perhaps for the first time but certainly not the last in these two texts, privileges an inner vision over the object-driven, physical act of superficial seeing. The goose, by masterly description in language, has made Damayantī present to him, clearly visible in his mind's eye. How so? Just what has Nala really seen? What is clear is that *kāṇṭal,* "seeing,"[23] is at its best when enabled or mediated by what is going on in the mind of a close companion, *tuṇai* (or friend, *suhṛd,* in the Sanskrit). But there is a slight (and in my view significant) difference between the two texts when it comes to what exactly the companion's mind is supposed to do. For Śrīharṣa it seems to be a matter of feeling, something transpiring literally in the heart *(svahṛdā).* For Ativīrarāmaṉ, the critical word is *karuttiṉāl,* "[seeing through] the mind"—but *karuttu* here seems to mean not merely "thought" or "mind" in a general way but rather the much more specifically conceived faculty of the imagination. When someone close to you imagines something, you, too, can perceive it by virtue of the empathic closeness you feel with that person and the deep trust you have in him or her. In short, seeing is believing (the Tamil commentary glosses this interactive process as *nampikkai,* "belief," made possible by the imagination). But true seeing is *not* the trivial business of looking at an external object; it is, rather, a matter of co-imagining.

In itself, this conclusion formalizes a theme we have followed through many of the classical sources. We know that visionary sight, transpiring in the mind, is often classed as more effective, closer to the reality of the envisioned object, than everyday modes of seeing. The Tamil poet, still true to his source, proceeds to explain the relative incapacity, even uselessness, of our eyes. The test of real perception, he says, is what we do with subtlety *(nuṇṇiyatu).* Our eyes aren't much good at discerning fine nuances—perhaps the single most important attribute of anything real in this perceptual universe—even if the fine object is brought very close. Nārāyaṇa, commenting on Śrīharṣa's verse, says: "Eyes can't even perceive the kohl applied to their edges or their own redness, and so on, so how can they grasp something that is more remote?" On the other hand, the imagination—at least as it is understood in sixteenth-century Tenkasi—seems perfectly suited for this critical purpose. The imaginative faculty, we may conclude, is predicated on subtlety and fineness; also, perhaps, on singularity. As I have said, the play of figuration and creative recombination in the goose's masterly depiction of Damayantī is clearly meant to conjure her up in all her uniqueness. She is beautiful, and her beauty can perhaps only be spoken of in the well-worn images and patterns available—yet the whole point of using these images lies in the poet's ability to reimagine them in unprecedented, sometimes shocking, sometimes playful and ironic ways. In addition, it is worth noting that in the Tamil passage the goose/poet asks his listener, over and over: "But to what object can I truly compare her? What is there for words to say?"[24]

There is, it seems, an intuitive flash of emotional insight that comes into play when a friend describes something.[25] The Tenkasi epistemology takes this notion a step further, toward the interactive imagination that can make something seem real to us, indeed more than real. You need two minds for this to work, and two engaged, interlocking imaginations, each quite personal and distinct. Interestingly, given such conditions, the empathic companion is apparently capable of creating something new in his or her friend's mind, as we saw in the case of Sīmantinī and Sāmavān.[26] The goose has produced an entirely new Damayantī for—better still, with the active help of—Nala. His imagination kicked in once the goose triggered it with the sophisticated verbal means at his disposal, including complex figuration (as in the example cited earlier); the result is that Damayantī has finally come to life for Nala, not just as one supremely beautiful woman but as a person with whom he can really fall in love. Here, again, is the Tamil commentator Tiruttaṇikai Caravaṇappĕrumāḷaiyar, summing up this trenchant statement:

> Our eyes are no more than an ornament for someone who sees with the help of his true friend's imagination. The word "true" *(mĕy)* occurs here to eliminate the possibility of doubt and misunderstanding. The friend's way of seeing is quite definitely superior to one's own sight. One can see everything that is, wherever it may be, through a friend's true statements and this friend's imaginative thought [*karuttu*]. It's impossible to see with one's eyes fine things—atoms, for example—no matter how close they may be; so the eyes [unlike the friend's imagination] are actually pretty useless.

We might take note of a variant reading for the middle of the verse: *naṇṇi mur̲ ṟonr̲um pŏruḷ uḷam piriyi' n̲āṭutar̲k' ariya vāṇ mukattir̲ paṇṇiya nokkam,* "if your mind [*uḷam*] moves away from what is right in front of it, then the eyes in your face [are only an ornament]." Our commentator thinks this is an inferior reading, very much opposed to the sense of the Sanskrit original. I agree. Still, even in this variant we see the clear superiority of the mind, capable of undermining direct physical perception and reducing the eyes (once again) to useless ornaments. In either case, what we see directly stands in a somewhat oblique, and inferior, relation to what we imagine.

Here is one tentative conclusion: a person sees, interactively, by virtue of an active imagination attuned to subtleties and hence to singularities. Seeing is not, of course, all there is to it. The *uḷḷam*—the interiority of the person as a whole; or, if you follow my suggestion, the mind—will have to process what the inner eye shows it. The *uḷḷam* also seems to know where imagination ends; it knows this because of the reality-force evident in the imagined object and absent or attenuated in mere verbal descriptions or physical perception. Once again, we note that certain knowledge of this kind is quite free from the material limitations of the body; when two minds are attuned, and the language that passes between them reflects this attunement, and a measure of receptivity is present, they share an existential dimension or space that is fully present only under such conditions of mutuality. We might posit the existence of such a dimension within all kinds of reality—how, otherwise, can we understand one another even in less profound moments?—but the deeper perception the verse describes requires the activation of a personal imagination, even two such imaginations.

We have here a striking example of how, in Ativīrarāmaṉ's hands, a particular passage in Śrīharṣa comes to serve a somewhat different purpose and reflect a different mental economy. We are in a milieu in which the active and interactive imagination, conceived as working in highly specific modes, is coming to be seen as central to any mature human experience. But the critical point has to do with the complex, interpersonal process of truly seeing and knowing. Nala cannot see Damayantī directly (at this point), just as the eye cannot really see even something quite close; Nala can only imagine her by imagining his friend's memory-based imagination of her. There are, apparently, degrees of imaginative force. To know fully you have to go through the intimate other's imagination—perhaps through several such receding frames—and you can do this because you and your friend belong to a single, living, resonant cosmos connected through the fine tissue of many distinctive imaginations. You are also breathing the same air as the other, in and out. This way of understanding perception also, incidentally, explains why what the imagination sees is objective, not in the modern sense of discretely contoured substances more or less independent of the observer[27] but in the sense that the imagined object is shared, consequential, and thus real. Damayantī's image—her unique face, eyes, hair, breasts, waist, and feet—exists and is, in fact, moving *into* Nala, breathed in, as it were, into some reservoir of personal being where it can deepen and grow, perhaps later reemerging to connect with, or superimpose itself upon, the living presence of Damayantī herself (or her imagination of herself). We will examine just such a moment shortly. All this depends upon the particular way the goose has chosen to depict her verbally, thereby activating Nala's *karuttu* via the goose's own vision.

But note the profound difference from the earlier, somewhat simpler *uyir*-based anthropology with which we began this chapter. The internal breathing in and out is no longer isomorphic with the external breathing of the cosmos. It is no longer a matter of the cosmic imagination recycling itself over and over, so that everyone is, in effect, breathing in the same cosmos in a similarly patterned way. Now the internal breath moves in accord with its own imagination as nurtured or motivated by the resonant imagination of the friend. There is an autonomy to the person that regulates the transition, so what comes from outside and what comes from inside create something else, something new, that is connected to the imagining other and therefore real (far more real than a direct perception). We could also describe this process more generally as an opening into depth, a resonant internal depth—but remember that the outside is also deep insofar as it, too, is breathing in and out. More to the point, as we will see, the cosmos out there adjusts itself to your creative act.

In short: Damayantī's image exists, it is moving into Nala, that is, into us, and back out of him and out of us into the world, because through his friend and ours we are able to imagine it, in all its singularity. Without this friend, we are blind. One could say much the same thing about the necessary presence of the poet in our lives.

8.4. Two Fantasies Embracing

Nowhere in the *Naiṭatam* is the new regime of the imagination more apparent than in the moment when Nala and Damayantī first come face-to-face. As it happens, ironically, neither of them actually identifies the beloved other at this juncture. Nala has been infiltrated into the women's quarters of the royal palace in Vidarbha; he is invisible, thanks to the magic of Indra and the other gods who have sent him on this invidious mission to Damayantī as *their* love messenger. Śrīharṣa elaborates the awkward scene with great ingenuity and humor in Chapter 6 of the Sanskrit text;[28] let us see the challenge he poses for his Tamil translator. Though they cannot see him, the women of the harem are deeply unsettled by his presence; he brushes against them, they hear him mumbling to himself, and they see the traces he leaves—his footprints in the dusty street, his shadow, his reflection in mirrors and all other glossy surfaces. As for Nala, though he is clearly if uneasily fascinated by the hundreds of women whom he, himself unseen, can study in their natural, intimate poses, his mind is mainly occupied with the vivid, hallucinatory images of Damayantī that it has produced. He sees her everywhere; her beauty pervades the space around him, so compelling that he is in no danger of identifying any of the other women with his beloved, as they are dwarfed by his consuming fantasy. But how does he know what she looks like? There was, you will recall, the richly satisfying, imaginative description by the goose. Aside from that:

> Had he met her somewhere before
> in the beginningless chain of lives?
> Was it because he had seen her in paintings?
> Or was it merely the magic of Desire
> that made her suffuse all visible space?[29]
>
> Helpless with longing, his heart despairing,
> with Desire lending a hand,
> he saw her—falsely—
> and, suddenly awaking,
> saw no more.
>
> Still, he started to speak of his mission
> to his beloved, imagined there *(vikalpohṛtām).*
> Only the murmur of women frightened
> by a voice unseen
> brought him back to his senses.[30]

Damayantī is in a similar state of overpowering love madness, her mind generating endless images of the absent Nala. Such are the circumstances in which the two lovers accidentally meet. Damayantī has paid a courtesy visit to her mother and has received from her a garland of flowers as a gift:

Bhaimī [Damayantī] bowed in reverence to her mother.
On the way back, she came together
with Nala, but he didn't know her
in the midst of all his delusional Bhaimīs—
and, being invisible, he couldn't appear
before her.

She tossed the garland of flowers
given by her mother
around the neck of the Nala
whom she saw in her delusion,
but as he was, in fact, standing
right there, it truly
touched him.

Please bear in mind that at the *svayaṃvara* ceremony where the bride chooses her husband-to-be, the sign of this choice is her placing of a garland around his neck. Damayantī's *svayaṃvara* is at this point still several chapters ahead of us; in effect, however, she has already made an unconscious (yet binding) selection, to the astonishment of both parties to the transaction.

He was amazed: "A garland,
the gift of a person
I have only imagined,
turns out to be *real.*"
She, for her part,
was also wonder-struck,
seeing the garland she tossed in the air
disappear.

They kept seeing each other
as if they were elsewhere,
though together they occupied one
shared space.
And while their two fantasies,
false, mutual, and internal,
gripped one another,
these two people
truly embraced.[31]

As always, we need to look closely at the language the poet has chosen to convey the meaning of this critical moment. Initially, things are fairly straightforward: he is looking directly at Damayantī, but he thinks she is only one more of the delusional images filling his mind *(bhrānta-bhaimīṣu)*; she, of course, simply cannot see him at all. She throws the garland at one of her fantasy images of Nala, and—this is the poet speaking—it truly falls around the real Nala's neck. She can't know this, however; what she sees is that a real, tangible garland has suddenly disappeared (like everything else that comes in contact with the invisible Nala). He, for his part, feeling the garland around his neck, the gift of a woman whom he assumes to be no more than a chimera generated by his mind, declares that it must be real, *satya* (real, not simply true). The "chimera" is *vāsanā*—not in the usual meaning of an unconscious karmic memory, but clearly an imagined entity (Mallinātha glosses it as *nirantara-bhāvanā,* "continuous imagining"); note the semantic displacement in the context of an implicit theory of the mind. Two overheated imaginations are working overtime.

Now comes a verse that is vintage Śrīharṣa, equally complex in thought and expression. The lovers embrace, still unaware of whom they are holding in their arms. Each thinks, the poet says, that the other must be somewhere far away. Still, the embrace is totally real *(tathyam)* and fully mutual *(mithaḥ)* in intensity. In fact—a touch of genius—there are two parallel embraces, not one. The imaginary lovers embrace inside the living lovers' minds (which of the two couples is more real?). The passionate fantasies are "false, mutual, and internal" *(*alīka-parasparântaḥ)*, a phrase only Śrīharṣa could have invented. The implication seems to be that *any* real embrace will normally—fortunately—be accompanied by its precise counterpart in the two interwoven imaginations.

The bizarrely joyful meeting that transpires on two parallel tracks, in body and mind, has immediate epistemic consequences, no less confusing than the cognitive point of departure:

> She had touched him—
> but, not seeing him,
> she thought it was all illusion [*bhrānti*].
> As for the king, though he really saw her,
> he froze, unable to hold it in.
>
> In the joy of touching, they thought
> it must be real. But as the moment

went on, they came back to their senses
and knew, falsely,
that it was false.
Again they touched each other,
truly, standing there on the path,
and, deluded, failed
to believe.

Like the flame of a lamp when too much oil is added,
the fire of desolate wanting, flooded by the joy
of truly touching, abated
for a brief second, then blazed up again
in their minds.

Torn between clarity and delusion,
her courage at war with her longing,
she went into her chambers.
As for Nala, he was sliding into madness,
seeing her everywhere before him.[32]

Physical touch should guarantee the reality (*satya* again, 53), and briefly it seems to do so, until the mind takes over and, with characteristic insistence, presents false knowledge as true. The two lovers have ample reason to believe what their bodies are telling them, yet they fail in this test of faith (*na śraddadhāte,* 53). We know this verb from our earlier discussion of attention; quite possibly the failure is not so much in "believing" as in paying precise attention *(śraddhā)* in the creative way that dependably generates insight. The result: madness accelerates, the imagination cuts loose from its anchor in the concrete encounter, and Nala and Damayantī embark on a tantalizing, sometimes excruciating game of identity probing that extends over the next three long chapters. Failure to pay attention invariably exacts a price.

What has Ativīrarāmaṉ done with his inheritance? Let us concentrate on the brief, dramatic moment of the embrace, condensed in the Tamil text into four remarkable verses:

"This garland came from a woman
whom I saw—as an illusion!"
That's what *he* thought while
she lost sight of the garland
and was bewildered.

He happily embraced her—the all-too-familiar
delusion. She clung to his chest, thinking
that was as it was.

Indescribable ecstasy welled up.
He let go of her, staring
at the brilliant vision.
She, grieved that she could see
no form, gently withdrew
her bangled arms.

Though he had held the dark-eyed woman
in his arms, he had let her go,
for to him she was illusion.
Now sorrow tortured him
like a man who has found great wealth
only to lose it.

Nala's first thought, directly quoted, is that a totally real, substantial garland has been given to him by a woman who, he is quite sure, is an illusion—what is called in Tamil *uruvĕḷittoṟṟam,* literally, an "apparition in empty space." Note that he knows very well that his mind has gone wild, that he is seeing things under the pressure of impossible desire (doubly impossible at this point—for not only is Damayantī not with him, but he is also committed to persuading her to marry one of the gods instead of himself). Damayantī, like Nala, is perfectly aware that her mind is generating images of her absent beloved; what she can't understand is how the garland she cast on one of these images could vanish into thin air. For our purposes, the key point is that both lovers seem to think of their own minds as self-contained, individualized entities that naturally, in certain circumstances, will give birth to illusions. Moreover, these illusions can, in theory, be distinguished from nonillusory reality. The ability to know that you are hallucinating, however compelling the delusion might seem, implies a theory of mind or consciousness as in some sense organized and whole.

But now comes a further surprise. Nala happily *(uvantu)* embraces the *uruvĕḷi* delusion. Why not? He thinks he knows what he is doing. He also has a specific, no doubt positive relation to his self-generated, interior image of his beloved (an image nurtured, we recall, by the goose). He thus thinks he is embracing an internal, imaginary person, in effect a part of himself, which he has projected outside. Damayantī has her own parallel or complementary conclusion. She, too, embraces the image. But the poet's phrasing is ambiguous. She thinks "that was as it was," *a<u>n</u>navā<u>r</u>' ĕṇṇi.* This could mean that she simply reproduces, on her own terms, the chain of thought that Nala has just produced. But our nineteenth-century commentator, undoubtedly continuing a line of traditional exegesis, thinks otherwise: *tamayantiy ā<u>n</u>avaḷ naḷa<u>n</u> uṇmaiy ĕ<u>nr</u>' u<u>nn</u>i pulli<u>n</u>āḷ ĕ<u>nr</u>uṅ kŏḷka,* "Thinking that [this] Nala was real, Damayantī embraced him." I think this way of reading the verse is persuasive and very much in line with the whole tenor of the passage and with the *Naiṭatam*'s implicit metapsychology. Damayantī cannot see Nala with her eyes, though he is right beside her; she sees the inner image with an intensity so overpowering that she trusts it more than she trusts her own eyes. All this fits very well with what we know about the compelling inner mode of perception.

Put more generally, these verses allow us to trace a continuum that stretches from actual external perception *(pratyakṣa)*, the simplest and most deceptive way of seeing, via the mental act of the imagination *(bhāvanā)* to abnormal states of possession, hallucination, and delusion *(moha),* with various gradations along the way. All these states are internal to the mind, which has both an inside and an outside. A strong notion of hierarchized levels of knowledge accompanies this discovery. There are things that we know, things that we think we know (but may not be sure), and things that we know we know. Often we know without knowing that we know. Look at the final verse in this short section. Nala is still convinced that he is embracing an illusion (this despite the indescribable ecstasy welling up), so he lets her go and is at once overcome by sadness, "like a man who has found great wealth only to lose it." On some level, he knows he has lost something real. In this last verse, an innovation of Ativīrarāma<u>n</u>'s vis-à-vis the Śrīharṣa original, a rather modern-sounding irony infuses the sad statement of our poet.

We thus have an interesting symmetrical (complementary) inversion. Nala sees the real Damayantī but thinks she is unreal. She sees empty space before her, filled with what she knows to be her own mental image, and thinks the latter is real. Nala lets go of the real Damayantī but goes on staring at her *pŏlivu*—the "brilliant vision" that he thinks has been produced by his mind and must therefore be false. We, on the other hand, outside the text, know the *pŏlivu* to belong to the real person. In terms of a more general theory of the imagination, we are very close at this point to a notion of real (that is, existentially demanding) fiction. Such a notion depends upon gradations of knowledge and their distribution over the standard set of poet, characters, and readers. In the new epistemic regime, we readers generally have privileged access to a wider kind of knowing than that available to the characters and even, in some cases, to the poet, who may be lost in his own fictions. This differentiation in modes of awareness is intrinsic to the notion of a relatively unified person as well.

Śrīharṣa offers us a subtle psychology of general applicability predicated on the notion that for a meaningful embrace to take place between two lovers, their mental illusions of each other must also (first) embrace. Ativīrarāma<u>n</u> takes us in the direction of two well-defined, autonomous, irreducible individuals, each with his or her own perspectivism built into their respective perceptions, who complement one another in both the images and the ideas they project outward into space. As I have said, this external space is, for the most part, only too happy to confirm the projection. In the Tamil text, it is no longer the illusion-based fantasies that embrace but rather the two individuals, each with a distinctive awareness: if Nala remains skeptical, Damayantī gives herself to her mental image of Nala, though she cannot maintain this stance for long. As the moment passes, "rational" cognition wins out over what we can only call "real imaginings." The mind subverts what the mind has created; as always, what is imagined is not a given, a datum, but something made and thus brought into being, though it cannot, in this case, be verified by the evidence of the senses.

8.5. Straight Speaking and a Visual Model of the Mind

Like its Sanskrit prototype, the Tamil *Naiṭatam* is a text of echoes and reflections. It also offers many instances of *śleṣa* paronomasia or split linguistic registers. Sometimes Ativīrarāma<u>n</u> manages to imitate a complex bitextual passage in Sanskrit with an equally complex statement in Tamil.[33] But, surprisingly, he turns away from the most famous of all *śleṣa* moments in Sanskrit *kāvya,* the so-called *Pañca-nalīya,* that is, Śrīharṣa's tour de force at Damayantī's *svayaṃvara.* Sarasvatī, goddess of language, introducing each of the suitors to Damayantī, comes to the four gods, Indra, Agni, Varuṇa, and Yama, who have assumed Nala's likeness; she presents them to the bride-to-be in verses that can be decoded in two distinct modes, one applicable to the god in question, the other to the human Nala. Damayantī's initial task is to figure out what the goddess is telling her in these verses, so as to identify the man she loves. When Sarasvatī comes to Nala himself, however, she speaks a single verse capable of being decoded in five ways, one for the mortal bridegroom and the rest for each of the deities—who together may make up the king's body.[34] As if this were not challenge enough, this verse also appears to state outright that this suitor is not Nala *(nâyaṃ nalaḥ);* Damayantī will have to find a way to make sense of this superficial negation.

In the *Naiṭatam,* too, each of the gods is first described in a verse that can also apply to Nala. But when Sarasvatī stands before the real Nala, she introduces him to Damayantī in the simplest, most direct manner possible, and without *śleṣa:*

potari nĕṭuṅ kaṇ'allāy pŏru cilai veṉilāṉiṟ
kotaiyar maṉamuṅ kaṇṇuṅ kūṭṭ'uṇuṅ kuvavu toḷāṉ
ṟāt' aviḻ kamalap potu malarnta pūn taṭaṅka'ṭoṟu'
mātar mĕṉ mukaṅkaḷ kāṭṭum vaḷaṅ kĕḻu niṭata vente// (12.167)

Listen, girl with long, streaked eyes:
Here is a man with powerful arms—
a definite improvement on the God of Desire—
who devours the hearts and eyes
of women. He's king in Niṣadha
with its many ponds replete
with women's faces or, if you prefer,
with lotuses rich in honey.

Try as one might, there is no way to turn this verse into a multiregistered statement of superimposed identities. Its very simplicity carries the decisive meaning most needed at this difficult moment, in stark contrast with the polysemic Sanskrit crescendo. True, the lotus ponds in Niṣadha might take a spectator aback with a transient, surreal vision of disembodied faces—but the figure hardly requires elaborate hermeneutic exercises. There's also the fact that Nala bears a striking resemblance to the God of Love and so is rather dangerous to the equanimity of young women, although for Damayantī the greater danger lies in failing to see him for who he is.

She is, naturally, still racked with doubt, *aiyam.* On the other hand, her mind *(uḷḷam)* is melting down, as is proper for a Tamil love heroine (12.167). In this heightened, bewildered state, she still has enough cognitive resources available to make a reasoned judgment:

ĕḷḷ' uṟav eṉaiyoraiy iraṭṭuṟa mŏḻitalāṉum
vaḷḷaṉ mārp' aṇinta tāril vaṇṭu vīḻnt' ararralāṉum
uḷḷ uṟap piṇittav aṉpiṉ ūḻviṉait tŏṭarpiṉāṉu'
naḷḷ iruḷ parukum paim pū ṇaḷaṉaiye naḷaṉ ĕṉṟ' orntāḷ (12.169)

Because the others had been described in doubtful, doubled language
and because bees were buzzing loudly
in the garland on *his* breast and
because of the ancient, fated, inner
connectedness of love, she knew
that Nala, his golden jewels drinking in
all darkness, was really
Nala.

Our commentator explains that the gods wear garlands of golden flowers taken from the Wishing Trees in heaven that, perhaps because they're made of gold, attract no bees. Then there is the matter of the deep, intrinsic connection between these two lovers. But the first thing that Damayantī notices, apparently with some relief, is the absence of *śleṣa* from the description Sarasvatī has given of this man. Strangely, and perhaps only for this crucial moment, unlike his Sanskrit model, Nala coincides only with himself—and Damayantī sees this and confirms it by making her choice. The goddess speaks straight—doubt (*ĕḷ*, an unusual lexical choice with connotations of derision and censure)[35] is ruled out, for once—and Damayantī acts with a similar unswerving clarity. The act is overdetermined: aside from its cognitive components (the escape from the irritating *śleṣa* statements and the inference drawn from the absence of bees), something within reality itself has bound these two people together from the inside *(uḷḷura),* connecting their minds *(uḷḷam)* in imaginative attunement to forces operating upon them from ancient time *(aṉpiṉ ūḻviṉait tŏṭarpu).* That is what the imagination is for; it has successfully completed its role. At the very last moment, at the start of the fourth line, Nala's name sparks an association with midnight darkness, *naḷḷ iruḷ,* but the meaning of this perhaps significant phonic linkage is best left for later in the story.

Before taking leave of the *Naiṭatam,* I want to explore one more verse that brilliantly articulates the themes we have been pursuing in this chapter, including the radical economy of perception that the poet has formulated. Consider, then, the opening verse of the "Chapter on the City," the *Nakarap-paṭalam.* This descriptive canto starts us off with a lyrical evocation of the physical setting of the work, as in most Tamil *mahākāvyas*. Such early verses are usually thought to adumbrate, in compressed and suggestive ways, major topics that will occupy poet and reader throughout the long text ahead. To the best of my knowledge, the following verse has no prototype in the Sanskrit source:

kuṭa vaḷaik kulam vayiṟ' uḷaint' iṉa maṇi kŏḻikkum
maṭuvil vāṉakar uruvu kāṭṭiyatu poṉ matil cūḻ
kaṭi kŏṇ mānakar an niḻal katuviṭāt' akaṉṟa
puṭai kŏ' ṇīr nakar uṭutt' alai pŏṅku per akaḻi (2.1)

In a pool teeming with pearls
spilled in pain from the wombs of conch shells
swollen as pots, you can see
the great city circled by walls,
a perfect image of the Heavenly City.
And the water that is not swallowed up
by that image is the moat,
ruffled by waves, that surrounds
that city.

The "great city" is Māvintanakaram, Nala's home, probably something like Tenkasi in the mid-sixteenth century (as we can see in the nineteenth-century lithographs that accompany the earlier editions). Outside the walls there is a pool *(maṭu)* that catches the reflection of the whole city (encompassed by fortified walls), which thus looks to the beholder like the true form *(uruvu)* of Amarāvatī, the city of the gods, brought down to earth. But this reflection takes up only part of the expanse of the pool. The leftover watery surface is just that—a liquid, shimmering mass. Or is it? Maybe it, too, reflects something, such as the moat surrounding Māvintanakaram, in which case we have water revealing water: the same eye that takes note of the moat encircling the city sees this same liquid expanse in the peripheral part of the pond, the part not occupied with the reflection of the walled town. Another possibility, the first that comes to the commentator's mind, is that the Heavenly City, Amarāvatī, must have a moat around it, too, and it is that celestial body of water that is, as it were, visible in the pond's periphery. In this case, since the core image is, after all, that of Nala's mundane city + the moat, we would have water (of the pond) reflecting water (of that city's moat) that is as if reflecting yet more water (of the moat in heaven)—a triple vision that includes a double superimposition. A vertical axis, imaginative and figural (Amarāvatī descends to earth in the pool), transects the horizontal axis of immediate, physical reflection (Māvintanakaram in the same pool). In a way, this vertical axis displaces the horizontal one; the imagined city is the one that demands the reader's attention.

The *Naiṭatam* thus opens with a mirror. As Charles Malamoud has noted, Nala himself is a kind of mirror image, perhaps of the God of Love, Manmatha (among others), to say nothing of the four mirror images of Nala that turn up at the *svayaṃvara*.[36] Yet it seems that we are being offered at the outset a specific theory of reflections, one strongly linked to the Tenkasi epistemic system. Let us follow the traditional explication of this verse. Caravaṇappĕrumāḷaiyar aptly tells us that mirror surface and reflection are mutually exclusive. When you look at your face in the mirror, the image takes up a certain space; beyond or around that space, you see the mirror itself. Similarly, when you look in the pond at Māvintanakar, you see a reflection—identified by an imaginative leap with Amarāvati—and, all around it, the reflecting surface itself. On the other hand, this reflecting surface, as we have just seen, may itself be multilayered, a palimpsest of limpid and partially coincident images. There is a certain thickness or depth to the mirror. The one-to-one reflection that we see on the surface may, in fact, be the most superficial perception of all. Better to look deep inside. What is more, the surface reflection somewhat aggressively swallows up or seizes *(katuvu)* much of the available space.[37] In a way, one might prefer to look beyond, outside, the reflection; the part of the radiant surface that is not preyed upon by the image may actually be the more promising domain, the richest in potential being and, for that matter, the more real. There is something irreducible about the watery remnant with its waves washing over the edges of the reflection.

Let's not forget that it is the mind that brings the Heavenly City into play. Some imaginative move, probably existing a priori, seizes upon the surface reflection and uses it to project the inner vision outward. Actually, what is physically perceived is the water of the pond and, in part, the reflection of the earthly city—that and the other images of the pond-mirror. How easy it is to forget that Amarāvatī is nowhere near. Once the imaginative projection has been articulated and externalized, it more or less takes over.

But we have failed to pay attention to the opening line of the poem. This pond is filled with pearls that are swept away by the waves, or that are cast onto the shore, or that somehow rise to the surface, or that can be sifted and examined and ultimately polished—all these are possible meanings for Tamil *kŏḻi.* You can take your pick. These pearls are all born from conches, one of the standard sources for pearls in Indian literature (along with the joints of the bamboo plant, the temples of elephants, etc.). The conch grows the pearl inside itself, just like any other pregnancy, and gives birth to it in pain. But we are talking about reflections and coming to the surface. The seemingly innocent metaphor is deliberate and expressive. This is how mirrors give birth to reflections. The seed, naturally embedded in the conch, grows into a tiny, shiny, reflecting surface, a mirror within the mirror. The process may have little to do with any external object waiting to be reflected; indeed, this object is probably both secondary to and later than the germinating process inside the mirror. The reflection predates its external source; it is held inside the mirror, complete, rounded, autotelic, before it emerges in pain.

I want to suggest that this whole set of interlocking images, in their specific logical organization, shows us one possible picture of the *uḷḷam,* the inner space that more and more coincides with the mind and that is, in sixteenth-century Tenkasi, the true site of the imagination, the natural, conch-like, embedded aspect of mind as a creative or generative force. More precisely, the imagination activates and inheres in the brilliant images *(uruvu)* it organically produces and projects, though not uniquely in them. These images, born in the deeply internal mirror space, expand to fill from within the wider reservoir of awareness. By implication, a verse like this also speaks to the analytical profile of the person in his or her more creative aspect. The *uḷḷam* is primarily a domain of limpid depth, a transparent pool. It can, of course, be churned up by various internal, endogenous forces such as thought and desire. It generates images that may come to the surface and even take over that surface; imagination drives this unending process. "Reflections"—that is, imaginative projections, rich in existential potential—are conceived, held and nurtured inside, but never exhaust the rich resources of the depth. Moreover, the pool—that is, the depth of *uḷḷam*—is not passive. It can also *not* reflect. That is the degree of real autonomy for any person. External reflections may enter into this deep reservoir, may even swallow up a portion of its surface; such reflections come in with the breath and are then breathed out, suitably reconfigured by the imagining mind. Or the pool may swallow them and make them disappear. In any case, the pool never gives itself over completely to its reflections. The verse thus speaks to the capacity of the human being to create worlds inside himself or herself without using up the leftover potential of nonreflective being, and also to breathe these worlds out into an elastic cosmos, which may then reflect them back inside, a secondary and derivative perceptual event.

This two-way movement of reflection—inside to outside, and outside inward—continuously reshapes each of the domains. The imagination, as we have seen many times, does not produce ex nihilo but rather combines in novel ways the external sensory material flowing inward with internally generated percepts and concepts. But even to state the matter in this way is to reduce a complex process of epistemic interlacing to two simple linear tracks.[38] It would be closer to the underlying axiology to argue that no external image would be visible at all without such imaginative configuration and projection. As for internal forms, invisible to the outward-oriented eye, they realize themselves, in the sense of making themselves ever more real, by this continuous intrapsychic negotiation. Normally, after ripening organically, they will eventually pass through the porous membrane that initially surrounds them and claim attention as solid, credible objects, like Amarāvatī as seen in the pool. Note that the wider cosmology within which these processes take place, minute by minute, could be called "realistic"; at no point is there reason to doubt the integrity of objects per se.[39]

The generative *uḷḷam* we are observing is at once bounded (that is, autonomous) and infinitely creative. Its imaginative aspect is pointedly configured as a mirror within the mirror, in the specific sense of a submerged and generative depth. In my understanding, the "pearl-like" reflections in the pool are always singular. This notion of singularity should include possible shifts in the terms of their internal composition, that is, in the relations among their component parts or among further, perhaps superimposed or interlocking reflections, exactly like the three watery surfaces flowing into one another in the poem. Indeed, the *uḷḷam* is often preoccupied precisely with mapping out and making sense of these relations, which may underlie experiences such as falling in love, choosing the right word ("doubled"? "doubtful"? "direct"?), or trying to decide what is real. Each reflection, whether internally generated from the depths of the reservoir or originating outside, involutes differently; imagined realities are not fully amenable to prediction, though they are extremely susceptible to patterned figuration, as we have observed. Once alive in the mind, these reflections for the most part no longer reflect any outer source, nor do they represent. They are, however, the stuff of what we think we see.

— 9 —

True Fiction

Fiction, as a cultural category, is always a discovery or an invention, never a given. It arrives late in India. I am not speaking of fiction in the trivial sense of any nonfactual narrative, which is amply attested in India, as elsewhere, from very early sources and classed as *ākhyāyikā* or *kathā*, among other terms.[1] Think, rather, of fiction as embracing a distinctive kind of truth-claim, something that is neither true nor false in the usual sense and which is recognized as such (something we could call a "true illusion"). We have met a series of features associated with this kind of claim and appearing together, in a defined and intelligible pattern, in the south Indian sources of the period that concerns us. Let me list them briefly.

We have the distinction, quite natural to English but possible also in Sanskrit, Tamil, and Telugu, between what is "real" and what is "true," the former enjoying a certain advantage over the latter. There is a notion of the imagination as operating with relative autonomy and of the seemingly autonomous, basically uncontrollable status of those characters whom the imagination invests with life. There is an implicit model of the mind that situates states of "illusion," "hallucination," or "possession" within a self-generating continuum that is entirely internal to the mind, integral to its everyday operations, and linked with imaginative production. We have discovered in the *Naiṭatam* a mode of external framing that gives the listener or reader a particular cognitive advantage over the characters inside the framed text and perhaps even over the author or poet who narrates it. In other words, there will be lesser or greater levels of awareness that are intrinsic to the operation of this particular cultural mode and which can be made explicit upon reflection—although there is also the countervailing tendency to what I have called "absorption," a very powerful indication that we have been enticed into this fictive mode.[2] One has to posit a new kind of audience that is capable of such absorption, always inflected in a highly personal way. I have also hinted that such developments require a professional poet or author who assumes personal authority for the text he or she has brought into being.[3]

I claimed in the previous section that the Tenkasi poets, and in particular Ativīrarāmaṉ, conceived works that were very close to the analytical category of literary fiction; in my view, the Tenkasi poets pioneered such works in Tamil. It is more than likely that they were influenced, in this respect as in others, by revolutionary changes in the Telugu literary world dating from the early sixteenth century, the height of imperial expansion at Vijayanagara, far to the north of Tenkasi. The first half of the sixteenth century saw the composition in Telugu of a set of closely related, heavily intertextual literary masterpieces usually referred to today as *prabandhas*—large-scale, integrated compositions, each by a single author, fictional in the modern sense, also realistic in a way, and meant to be read through from beginning to end, as one might read a novel.[4] This literary explosion in Telugu was profoundly linked to the new interest in the imagination and to an analysis of its prevalent modes of operation, as we will see. Our primary example is itself a bold attempt to define the human as a cultural domain and to explain the origins and dynamics of this domain: this is Allasāni Pĕddana's *Story of Man* (*Manu-caritramu*), composed during the reign of the famous king Kṛṣṇadevarāya (1509–1529), himself a major poet.[5]

The *Story of Man* is the kind of book that miraculously articulates the vision of an entire civilization at a particular moment in its history. However, Pĕddana did not invent his story. He took it from the classical *Mārkaṇḍeya Purāṇa* (chapters 58–63), which he must have read either in the Sanskrit original or in an early Telugu version by Māranna. He adheres for the most part to the original story line, though everything else is radically transformed. I am going to review this story only up to a certain point, which happens to coincide with the part of Pĕddana's poem that is seen by the Andhra tradition as a relatively self-contained unit of exquisite poetic power. Our interest lies less in the narrative than in the particular poetic vision and its textures and devices, but to understand those, we need to know how the tale begins.

This, then, is the story of the first human being; more specifically, it is a story about how one might begin to generate such a being—what elements are necessary, and in what kinds of permutations and combinations. The human being in question is Svārociṣa Manu, the First Man of an earlier *manvantara* or cosmic age. His story resonates strongly with those of other Manus, especially Vaivasvata Manu, the First Man in our own segment of cosmic time; also with far more ancient, Vedic anthropogonies.[6] As we will see, the First Man is not first in a chronological sense; many human beings preceded him. He is, however, a model for what constitutes the human being, especially in terms of his awareness and its convoluted genesis. In this respect, the pivotal figure in the text is Manu's grandmother, the divine nymph Varūthini.

9.1. The Frame: An Innocent in the Himâlaya

There was once a Brahmin named Pravara, who lived in the city of Aruṇâspadam, on the banks of the Varaṇā River, somewhere in the plains of middle India. This Pravara suffered greatly from wanderlust. His deepest longing was to see the famous pilgrimage sites he had heard about, especially those in the high mountains. One day a wandering Yogi gave him an ointment that, smeared on his feet, would allow him to travel throughout the world. Pravara took off at once for the Himâlayas. But after an hour or two of wandering over the cold slopes, where he was amazed by the novel sights and sounds, he was ready to go home for lunch. Alas, the ointment had washed off his feet in the snow; Pravara was stuck. In his distress, he came upon an *apsaras,* a divine courtesan, playing the *vīṇā;* thinking she could perhaps direct him southward, he ventured to speak to her. But this woman, Varūthini, at once fell in love with the radiant and handsome Brahmin. She used all her womanly arts and eloquent words to seduce him, but Pravara steadfastly refused her invitation, even pushing her away violently with his hands. He then prayed to the god of fire, begging him—in what is called an "act of truth," *sat-kriyā*—to take him home; Agni agreed to this request and spirited Pravara back to Aruṇâspada. Exit the hero of the first two cantos.

Varūthini was left aching with unrequited love and desire. Each passing moment, each subtle shift in the natural rhythm of day and night, only intensified her pain. But at this critical juncture, as her life hung in the balance, a divine *gandharva* (who once had wanted her but had been rejected) saw his opportunity. Magically adept, this *gandharva* took the shape of the absent Pravara and presented himself to Varūthini, who was, of course, overjoyed. This false Māyā-Pravara declared himself ready to sacrifice his body, and his dharmic scruples, to save Varūthini's life—on condition that she fully satisfy him and that she keep her eyes tightly shut during their lovemaking. She agreed:

In a rush of passion, she held him
with her burning breasts,
and they kissed, searching
for the very roots of their lips.
Flooded by desire, she bit him,
fell, exhausted, to the bed,
and now she was begging him
as gently he slapped her cheeks
to draw out her moans,
and there was anguish, still, and absence,
given voice in words
though her whole body thrilled to his touch
and her mouth was crying out in joy
until slowly, little by little,
the sounds of praise grew softer
and she lay quiet, eyes closed, cheeks glistening,
her movements now controlled,
while her jewels and bangles also
ceased their wild ringing.

That was the first time: and he
flowed like water in her loving. (3.116)

Soon Varūthini became pregnant with the physical seed of her *gandharva*-lover that fruitfully combined with the burning image of the real Pravara in her mind. Māyā-Pravara was bored and restless—and also afraid that she would somehow discover his deception and curse him. So he took his leave with disingenuous, brutal phrases: "Neither union nor separation are permanent states. Don't lovers come and go? If I go, will my devotion to you diminish?" Once our debts to the past are paid—this is the poet speaking—even a love as dear as life itself will fall away.

Eventually Vāruthini, doubly abandoned, gave birth to a boy, Svarocis, who, after many further twists and adventures that I can't pursue here, fathered Svārociṣa Manu, the First Man.

What does it take to produce a human being? One needs, of course, the material, biological component, here supplied by the disguised *gandharva.* But probably even more crucial to the enterprise is the mental, imaginative component—the image of the beloved Pravara that has been imprinted on Varūthini's mind and which remains there, alive, active, and potentially generative, exactly as the classical Nyāya model of perception would have it.[7] But something has changed dramatically in relation to the classical model. The *saṃskāra* impression buried in the mind now has to be projected outward onto an external simulacrum, an ersatz figure capable of carrying the projection forward, extending it, fleshing it out, and folding it back into the internal, physical space of the projecting subject. Indeed, the poet's whole attention is directed to the meaning and implications of this mental process, with its intrinsic delusional aspect. The logicians' *bhāvanā,* a causally effective feature of the mind capable of allowing the initial impression to resurface in all its vividness, has become an act of the projective imagination, *bhāvanā,* in its sixteenth-century configuration. Unconscious cognitive error is now a normal, apparently necessary part of conception. A human being is born when a physical, sexual event meshes with a metaphysical, imaginative one through displacement and delusional projection. Moreover, the subject whose mind enacts such a trajectory remains unaware of what has happened; only those outside the story, the readers and observers together with the poet, can see it.

All this is spelled out for us by Pĕddana in several lucid verses. Listen, for example, to how he describes Varūthini at the cruel moment Pravara—the "real" Pravara—disappears:

> The Brahmin had gone, but *she*
> fixed his perfect image
> in her mind as, drowning
> in grief, her self-possession badly shaken
> by the constant twanging of the bowstring
> in the hands of Love, unable to stay still
> in that place, she wandered over the mountain slopes
>
> searching for the Brahmin's footprints,
> searching for some trace and finding
> none. At last she turned back
> with her companions, but in her mind . . . (3.3–4)[8]

This is the opening to the long passage that brings us deep into Varūthini's mad world of unappeased desire—the passage that will most interest us here. Dozens of complex verses reveal what exactly is going on in this woman's mind. But the very first thing we learn is that she has kept alive the image of her lost lover, an image that she actively fixes in her mind, *bhāvambuna nilpi,* as if engraving it in some receptive material, storing it for future access. She is the agent here, not at all a passive victim of the Love God's attack from the outside, as it were—though she is unsettled by the "constant twanging" of his bowstring. *Bhāva,* "mind," is, first, the domain of crystallizing feeling—not yet quite "imagination," *bhāvanā;* we are at an early stage, before the appearance of Māyā-Pravara. In any case, we can see that Varūthini is entirely caught up, even possessed by a private vision—that she cultivates and intensifies this vision in an internal space of her own. Remember that we have been speaking about a certain capacity for "absorption."

Now look at the moment, or process, of conception:

Her celestial lover, who made love to her
in that Brahmin's form,
had ordered her to close her eyes—
for *he* was afraid.[9]
She, clinging to him
in the fullness of her desire,
had agreed—so this condition
was fulfilled, in an overpowering excess
of joy. And through that experience of deep delight,
the flame that was burning in Pravara's body
became magically kindled
in the *gandharva*'s form, now held fast
in *her* unwavering mind.
Thus the child, a glowing fire,
was conceived and grew to ripeness
during nine months in her womb.[10]

So there is a hidden flame or glow, *tejas* or *dīpti,* linked with an externalized act of magic but nonetheless securely fixed in some imaginative space internal to the mind. Clearly, nothing could have happened without the fire that was lit in Varūthini's mind by Pravara's beauty—without, that is, her passion for him and the mental image seared into her consciousness.

This mental image continues to produce real effects even in the absence of the living person who inspired it. Creativity is not a technical achievement. Some deeper engagement, fueled by desire and fed by imaginative process, is required.

Actually, I have to confess that the more I read this text, the less certain I am about Varūthini's failure to sense that something a little irregular is going on. That is to say, I am not entirely convinced that on some level, below the threshold of articulate awareness, Varūthini does not actively invest in the adventitious and rather useful illusion. But for the moment let us stick with the assumptions I have spelled out (which are shared by all Telugu commentators and critics) and allow her to imagine that Pravara is the father of her child.

9.2. A Map of Poetic Projection

In fact, we know a good deal more about Varūthini's consciousness. In a sense, it is the central concern of the whole poem—certainly of the third canto, the core of the story and by all accounts the peak of the poet's craftsmanship. Anyone who comes to these verses while reading straight through the text immediately notices a change in style relative to the earlier, conversational passages (Varūthini's unhappy dialogue with the first, real Pravara). Suddenly we find ourselves in a densely surreal world, where everything that happens—the simple daily dramas of sunset, darkness, moonrise, moonset, dawn—takes on a charged, almost lurid quality. We see these natural events through Varūthini's staring eyes or, rather, feel them through her body, aflame with unappeased desire. It is as if the outer world were coursing through her, each intricate inset of landscape or skyscape correlated quite precisely to the painful excess that is flooding her mind—so all that the poet reports to us, his extraordinarily complex ornaments and figures, although ostensibly keyed to the exterior, actually paint a very lucid picture of Varūthini's inner state. We know this principle well: the ancient Tamil poets called it *uḷḷurai uvamam,* the "interior landscape" that A. K. Ramanujan made famous in the West, that is, the mirror-effect of inner *(akam)* and outer *(puṟam)* states.[11] The operative assumption is that inner and outer domains should correspond in experience, or in the perceptual and emotional field the poet portrays. But Pĕddana has taken the technique in a startlingly new direction; he wants us to see into Varūthini's mind, to observe the sudden transitions, the subtleties and nuances, and the attendant bodily states, via the indirect projections of these perceptions onto the exterior—the very same mechanism that will eventually allow Varūthini to identify (actually misidentify) her lover and, in the end, to conceive a child. We thus find ourselves in the domain of a new psychology, one in which imaginative projections can be studied as such, in all their intensity and specificity. Here is one key to the freshness and innovation of Pĕddana's poem: speaking in his own narrative voice, the poet presents us with a map of his heroine's imagination, which happens to coincide with his own.

Pĕddana and Varūthini seem more or less equally absorbed in their shared fantasies. There is even a verse that makes it clear how closely the poet has identified with his heroine:

> "Though she loves no other man,
> that cruel, self-centered
> scoundrel of a Brahmin
> has gone away and left her prey
> to the tortures of Desire, her body
> helpless against his lethal
> arrows of flower." As if in rage
> and terror at this thought, the sun,
> heaven's glowing jewel,
> turned red. (3.10)

In other words: the sun began to set. This is the figure known as *utprekṣā*, which we studied earlier.[12] The sun turns red as if in anger at Pravara's unfeeling act of desertion. For us, the point is the poet's disclosure of his own sympathies. He is clearly on Varūthini's side. So unambiguous is this statement that many Andhra connoisseurs insist this verse must be an interpolation: how could Pĕddana show such anger toward a Brahmin who was, after all, only sticking to the dharmic path, probably because he was interested not in some merely physical and transient pleasure (*bhautikânanda*) but in an enduring mental ecstasy (*mānasikânanda*)?[13]

It is not only a matter of sympathy, however. The deeper point, which has strong metapoetic implications, has to do with the nature of a shared intoxication and the operative modes of the imaginative faculty that has produced this state. Pĕddana shows us the world as Varūthini perceives it, that is to say, in an exuberance of lyrical distortion that has made this passage one of the most famous in classical Telugu literature. A set of discrete epistemic vantage points helps to shape Pĕddana's poetic experiment. To see what this means in practice, we are going to look briefly at four examples, one for each moment of natural transition from sunset to sunrise in the course of Varūthini's endless night of longing (*viraha-vedanā*).

9.2.1. *Sunset*

Tigers sleeping in deep mountain caves
  wake to drink at blood-
  red streams.
Deer roaming the grassy slopes
  tremble at the sight of a sudden
  forest fire.
The highest branches of the trees seem to be hung
  with the ochre clothes of a million
  wise men.
The gods flying above
  these craggy peaks
  come down to land on what they think
  must be the Golden Mountain.

With gentle flames
red as *kiṃśuka,* as coral or *kuṅkam* petals
and other bright red flowers,
a dying sun burnt that
unmoving mountain. (3.11)[14]

To understand the verse, one has to know that red, ochre, and gold are all variants of the same color in the south Indian chromatic universe. Like all of Pĕddana's depictions of the natural world, this poem is charged with a mantic quality derived from the mathematical and musical properties of iconically ordered sounds. Such verses are, in other words, hardly "descriptive" at all, in the ordinary sense of the word. Rather, they enact their own discursive contents. Notice, for example, how the poet's eye (seeing through Varūthini's eyes) slowly moves from the ground up—from the grassroots level of the mountain streams to the grassy slopes, then up to the higher branches of the trees, and finally to the peaks. Pĕddana follows the dying sunlight, its angle rising as the sun itself sinks lower, as if language itself were pitched on a diagonal and continuously in movement. In fact, the external movement gradually accelerates and intensifies as the poem reaches, almost literally, toward a climax.

Note that the initial four "sentences" (syntactically and metrically distinguished from the final segment) are each structured around the figure of *bhrāntimat,* "misperception"—actually the master trope for the entire *Manu-caritramu.*[15] Thus the tigers think the streams bathed in the red of sunset are flowing with blood, the deer think a forest fire has broken out, and so on, but they are wrong. The reader knows something that those who are inside the poem do not, and the charm of the verse depends on this gap in knowledge. A similar gap positions the reader in a privileged vantage point vis-à-vis Varūthini more generally as she slips further into madness.

The contrary movement of sun and light suddenly collapses in the final segment, and the meter also changes (to *teṭa-gīti*). We are subjected to a jumble of objects of comparison (*upamāna*), all familiar standards of redness. The very cumulation suggests that such similes have been superseded—as if redness had overwhelmed all conceivable vehicles, had transcended similarity itself. That is how red the landscape looked. We could also say that language is sometimes capable of intense supralinguistic effects—in part by turning back on itself or into itself. In the nascent fictive world of this Telugu *kāvya,* a self-contained space has been carved out somewhere in the depths of language, a space where, though cut off from normal reference, everything that happens, however distorted or seemingly surreal, is utterly real in terms of perception and affective texture, and perhaps in a wider or deeper sense as well.

Finally, the translation seeks to capture the fact that the point of greatest tension in this verse, like in most Telugu poems structured around head rhymes, is in the opening syllables of the final line: *an-nagambuna,* "that unmoving mountain." Sanskrit *na-ga*—"not moving"—is a common synonym for "mountain," and its appearance here is clearly meaningful. A verse dramatically alive with movement comes to rest on something that never moves. Perhaps this culmination reflects a more pervasive tension situated in the depths of the mind (Varūthini's mind? The poet's? The reader's?).

9.2.2. *Nightfall*

Blacker than the blackness
of the Tribal Hunter in disguise,[16]
who smeared her whole body
with black musk,

accepting homage from the black beauty
of Lotus-Eyed Krsṇa,[17] dancing with black
peacock feathers on his crown,

unsettling the pride of the Black River[18]
with its flocks of black geese,

swallowing up the slopes of Black Mountain[19]
and all the forests of Night Trees,

darkness spread the deepest
black brilliance of crows, peacock's throat
and cuckoo, elephant herds,
blackbirds, or massed monsoon clouds
through all concave space.[20] (3.19)

The commentators class the dominant figure as *nidarśana,* "exemplification," "pointing," or, better, "modeling"—one of the more complex and opaque of the traditional figures. An implicit comparison is set in place between two quite unlike (even impossibly unlike) items whose qualifying features can be shown to mirror each other (*bimba-pratibimba-bhāva*). Mirroring goes beyond mere similitude in the direction of a well-integrated, complex, and dynamic set of shared or parallel features, a systemic congruence. The blackness of night thus shares with the great variety of objects of comparison the qualities of density, depth, continuous expansion, and so on.[21] For our purposes, what matters most is the logic of iconicity present in the opening segment. We could formalize it as follows: A certain black feature or attribute (e.g., musk, peacock feathers, etc.) is superimposed on a black object of comparison (*upamāna*—e.g., the hunter's body, or Krishna's body), thus intensifying the blackness—which is then explicitly superseded by the subject of comparison (*upameya,* which only appears at the very end of the poem). So: X is black. Y blackens X further, on the surface. Z (the true subject) is thus not unlike X + Y but actually much blacker (also much blacker than all known or possible X's). (As in the previous example, this verse crescendos in a list of black standards of reference that effectively shreds the standard mechanism of the simile.) So Z is actually singular, though we know this singularity only by contrast with all previous, less-than-singular objects of comparison. It is as if one went *through* the primary subject and beyond all the usual ways of speaking about it, into an experiential or perceptual domain quite resistant to comparison or, for that matter, to description of any kind. By the end, space itself has become concave, thus receding into infinite depth, and profoundly black, though this blackness varies in intensity. But what space are we talking about? I think we have entered into Varūthini's mind, with its embedded pools of darkness opening up into ever deeper and darker recesses.

9.2.3. *Moonrise*

> Time smears his eyes
> with the magic of darkness,
> makes the stars his grains of rice,
> mixes in the red quiver of moonrise
> that could be a hapless traveler's blood
> and sprinkles this offering in the eastern sky.
> Now he can see the spot marked
> by the black banyan in the moon, and sure enough,
> digging there, he uncovers
> the hidden treasure, glowing
> with gold, that *we* call the moon—a gift
> set aside for the God of Love.[22] (3.21)

A complex series of metaphorical identifications (*rūpaka*) is extended to the limit and rationalized by a rudimentary story. Here is the basic idea. A person looking for buried treasure is supposed to smear his eyes with the magic ointment of collyrium that produces a sort of X-ray vision. He can now see where the treasure must be buried—by the sign left to mark the spot by the original owner/robber, in this case, as often, a tree. Normally, a hungry demon or two will be guarding the treasure, and in order to distract them or appease them, the treasure hunter will make an offering of white rice mixed with blood (perhaps that of an unfortunate passer-by), just the kind of food demons adore. Once the demon-guard has been disposed of, the treasure hunter can proceed to dig up the hidden gold. All these elements are spelled out in relation to embodied Time, Kāla or Kāla-puruṣa, searching for the gold he knows must be there close to the dark mark in the moon (variably identified as a hare, a deer, or a banyan tree). Possibly Time has come back to reclaim a treasure he once hid and forgot. Darkness serves as his collyrium, the red tinge of moonrise is the blood added to the white rice composed of stars, and the treasure ultimately revealed is the golden moon itself—here offered, probably in vain, to the

God of Love in the hope that the latter might desist from his habit of torturing separated lovers (like Varūthini). Please forgive me for spelling this out, thereby ruining the charm of the poem.

We can observe, in passing, that this verse condenses themes that color the entire passage of Varūthini's love madness. It combines, almost nonchalantly, the elements of a violent innerness, twisted and lurid perception, rituals of sorcery (including the sorcery of poetic speech), a meditative and painful awareness of space and time, and the strong sense of uncovering or revealing a hidden reality that is far beyond the bounds of sanity and that is at work in the heart or mind. Once again surreal figuration convincingly claims for itself an indubitable psychic realism. A world is being built up for us, one strangely autonomous, emotionally viable, real enough in its own terms, yet also deliberately distorted relative to the familiar world that we inhabit when we are not reading poetry.

Time, the grammatical subject of the verse, probably repeats the search for hidden treasure, a little pathetically, night after night. Perhaps Time is driven by greed. At several points Pĕddana introduces us to Time as a thinking agent, a living person equipped with intention—usually in the service of desire, as in this verse (but why should Time have to make an offering or give a gift to Desire?). In the present instance, it is as if the tortuous hours of Varūthini's night alone had crystallized into a specific, rather menacing presence. Recall what her lover, Māyā-Pravara, will later say to her as he leaves her: "Neither union nor separation are permanent states. Don't lovers come and go?" Peddana's characters inhabit a world heavy with temporality in its several modes—the very opposite of the unchanging, timeless universe of poetic essences that is sometimes, wrongly, said to inform classical Sanskrit *kāvya*. Here Pĕddana, moving toward something akin to "fiction," thematizes the uneven time of human experience as something intrinsic to any conscious world. Even more striking is the nonexplicit yet pressing sense that Māyā-Pravara is speaking for, or as, the poet himself, the purveyor of illusion of another sort. How precarious is his delusion, and how potentially creative! The poet can leave us stranded at any moment. In effect, he promises to do just that. This is the risk we take as readers and one of the dangers embodied by a good poet—a danger much more severe, in my opinion, than what Plato warns against. Viewed in this light, the complex verse we have just read is yet another metapoetic statement about perceptual displacement and the generation of a certain type of evanescent yet precious, indeed priceless, experience. The gold, that is, is real.

9.2.4. *Dawn*

Look at this row of lamps:

Yesterday, at sunset,
  they stole the Sun's red glow.
Now he's coming back
  to claim it.
So they've hidden it in the corners
  of the eyes of women
  worn out by a night of love
  (who owe them something for the daily gift
  of soot for their mascara)
and in exchange have taken on
their paleness
as a mask.[23] (3.56)

It is dawn, just before sunrise. The lamps are soon to go out, and already their light pales in the glimmer of morning. The poet (speaking through the mouth of Varūthini's companions) explains. There is a certain red glow, another precious treasure—in this case, the one that naturally belongs to the sun, but which has been stolen from him the previous night at sunset. This is a very old theme in India. The *Brāhmaṇa* texts tell us that the light of the sun is fragmented at nightfall into the many fires lit on earth; one purpose of the morning rituals is to reassemble these fragments into the rising sun.[24] Here, however, the lamps are reluctant to relinquish their treasure or to restore it to its rightful owner, so they look for a place to hide it. Very fortunately, young women who use the black lamp soot each day as kohl or collyrium to make up their eyes owe the lamps a favor—so, repaying the debt, they agree to let the rubescent cache of light lurk in the corners of their eyes. Now we know why women who stay awake all night making love have red eyes.

I think this slight verse is the most beautiful of the four I have selected. In any case, we have, once again, an *utprekṣā* based on a delightfully improbable causal sequence (also on naturalistic observation of what happens to oil lamps at dawn). But see how close we are to Varūthini's own, still hidden destiny, with its necessary masking, hiding, and creative delusion. As in the *Brāhmaṇa* example just mentioned, here, too, we find the idea of a necessary and creative exchange that keeps the gift somehow alive and accessible—that provides the conditions for sunrise, on one hand, and for fulfilled (displaced) desire, on the other. Put schematically, the vital glow is stolen, appropriated, then further displaced and disguised before it re-emerges as the light of day: the same series of acts that produce the new human being or, perhaps, the new poem.

9.3. The Limits of Fantasy

What is different or new about this early sixteenth-century essay on being, or becoming, human? What marks off these verses from the daring and often wildly surreal tropes of the great Sanskrit poets such as Bhāravi and Māgha? Many of the figurative techniques are clearly quite similar, even if Pĕddana is the first to produce such complex textures in Telugu. The materials were all present before him. And yet Pĕddana's "Story of Man" does constitute a kind of breakthrough—in effect, the creation of a new genre or, if you prefer, of a proto-generic mode of imaginative enterprise. I want to spell out several defining analytic characteristics of this new mode that seem to me to be critical to a strong notion of literary fiction in its south Indian guise.

1. *The personal and individual character of imaginative perception.* Each of the verses we examined ostensibly deals with externality—the temporal progression of a single evening and night. But each of them turns out, on closer inspection, to reveal an aspect of internality, as if the outer world had been conscripted to reflect the mind of the observer, the true subject of the canto as a whole. We can enjoy the brilliant images of sunset and nightfall in all their hallucinatory intensity, but it is Varūthini who interests us most of all. We are seeing the world through her eyes and with something of the texture of her feeling. Once again the principle of singularity becomes important: the figurative techniques may be familiar, as are some of the themes, but their particular configuration, linked to a nonrecurring perception, is in each case unique, like the lovesick heroine herself. Thus the ancient south Indian axiom that outer and inner domains must be powerfully connected, resonant, and mutually reinforcing is taken to a new level, which explains and rationalizes the linkage: the irreducible individual sees the world in his or her particular (often distorted) way. No wonder, then, that we find a correspondence; nor do we need to look far to find its source.

2. *Perceiving as imagining.* Such acts of seeing are never simple records or reproductions of external impressions. Nor are they reflections in the usual sense of the word in English (they may, however, be the stuff of reflections in Tamil, Telugu, or Sanskrit, that is, creative crystallizations

from a deeper reservoir of seeing and knowing, as noted in the previous chapter). Rather, they—indeed perceptual acts of any kind—are organized imaginative ventures. Generally, they take the form of projections outward from an active, image-producing mind. In effect, under the heightened conditions of her madness, Varūthini sees what she imagines. But madness, though perhaps helpful, is not a necessary condition for such projective acts, which are probably normative for everyone, though we pay them little attention.

3. *The generative, that is, consequential, nature of the imaginative act.* The explicit themes of the book repeatedly enact this basic principle. Varūthini fixes the image of her absent lover in her mind; all that subsequently unfolds depends on this first mental movement on the threshold of further imaginative work. As the process accelerates, it rapidly drifts into consequential distortion. Just as sexual generativity requires a dimension of mental and physical displacement, so does the life of the imagination—anyone's imagination, with its inherent singularity—depend upon just such twists and folds. Sexuality—fantasy-driven desire—happens first, and most crucially, in the mind. Distorted cognition seems to be intrinsic to it, as it is to the more severe, indeed pathological states that the imagination may induce and sustain (such as Varūthini's continuously intensifying hallucinations). Let me say again that all these states are now seen as endogenous phases of a single continuum ranging from what could be called "correct perception" to much more extreme experiences of love madness, imaginative deformation, and, at the end of the scale, psychosis or demonic possession. None of these states comes from the outside, and none is entirely marked off from the others. They offer vast scope to the poet, who studies the projections and displacements that shape the self-awareness of his heroine or hero in their profusion, variety, and creative power.

Thus the the mind—bounded, integrated, and whole—becomes the primary domain of application for the poetic endeavor, the proper workshop for "true illusions," and the natural subject matter for the poet. Moreover, the integrity of the mind now matches the integrity and the operational dynamics of the singular poetic text. Standing back a little from our source, we might say more generally that it is "fiction" itself, in this integral form, that motivates and sustains the generative moment. Or we could say that the poet, while deluding us, gives us something real that could also perhaps be true. One telling sign of the formative presence of fiction as a self-conscious category in a text such as Pěddana's is the transition (in

Canto 4) to a strikingly realistic mode: the poet describes in a graphic way never before seen in Telugu the violence and terror of a royal hunt. Once fiction is in place, realism also becomes conceivable.

4. *Heightened tension between real and unreal.* Fiction comes with an ontic claim, which can be formulated in more or less compelling terms. A mild statement would follow the logic of (2) above. Since perception is itself an imaginative act projected outward onto an existing world, its internal shaping imparts the sense of reality to what is seen. A stronger formulation would do away with the inner-outer divide altogether or relegate the outer sphere to the role of epistemic detritus; what is real is real *because it is imagined.* Unimagined objects are utterly unalive; they may be the only things not alive in the natural world of the sixteenth century in south India.

The integrity of the visionary world does not require a comparison with external objects that one might presume to be real. Precisely in this sense—*because of* the overriding ontic claims of the imagination—a tension between the notions of real and unreal survives, and may become still more intense than it is, for example, in the metaphysical world of the later poeticians. We saw how Ruyyaka and his successors insisted that if, in a work of literary art, the tension between real and unreal is resolved—either in the direction of seeing the poem or the poetic figure as a kind of mistake or misperception or in the direction of seeing it as entirely real and correct—then poetry itself disappears.[25] We can now go beyond this way of posing the problem, suggestive as it is. It is apparently the very twist or displacement inherent in extreme forms of imagination that, in Pĕddana's world, produces real results (the conception and birth of a human being). In other words, the implicit tension has defined empirical results. What Varūthini sees, and what we see through her eyes, is both entirely real and powerfully distorted.

5. *The person ruled by fantasy.* Take Varūthini as exemplary, a person inhabiting a world whose contours are continuously drawn and redrawn in the mind. Is there a constraint upon her fantasy or a limit to her projections? Yes: she suffers (twice) the sorrow of being deserted. She is not so mad as to be immune to such pain. Moreover, her dramatic imaginings, while personal in character, are heavily patterned; they draw on an available stock of themes, conventions, syntagmata, and poetic figures. Nonetheless, given these constraints, her life is ruled by recalcitrant images deeply rooted in her mind. She is, we could say, living these fantasies from minute to minute; they are the stuff of her awareness and, consequently, of

her experience; they structure the story she tells herself (and which the poet tells us in her name); they impart continuity and coherence not merely to her perceptions but to her very existence. (In this, Varūthini is no doubt very much like all the rest of us.) She thus has, in Pĕddana's presentation, a fictive self, real in exactly the terms just mentioned—though possibly not entirely subsumed by its own fictionality. We have arrived at a question worth pursuing in the remaining sections of this book.

6. *The systemic reorganization of the triad of poet-character-reader* so as to privilege the latter two members of the set. As we have seen, Pĕddana is present in his work via his identification with two of his characters—Varūthini, whose hallucinations he expresses and seems possibly to share, and the deluding Māyā-Pravara, the unstable, unreliable lover. Given these two personae, there is a sense in which the author is at once both internal and external to the frame of the work, both a purveyor of and subject to the illusion that constitutes its core. As Varūthini, the poet is utterly deluded, yet fertile; as Māyā-Pravara, he is sober, calculated, ostensibly clear-sighted, and fertilizing. More to the point, however, are the differing levels and degrees of knowledge that are now in play.

Let us try to spell them out. Varūthini, the subject of the chapter, is absorbed, first, in love madness that shapes the external world to its own contours and then, after night has given way to dawn, in an active delusional projection (she sees Māyā-Pravara as the original Pravara). She knows, explicitly, that she is suffering, that she is jealous of mortal women, that the Moon and the southern Wind are torturing her, and that things are getting worse—until suddenly they get better. The poet shows us her overheated, deteriorating states from his seemingly omniscient vantage point; he, of course, knows very well that her lover is a Māyā-Pravara, not the "true" Pravara. He tells us clearly that this is the case. And yet, as we have seen, Pĕddana is, like Varūthini, caught up in an intense, lyrical, intoxicating self-absorption. The technical content of his knowledge is perhaps less crucial than his surrender to the visionary reality of his mind, so attuned to hers—the mind of the character that he himself has created. Pĕddana, one might say, *knows,* only to forget. Though he has created this text and, in the introductory *avatārika* section, even explains the circumstances that led to his taking on the task, one can easily see those points at which he loses control.[26] These are the same points where his characters, although encumbered by an inherited narrative that cannot be changed in its essentials, take off on their own imaginative trajectory, dragging the poet along with them.

But what about us, the listeners or readers of this compelling text? We are clearly drawn into the hallucination—indeed, in a way it is this talent for absorption that in Pĕddana's world apparently makes us human and infuses the desire that activates both our listening and our loving—but though we are inside it, a part of us lingers outside. We, the listeners/readers, remain aware of the precarious, singular status of the imaginative reality that has enticed us. In this sense, we may even have a certain advantage relative to the author. We, too, are capable of being carried away—this is one reason we read books or listen to poetry—but we seem almost always to know where the boundary lies. We recognize fiction for what it is. Put somewhat differently, it is the reader or listener who sustains the highest degree of tension between real and unreal, with its attendant irony, its claim to imaginative autonomy, and its psychic or existential consequences. Might not the same be said for the reader of Cervantes, Pĕddana's near contemporary?

9.4. Summary: Toward the Novel

Pĕddana uses the inherited tools of the professional poet, including, above all, the available modes of figuration, to produce a self-contained narrative essay presenting the self-consciousness of its heroes and heroines as its primary subject matter.[27] Such a theme, and the particular techniques, framing devices, and hierarchies it seems to favor, requires at least a minimal notion of fiction as distinct from other modes or genres—the much earlier epic, for example, or the literary romances such as Subandhu's *Vāsava-dattā* or Bāṇa's *Kādambarī*,[28] or the contemporaneous explosion of historiography (*caritra, varalāṟu,* etc. in Telugu and Tamil). Perhaps it is not by chance that the discovery of fiction and a vogue in historiography appear at the same moment. Concomitant changes in the self-presentation of the poet, his or her relations with patron and audience, and the domain of operation natural to the poem are intelligible in the light of the novel articulation of imaginative process that occasionally breaks through the surface of Pĕddana's masterpiece.

Once the *Manu-caritramu* was present as a model, the way was open to much more radical experimentation. By the end of the sixteenth century, the new mode has firmly taken root. In effect, as I have hinted earlier, the literary tradition bifurcates in both Telugu and Tamil, so we find, on one hand, discursive novels (in verse) and, on the other, works of "pure" musicality almost cut off from referential language. (The latter type dominates the field in Tamil, the former in Telugu.) We might note in passing that both vectors are still twined together in Pĕddana in a manner oddly suited to his great theme of effectual illusion or creative misperception, with its implications for future poetic praxis.

Someone, I suppose, has to know the truth about the superimposed fantasies that drive our bodies and our hearts. If Pĕddana's heroine fails to understand this—to the end, she is gripped by a necessary delusion—at least the poet can see it and help us to see it with him. On the other hand, not even the poet can control his or her character to the end: this is in the nature of imaginative generation. Varūthini thus offers us an image of imaginative excess, rooted in displacement, that takes the form of extreme self-absorption; it is, I think, impossible to read this part of the *Manucaritramu* without discovering in ourselves something of this same heightened state. In this sense, the work is, exactly as its name implies, about us—about what it is to have a human mind that is capable of such compelling fantasy, now the hallmark of the mind's maturity and wholeness and, it seems, its implicit telos. To have identified this capability as a defining human achievement and to place it at the center of an integrated poetic work are indications of a profound cultural and conceptual shift. It would take only one more generation before Telugu poets could address more directly the question of the fictional character's final independence from her creator—before that is, the full-fledged novel could appear.

9.5. Penetrating the Image and Impacting upon Nature

Developments in both Telugu and Tamil in the mid- to late sixteenth century assume fiction as an available cultural category unambiguously linked to the autonomy and effectuality of the poet's imaginative acts. Moreover, as we have already seen, the imagination as a distinctively human mental capacity is explicitly thematized and explored in the novelistic works from this time. Such explorations sometimes take surprisingly rigorous and highly original forms. Piṅgaḷi Sūranna, active in Nandyāla and Ākuvīḍu in the southern Deccan toward the end of the century, is particularly interested in the reality-quotient of artistic creations: thus his heroine Prabhāvati falls in love with her lover-to-be, Pradyumna, when she dreams his image as painted by the goddess Pārvatī on a wooden board. This dream painting, a pure product of the goddess's own imagination (*saṅkalpa-mātra*), then emerges, entirely tangible and externally visible, into the everyday world of experience.[29] The next step in the ontic sequence is taken when Pradyumna himself, halfway through the novel, steps out of the painting as a living, feeling person. He has, by the way, gone through his own extended training in imaginative visualization, in the course of which he constructs a wholly mental but precise and perfectly real image of his beloved from the scraps of description and somewhat conventional metaphors he has garnered from various quarters (above all from a talking goose, Śuci-mukhi). Since we have discussed these passages at length elsewhere,[30] particularly in relation to the author's implicit theory of *bhāvanā*, it may be enough at this point to articulate the main principle involved: for the imagination to work as it should—that is, for the fully alive lover to turn up—the active imaginer has to penetrate through the visible, artistic image, whether situated in the mind or externalized in some tangible form, and reenvisage the imagined other in some always personal and singular way. A certain transparency, a regular and perhaps necessary feature of mental images evolving into substantial objects, thus comes into play.

Transparency—because one starts with the available surface, a conventional one, and penetrates through it to an unconventional reality. Here the *bhāvanā* of the Telugu novels diverges from the Yogic *bhāvanā* of the *Wave of Beauty;* the latter makes the imaginer over into the imagined as defined a priori (although, as we have seen, each such "engoddessment" entails its own singularity). For Prabhāvatī, however, successful imagining empties out the opaque image of the beloved so that another, newer image can begin to take shape. Everything depends on seeing through the shapes and contours of what was given (painting, verbal description, dream). This is not to suggest that the singular person who emerges—who is seen or imagined into being—has been created out of nothing; on the contrary, he or she exists within those very shapes and contours before they are dissolved by the imaginative force of the creative observer. Once dissolved, the pieces are normally put back together and enhanced or intensified by this same observer. But the person imagined in this way has a life and a mind of his or her own. Thus we, the active imaginers, always encounter a no less active imagined—engaged, we may be sure, in imagining us.

I hope you haven't forgotten that we are dealing with a work of fiction. You and I probably don't usually walk out of paintings. It is, however, possible that we bring a very real dimension of creative imagining, figurative and integrative along the lines just described, to the perceptual and interactive world of our everyday transactions, including our most intimate modes of being and relating to others. To envision a reality more real than any surface perception is the easy part of this process. Anyone can do it. (A minimalist view would assert that much if not most of our mental life is taken up with just such activity, much of it unconscious.) In the last analysis, the Sanskrit poeticians got no further than this point.

A truly radical model of the imagination emerges empirically, accessible to inductive generalization, only in the works of fiction in Telugu and Tamil in the late sixteenth century. In these works, the personal aspect of imagination reaches its full flowering. Whatever is deeply imagined must, by definition, be singular, irreducible, and personally configured. As such, it is also real—that is, if we are speaking of people, fully embodied in a living individual who is at least in part activated, even brought into being, by such visionary projection. What begins somewhere in the recesses of the mind eventually extrudes itself and becomes visible in the routine mode of external perception that at the end of the day may graduate from its relatively devalued status to a somewhat more honorable place in the hierarchy of perception. The rule, adumbrated in our previous section, would be: If we can see it, we must also have imagined it—that is, following Sūranna's logic, we must have seen through an original, rudimentary surface to a core that is now transparent, and at the same time resistant and quite autonomous. But even this description is inadequate to the conceptual world we are trying to define, on at least two counts: it reduces the process to a false unidirectionality, as if the standard evolution was from the inside outward, when in "reality" it clearly operates along both vectors, often recursively; and it fails to come to terms with the interlocking sociality of these imagined beings, that is, with the contingency of their coming into existence through concurrent or mutually dependent imaginings occurring either simultaneously or with a meaningful time lag in more than one effective mind.

In any case, it is clear that such a practiced and effective mind will impinge consequentially on its natural surroundings, in ways that go far beyond Varūthini's subjective, internal hallucinations. Let us take one last example, this time a single verse—the invocation—from Bhaṭṭu-mūrti's great work, the *Story of Vasu* (*Vasu-caritramu*), arguably the finest achievement of the sixteenth-century Telugu renaissance. This text was composed in Penugonda, near the southern border of the Andhra country, under the patronage of King Tirumalarāya some years after the major military débâcle of Tallikota and the loss of the imperial capital, Vijayanagara (1565).[31] Far from showing signs of a post-traumatic origin, the *Vasu-caritramu* is an exuberant work of daunting complexity and daring; and, like all the sixteenth-century Telugu masterpieces, it, too, is profoundly concerned with the imagination, as its opening verse states explicitly.

To understand this poem, one needs to know the following facts, taken from the classical tradition (in particular, from the first book of the *Rāmāyaṇa*). Indra, king of the gods, fell in love with Ahalyā, wife of the sage Gautama. Indra craftily found a way to get Gautama out of the house and then, after magically assuming the latter's external form, made love to Ahalyā. The absent husband, however, discovered what had happened thanks to his superhuman powers of visualization; enraged, he cursed both of the illicit lovers. Indra's body was covered by a thousand vaginas (eventually converted into eyes—hence Indra's title, Sahasrâkṣa, "Thousand-Eye"), and Ahalyā was turned into a rock. Fortunately, all such curses have an expiration date; Ahalyā was promised release from her petrified state when the man-god Rāma's feet came in contact with the rock. So when the adolescent Rāma, walking with his brother Lakṣmaṇa and the sage Viśvāmitra on the outskirts of the city of Mithilā, stepped on this particular rock, the lovely, suitably chastened Ahalyā instantly arose. Rāma then went on to win Sītā in Mithilā and to marry her shortly thereafter. We can assume that at the time of the wedding, Ahalyā's miraculous restoration was fresh in everyone's mind.

It may also have been particularly close to the surface of Sītā's consciousness:

śrī-bhū-putri vivāha-vela nija-mañjīrâgra-ratna-svalī-
lâbhivyakti varâṅghri-reṇu-bhava-kanyā-līlay añcun madim/
tā bhāvimpa śubhakramâkalanace dad-ratnamum gappu sī-
tā-bhāmā-pati provutan dirumalendra-śrī-mahārāyanin//

It is the moment of Sītā's wedding,
and suddenly she sees her own reflection
in the jewel set in her anklet,
and in her mind she imagines
that another girl has turned up,
touched by the dust on her bridegroom's feet,

but as the rite proceeds
he covers that jewel
with his foot.

May he, Sītā's husband,
protect our king.

An intricate vignette has been compressed into four dense lines that are meant to provide an auspicious beginning to the long work ahead. What could be more auspicious than a wedding? During the Hindu wedding ceremony, the bride and groom circle a blazing fire; the bride is also made to place her bare foot on the *sannikallu* or grinding stone (sometimes the groom does so as well). What is going on in the minds of Sītā and Rāma at this highly charged moment?

Sītā wears anklets studded with polished jewels. In the light of the fire, her own face, or perhaps the whole upper part of her body, is reflected off one of the jewels, no doubt on her right foot. But Sītā, like any young bride (she's only about fifteen or sixteen), is a bit flustered and excited, so it doesn't actually occur to her that what she sees when she looks down at her foot is her own reflection. She doesn't recognize herself (she's in her bridal costume, something quite new in her life). But she does see a woman, a stunningly beautiful one, and her mind immediately conjures up a slightly unnerving explanation. She has certainly heard what happened with Ahalyā not long before this day: how the dust clinging to Rāma's feet had touched the black rock, immediately turning it into that radiant figure. If this happened once, there's no reason to believe it couldn't happen again. Maybe every time her new husband steps on a rock, the rock comes to life; maybe every time this happens, there's another young woman and potential rival nearby, someone who has already been touched by Rāma and may have some claim on him. What kind of a life awaits her, with this vast host of rock-born, lightly dusted young women clamoring for Rāma's attention, hour by hour?

Panic sets in. All this, the poet tells us, in an act of imagination (*tā bhāvimpa* < *bhāvanā*) sparked by the misread reflection. Such reflections have an existential charge normally consequent upon an imaginative act or series of acts. So Sītā does have reason to be worried. We are halfway through the verse.

Now the solution emerges. Rāma, circling the fire with his bride, apparently realizes what is going on in her, and he acts to put her mind at rest: when the moment of stepping on the grinding stone arrives, he takes care to cover the disturbing jewel with his foot, so the reflection disappears, and with it any potential rivals or cowives also vanish. How does he know to do this? The precocious husband is fortunately endowed with the kind of empathic insight that his nervous young bride desperately needs at that moment. What is called for, the real point of the whole business of falling in love and getting married and all the rest, is to produce a person who is capable of that kind of imaginative and empathic knowing *without having to be told*. That, I propose, is what husbands (Telugu husbands, but they are not alone) are for.

But there is a more general and, in the end, more incisive point to be made. In the Ahalyā story as we find it in text after text, the transition from stone back to woman has a somewhat automatic aspect.[32] Usually it requires absolutely no intentionality on the part of Rāma himself. There is a curse, a linguistic template that operates within its own structured field; even God himself can only wander innocently into that field, and he, too, tends to be amazed by what happens. It's as if he had no part of his own in the miracle, which, in fact, is almost not a miracle at all; it's more like the operation of a natural law. Painful objectification—stony paralysis—gives way to reanimation when the prescribed trigger is activated. But in our Telugu verse, there is at least the possibility of a much more radical human intervention in the natural world. The trigger is no longer mechanical, and the transition itself not quite so innocent. Sītā's nightmare cannot simply be ruled out; to overcome it we need the interactive imaginations of both young people, with all the attendant anxiety, on one hand, and all the hoped-for empathy, on the other. But this is the easy part.

The more interesting suggestion, in my view, is that Rāma's act is no longer beyond our—and his—understanding, without any real personal involvement on his part. Sītā is not the only one endowed with an imagination. Nor is she the only person worthy of imaginative empathy. As we have seen, human beings, in all the great Telugu *prabandhas*—and very conspicuously throughout the *Story of Vasu*—are continuously projecting imaginative materials onto the world, always to substantial effect. Ahalyā's revival may thus have required, on some unspoken level, an imaginative investment or unconventional perception on Rāma's part, as if Rāma's mind were now an integral condition to such transitions in state—which is why Sītā needs this mind to be working for her, to be on her side. Indeed, her more serious anxiety would be prospective rather than retrospective: she has reason to be afraid that Rāma will be imagining young women into life moment by moment. Such things transpire in any living mind, in Rāma's no less than in hers; she knows this, and by his own experience of himself he knows that she knows it. Hence his eagerness to soothe and reassure her before things get out of hand. By covering up the reflecting surface, he temporarily puts an end to the threatening imagined reality that surface conjured up, a reality that had immediately taken on a life of its own in Sītā's mind. Imagination requires a limit precisely because it is so effectual even, or especially, when it feeds into a misperception. Crucially, Sītā's imagination (which dominates the first half of the verse), set in motion by her failure to recognize her own image, reveals by implication something of the liveliness and power of Rāma's imagination, and not only in the moment the verse ostensibly describes. He has, we can assume, the gift of seeing, or attending to, the woman locked in the rock (any rock). It is a gift he shares with Sīmantinī and other skillful imaginers.

Put more simply: we can glimpse a natural domain—perhaps defined in this period as both autonomous and rule-governed in a new way—that is impinged upon by human action, in particular internal, visionary, affective, and imaginative action, the most consequential kind of all. In both poetic and psychological terms, the entire verse rests on the critical moment at the opening of the third line where the poet tells us that we are dealing with *bhāvanā,* Sita's projection of mental contents, via the visible reflection, onto a relatively pliable and accessible natural reality. Something has intervened—some definitive human faculty—in the way this reality works. Rāma, who is only intermittently aware of his divinity (just as Sītā is unable to identify herself in the reflection), is probably, by this very configuration of his identity, more capable than most of practical imagining. Wherever he goes, reality changes around him. But he is also the closest model we have in this period for a fully active, thinking human being, a person imagining his or her way through a world partly shaped by such mental events.

Further conclusions flow from this exegesis. Please bear in mind that the verse in question, like all such invocatory statements, is thought to condense and articulate all the major themes of the work as a whole. The unrecognized, lucid self-image that is ultimately made to vanish is certainly a metapoetic statement about the kind of reality poetry can generate, about how we perceive or misperceive it, and about the way such a reality tends to evolve, its end always inhering in its beginning, and vice versa.[33] The sixteenth-century poets, perhaps like all writers of fiction, are given to such metapoetic touches, as if reveling in the freedom of imaginative production and eager to share this discovery with their readers. Such metapoetic reflection always has the further effect of deepening and reaffirming the ontic claim implicit in each crafted verse and in the lyrical narrative taken as a whole, that is, as an attempt to engage, on its own terms, with the issue of what is real.

A revolutionary regime of the imagination clearly took root over a period of two or three generations both at the imperial capital of Vijayanagara and at its peripheral extensions and epigones in the southern Deccan and in the far Tamil south (Tenkasi). Moreover, at roughly the same time that this reconfigured cultural world gave birth to a range of experimental works of literary fiction, all clearly aware of one another, it also produced reflective essays, in a variety of genres, on the mind and its newly defined capacities. We turn now to a Sanskrit work from a small court in northern Tamil Nadu of the mid-sixteenth century, a work that falls into this second group of texts and applies the logic of imaginative embodiment to imagination itself.

— 10 —

The Marriage of Bhāvanā and Best

10.1. An Allegory on the Mind

Once upon a time there was a king. He had a name: Best of All Males. In the context of our story, this name identifies him as a god, or as God—Viṣṇu-Puruṣottama. I'm going to call him King Best. Like all Indian kings, King Best had a harem full of beautiful wives that included the goddess of wealth and prosperity, Śrī/Lakṣmī, and the earth goddess, Bhū-devī, among others. This plethora of female companions didn't stop King Best from falling in love again, more passionately than ever before, with a young princess from a good family, a typically innocent but no less passionate creature named Bhāvanā, that is, Imagination. Like all good love stories, this one has its ups and downs, its moments of grave danger and imminent collapse, its confusions and alarms, as well as some—actually, rather few—playful and more or less happy scenes. I won't tell you yet how the story plays itself out in the end, but I'd like you to begin thinking about what it means for a man, and in particular a king with romantic inclinations, to fall in love with his imagination, a highly concrete, tangible, and personal (female) entity—or, one might say, with his own imagination of a woman, of the world they might share, and of himself; and to fall in love also with her developing imagination of him and love for him. For Bhāvanā, Imagination embodied, is equally in love with the man whose mind, or heart, she inhabits—that is, with the imaginer himself. Together, this couple shows us the mature south Indian theory of imagination in very tangible, intelligible form.

We'll be spending the next pages with King Best and his beloved. Our text is an allegorical play, very much in the honored tradition of Sanskrit dramatic allegories, by a south Indian Sanskrit poet from the first half of the sixteenth century, Ratnakheṭa Śrīnivāsa Dīkṣita. The play is called *Bhāvanā-puruṣottama* ("Imagination and King Best"); it is one of the few works by this highly prolific, erudite, and rather daring author to survive. By south Indian standards, we know quite a lot about Śrīnivāsa Dīkṣita and about the social and institutional setting within which he lived and wrote.[1] He was born in the Brahmin village of Tuppul, near the famous city of Kāñcipuram in what is today northern Tamil Nadu. Trained in the traditional arts and sciences, with a strong philosophical bent and a taste for rigorous nondualism, Advaita, he served as the court poet of one of the early Nāyaka kings, Sūrappa Nāyaka of Senji (Gingee—mid-sixteenth century), who gifted to him the whole village of Sūrappa-samudram.[2] Among the official titles this poet either received from his patron or invented for himself are Ṣaḍ-bhāsā-catura, "Proficient in Six Languages"—in itself an accomplishment not so unusual at these small, polyglot courts in the early premodern period in the south—and, perhaps more striking, Pratidina-prabandha-kartā, "Author of a Book a Day." We know the names of many of his lost works from the commentary by Bāla-yajña-vedeśvara (early nineteenth century) on a long poem by our poet's son, the famous Rāja-cūḍāmaṇi Dīkṣita, the *Rukmiṇī-kalyāṇa*. Like his father, Rāja-cūḍāmaṇi Dīkṣita fit the prototype of the prolific late-medieval polymath scholar-poet; his brother, our poet's second son, Ardhanārīśvara Dīkṣita, wrote a commentary in the Tantric mode on a popular work praising the goddess Tripura-sundarī, the *Ambā-stava*. This latter fact is significant, as it suggests that the family had leanings toward the Tantric cult of Śrī-vidyā. There is one more family connection of great importance to be noted. Appayya Dīkṣita, one of the true luminaries of sixteenth-century India, a scholar whose works spread throughout the subcontinent and revolutionized whole domains of knowledge,[3] was Śrīnivāsa Dīkṣita's son-in-law.

It is a matter of some importance to our argument that a highly sophisticated author such as Ratnakheṭa Śrīnivāsa Dīkṣita should have chosen the imagination, in the protomodern sense we have been exploring, as a topic worthy of a long essay couched in quasi-philosophical, allegorical form—just as we found it meaningful that Pĕddana, two decades earlier, had chosen the *Story of Man* as the frame for his essay on the new anthropology. By its very nature, however, and the constraints of the chosen genre, the *Bhāvanā-puruṣottama* is more directly discursive than Pĕddana's poem. In terms of our method, it is thus somewhat easier for us to extrapolate and abstract the conceptual propositions driving the author of this play. At the same time, we find these propositions for the most part in raw, dramatic form, not as honed philosophical or metapsychological statements. It is crucial to keep in mind that everything enacted here by or in relation to either the heroine, Bhāvanā, or the imagining hero in whose mind she resides tells us, often rather obliquely, something about the roles and functions of the imagination as Śrīnivāsa Dīkṣita and his readers or audience understood it. One of the merits of the play is the compelling quality of the story it tells; at moments it is quite possible to forget the metaphysical register that gives it a deeper meaning.

Thus the *Bhāvanā-puruṣottama (BP)* differs from some earlier Sanskrit allegorical plays, and in particular from Kṛṣṇa Miśra's eleventh-century *Prabodha-candrodaya*, the prototype and pinnacle of the genre, in the relative lightness of its touch.[4] Practically every line of the *Prabodha-candrodaya* is saturated with direct allegorical content; when characters such as Ahaṅkāra, "Ego Identity," or Mahāmoha, "Vast Confusion," or Śānti, "Peacefulness," speak, they almost inevitably give voice to the set of abstract traits or features implied by their names. Something of this Bunyan-like embodiment naturally survives in the *BP*, as does the polemical and heresiological tendency so pronounced in Kṛṣṇa Miśra; but the *BP* also allows for development of character and a certain lyrical expansiveness, particularly in Acts 2 and 5, as we will see.

10.2. Openings

Let me set the stage (as the Sūtra-dhāra or Stage Manager does in the opening scene). Here's the problem. Bhāvanā, Imagination, daughter of King Lord of Life (Jīva-deva), has a bad case of lovesickness. Her father is ruling in Nava-dvāra-pura, the Town of Nine Gates (that is, the nine orifices of the body), and is married to Hidden Memory of the Truth (Tattva-vāsanā). With parents like these, Imagination comes by her metaphysical inclinations honestly. She is in love with King Puruṣottama, Best of All Males, whose picture *(ākāra-lekhā)* she once saw when it was conjured up by a wandering ascetic woman named Knowledge of Yoga (Yoga-vidyā), in special circumstances: two playwrights, Slave of the Goddess and Slave of God (Śrī-dāsa and Viṣṇu-dāsa), were arguing over the merits of their two plays, presented at the royal court—one titled *God in the Mind (Cintā-mukunda)* and the second, *The Birth of the Elixir of Freedom (Apavarga-sudhodhaya).*

We know how jealous playwrights can be. Apparently, Knowledge of Yoga had produced the picture of King Best to help resolve the dispute, but the result was that the king's daughter saw it and was immediately stricken, rather like Prabhāvatī in Sūranna's novel. For someone gifted with an active imagination, a painting is always a rather dangerous contraption—a fortiori for someone who is Imagination itself (herself). In these dire circumstances, Knowledge of Yoga, taking full responsibility, has decided that the best solution would be to make King Best fall in love with Imagination. To this end she has sent a trained and articulate messenger named, as we might guess, Haṃsa, Goose, to Best's court with instructions to speak at length of Imagination's virtues.

The plan, we discover at the outset of the play, has worked perfectly: thanks to Goose's eloquence, King Best is prostrate with a lover's longing, exactly as Knowledge of Yoga had hoped. But a new difficulty has emerged. One of those heavenly voices that have a way of calling out of nowhere from time to time has announced to Imagination's father, Lord of Life, that his daughter would marry none other than the Lord of the World (Jagad-īśvara) and that the new son-in-law, because of his intense love for his bride, would make his father-in-law the Emperor of Lucid Discrimination (Viveka-sāṃrājyâdhipati). Moreover, as a result of doing away with darkness through various useful (ritual) means, Lord of Life also would become ultimately happy. Ever since Lord of Life heard this rather prolix, anonymous message, he's been trying to figure out just who the real Lord of the World might be, since, lured by the promise of becoming emperor, he's more than eager to give his daughter to him. But since the Town of Nine Gates seems to be a veritable hotbed of philosophical claims and counterclaims, there are quite a few candidates for the coveted title, and these days the court is given over entirely to heated metaphysical debates, as a royal court ought to be. How else would a typical Tamil king want to spend his days? As you might expect, Knowledge of Yoga has another plan to solve this crisis. She has seen to it that her elder sister, Voice of the Teacher (Guruvāṇī), is hired as Imagination's close companion (or nurse, *dhātrī*), so that she'll be on hand to reveal the truth at the suitable moment.

So things are looking up, in a way, except for the fact that both Imagination and King Best are so miserable. When he can't take it anymore, Best decides he'd better divert his mind by doing what kings do best—that is, hunt wild animals in the forest—so he's gone off on his great eagle,

Vainateya, to a wilderness called Heart of Everyone Stuck in the World (Saṃsāri-hṛdaya). This hunting zone is not far from the Town of Nine Gates, and Best is also hoping that he might somehow get a glimpse of Imagination's face. With him is his crown prince, Vedic Man (Veda-puruṣa). As we first see him, Best and the prince are pursuing a male deer named Natural Order (Dharma), who has been enticed and deluded by the beautiful doe named Desire (Kāmanā). Knowledge of Yoga, who is masterminding this scheme, observing all this in her mind's eye, sends her favorite disciple, Purified by Truth (Sattva-śuddhā), to enter the male deer and ensure that he leads Best and his party directly to the shrine of the goddess Tulasī on Añjana Mountain, where Imagination will also turn up shortly.

Allegory is always a little tedious. You can, if you like, put aside all the names and focus on the essentials. Imagination is yearning for a man—who happens to be a king who is God—after seeing his painted portrait. Best, the beloved, is similarly obsessed with Imagination, whom he has seen only in the verbal depictions of the messenger. Sooner or later, the two are bound to meet. As usual, this meeting is certain to evolve out of a doomed displacement. Best, who really needs to find Imagination, is out hunting someone else. Not by chance, since we are dealing with the imagination, a goddess is on call nearby.

10.3. Act 1: On Triggering and Revealing

We know about these wild-deer chases. Kālidāsa's fifth-century *Abhijñāna-śākuntala,* the most famous of all Sanskrit plays, opens with just such a scene (King Duṣyanta pursuing a deer in the wilderness), and this is by no means the only example in Sanskrit literature. Always the verses attached to this first appearance of the hunter-hero on stage deal with the strange compression in the space-time continuum that rapid movement engenders. Consider first the well-known Kālidāsa verse, spoken by the king (to his driver) as he stands on the back step of his chariot:

> What at first glance seems minute
> rapidly extends to vast proportions.
> What is cut in two
> is soon reconstituted.
> Whatever is naturally crooked
> straightens its lines

before my eyes.
Nothing remains far from me
even for a moment,
just as nothing
stays near.[5]

The *Śākuntala*, we might say, is all about reconstituting what has been cut in two—also about the familiar, rather lonely state in which everything is neither far nor near. Now compare this classical precedent with Śrīnivāsa Dīkṣita's statement, uttered by King Best:

yad drāghīyas tat tad eva hrasīyo
yan nediyas tad davīyas tadaiva/
yat kṣodīyas tan mahīyas tadānīṃ
citrâkāraṃ dṛśyate viśvam etat// (1.24)

Whatever is long
is truly short.
Whatever was close
is suddenly very far.
The tiny has become
immense, and everything
looks to me
like a painting.

We might take a moment to observe how Kālidāsa's vision of rapid movement—nothing remains either far or near, the crooked straightens itself out, and the discrete merges into a wider unity—is transposed in our text to a somewhat simpler and starker statement: close things are distanced, the extended is shrunk, the minute is enlarged. We could also translate the final line "Everything looks quite weird" *(citrâkāram),* but for reasons that will soon become clear, I think it's better to stick with the idea of a painting and the potential distortion, or freedom, that it offers the painter and viewer. Still more important for our purposes is the way this intertextual elaboration, with the inherent complexity and depth produced by the transparent reference to the intertext, feeds directly into the primary themes of the work as a whole. Suppose we take this verse as a statement about the qualities and mechanisms of the imagination, its potential for turning one thing into another (its opposite), and its relation to some form of artistic expression. Let me repeat: at virtually every step in this long drama, consistent but largely implicit statements fill in the ground against which the primary allegorical figure is played out.

As Knowledge of Yoga has planned, Best is led by the possessed deer—which, says Best to his driver, is far too beautiful to be slain but must be captured alive, to become a pet deer in his harem—to Añjana Mountain, near the river Kuñjarā. The mountain is also referred to as Śrīśeṣa-bhūmi-bhṛt (1.57), Snake Mountain, so it seems we are near the great pilgrimage site of Tirupati-Veṅkaṭam on the Andhra-Tamil border. Here there is an ashram named after a sage, Siddha, Perfected; also the temple to the goddess Tulasī, one of Lord Viṣṇu's wives, as we have seen. Best correctly conjectures that Imagination must be somewhere close by. He orders his mount Vainateya to take the form of a Clown companion, the Vidūṣaka; Best himself announces that he will put aside his extraordinary *(aprākṛta)* four-armed body and become a "human hero" *(mānuṣa-nāyaka)*—all this in the interests of finding Imagination. The change is immediate: Vainateya announces, in Sanskrit, that he has become a Vidūṣaka; from now on he will speak, as Clowns do, only in Prakrit. Best, for his part, declares that he is fully human *(aham asmi mānuṣa-nāyakaḥ).*

They find themselves in utopian surroundings. Deer delight tigers by licking them all over with their long tongues; young hawks feed wild rice to roosters, grain by grain; lions generously scratch the backs of female elephants that are fanning with their huge ears the many Yogis exhausted by their severe exercises. Interestingly, in this idyllic setting the mind calls up forgotten memories (of life in the holy city of Vārāṇasī, 1.29). But most intriguing to the two visitors, King and Clown, are the deer near the temple: they seem to be listening to something, heads bent, their eyes half closed and weeping. It soon becomes clear that they're mesmerized by a vina performance: some woman in the temple is playing the instrument with consummate skill and singing a plaintive song, a prayer to the goddess:

> Great goddess Tulasī, beloved of Viṣṇu,
> you who grant anyone's wish:
> please make *my* wish
> come true. (1.34)

Hidden in the bushes just outside the temple, Best and the Clown hear this woman's confidante complaining to her: "You've been playing that vina for ever so long, and still the goddess Tulasī hasn't given you what you asked for. She must be a heartless goddess." The Clown is ready to rush in at this point, but Best prudently suggests they wait; he doesn't want to shock the girl, though, glimpsing her through the branches, he is already responding with all the usual symptoms of advanced love madness (bulging eyes, copious sweat, and so on)—as the Clown readily perceives.

The girl's friend tells her again to put an end to the futile musical performance. No, says the young lady; this very day she has heard a miraculous, disembodied voice *(upaśruti)*—undoubtedly that of the goddess herself—promising that her wish would be fulfilled very soon. The Clown, always happy to take credit, rightly or wrongly, for some positive development, whispers into his companion's ear: "Wow! My cleverness really paid off. I'm the one who said that while hiding here behind the temple!" But the confidante is fully persuaded: "That means you'll certainly get your beloved." Best has the usual panic reaction of a hero in love: "Who is that lucky guy?"[6] His doubt is instantly dispelled by the girl herself: "Yes—but the Lord of the World, King Best, could he really be somewhere near? Still, what the goddess says can't be wrong." And as if that were not enough, the confidante addresses her friend by name: "My dear Imagination, I was also thinking the same thing."

Now that these tricky identity problems have been cleared up, at least for the moment, the Clown, with characteristic impetuousness, barges in:

CLOWN *(pulling Best by the hand and showing him to the two girls):* Madam, you're quite right. The Lord of the World might just be right here.

IMAGINATION *(scared out of her mind, but staring shyly and longingly at Best; to herself, reflecting):* So the Lord of the World might just be right here. But one might conceive of [*sambhāvyate*] some other king having just this sort of beauty. My eyes keep seeking him out. But I am totally determined[7] that only Best will be my lover. What shall I do? *(Aloud)* We'd better go. What's the point of staying here? *(Takes a few steps away, still looking with mixed shyness and hope at Best.)*

Best looks at the Clown.

CLOWN: Madam, is it right for you just to walk away without saying anything when the Lord of the World is right here?

Imagination looks meaningfully at her friend.

FRIEND: Sir—it's not just any old Lord of the World who will be this girl's lover. It has to be that Lord of the World who is bigger and better than Brahmā the Creator and Lord Śiva; who has totally trounced

> all demons and anti-gods, who is handsome as ten million Love Gods all thrown together, who has the skill to create the cosmos, and who has the most wonderful personality anyone could ever want.

CLOWN: You're talking about Viṣṇu the demon-slayer?

FRIEND: Who else?

CLOWN: In that case, this man could well be him.

FRIEND: What, a *man* could be *him?*

The girlfriend's skepticism is surely on target. A break in the conversation is urgently required. Perhaps the Clown thinks things are going nowhere, or perhaps he fears that the direction is a little confusing or even dangerous, touching as it does on the critical oxymoron of Best's identity. In any case, he wants to make sure that the girl doesn't disappear, so he complains that, whoever he and his friend may be, they haven't received the usual offering given to guests who turn up at an ashram. The girlfriend, who can see that Imagination is already overcome by passion, like a goose longing for the lotus pond, adopts the Clown's suggestion with alacrity and asks the two men to take a seat. The Clown takes his cue: "Actually, I think I'll just check out how all the trees are doing in this ashram. I'll be back soon."[8] And he exits, leaving King Best alone with the two women.

The king turns to the girlfriend: "Could you tell me what that Best Man whom your friend desires really looks like?" "He's well known," says the single-minded (and quite literal-minded) girlfriend; "he's got four arms, he's black as a monsoon cloud, he wears golden clothes and holds in his hands a conch and a discus—and he has a jewel on his breast." At this our hero, hearing himself described in his deeper or truer form as Lord Viṣṇu, is overcome with longing, so much so that he half reveals his divine body, exactly as she has just portrayed it. Imagination is shaken: "Either this young man is a fantastic magician," she whispers to her girlfriend, "or else he really is Best who has hidden himself in a human body." The girlfriend has come to her own conclusion: "Otherwise how could this young man be so dark, so handsome, so debonair . . . ?" And by now Imagination is sure, too: "My eye has never found such happiness in seeing another man, not even in a dream. This is the man Knowledge of Yoga predicted would be mine. There's no doubt."

The work of Act 1 has been accomplished. The two lovers have met and successfully negotiated the passage from a purely mental image of the beloved to the superimposition of that image onto a living, present, visible person. An interruption is clearly in order, and it comes when an urgent cry for help is heard offstage: "Come quickly! This ghoulish ghost [*brahma-rākṣasa*] is muttering something scary." King Best immediately understands: his bumbling, always famished friend the Clown has mistaken a dark Tamāla-Sāla tree for a ghost. The king will have to save him from his illusion. Anyway, says Best, it's time for the girls to go off to perform their midday tasks. High noon: the bees are resting inside the lotus buds, the geese are sleeping in the reeds on the riverbank, and even the Sun himself has plunged—in the form of his own reflection—deep inside the ponds.[9]

We can also take a short break. The complexities of Act 2 await us, but already we can see parts of the template the poet has put in place for his intricate essay. Inevitably, there is something here about reflections (also about painting, whether with colors or with words) as they are perceived in the mind with the galvanizing aid of the imagination. Does it make sense to ask if the Sun is "really" inside the ponds? Yes: the burning source of all heat is too hot for his own good and seeks relief. The Lord of the World is also too much for himself, and very much in need; he seeks help by shrinking himself into a manageable human form in which he may, if all goes well, meet the girl he longs for. A more abstract formulation would show us a great god looking desperately for an imagination or, perhaps, for his own imagination, which apparently exists autonomously somewhere outside of him. Were he to fail to find it, he would continue to suffer. Moreover, in his reduced, human persona, God is immediately assailed by doubt, a dependable feature of the human mind.[10] Can Imagination want *him?* She clearly wants somebody, but could it be *him?* When it turns out that she does indeed want him and only him, it is her turn to feel doubt. What to make of this human being who stands or sits before her, when she seeks someone fully divine? Perhaps imaginations are like that. Maybe it's all a kind of hocus-pocus. But no: she knows that what she is seeing with her eyes must be real.

"Real"—that is, present, tangible, palpable, knowable. As we know by now, the real is not isomorphic with the true. And Imagination, as I have argued, is mostly concerned with what is real. This is the first but not the last time that we will be seeing this theme in our play.

The most striking element in all this is the moment of revelation as it transpires suddenly within the god. Imagination describes him through the good auspices of her girl friend; describes him as she imagines him to be and as he knows himself to be, though he knows that he now looks quite different from this iconic portrait. Trapped in a human-divine amalgam of his own devising, driven by an unexpected and urgent impulse and infused with longing *(autsukya)*, he half shows his fuller, perhaps truer self. Only half: the complete self is not available anymore, at least at this crucial juncture. God, imagining himself as X as projected by himself (or a part-self) Y, knowing himself in his twofold nature, cannot bring more than half of himself into play. This subtle splitting or semiemergence seems integral to the work of the imagination at this early stage. A residue of being remains unrevealed, just as we saw in the mirror-model of mind in Ativīrarāmaṉ's *Naiṭatam*.[11] But the movement from a lesser form or a partial self toward a fuller, more complete mode of being depends entirely on and is triggered by the doubt-filled meeting with Imagination. Once again, a pronounced autonomy is in evidence when the imagination meets its (her) desired object. It is the imagination that conjures up the real, penetrating past its outer guise, working on—actually half dispelling—its surface manifestation with the verbal means at its disposal.

Sanskrit romantic dramas normally bring about a tentative revelation toward the end of the first act. The lovers declare themselves, not always explicitly, but clearly enough to set off a far more heated meeting in the second act, with the Clown usually present as witness and, sometimes, as the bumbling fool needed to move the plot forward. Our allegorical play has seized on this template to make a strong statement about incipient movements inside the imagining mind. How does imagining begin, and how does it develop? The initial image, sparked by a painting, is vivid, indeed overpowering. It is also deeply unsatisfying. It follows a formal teleology that strives to exchange the purely mental content for a visible, objectified being, in this case a full-fledged person on whom the image can be superimposed, after which, if all goes well, the image can be discarded. Severe doubt accompanies this transition. The coincidence of image and living being is not complete. The imaginer is not yet one with his own projected, and desired, image of himself. Is it possible for a more complete coincidence to take effect?

10.4. Act 2: Excess

An honest, rambling soliloquy by the Clown, immersed in oral obsessions, opens the second act, as is often the case:

CLOWN: I thought that Tamāla tree was a ghost—just because I was so hungry. My heart is still pounding. My friend must really love me. Within a second he stopped his ecstatic swimming in the ocean of Imagination's beauty and came to save me. Good thing, too. I satisfied my hunger a little with the buds that were left on his shoulders from the Tulasī garland. He disabused me of my illusion and calmed me down. *(Remembering)* Anyway, it's not bad here. I go from vine-hut to hut, and everywhere I am fed by Knowledge of Yoga's disciples, Non-Violence, Compassion, Freedom from Envy, Exploration of Hunger for Freedom and Hunger for Knowledge, and many others; they give me wild rice and sweets, fruits and roots. You won't find here any dissolute playboys or drunkards or fools or slanderers or thieves or chatterboxes or greedy and envious and unwashed people who would be hostile to Brahmins. This hospitable ashram is just the right place for a detached, dispassionate Brahmin like me. If my friend could manage to stay here happily for twelve or thirteen days, I, with my fondness for sweets, could develop a little tummy. . . . Fate has been kind to me in arranging for my friend to catch sight of Imagination, Lord of Life's daughter, here in the ashram. He seems to have fallen in love with her, and she with him. Well, let's see where my friend has gone.

As it happens, King Best is debriefing the crown prince, who has been out hunting again in the Heart of Everyone Stuck in the World forest together with Best's two grandsons, Understanding of What Must Be Proved (Sādhyâvabodha) and Understanding of What Has Already Been Proved (Siddhâvabodha). Using the deadly weapons of logical analysis, the two boys have killed off rather a lot of troublesome beasts such as the Tigers of Wrong Opinions and Doubt about the Existence of God. Among other adventures, there was a fierce battle with a horrific demoness named Bad Karmic Memories, said to be the cause of the vast chain of suffering rooted in false knowledge. Understanding of What Must be Proved engaged her first, but it was Understanding of What Has Already Been Proved who finished her off with the weapon called Mentioning God's Name *(bhagavan-nāma-grahaṇa-brahmâstra)*. This great feat accomplished, the young hero renamed that wilderness the Garden of Good People's Thoughts *(saj-jana-mānasodyāna)*. Civilization has domesticated the wilds: it is in this reconfigured garden that today's romantic rendezvous will take place.

Our hero is happy with this report from the front but, as the Clown instantly perceives, his heart is elsewhere. Best is, in fact, out of his mind with lovesickness, his imagination given over to rather lurid erotic fantasies (we should bear in mind that Bhāvanā is ostensibly a demure adolescent girl whom Best has met only the day before). Like Nala in Damayantī's palace, Best sees his beloved everywhere:

tan-mukhaṃ sa dṛg-añcala-kramas sā ca vākya-racanā-camatkriyā/
tāni tāni hasitāni subhruvas santataṃ manasi saṃcaranti me// (2.2)

Her face, the charming corners
of her eyes, that amazing way she has
of putting sentences together,
all the different kinds of smiles—
I see them all, without cease, wandering
through my mind.

At least he seems to know at this stage that these hallucinations are internal, generated from within. "Amazement," *camat-kriyā,* here linked to verbal proficiency, recurs often throughout this long passage (see verses 10, 14, 15)—a strong imprint of the poeticians' world, where *camat-kriyā* or *camatkāra* is the very heart of the poet's endeavor. To be in love with the imagination is, one might conclude, an apt definition for a poet.

In nearly forty unbridled verses, Best pictures the girl in all the wilder poses and tableaux of the south Indian erotic arts, with a particular fondness, right from the start, for the *puruṣāyitam* position, in which the woman assumes the male role.[12] He "remembers" her vividly in this delightful pose (10, 13, 15): "God, how long she played like that on top of me!" (*cirāya puruṣāyite śiva śivâbalā khelati,* 13; has he forgotten that *he* is God?) Eventually this theme is replaced by images of the bold *abhisārikā,* the mature lover who secretly makes her way, usually in the midst of a violent nocturnal thunderstorm, to the tryst:

dūrī-kārita-mekhalâṅghri-kaṭakā dhārārdra-cīnâṃśukā
dhautâṅgī taḍitâvadhārya padavīṃ dūtī-janâveditāṃ/
saṅketa-sthalam etya vāri-jaṭilān uddhūnvatī kuntalān
dvāra-sthâham iheti kaṅkaṇa-jhaṇatkāreṇa sâsūcayat//

She's taken off her belt (with its tingling bells),
also her jingling anklets.

Her silk sari is soaked through—her body, too,
to the bone. Thank God
for the lightning flashes:
they show her the path,
the one her messenger described.
Now she's arrived. She stands there
tossing her long hair, drenched by rain,
bangles ringing as if announcing:
"I'm at the door!" (2.28)

Though she's afraid the anklets and belt will give her away during the trek to her lover's doorstep, apparently she's just not willing to take off her bangles. Best is imagining a self-possessed, experienced (and possibly married) woman—and, like any other imagined object, this one is highly determined by convention. Still, it's a lovely poem, taking us step by step with the determined *abhisārikā* and painting her with clear strokes: we can see her threading her fingers through her disheveled hair as she shakes off the raindrops, and we can hear her bangles ringing. Verse 30 takes up the theme once more: the path is slippery and muddy, the darkness dense, and our heroine, Imagination, is terribly alone *(ekākinī):* all this is doubtless the result of the magical skill *(cāturī)* that only Love can put to such effective use.

The Clown, meanwhile, is enjoying this "overflow of expectation" (or of hope and desire, *āśā-nadī-parivāha*). When Best launches into yet another *abhisārikā* verse, this time describing the dark blue camouflage sari the girl is wearing, the Clown remarks: "Quite proper dress for your lover" *(yujyate yujyate tava vallabha-vadhū-pallavasya eṣa vāsanā-vilāsaḥ).* His friend hears the words but misunderstands them: "What, that too?" He apparently takes *vāsanā*, "dress," as the homophonous word for unconscious karmic memory, the major part of everyone's mental reservoir of impressions and thoughts—or possibly, as we have seen, for the personal imagination, thus yet another veiled reference to Bhāvanā.[13] The Clown says: "You should know!" Best tries to think this through and comes up with a verse: "What's rolling around in my mind [*cetasi*] is the way she turned back and looked at me from the corners of her eyes when I took hold of her skirt with my hand" (2.34). Then, meditating further, with a sigh:

ayi sarasija-netre gaccha te svasti bhūyān
mama hṛdayam idānīṃ vāsa-bhūtaṃ bhavatyāḥ/

malaya-giri-samīrair vardhitābhiś śikhābhiḥ
kabalayati nikāmaṃ kāma-kālânalo 'sau// (2.35)

Fine, lotus-eyed lady, you can go now.
Good luck to you.
Clearly, my heart has become
your home, set aflame by the deadly
fire of love, fanned by the gentle
southern breeze.

The chain of association seems to lead from the double-edged *vāsanā* to *vāsa,* "home." It's as if we were watching a charged imagination at work—restless, overflowing, casting about for whatever materials are available, catching hold of double entendres and other verbal devices and teasing out their potential meanings, following the associations wherever they may go. This is the imagination as dream or daydream, subject to familiar processes of condensation and displacement that a much later and very distant modeler of the mind has taught us to look for. But at this point the heart has apparently subsumed the mind along with its hyperactive imaginative component; by the logic of the verse, Imagination, or the king's imagination, must be suffering, as he is, from the raging fires within.

Concluding this passage, the reflective awareness finally breaks through with a pointed question:

hanta hṛdayasyâkṛtârthatā

vikalpenodbhūtāṃ satatam api paśyasy anudinaṃ
parīrambhaṃ tasyā racayasi tayā jalpasi samaṃ/
mukhaṃ vrīḍânamraṃ pibasi rati-sarvasva-madhunā
tathâpy utkaṇṭhā te kim iti hṛdayodañcatitarām// (2.37)

How unsatisfied is the heart!

You see her every minute, conjured up as you imagine.
You arrange for me to embrace her, you speak with her,
you drink the full and final essence of happiness
from her lips as she shyly bends her head,
so why, my heart,
are you still so furiously driven
by longing?

Notice the word Best chooses for the imagination, *vikalpa,* though he is thinking about Imagination/*bhāvanā*—probably, as I have said, a wider and more powerful faculty than those designated by the more intellectually oriented derivates of the root [*vi-*] √*kḷp.* Again, our poet is deliberately echoing a statement by his great predecessor Kālidāsa, who also connects longing, *paryutsukatva,* with the overflow experience of fullness (in Kālidāsa's famous verse, the fullness one feels when seeing something beautiful or hearing beautiful sounds).[14] The intertextual reference underlines a point of consequence: imagination, like the intense sensations mentioned by Kālidāsa, operates effectively under what might be called "conditions of saturation" no less than in states of separation and absence.[15]

A wider mental economy is intimated in these verses. Thought *(cintā),* the king tells us, is the love messenger that keeps bringing his beloved before his eyes; at the same time, some inner, swelling despair *(prabala-pariposạḥ . . . viṣādaḥ)* is wreaking havoc with his awareness (*caitanya,* 2.38). He thinks of all of this as a kind of sorcery *(mahad indra-jālam).* Within the bewitching business of hungering after the imagination, his mind produces stark naturalistic descriptions and conclusions of a general nature about how desire is nourished and continuously enhanced (it's not the beds of flowers, the lamps, or even the nights of lovemaking; it's some kind of self-generating excess of feeling, *rāgâtireka,* 2.20). One result, perhaps unexpected, is that he feels himself assuming the same form or body as his beloved—achieving, that is, *sārūpya,* a coincidence of self and image, with his imagination (see prose after 2.38). Perhaps this goal fuels the entire process from the beginning, as I have suggested. Thus his body is emaciated, worn away almost to nothingness, like her nearly invisible waist; on the other hand, his depressive feelings *(kheda)* are as big as her breasts, and his anxiety or obsessive mentation *(cintā)* is more or less equal to her full buttocks (2.39).

Eventually the Clown interrupts with an announcement: Knowledge of Yoga has asked Best to remain in the Garden of Good People's Thoughts for the next two weeks, to ward off demonic influences. Best—very relieved at this development—sings a remarkable verse:

yad-āloke sadyas samudita-parânanda-laharī-
parivāhe magnaṃ hṛdayam idam āsīd atitarāṃ/
sakhe bhūyas tādṛk taruṇima-camatkāra-garimā
dṛśor adhvanyaś cet ka iva tadā syām ayam aham// (2.40)[16]

Seeing that depth of youthful wonder [*camatkāra*],
my heart dived in and nearly drowned
in a flood of ecstasy. If now, my friend,
I see it with my eyes, who, just who,
will I be?

Best has seen the girl over and over in his mind, has nearly drowned in the ecstasy of longing for her; what will happen to him when he sees her again with his own two eyes, as he of course wants and needs to do? A strong deixis highlights the first-person pronoun *(ayam aham)* that seals the verse. He's not at all sure what, under those circumstances, the word "I" could possibly refer to.[17]

10.5. Paramârtha: When Truth Turns Real

But where is Imagination herself? In the garden, of course, where she has taken refuge with her girlfriend after being tortured by moonlight and the southern breeze. Best and the Clown shamelessly eavesdrop on their conversation. The girl confesses that she can no longer see the image of her beloved in her mind *(cintā)* and asks for paintbrushes, a board, and paint so she can reproduce his beauty from memory. The girlfriend has, it seems, anticipated this emergency, and all the tools are at hand. Somehow or other, with trembling hand, Imagination paints the image. Best, who has deduced what Imagination is up to, and still tormented by lingering doubt, longs to see the fresh painting *(phalake katham iva mugdhayā kula-pālikayā vyalekhîti draṣṭum utkaṇṭhate cetaḥ).* "Leave it to me," says the Clown. He has a pill that, if swallowed, allows him to assume another body—in this case, that of a monkey. The two girls are terrified by the sudden appearance of the monkey and run off; the Clown grabs the painting and delivers it to Best. The king immediately identifies himself, to his surprise, on the painted board; the Clown, who seems to have hidden talents, quickly paints an image of Imagination beside the king's image, but Best protests, "How inappropriate! You didn't paint me prostrating at her feet." So much for the Clown's empathic understanding.

Imagination, meanwhile, has realized the immensity of her loss:

IMAGINATION: Alas and alack! Where have you gone, beloved, without even saying a word? Why are you not embracing me? Come quickly. *(Breaks into tears.)*

BEST: Friend, this is our chance to approach her. *(Takes the Clown by the hand.)* Dearest, where have you gone without even saying a word? Why are you not embracing me? I'm coming, I'm coming. *(Moves forward.)*

IMAGINATION: Help! Some king or other is approaching, holding a monkey by the hand. Let's get out of here. We can hide behind that Aśoka tree and see who he is. *(Takes a few steps.)*

GIRLFRIEND *(to Imagination):* Wait a minute, why go somewhere else? They can't see us, remember? The sage told us that, at the request of all the women in the ashram, for the fifteen days that *he* is here, in human form, no woman will be visible to him. So let's go bathe and finish our other tasks; there's no need to be afraid of that king who's just come back from hunting.

IMAGINATION: Thanks for reminding me. We'll stay right here.

Absence escalates: if the painted image is missing, the lover, too, is gone.[18] The king, it now transpires, has the same problem as the girl, only worse. He can't see her directly, for the reason just explained, but he *does* see her reflection on the glossy moonstone where she should have been—because, as we know from Śrīharṣa's version of the Nala story, a person who has become invisible still casts a reflection (or a shadow) on any polished surface.[19]

Once again we are poised on the brink of a complex meditation on "reflections" as a particularly salient form or aspect of the imagination. The present case goes, in some ways, even further than our earlier examples of this equation, since here Imagination herself appears as a reflected image, as if to show us what is and is not possible when a mental, visionary image—or the imagination as an abstract faculty—is projected onto a glossy surface. By now we know that we are dealing not with merely superficial or technical acts of mirroring but with a process of emergence from, and possibly reabsorption within, some generative domain. In theory, the imaginer in question—the prototypical King Best—should be able to see his imagination at work, externalized as a visible reflection. By the same token, the imaginer could be said to be staring deeply into the mirror that holds his imagination hidden inside it. Let us see how he does under these laboratory conditions.

Best studies the reflection, which he assumes to be his beloved in the flesh: it is every bit as vivid and compelling as the girl he saw in Act 1. But

Imagination is showing the effects of unrelieved lovesickness (in marked contrast to the way Best has just been obsessively imagining her). She's as thin as the tiniest of atoms, so pale that by comparison even moonlight looks black; she's crying so hard that, again relatively speaking, the seven oceans seem hardly more than a few drops. He can't stand it; he embraces the reflection passionately, certain that it is real (unlike Nala, who embraces the real Damayantī while convinced that she is no more than a hallucination). "Hey," says the girl at this point, watching from nearby, "it's him!" The girlfriend wonders why he's stretching out his hands to no purpose:

> BEST: Friend! I hear someone talking, but I don't see anybody for real [*paramârthataḥ*]. It's only a transposition to the moonstone that delights my eyes; the touch is utterly frustrating. Maybe this is some magical apparition; or some dream concoction; or the ripening of a visualization through meditation [*nididhyāsanâbhyāsa-paripāka*].
>
> CLOWN *(studying the image carefully):* It's just a reflection [*pratibimba*].
>
> BEST: In that case, let me look for the original.

We now have a clear epistemic divide between the truly real *(paramârtha)* and a mere reflection of the absent real. For a brief moment it looks as if, for once, a reflection may be no more than a reflection. As anyone who has ever embraced a rock can attest, it's not quite the same, at least at first, as embracing a living human being.[20] Best thus hunts for Imagination all over the garden but can't find her; sighing, he comes back to stare again at the shiny moonstone. His conclusion: "It's her all right, tortured by my absence. She's gone deep inside the moonstone in order to cool her burning heat" (48). Moonstones, which have the marvelous faculty of turning to water at the touch of moonlight, are common refrigerants; Imagination is in the same situation as the Sun at noon, immersing himself, as a reflection, in the pools (see the previous section). Our hero, however, cannot resign himself to this situation; he again stretches out his arms to embrace the reflection, again recoils in disappointment. He thinks for a moment: "It's a reflection, no doubt about it; but in that case, the original has to be somewhere close enough to touch." He gropes around and, indeed, suddenly bumps into the invisible Imagination. His body breaks out in goose bumps, a sure sign. Imagination, for her part, smiles and moves just out of range of his hands, to the dismay of her girlfriend, who has no patience for these games.

We should remember that, as in several Sanskrit precedents for our play (notably Bhavabhūti's *Utttara-rāma-carita* III), the audience can clearly see characters who are invisible to others onstage. We have a typical and peculiar form of dramatic irony, with the spectators in a highly privileged position. Poor King Best is left to grope blindly at the periphery of one reflection and, in effect, in the gaps between several others. The Garden of Good People's Thoughts is a tantalizing house of mirrors. You might think Imagination would take pity on her lover, reduced to such humiliating circumstances. But no: she is suddenly assailed by corrosive doubt of a type that seems only natural in this setting. "My heart," she says, "is swinging back and forth. I can't tell if I feel real love for this particular person or for someone else who has assumed a similar human form."

Not a bad question. Probably all lovers know about it. Is the surface image correlated or identical to the one held in the mind? And a still more urgent question: is the one in the mind truly related to the particular, autonomous person with whom you've fallen in love? These are questions that Imagination is asking herself, as any active imagination might. Stated more generally: Is what she feels commensurate with what she sees? How real is what she sees? Does it have the depth at least of, say, one of those reflections sunk inside the mirror? Is certainty possible? While she is deliberating, the king, for his part, wants to have another look at the moonstone. To his dismay, the reflection has vanished (the girl, we know, has moved away).

Best can't touch the real Imagination unless he runs into her by accident. He can, presumably, still see her in his mind, but even the secondary image on (or perhaps inside) the moonstone—the one that he has now twice tried to embrace, that has the advantage of concrete visibility—is no longer present. He is experiencing absence of the second order, a compounded form of the stony absence he keeps discovering to his dismay. Of course, we know that she is there right beside him, because we can see her. But even the Clown is puzzled: "That image [*pratikṛti*] of a young girl, like the new moon, with Tulasī flowers as her earrings—where could it have gone?" It's one thing not to have access to the original, quite another to lose even its shadow or reflection; the Clown, himself a kind of distorted but highly expressive reflection of the hero, knows something of what this might mean. As for Best, this last disappearance drives him over the brink and into madness *(unmāda)*. He tears furiously through the garden; he now sees Imagination in every vine and creeper; he addresses the latter as if they were his lost beloved; he embraces each of them in turn. We are watching madness as projected identification followed, time after time, by a rude awakening. The Clown is deeply worried about his friend's state of mind: "This is what comes of thinking too much" *(aho vicāra-śīlasyâpi eṣā daśā).* Another possibility: "It's all because of this miserable [human] form" *(eṣā malinâkṛtiḥ).*

Maybe he's right. Maybe being human produces these imaginative flights, with their attendant skeptical and ironic overtones. Maybe having an imagination is what being human is all about. Maybe we are all grasping at reflections and writing poems to them. Maybe all such poems are, on principle, ambiguous, open to doubt. Guess what happens in the Garden of Good People's Thoughts. King Best returns, despairing, to the moonstone. Lo and behold, the reflection is back: Imagination, filled with remorse, has come close again.

The king, overjoyed, improvises a verse under the influence of a lost memory of happy enjoyment during a dream (*svapna-samayânubhoga-vāsanā-vaśena smaraṇam nāṭayan*), with the girl outside and beside him sniping at him, presumably inaudibly (for him), with her comments on every line:

premârdreṇa pacelima-praṇayinā prollīḍha-rāgeṇa mām
Awash with love that was ripe and ready, it was me—

IMAGINATION: What's he going to say?

śāntaṃ vīkṣya dṛg-añcalena—
exhausted, that she saw from the corner of her eye,

IMAGINATION: That is, I saw that he was just too tired. . . .

kabarīm udgrathya hārālibhiḥ/
and binding her braid with her pearl necklaces

IMAGINATION: Just what does he think I did then?

āruhyoru-talam—
she climbed on to my lap

IMAGINATION: I shudder to think what's coming next.

tadā rahasi yad vâtāni—
and did such wonderful secret things,

IMAGINATION *(jealously):* I think this crooked poem is about Śrī or Nīlā![21]

hantaitayā
sākṣī tatra sa eva pañca-viśikho vācaḥ sakhe mudritāḥ
as the Love God is my witness—but my lips are sealed, my friend.

Let us take a moment to look at the verse as a complete unit, without Imagination's comments:

Awash with love that was ripe and ready, it was me,
exhausted, that she saw from the corner of her eye,
and binding her braid with her pearl necklaces
she climbed on to my lap and did such wonderful secret things,
as the Love God is my witness—but my lips are sealed, my friend.

Not bad for an improvisation on the spur of the moment. We almost forget that Best is reporting on a dream. Imagination, too, for her part, responds as if her would-be lover were disclosing intimate secrets: "Who needs this guy? He's in love with some other woman who looks like me. I'm out of here."

The imagination, it seems, has its limits.

Or does it? Why is she so angry? Why is she so sure that he's in love with someone else? But we have reached a boundary point. Imagination is so incensed that she wants to renounce the world at this very moment. She's already putting on the ochre robes of the wandering ascetic when her girlfriend, frantic, prays to the lord: "Help! Help! Save my dear friend Imagination, O Best of Males, Lord of All the Worlds, four-armed Ocean of Compassion, with the *kaustubha* jewel on your breast!"

It's an appeal that Best cannot resist, for more than one reason. Just as at the dénouement of the previous act, the god-king makes a transition into his true or natural form *(svābhāvikâkāra),* together with the Clown, who reverts to his role as the eagle Vainateya—and this time the revelation is complete. "Proud lady," he cries, taking her by the hand—he can see her now, as he is no longer quite human—"if I have gone wrong by speaking of private things relating to the sexual pleasures you experienced in a dream, then I should be punished by the measures laid down in detail in the Royal Code of Love [*madana-rāja-nīti-śāstra*]. I'm at fault. But that's no reason for a beautiful girl like you to say goodbye to the world."

By the way, whose dream are we talking about—his or hers? It seems, on the surface, to be his dream of her pleasure, a happy male fantasy; that is, she inhabits a space inside the memory trace *(vāsanā)* left by his own dream. Yet she is embarrassed and incensed by what he reports, and his apology leaves us with the impression that he was speaking (to her) about a dream *of hers*. Or perhaps the two dreams have coincided, as happens not infrequently in the Indian sources[22]—in which case we have a first, very promising convergence of these two imaginations (or, if you prefer, of the imagining person and the imaginative force independently operating within him) within the arena of a shared dream. Note that the game ends, as it should, with the two players successfully, though only momentarily, finding each other. Some moments are definitely more real than others. Imagined moments, lived through, are the most real of all.

For all intents and purposes, in formal terms, these two—God and Imagination, or King and Princess—are now married; he has taken her hand. But the play is not over yet. As the girlfriend points out, the marriage should come out of the bridegroom-choice, *svayaṃvara,* set to take place in a day or two in the royal audience hall *(sabhā).* All kinds of heretics *(pāṣaṇḍa)* have turned up as candidates for the match; King Best should defeat them and show everyone that he is the real Lord of the World. Best accepts this scenario and departs, leaving Imagination to wonder how she is going to survive the next hours, each minute as long as a cosmic eon.

Let us stop for a moment to attempt an abstract, analytical formulation of what we have learned from this short scene, which I have condensed considerably for the purposes of this chapter. Already it is clear that the text presents us with a nuanced, coherent understanding of imaginative process, with linked, secondary observations that are new to our discussions. For one thing, imagination turns out to be a private affair. It has its secrets, which include dream-memories, and it can feel violated when something of the intimate space spills out into words, even crafted, suggestive, poetic words. Such a violation may be severe enough to make a person turn away from life altogether. Indeed, the potential merging of imaginations, or the coincidence of any given person with his or her imagination of self, and with his or her name, takes place on the very edge of aliveness. It is, judging by the story, a matter of life or death. It consistently triggers a revelation of a fuller way of being, a deeper selfhood. It brings us into active relation to the divine component of our nature—a part accessible first and primarily (and possibly uniquely) to the imagination. It also has a political aspect: imagination belongs to this world and, within the human sphere, to kingship. In a sense, imaginative process is pure political science, *rāja-nīti,* as the hero himself says. Moreover, the imaginative flights of the royal paragon, these exercises that constitute the major part of his daily experience and that define his quandaries, are explicitly linked with a notion of what is finally and believably real *(paramârtha).* Here is one particularly pressing duty of a king. We might posit, as a working hypothesis, that the south Indian king has to imagine large pieces of the world into existence and then, once they have come alive, to determine what degree of reality attaches to each of them.[23] I will return to this point.

Note that each partial revelation, perhaps each crystallized visualization, has its dependable skeptical counterpart. Two imaginations don't just flow into each other without doubt; for that matter, even a single imagination seems not to flow back into itself, or into the inner spaciousness that has generated it, without mental pain and cognitive conflict. When the imagination is called into play, there will always be a lurking question about what is and is not real—and also, it seems, about *who* is or is not real. Various modes and media—the mirror, the dream, the poetic figure, the painted canvas, the musical performance (with or without words), the buried karmic memory—are linked by this courtly culture both to the politics of imaginative action or feeling and to a notion, or an experience, of collective and/or individual depth. It looks as if the imagination, guided, interpersonal and reflective, is the most reliable mechanism this culture knows for experimenting with the elusive reaches of the mind.

I want to venture a further abstract extrapolation, in several parts. In the scene we have just studied, the visible image is, in terms of its reality-content, a "mere" reflection; perceived imaginatively, however, this reflection dependably supersedes the invisible original. The reflection is, as Best himself tells us, buried deep inside the surface; because of this depth, it tends to be more potent than the unseen original. In effect, it stares back at us as we perceive it. If you prefer a linear sequence of a metapsychological tenor: the mental image, hidden somewhere in the mind (the unknown imaginative faculty, imagination itself), generates the surface reflection, which, invested with life by the imagination in continuous play, reconstitutes and thus enriches the initial image. This process is personified by the rather moving portrait of a man searching frantically for his lost imagination; he can't see it, but he does see its reflection inside the surface and, rather pathetically, repeatedly tries to embrace it even as it, or she, watches him from a vantage point laden with doubt. Note the reciprocity of this interaction—who, exactly, is imagining whom? Here we have the central problem worked out by the dénouement of our play.

Before turning to this dramatic conclusion, let us reiterate the "facts" as we have seen them in operation in Act 2. Best is in love with his imagination and wants to marry, or in any case to have or hold, it (her). She, however, goes off on her own lovelorn way. Once Imagination is set into movement, she has an irreducible autonomy. He catches glimpses of her. He knows she must be there, but he has difficulty touching her. In *truth,* there is no absent original; in *reality,* by definition, the original must be absent, or available only in embedded and reflected forms that require imaginative enhancement. Note that Best doesn't really care about the truth—he wants her for real, and his claim is that she *is* real. She, on the other hand, does care, in an odd way; she moves toward him, pulls back, succumbs to doubt. In any case, the distinction between real and true takes on an urgency that borders on the existential. From his perspective—that of the active imaginer seeking his imagined imagination—the realness of the real has become so real that truth (the original embedded as image in the most concrete existent of all, the moonstone) is somewhere inside it. But from her point of view as well, Imagination is in, or all about, the real, as we see from her response to the dream. If they are to coincide, it will have to be on that level of hypertrophied, interactive reality in which he imagines his imagination as imagining and thereby finding him and she imagines herself imagining him, or rather his imagination of her imaginative act. This is one possible working definition of the real.

Consider the following propositions, inductively formulated on the basis of Śrīnivāsa Dīkṣita's text. (1) A person is not isomorphic with his or her imagination of himself or herself. (Best knows his imagination is present even if he cannot see it or deliberately touch it; he can bump into it, if he is lucky, but it lies somewhere beyond his control and mostly out of reach.) (2) What is real is rarely, if ever, isomorphic with the visible, unenlivened surface. (Imagination comes and goes, and even its reflection suffers from differential intensities and perspectives. In particular, something happens to the reflection as a result of someone's seeing it; the same is true, no doubt, of the image viewed inside the theater of the imagining mind, which generally seeks to enhance and then to project this image onto some more visible screen. If enhancement or amplification is what the imagination normally does to its images, then obliquity, indirection, and instability may be the mechanisms available to achieve this goal.)[24] (3) Given the reality of reciprocal, mutually determining projections, each undergoing continuous amplification along the lines just stated, any individual—even God himself—is actually more, much more, than he or she imagines himself or herself to be. But only the imagination can bear witness to this insight. (Best assumes his full personhood, a divine one, when the limits of imagination are reached.)

Finally, let me state a rather important corollary to the above. What is the antithesis of imagination in the text we have been studying? Certainly not reason or logical argument. The antithesis of the imaginary is, I propose, illusion.[25] The very richness of illusory forms, or such forms as may appear (repeatedly and finally falsely) to be false—a painting, a surface reflection, a contingent and improvised poem—is the surest evidence we have that something else must, in contrast, be very real indeed. Thus we find in the Senji court of Śūrappa Nāyaka, as in Tenkasi and Nandyāla, what we might call a realist theory of imaginative production. The final act of our play clearly bears out this conclusion.

10.6. Choosing with Open Eyes

Most of Act 4 is taken up with the persistent attempt on the part of Imagination's father, Lord of Life, to figure out who the Lord of the World—his son-in-law-to-be—might be. To this end, all the philosophers in south India (who turn up in the Town of Nine Gates in Act 3) debate before him; five of them submit written statements *(cīṭikā)*[26] of their positions, which Voice of the Teacher (Guru-vāṇī), Knowledge of Yoga's secret agent at the court, evaluates, always negatively, for the somewhat muddle-headed king. The Cārvāka Materialist suggests in his letter:

> If Your Highness is determined to give his daughter to the Lord of the World, then he should marry her to some king or other, someone courageous and skilled in the science of punishment—for the king is the real Lord of the World. Any revelation of some other Lord of the World is no more than a magical production by that evil-minded Voice of the Teacher; the truth is that nothing at all exists apart from the people and the physical world you can see with your own eyes. You have a lot of fine kings to choose from: the Cera, the Cola, the Pāṇḍya and others are all coming to the *svayaṃvara*.

Voice of the Teacher merely smiles when she hears this document read out; it is, clearly, the utter opposite of the view this text, taken as a whole, is striving to articulate. Something, apparently, does exist apart from "the physical world you can see with your own eyes." In any case, by the end of the act, the true heretics have been more or less eliminated: they will not be allowed even to participate in the *svayaṃvara* bridegroom-choice ceremony, while only five seats will be set aside in the hall for all those who have argued for a bodiless, formless god.

As Act 5 begins, the hall is packed with suitors. All the gods have come, hoping to win Imagination's hand, and there are also vast numbers of mortal kings representing the many regions of India as well as Huns and the ruler of Gandhara to the northwest; even a few hopeful anti-gods and demons are present. Only Best of All Males has not yet arrived when Imagination, garland in hand, enters the hall together with her companion, Voice of the Teacher. As always on such occasions, it is the duty of the companion to introduce each of the suitors to the prospective bride. Voice of the Teacher begins with the mortal kings, at the bottom of the hierarchy. Imagination is indifferent to all of them. Voice of the Teacher proceeds to present the gods, one by one, beginning with Indra, king of the gods, whose qualifications include seducing the wife of the sage Gautama and his victory over the demon Vṛtra. Imagination looks away. Agni, god of fire, fares no better—Imagination can't stand the thought of him touching her—and Yama, god of the dead, scares her. She holds her nose when they approach Nirṛti, lord of the demons, a happy blend of the terrifying and the horrible (one begins to suspect that Voice of the Teacher's descriptions are not quite impartial). Imagination doesn't give a second look to Varuṇa, lord of the seas, and when she approaches the wind god, Vāyu, she flicks away a speck of dust that has lodged in her eye. Kubera is too ugly, Īśāna has bound his matted hair with repulsive snakes, and even the Moon has a blemish that rules him out. Only the Sun gets a respectful glance from the girl before she moves on.

Maybe to save time, Voice of the Teacher expresses a logical deduction: "If you're not interested in all these deities, then, a fortiori, you probably won't want any of the great anti-gods like Bali." Brahmā, the creator of the world, is respectfully rejected. But what about Śiva, particularly in his ravishing local form in Kāñcipuram as a *liṅga* of light at the foot of the mango tree? No chance. They pass on to the five empty seats reserved for the proponents of the theory that God has no form. They seem to hold little interest for this full-blooded young woman. This is the moment she has been waiting for. A voice from behind the curtain announces, to the accompaniment of drumming, that the great master *(dīkṣā-guru)* who gives life to the entire cosmos has arrived, riding on his eagle. "Demons," says the voice, "go hide yourselves in darkness. Anti-gods, depart for the netherworld. Heretics, head for the hills." Voice of the Teacher correctly concludes: "This must be the Best of All Males, the Lord of Vaikuṇṭha, who has come separately from all the others [*pṛthag eva*] but together with the crown prince." She bows to him, the self-luminous, the highest god, the one who always contains all that exists as his own body *(śaśvad-viśva-śarīra)*.

Best enters the court and takes his seat. Imagination looks at him shyly from the corners of her eyes. She is thinking about something, apparently something wonderful *(mānase kim api kim api tanvatī)*. Voice of the Teacher eggs her on: "What are you waiting for? Throw the garland around his neck." We have reached the critical moment of choice. Imagination knows what, or whom, she wants. Doubt has dissipated. She has also seen her bridegroom-to-be in his true form. She opens her eyes wide. Now the real problem occurs: suddenly each of the gods in the audience hall looks exactly like Best of All Males.

This predicament is by no means unique to Imagination. As is well known, the great heroine Damayantī faced the same problem at the *svayaṃvara* where she hoped to choose the mortal Nala for her husband; the four gods of the cardinal directions assumed Nala's exact form, so that the poor girl was unable, initially, to distinguish among them. Śrīnivāsa Dīkṣita has followed his intertext faithfully; he also has a theological point to make, one relevant to the workings of the imagination. Voice of the Teacher formulates the dilemma in a slightly unusual way: "The gods are so much in love that when they saw that this girl was not in love with *them*—or not in love with the true self [*ātmani*]?—they took on *his* bodily form. Or maybe it's all yet another trick of that magician? Anyway, what shall we do now?"

Imagination looks helplessly at Voice of the Teacher. Thinking hard, this resourceful companion makes her recommendation: "Listen, my child. If the goddess Tulasī is pleased with you, then may this garland fall around the neck of Best of All Males. Throw the garland now." Imagination does so, looking at, or for, her lord as she takes this leap of faith. After a moment her eyes widen in astonishment. Now each of the suitors in the audience hall has a garland around his neck.

In extremis, Voice of the Teacher meditates, with eyes closed, on the goddess Tulasī, who enters flying through the sky. She takes a few Tulasī leaves that were scattered at the feet of Best and rubs Imagination's eyes with them, revealing the Lord. The goddess disappears. Imagination peeks out again from the corner of her eye—shy, frightened, curious, eager, but apparently confident now about what and whom she sees.

There is still a little business to be transacted. Now that the bridegroom-choice has succeeded, despite all impediments, many of the rejected suitors protest violently, as is customary at such a moment. The heretics, in particular, remain a problem. Best sends the crown prince to do battle and waits impatiently for a report from the field (God, clearly, has no idea what is happening just beyond the range of his vision). As we know, the crown prince is a skilled warrior, and the results are mostly satisfying: some proponents of views that are not so far from the truth—Madhva dualists, for example, and those who believe in a formless god—end up converting to Vaiṣṇavism, but the Buddhists and Materialists are badly mauled by the arrows of True Memory *(abhijñā)* and the spears of Unity in Diversity (*bhedâbheda*). Best is pleased by this report—and now it is time for a wedding.

So Imagination ends up married to her beloved, as he—like each of us—is wedded to her, that is, to the imaginative part of his own mind. But look at what we have to go through before this marriage can be consummated; look, in particular, at the inevitable cognitive and perceptual diversions and confusions that precede it. What happens at the penultimate moment in the hall is far from accidental. The Hindu god truly comprises all the visible pieces and parts of his universe; the garland aimed at his neck *must* fall around the necks of all the others; the imagination that finally sees this god, seeing through his surface, will inevitably see him in everyone and everyone in him. It has taken quite a long time for Imagination to see, to know, and to choose the lover she has wanted from the start, from the moment she saw his painted likeness produced in a play. Similarly, King Best has also suffered long delays and recurrent displacements before he can fuse with his beloved. Here is one tentative conclusion from the way the plot has unfolded: however much a person may want to find his or her own imagination, and no matter how much that imagination may seek to explore the mind that encompasses it, the process of rapprochement is heavy with indirection and in constant danger of failing. We are not simply at one with our imagination, and our imagination, exceeding our own natural limitations, may not even recognize us, the imaginers, at the moment of truth.

10.7. Beyond the Subject-Object Divide

Clearly, for readers or spectators of the *Bhāvanā-puruṣottama,* the imaginative faculty was worth thinking about. Clearly, too, for such connoisseurs the mind, to say nothing of the person, was wider than any single mental faculty and could not be subsumed by any part of the larger whole. One implication of this fact, very evident in all that we have seen of this play, is that imagination and mind sustain relations that are at least partly disjunctive, although there is also an overlap of certain central, core functions and a shared teleology of desire.

As we know, the problem of the imagination is not, in this south Indian system, to invent something new. It is far more a problem of recognition, in a strong sense of the word. The imaginative task is to see what is there—to see it in its concreteness, to discover it insofar as it is veiled or constricted, to identify it in relation to the act of seeing and imagining, and to trigger, perhaps by seeing through it, a fuller state of self-possession. In other words, the imagination can be said to see what is there *as it was imagined* and, by so seeing and knowing it, to enhance what is there so that there is now more there. In this sense, imagination does create newness. The coincidence of the (internalized) visionary image and the external surface produces just that sort of enhancement, and the cognitive addition of recognition, always a metaphysical move, dependably inflates and intensifies things further. It is not the original image that the imagination finds but, through the finding, something much fuller, something the imagination has itself driven to the surface and then shaped and deepened by seeing or reimagining it. That is why one needs the whole panoply of mirrors, memories, paintings, poems.

Examining itself, imagination hides from itself, recedes, becomes invisible, as we saw in the moonstone scene. That is, imagination is not a thing. Not by chance is it embodied here in a coy and somewhat moody but self-driven and determined young girl. Note the final autonomy of this function: Imagination has to make a choice. Everything she does and feels moves her closer to making the choice. That she does so on the basis of an initial perception, perhaps somewhat abstracted, of a painted image only strengthens our sense that the business of recognition is critical, complex, informed by artistic or other mediations, subject to conventional patterning, and riddled with doubt. It is also of great importance that she ultimately chooses a particular, singular individual—Best in his most complete, undisguised mode of being—though the choice takes place under conditions of radical identity diffusion and displaced perception, like most consequential choices.

If I had to pick a single sequence as emblematic of what this text is telling us, I would choose the king's futile attempt to embrace the reflection of his absent lover. He is in love with his imagination but can reach out to only a derived image of it, locked in a glossy surface, incommensurate with both the reflected reality and with the internal image the king has conjured up by himself. Best can't see his beloved imagination, but he knows for certain that it (she) is there. Sanskrit plays famously show us heroes, such as Duṣyanta in Act 6 of the *Śākuntala,* who direct their whole, desperate passion at a painting, forgetting that it is not quite "real." Trying to kiss a reflection is a little different from the latter case, however, particularly given the fact that the reflection reflects the act of reflection itself—in both senses, a radiation outward from a shiny surface as well as the attempt to understand what is happening. It is Imagination, fully concretized and humanized, whose reflection the king can see; in this context, reflection is the imaginative act par excellence and, as such, in its own way at least as concrete and effective as its constantly disappearing original. Here the notion of reflection has evolved beyond the axiom of a generative, inexhaustible mirror space, as we saw in the *Naiṭatam* and still earlier sources, to a more precise theory of perception and its discrete stages. Though we cannot touch our imagination, apparently we can see the detritus it leaves behind on some visible surface such as the inner canvas of the mind. Seeing it, recognizing it as such, we may begin to see through it to the living presence that has created it, thereby amplifying that presence. "Don't look at what is before you," say the Tamil Śaiva poets; "look at looking."[27]

Reflexivity of this special sort, of the second or third order, neither splits perception from the perceiver nor reframes the perceived: it distinguishes what is real from what is not, or the more real from the less so, but more important is that it shows us, in place of objects, a creative and visionary movement in the mind, always receding, always autonomous, always particular in revelation, driving the mind toward recognition of itself from within. Reflexive imagining is the weapon of choice for attacking the subject-object divide. It is not so easy, however, to achieve a satisfying result. Recall that True Memory, *abhijñā,* is the doomsday weapon that finally puts to rest the heresies of materialist hedonism and the Buddhist doctrine that the world is a chain of mostly meaningless moments *(kṣaṇa).* All this happens, of course, *after* Imagination makes her selection and, having made it, follows the helpful instructions of a goddess.

Another way to describe imaginative process as it builds toward a climax in Act 5 is to focus on its consequentiality, the most reliable index of what is real. Imagination sees a world of sameness—her lover replicated infinitely before her eyes—and, instructed by her companion, no doubt an inner voice, she acts upon this world with a certain blind faith. At first the sameness persists: each of the replicas has the same garland around his neck. Imagination, as we know, is profoundly patterned. Then singularity triumphs. The illusion is dispelled. One might say that Imagination has conjured up a world and forced it to give way to her need for certainty, corroboration, and other personal concerns. That is, this world is generated—*bhāvita*—as a result of *bhāvanā*, the imagining that brings something into being, on the one hand, and then sees *through* it, on the other. Instability haunts such a process, but its effects are utterly real, not merely true; the recognition that emerges is a particular kind of knowing, the kind that can replenish one's entire being, triggering a transition to a greater experience of fullness. Of course it must be possible, in theory, for this sequence to fail or to become stuck halfway; there is no guarantee that Imagination will marry Best. That is the beauty of this play.

And yet the culmination we have described again abstracts a complexity. For it is not just a matter of the imagination's ability to see through, to penetrate the visible. After all, at the height of the *svayaṃvara* Imagination opens her eyes to the god-lover as he truly is, that is, as everyone and everything. It is this truth that she finds unbearable. Going beyond it, she strives for the tangible singularity she desires, Best as the irreducible being she knows; it may be less true, though it may feel more real. The distinction remains critical. It could also be described in terms of redundancy. Think of the initial problem the two lovers face. Her imagination of him sets up a discrepancy between what she sees in the ashram and the fullness of form and being she has conjured up in her mind, while his imagination of her wavers between the violent expansiveness of his erotic fancy and his frustrated inability to see her at all, in the flesh. Even when the two imaginations come together, at the end, they leave a residue of incompatibility and apparent asymmetry. One expression of it is the strange passivity, even helplessness, of the imaginer/hero who can, in the final analysis, only wait and hope. His imagination, by now fully autonomized, has taken over and will have to act.

Somewhat unexpectedly, we end up with a demonstration of Realpolitik and a new empiricism. Hindu kings, at least the little kings of this period, quite rightly spend their days embracing shadows and reflections. We have a negative image that confirms this positive: the Materialist in the play recommends "someone courageous and skilled in the art of punishment" as a suitable husband for Imagination, because in the eyes of the Materialist, the king is the true Lord of the World, and the world is coterminous with crudely visible objects and forms. King Best is the exemplary refutation of this skeptical fallacy. He shows us a Hindu king doing what a Hindu king is meant to be doing: allowing his fancy to wrap itself securely around the contours of imagined objects, comparing the latter with the externalized reflections he encounters, composing poems on the evident disjunction between these two domains, actualizing the divine components of his identity in response to various experimental conditions, playing with the pronoun "I" and its possible meanings—in short, bringing a world into being. It is no less serious a task than winning (or losing) wars and amassing money. Note that the "I," or for that matter the royal "we," dissolves to some extent in a successful act of imaginative seeing, or of seeing the imagination. On the other hand, such an act depends entirely on a strong notion of tangible particularity, or of personal investment in this way of seeing.

A certain elasticity is built into such a world, where everyday perception tends to flatten out the contours of imagined space; only the ongoing play of the imagination itself can deobjectify the categories and boundaries this same faculty has generated, linking them to their already existent counterparts in some visible dimension of experience. This movement within the mind in relation to the visible is always an exercise in imparting depth. As we have seen, one of the very first things King Best tells us as he enters the stage in Act 1 is that

Whatever is long
is truly short.
Whatever was close
is suddenly very far.
The tiny has become
immense, and everything
looks to me
like a painting.

You can see why I preferred this translation of *citrâkāram* in the concluding line. To this divine-human hybrid, everything looks at first glance as if it were endowed with both tangibility and the relative freedom from constraint of a painted image. He sees rapid movement as analogous to the artistic imagination at work. He sees all objects changing their shapes: perspectivism gone wild. Precisely parallel to this statement is the narrative we are given about how Imagination first fell in love—by seeing a picture brought alive by Knowledge of Yoga in the context of two competing dramatic performances. Like the reflection in the moonstone, a play—more specifically, in this case, a reflected artistic reality informing two performances—sets something in motion; in effect, it activates the slow, precarious process leading to the eventual merger of the imaginer with his imagination, however transient this result may be. The hero of the play, the imaginer, has lovingly imagined into existence the autonomous inner faculty that will reciprocally imagine him into being, the same faculty that, at moments along the way, lifts him from a more constricted mode of self-awareness to a less constricted one—that is, to a more elastic mode of imagining himself. This conclusion, at once skeptical and empirical, rooted in disciplined metapsychological experimentation, rests primarily on a strong notion or repeated experience of effectual imaginative process.

— 11 —

Toward Conclusion

11.1. First Attempt at a Summary

There is nothing mystical or arcane about the sixteenth-century imagination in south India. If anything, it belongs to a conceptual world that is mostly realist and empiricist. This world and the emergent model of the mind that it privileges draw, of course, on much earlier materials, including theoretical statements on the imagination that crystallized in the classical philosophical schools, the discursive works of Sanskrit poeticians, Tantric and temple-oriented ritual praxis, and the implicit theories about mind and self that we find in much earlier literature in Tamil, Telugu, and Sanskrit. We have studied samples of all these sources and can trace their influence. Nevertheless, the sixteenth-century model clearly has a specificity and originality that go well beyond any of its possible precedents.

Look again at the nature of our late medieval and early modern sources. It is important that we see them for what they are (also for what their authors intended them to be) as we attempt to formulate our conclusions, largely inductive in nature yet potentially wide-ranging in scope and application. Conventions of genre should not mislead us. For example, *Imagination and King Best* is, formally, a courtly drama, probably composed not for live performance but for some form of public reading; as we saw, it has close affinities with the powerful allegorical dramas in Sanskrit that shaped this literary genre. However, I think we would do better to see it as a sustained essay on the workings of the human mind, thus philosophical and theoretical, and indeed empirical, in its expressive aims. Its closest analogues are scientific: think, for example, of the medical allegory—also metaphysical and psychological in character—known as the *Jīvânandana*, composed by Ānandarāya at Tañjāvūr c. 1700.[1] As in the case of late medieval historiography in southern India, discursive scientific treatises from this period often adapt existing literary genres to their purposes, even as the great literary works engage with emerging scientific and empirical themes.[2] The crystallizing anthropology of Senji, Calicut, and Nandyāla was profoundly interwoven with other innovating disciplines belonging to natural sciences such as medicine (Āyurveda), botany, metallurgy, and chemistry. For example, underlying the exhaustive compendia of Indian botanical species produced in the seventeenth and eighteenth centuries by the great European scholars recently studied by Kapil Raj[3] is a scientific literature in Sanskrit, Tamil, Malayalam, and other languages, still largely unexplored.[4] I would be prepared to argue that a strong notion of "nature" as a distinct domain amenable to observation and analysis crystallizes for the first time in South Asia at this period, and primarily in the south; for present purposes, the crucial point is that this domain is, as we saw in the invocatory verse of Bhaṭṭu-mūrti's *Vasu-caritramu,* highly susceptible to the impact of imaginative acts.[5] Why should this be the case?

We could start with the relatively minimalist claim that *bhāvanā,* in the sense of an individualized, personal, imaginative process aimed at bringing something into being, functions first on the level of perception. Again and again we have seen how perceived realities include a strong imaginative component—so strong that in the absence of imaginative investment, perception itself is put in doubt. Nala, entering Damayantī's palace, sees her directly before his eyes but fails to recognize her because of the presence of an infinity of imagined Damayantīs. Eventually these two levels coincide. Varūthini, like any *kāvya* hero or heroine, sees sunset, sunrise, and other natural events through the distorting lens of her love madness; her hallucinations, however, ring true and are followed by the conception of a (real) child, again via an act of displaced imaginative projection. Prabhāvatī sees through the painted surface of a wooden board to the living person hidden behind it. Such events are staples of sixteenth-century poetic novels in Telugu and Tamil. But far less dramatic perceptual events that fall within the realm of normal mental activity are also shaped, informed, and energized by the perceiver's imagination. We have come a long ways from classical Indian theories of vision, which assume that the eye emits subtle rays in the direction of the seen object and that these rays come into physical contact with the object and assume its contours before returning for processing to the eye. In the new economy of the mind, each perceptual act is a negotiation between internal visionary projection and whatever external reality attaches itself to or is informed by that vision. *I imagine, therefore I see and know.*

In itself, this way of thinking about perception, while far-reaching in implication, does not yet constitute a radical departure from the past. It is the next step that makes a real difference. Abstracting from the materials we have studied, we are driven to the conclusion that imagination-driven perception is, in effect, a theory of causality. (The same, by the way, could be said for metaphor generally.) Sīmantinī sees, through *bhāvanā,* the female person hidden within Sāmavan, thereby turning him into the woman Sāmavatī. Nārada's transformation at Sarpavaram in the Godavari Delta follows a similar logic. By some such mental process Rāma extracts Ahalyā from the rock that encases her. Attention, the handmaid of imagination, has a role to play in all these events; it serves categorical objectification and could be called the objective component of imaginative process. Analogous transitions may take place if one sees not with the eye but through the eyes of a friend, that is, by joining one imagination to another. Our world is largely built up of just such overlapping, not necessarily congruent mental acts. Such causal sequences are taken seriously; it is not that we perceive what is there, but rather that what is there exists, in perceptible form, largely because of the way we imagine it. A profound perspectivism, causal through and through, fueled by imagination, inheres in such a system. Existential claims may follow, by nature usually interactive or interepistemic. In such a world, *I imagine, therefore I am.* Even better, as in the cases we have seen: *I imagine, therefore you are;* or, if you prefer, *You imagine, therefore I am.*

What kind of existence are we talking about? Here a continuum unfolds. Unimaginative perception, if such a thing were possible, would atrophy, leaving us with the detritus of a once-living world. Seeing, especially a visionary, inner-eye seeing, is a compelling criterion of reality (not simply truth). In this sense, *pratyakṣa,* "direct vision," the ancient Indian criterion of secure knowledge, comes back to life. Such forms of vision are amenable to empirical correction, but in general, products of the imagination appear to have a truth-value of their own. They may, as the Sanskrit poeticians have taught us, incorporate an unresolved tension between real and unreal, as if they were balanced on a fine mental point, sometimes swaying toward either pole but never succumbing to such a movement. More often, imagined entities overpower lesser realities. The very act of perceiving them and projecting them outward enhances their reality-quotient.

It is at this juncture that, if we are to be true to our sources, we have to make room for a more far-reaching ontic claim. We are dealing, let me say again, with realists, not idealists, although no doubt we could find points of contact with a theory of cosmos as conscious, or as consciousness itself.[6] The south Indian poets are not, or not usually, asserting that any kind of materiality is no more than a mental production or projection. But they allow for the possibility that what begins, so to speak, as a mental image, pregnant with externality, can solidify or crystallize into object status and, as such, assume autonomy and, if we are talking of a person, full-fledged subjectivity. The world is one, with no external boundary. Mental acts are no less karmically effective than any other kinds of acts. There is no reason that an intimate vision should not evolve, as other objects and beings evolve, from a more subtle state to a less subtle one. In any case, internality and externality are somewhat artificial divisions given their tremendous interpenetration and mutual embedding (as is already the case in the ancient Caṅkam poetry). The specific late medieval south Indian addition to this rather widespread and general principle lies in the protomodern claims that (1) a well-defined mental function, that of imagining, holds the key to such an evolution, with observable phases and stages, and (2) this imaginative creation, interactive by definition, nonetheless regularly tends to the personal and the singular. This same mental function is also capable of destabilizing objects, which may dissolve under the force of further creative imagining.

Imaginative production can thus objectify itself, but it can also deobjectify itself. We have returned to our point of departure: remember Pūcalār's creation of an operational, entirely real temple in his mind. Objectification is an inherent property of the mind, in several senses. Minimally, it is a linguistic or definitional business. More strongly, it is a visionary procedure that informs all of perception and is never purely or simply internal. As such, it does not belong solely, perhaps even primarily, to the mind. That imagination should impinge to dramatic effect on the natural world is thus a necessary corollary to a culture-specific notion of objectivity, one in which objects, like thought, grow and ripen both inside and outside any living person.

The world is interesting not as transfigured—a rather trivial matter—but as ordinarily figured. Ordinary imaginative figuration, as we saw, has limits and constraints. A capable imaginer quite often comes crashing against them. One of them, the irreducible autonomy of the imagined being, came through clearly in our allegorical play about imagination. Another one derives from a pattern of recursive mutual determination: internal to the imaginer, the imagination imagines him or her into being and action. More simply, not everything is visible even to the mind's eye. Basic lines of force and objective patterns preexist the imaginative moment. Still, it now appears that Ingalls understated the principle when he wrote: "It is as though our authors thought of the objects of the world as existing in a pattern which rendered them amenable to mutual suggestions when viewed by a great poet. The poet's imagination, in this view, would be the medium, not the primary cause, of the creation of new worlds."[7] Here we have one striking difference from the poetic world of the sixteenth century in the south. The imagination—not, incidentally, only the poet's—is much more than a medium. Although it governs perception, it is also a cause, possibly the main cause, of what passes for reality. As in the Kūḍiyāṭṭam performances, as in the Yoga of imagination, but above all as we see it in the early Telugu and Tamil novels and poems, the work of the imagination presents us with fundamental reality claims. Such claims are, in the final analysis, based on precise, empirical observations of efficacy.

Autonomy, singularity, effectuality, reality—such are the hallmarks of an anthropology organized around the imagination in texts from all over south India at this period of civilizational change. The sheer consistency of the theory, particularly in the sixteenth-century sources, is impressive, though it was never fully formalized in philosophical language or in a systematic economy of the mind such as we find in Tibet or, much later, in Western Europe. The closest we come is in Śrīnivāsa Dīkṣita's drama-cum-essay, though there, too, we had to proceed largely through induction. But then primary cultural intuitions are only rarely rendered explicit. They thrive on indirection. We have been trying to identify one such intuitive complex within the ramified cultural production in the various languages of late medieval south India, and to identify change. We may now want to ask ourselves how this model differs from others from outside South Asia. In what follows I offer a brief comparative excursus focused mainly on the Western European trajectory beginning, as usual, with the Greeks. We will look at the prehistory of several relatively familiar cultural models with the aim of highlighting the distinctiveness of the south Indian case.

11.2. Comparative Notes: From Aristotle to the Tripartite Model of the Brain

11.2.1. *Phantasia*

"These [sensations] are always true, while imaginings are mostly false" *(eita hai men alētheis aiei hai de phantasiai ginontai hai pleious pseudeis).*[8] Aristotle, the first in the Greek world to thematize imagination as a defined part of mental economy, already articulates the suspicion of, even outright hostility to this function of the mind—an attitude that turns up in European sources, with remarkable resilience, right up to modern times. At the outset of his essay, Aristotle asks himself if thinking in general *(to noein)* might not itself be *phantasia* or, minimally, might not ever take place without *phantasia,* in which case thought could not exist independently of the body (1.1 403a9). Here, too, he adumbrates a long philosophical debate in the West: can thought do without images?[9] A little later, he takes an unequivocal stand: the soul *(psuchē)* never thinks without an "image" (*phantasma;* 3.7 431a). But what does he mean by *phantasia?* Clearly, the mind's habit of generating powerful visual images *(phantasmata)* is part of the discussion; Aristotle knows that, unlike the products of pure sensation *(aisthēsis),* which is either a potential *(dynamis)* such as sight or an activity *(energeia)* such as seeing, images can appear in the absence of direct perception, as happens in dreams. Hence, for Aristotle, their falseness (it is sensation or direct perception that is, as a rule, true). But as has often been noted, for Aristotle "the metaphorical sense of the term 'imagination' is that which connects it with appearances rather than images (*phainesthai* rather than *phantazesthai*)."[10] Even Aristotle, who thinks that there is such a thing as imagination and who tries, not quite rigorously, to differentiate it from other mental processes such as sensation, intellection, and opinion, regards the images produced by the mind as somehow aligned with the classical Greek theme of phenomenal "seeming," the glistening surfaces that captivate both mind and eye and may lead both astray.[11]

But even this business of "seeming" may fail to do justice to Aristotle's *phantasia:* like Sanskrit *saṃskāra,* a *phantasia* may be no more than a "single, isolated impression."[12] Such impressions have physicality and may or may not translate into images; they record what appears to us, what presents itself to our awareness, whether waking or sleeping and, as we just saw, they tend to be less than true. Nussbaum thinks that "the basic insight underlying the theory is the important one that perceptual reception is inseparable from interpretation," *phantasia* thus being an inevitable interpretive activity beyond simply "receiving" or "imprinting."[13] I wonder, however, if there is room in this ambiguous and capacious term for imaginative intellection more generally, imaged, imageless, or something in between.

We know, or think we know, what Plato thought about "seeming": images *(eidōla)* of whatever kind—objects generated by the craftsman, artistic and musical productions, spoken approximations of truth *(eidōla legomena)*, and so on—are mere semblances of true being, mimetic replicas that, metaphysically, verge on "a really unreal nonbeing [*ouk on ouk ontōs estin ontōs*]."[14] The gulf between being and seeming is a wide one, and for Plato, unlike the Sanskrit poeticians, no imaginative act could possibly help us to bridge it. As Vernant says:

> We will not be surprised that in his [Plato's] work the term *phantasia*, derived from *phainein* (appear), does not in any way signify the imagination as a faculty, the power of constructing or using mental images. . . . *Phantasia* is that state of thought where spontaneous assent is given to the appearance of things in the form in which they are viewed, as when we uncritically yield to the spectacle of a stick placed in water that seems to us to be bent.[15]

The visible surface is thus inherently compelling; mimesis, ontologically degraded, deludes us; images, in general, will get us nowhere; pure intellection is our only hope. What is unreal can only be "fictive and illusory."[16] Plato is in all ways far removed from the south Indian assertion that what is imagined must be real *because* it is fictive. To sharpen the contrast, think also of the difference between classifying images as bewitching *(< thelgein)*, casting a spell on the spectator at a literary or theatrical performance, for example, and the rich play of the imagination in the Kūḍiyāṭṭam theater of Kerala, where a shared mental universe is danced into existence by the actor and survives as an integral and compelling reality, no less real than any other, for the duration of the drama.[17]

There is no need to belabor this point about Plato, which has been rehearsed by scholars for centuries. But does it explain the striking impoverishment of theoretical discussions of the imagination in classical Greece compared to what we have seen in India? Perhaps not. On one hand,

Greece ascribes to images both too little and too much substance, as if sealing off the Indian understanding of imaginative process from either side. Archaic conceptions of the image *(eidōlon),* as in Homer, treat it as entirely real, though insubstantial: it is a phantom form of the person appearing in a dream, or as a waking revelation, or as the disembodied spirit of the dead *(psuchē).*[18] Such *eidōla* allow for highly consequential interaction and claim credible forms of existence. There is no room here for intervention by a shaping, generative faculty active within the mind, whether of the perceiver or the perceived. Facts are facts. Plato, for his part, wary of illusion, deprives these and other images of their factuality, emptying them entirely of reality. Facts are still facts. What is real, in an ultimate sense, can never be anything even approximating an image, let alone a mere reflection.

On the other hand, it is surely a mistake—ours more than Aristotle's—to constrict discussion of the imagination to images per se. We may, in fact, do an injustice to both Plato and Aristotle by holding to overly narrow definitions of the human mind's visionary capacities. For us, a moment's reflection should suffice to show that imagination need have little, if anything, to do with an image.[19] Think of the mathematician or musician whom we praise as imaginative. Certainly from the comparative perspective our tour of the Indian sources has enabled, the Platonic *idea*—actually, it is more like the *idea of an idea*—could easily be seen as an imaginative achievement in its own right and, as such, potentially part of any implicit or explicit theory of "soul" or mind. In this sense, the rather limited discussion of the imagination that we find in Aristotle may itself be misleading, a semblance of a deeper and more compelling theoretical concern. Once again: could pure intellection, a mythic notion in its own right and possibly never entirely realized empirically, be classed as imaginative production? Can it relate to *phantasia* only as truth relates to seeming? Aristotle's God, granted, does not apparently think in images.[20] I leave it to others to decide if this means that God, like Śaṅkara's *brahman,* lacks an imagination, broadly defined.

11.2.2. *Khayāl*

Aristotelian *phantasia* eventually evolved into Late Antique *imaginatio*—no longer a devalued mechanism of mimesis but a creative mode of knowing invisible truth.[21] In Plotinus and Porphyry, this mode has profound metaphysical implications: the soul veils or wraps itself in the images it conceives, thus modeling the cosmogonic habit of the Demiurge creator. Cognitively or spiritually, "the imagination *(phantasia)* is a kind of mirror in which the soul can see its own image, and that of the eternal Forms which it previously contemplated intellectually."[22] But there are also what could be called practical consequences to imagining: "The imagination produces what is visible by simple inner vision. . . . To imagine is already, in some way, to make things real."[23] Neoplatonic notions of the imagination have almost an Indian flavor and invite systematic comparison, which we cannot attempt here.

Still, *phantasia* as a defined, relatively constricted mental faculty, to be distinguished from "perception," lived on in the neo-Aristotelian philosophers of medieval Islam (al-Farābī and Ibn Rushd, among others). For a more positive and daring valuation of the imagination, we would have to turn to the early Sufi mystics; above all, it is with the great Andalusian Sufi master Ibn al-ʿArabī (1165–1240) that we find perhaps the most elaborate metaphysics of the imagination in the history of human civilization. For Ibn-al-ʿArabī, imagination *(khayāl)*[24] is, in a sense, synonymous with existence itself. God, though axiomatically beyond the imagined—and identified with pure Being—imagines the cosmos, which is both God and not-God, into existence.[25] The cosmos, that is, is coterminous with God's imagination, and its peculiar, profoundly paradoxical truth-status derives directly from this assertion. Ibn al-ʿArabī did not shy away from the question that we wanted to direct to Aristotle; in a sense, he reworks both Platonic and neo-Platonic theories of the mind to allow for imaginative intellection as a primary cognitive (indeed, metacognitive) move operative on all levels of being and knowing.

To give only the slightest taste of what a truly bold theory of imagination can look like, here is one way to depict Ibn al-ʿArabī's cosmos in its main divisions. The cosmos inhabits a domain, so to speak, between Being and Nothingness. In his language, drawing on classical sources, this domain can be pictured as a horn of light, very narrow in its upper reaches, increasingly wider as it descends or unfolds into knowable reality.[26] The horn—that is, the cosmos as a whole—is divided into three separate "worlds" or, better, "planes" *(ḥaḍra)*,[27] distinguished by a descending hierarchy of substantiality and obscured luminosity: one of spirit or spirits, one of the imagination proper, and one of corporeal existence.[28] How does the middle plane, which (ever since Corbin) is sometimes referred to as "imaginal" in order to avoid the connotations of "imaginary," differ from the wider domain of the imagined cosmos? Ibn al-ʿArabī has a precise terminology keyed to what might be called the differential existential gravity of these levels. The cosmos in its entirety is "absolute imagination" *(al-khayāl al-muṭlaq),* unlimited in scope, a godly business; the crucial middle plane, by way of contrast, is "delimited imagination" *(al-khayāl al-muqayyad),* an autonomous domain continuously open to the play of "meanings" and other spiritual forces. This middle plane—eminently real for Ibn al-ʿArabī and accessible to us in dreams and mirrors, among other media—is also called "discontinuous imagination" *(al-khayāl al-munfaṣil),* in the sense that it persists even when the subjective, individual imaginer disappears. The human soul *(nafs)* can then be defined as constituted by "contiguous imagination" *(al-khayāl al-muttaṣil),* a derivate of the discontinuous variety. Note that the soul of human beings, awkwardly balanced between spirit *(rūḥ)* and body *(jism),* is defined by its imaginative faculty and naturally inhabits the middle plane, the site of imagination in its defined or delimited mode.

These distinctions of level, while sometimes critical, can easily conflate in a constantly proliferating metapsychology of imagining, with its distinctive truth-value, operative modalities, and spatial or topological features. The truth-value is, by definition, paradoxical. Reason, *ʿaql,* abhors the union of opposites *(al-jamʿ bayn al-aḍdād),* whereas imagination delights in it. An astonishing inventiveness works itself out in the repeated attempts to formulate the evident paradox, which, again by definition, is far closer to truth or to the divine reality *(al-ḥaqq)* than anything reason can achieve alone. Corbin famously insisted in his study of the *imagination creatrice* in Ibn al-ʿArabī that the truth embodied in imaginative acts is autonomous and irreducible—in a manner reminiscent of what we have discovered in the Sanskrit sources.[29] What is more, whatever is imagined is inherently sound by virtue of the radiance, inherent to the imagination, that allows the imaginer to imagine in the first place (this principle, too, recalls classical Indian notions on the self-validity of perception).

Ibn al-ʿArabī is fond of using the language of the possible and impossible to get at the peculiar, highly dynamic, always consequential activity of the imagining soul:

> Which faculty is more tremendous than that which makes the thing which cannot possibly exist into an existent sensory thing which can be seen?

> For example, a corporeal body exists simultaneously in two places. . . .[30] The levels have interpenetrated, and the impossible thing has been made into the possible thing, that is, joined to its level, while the possible thing has been joined to the level of the impossible thing.[31]

Another way to describe the actual situation in the imaginative sphere is to cite Abū Saʿīd al-Kharrāz, who when asked "Through what have you known God?" answered: "Through the fact that he brings opposites together."[32] We have some idea which opposites Ibn al-ʿArabī thought were relevant. What felt real to him required the thorough interpenetration of the impossible and the possible. There is an existential integrity to the impossible that the possible can only envy.

"All of existence is imagination within imagination."[33] An imagination inhabiting a space within imagination[34] is an imagination that moves or winds through itself, weaving the seemingly distinct conceptual levels together and thereby intensifying their effective power *(quwwa)* and their impervious autonomy. There is no outside to impinge upon such a domain. Or: the false outside, like the felt reality of the inside, is interior to each imaginative act. This hypertrophied functioning of the imagination, identified variably with the cosmos, with God's self-knowledge, and with the deeper contents and fundamental conditioning of all human awareness, seems remarkably similar to the radical vision of the *Yoga-vāsiṣṭha-mahā-rāmāyaṇa* and to the cosmogonic or theogonic Yoga of imagination.[35]

Did this Andalusian mystic know, indirectly, something of Indian speculation and, more specifically, of the role of imagination in Indian metaphysical models of the mind? This is a historical question, probably of little import, that I cannot address. It is very clear that for him imagination is infinitely more than a mere form or extension of perception; as in India, it functions, above all, as a causal force generating the worlds, and indeed as the primary mechanism and inner logic of all creation per se. Moreover, imagination, he tells us, is something no one can deny, since all of us find imagination in ourselves[36]—an argument familiar from Indian sources as well. Our personal, intimate experience of imagined and effective truth serves as a sufficient epistemic guarantee of its truthfulness (better, its reality).

One could easily continue in this vein, discovering further striking parallels between Ibn al-ʿArabī's lyrical yet utterly idiosyncratic Mediterranean sensibility and the themes that have occupied us throughout this book. Perhaps a word on the rather different texture of the discussions is in order: the south Indian texts, for all their color and drama, have a rather matter-of-fact way of presenting their understanding of the mind and its powers, and they are not so given to a metaphysics of irreducible paradox as is the Andalusian master. In Vijayanagaram and Tenkasi, the causal impact of imaginative perception on the world is a relatively straightforward matter, not much different from the normal process that leads to the solidifying of any subtle word or thought into a "thing." I will return to this point once more below.

11.2.3. Animal Spirits

The sense of kinship we feel when we come to Ibn al-ʿArabī from the *Wave of Beauty* or the *Yoga-vāsiṣṭha,* or even from Ruyyaka and Ativīrarāma Pāṇṭiyaṉ, is absent when we juxtapose our south Indian sources with major texts on imagination from early modern Europe (despite the formal and thematic affinities that we observed between the sixteenth-century Tenkasi poets and Montaigne). It seems that India and Europe arrived more or less at the same time at a critical crossroads and took highly divergent paths as far as primary cosmological paradigms are concerned. In Europe, the ancient dichotomy of mind and matter hardened into a fully desubjectified theory, or evolving set of theories, about the status of objects within an external, natural world. In India, the dichotomy itself is questionable, and the metaphysics of inner and outer took another course. Broadly speaking, in one conceptual system the imagination became increasingly associated with pathology, while in the other it tended to be understood as therapeutic. As this book moves toward conclusion, I want to put in place at least the scaffolding of a possible historical comparison that would take seriously two sets of incorrigible intuitions crystallizing in novel forms at the same extended historical moment.

An inviting point of departure is the strong notion, prevalent in early modern Europe and reflecting a "compound of Greek, Arabic, and Christian Latin sources,"[37] that the imagination and its modes of operation are entirely material and also directly correlated to the functional structures of the brain. As Aleida Assmann has shown, the ancient tripartite or tricameral model of the brain survives well into the modern period: images are produced and processed in the frontal area (the site of *imaginatio*); the middle "compartment" is the locus of *sensus communis* and the integration of sensual data into an ordered, rational, and reflexive awareness;[38] at the back of the brain we have the storage system for *memoria*.[39] A simplified and somewhat modernized version of this scheme is offered by Francis Bacon (1605), who speaks of reason, imagination, and memory as the primary mental functions—still seen as physiological realities—and who also situates poetry and art in the imaginative domain.[40] But whether we are looking at Montaigne, Bacon, Milton, or even Voltaire, the basic mechanism of the *vis imaginativa* is suffused by a Renaissance model of hydraulic materiality beautifully summarized by Daston:

> Animal spirits [which fill the hollow nerves connecting the brain with the rest of the body] are concocted from the vital spirits produced in the heart from blood and air supplied by the lungs and which distribute heat throughout the parts of the body via the blood. The animal spirits are a further refinement of the vital spirits, and stored in the ventricles of the brain, from which they flow via the nerves back and forth from the sense organs and muscles to the brain. Via the animal spirits the soul transmits commands to the muscles to move and receives impressions from the outward senses of seeing, hearing, smelling, tasting, and touching. Just as the imagination received impressions via the animal spirits, it could also transmit them by the same means, sometimes causing disturbances in the animal spirits that could in turn disrupt bodily functions. Vivid images, reinforced by strong passions like fear or anger, could so stir up the animal spirits that they overwhelmed the heart and brain, causing madness or even death. In extreme cases, the animal spirits agitated by the imagination might overflow the body, conveying the potent image to nearby bodies.[41]

Imagination thus works on and through the "pure, subtle, rarefied, vaporous, flowing, active, penetrating, malleable" stuff of a physical interiority capable of carrying and transmitting sensations crystallized into perceptible form.[42] As effluvia, so subtle they can easily enter dense bodies without being noticed, the animal spirits can spread visible images far beyond the individual, thus explaining scientifically phenomena we might today class as mass psychosis. But the effects of such contagious visualizing need by no means be negative. A wise person develops a sensitivity to these inner forces, and there are those—such as pregnant women—who can use them effectively to imprint imagined contours on reality (as we saw in Montaigne).

The process depends, however, on a belief in the receptivity or impressionability of the pliant substances in which the mind's images could be embedded—notably the human embryo, but also other soft parts of the body. "The original projections of the imagination were literal: streams of subtle matter flowing from the brain to other organs of the body, to the foetus nestled in its mother's womb, or even, in the case of the most ardent imaginations, to external objects—other people's bodies, but also clouds, vapors, or any other soft, yielding material."[43] Daston links this theory to an astonishingly persistent fantasy of perfect passivity as well as to later theories of psychological projection. It is as if somewhere in the world, in malleable media accessible to ordinary experience, there simply must be noncontingent, nonsubjective, entirely faithful presentations of the real, including the real but delicate images conjured up by the mind. And while the fantasy eventually shifts its modes and metaphors—by the late seventeenth century the expressive and formative effluvia give way to optical projections through a lens onto a blank screen and later to a fully psychologized model of projecting onto the wholly internal screen of the mind—a residual, almost primitive materiality continues to haunt European discussions of the imaginative. Either the imagination is itself a material business mingling with and acting upon other material domains in chemical, physiological, or mechanical ways, or it is a purely mental production utterly cut off from the world of objects and hard, natural facts. A materialist dualism seems integral to the whole theme of imaginative effects. For eighteenth-century thinkers such as Locke and Condillac, the imagination had become more and more subtle, internal, and, most important, entirely mental. A highly modern skepticism reinstates the stark division of inner and outer; fully situated in the former, the imagination is effective only in menacing, pathological ways that depend on the assumption that, as Aristotle claimed so long ago, "imaginings are mostly false."

The wariness of the imagination that we find in Condillac, for example, goes far beyond its ancient roots. There is a new ring to it, a commitment to a nascent theory of objectivity: the imaginative mind, turned in upon itself, is both susceptible to the continuous disorder of randomly associated ideas and impressions and capable of spinning entire, quite autistic (though orderly) systems of thought utterly cut off from the real world outside.[44] Sealed into a self-contained universe rife with chaotic imaginative productions, the fragile self becomes prey to its own imagination, which Voltaire described as "an interior sense that acts imperially."[45] The profound danger of—perhaps also a lurking passion for—passive receptivity meant that in the Enlightenment "the finest minds were thought to be in constant peril of mistaking their own theoretical systems for nature."[46] Imagination is thus in effect criminalized, its most characteristic role that of a terrorist who has infiltrated the rational self and can hold it for ransom. And while the dream of perfect passivity is eventually harnessed to the service of the newly emergent scientific objectivity—the scientific observer aspires to a state of pure receptivity utterly unmarred by personal impulses, wishes, memories or, God forbid, flashes of imagination—the fierce division of inner and outer grows ever more axiomatic. Romantic poets of the nineteenth century such as Baudelaire and Shelley might protest such attempts to exclude the imagination from the domain of intelligible truths, and a newly fashioned theory of subjectivity would pit itself against the rigors of a militant, "pure" objectivity; but the opposition itself speaks to the triumph of a crystallized European axiology, still very much a part of our own imagined worlds.

11.3. Second Attempt

Look once more at the historical template we have followed in presenting the Indian materials on the imagination. A fascination with imaginative practice and its place within a wider mental economy is clearly evident in some of the most ancient Sanskrit texts. Vedic ritual itself offers room for forms of disciplined visualization that may supersede pragmatic performance. We have seen how such practices and their analogues in classical literary and other artistic media inspired a critical theoretical literature in Sanskrit and, linked directly with the latter, various subtly articulated models of the mind.

But something happened in south India in the late fifteenth and early sixteenth centuries that pushed the analysis of the imaginative capacity of the mind to a new level and profoundly shifted the assumptions on which that analysis rested. On one hand, the imagination was identified as perhaps the single most crucial aspect of human thinking and feeling. On the other hand, imaginative pragmatics were now systematically explored in a wide range of texts and contexts, artistic and discursive. We cannot easily explain why this change occurred—although it is clear, as mentioned above, that it is part of a much greater civilizational shift, a Renaissance-like reimagining of human life in all major domains together with radical experimentation in the forms and modes of political and economic life. I think it likely that one vector in this complex field of forces is the victory in this period of a powerful Deccan culture, and of the elites that embodied it, over the older Deltaic institutions and their classical cultural forms. Notions of individual autonomy and singularity, along with the social mechanisms that express them, can be shown to belong naturally to the historical Deccan systems from Kākatīya times (eleventh century on) and even earlier. Such notions, or the values derived from them, have an intrinsic and logical connection to the understanding of human capacities that crystallized during the period on which we have focused. But this is the not the moment to speculate on causes.

Still, in the interests of clarifying a little further the specificity of the south Indian views that have concerned us, let me, in conclusion, formulate a few appropriate questions. What if the language of projection, which I, too, have used, is actually rather unsuited to descriptions of imaginative production? What if the solidity of objects—what Daston nicely calls the "proverbial recalcitrance of things"[47]—were not a given but a kind of perceptual error or teleological habit that could, under certain conditions, be superseded or reversed? What if this same recalcitrance were itself an imaginative production? What if the obsession with a mechanistic materiality were no more than another variant of the pervasive European fantasy of the blank, noncontingent screen?

Or, rephrasing the latter question: What would a nondualistic theory of the imagination look like? Is this what we have seen in the south Indian sources?

Perhaps—though I don't want to overstate the claim, and we have clearly and repeatedly seen that the Tamil and Telugu texts presume a newly defined notion of the mind as a systemic and relatively autonomous entity, embodied yet distinct both from other constituents of the person and from a natural domain outside and enveloping it and upon which the mind may have some consequential impact. In any case, we need to revisit the problem of how imaginative causality—the heart of the matter—works. So let us first ask ourselves again, following the materials we have seen, just how one can bring something into being *(bhāvanā)* and why the imagination, called by this same name, is the privileged instrument for this process.

Bear in mind that *bhāvanā* reflects the causative verb *bhāvayati,* "to cause to be." The causative requires a subject, and in our case it is the imaginer, whose internal vision instantiates itself in an object or process. At times "causing to be" coincides with a wish or need to come into being, *bubhūṣā* (the desiderative noun). Such a wish may be directly linked to artistic production: thus as Rāma listens to his two sons (whom he has still not recognized) sing his own story, the *Rāmāyaṇa*, he is overcome by the wish "to come into being" through that story.[48] The artistic reality allows the listener to become himself or herself in an intensified ontic mode, by no means purely a mental construct; this is *bhāvanā* in normal operation, akin to the uses of the embedded paintings or other artistic media, including the plays-within-plays, that are so prevalent in the literary sources. There are, then, points or moments in which the generation, imaginative or other, of "objects" or "beings"—including living persons—will coincide with those objects' own internal telos of manifestation. In such cases, the imaginative vision is causal largely by default; it rides upon a process driven by other energies and aims.

If, however, we want to come to grips with the causal logic underlying the more common instances of imaginative creation as they emerge in the south Indian sources, we will have to revisit briefly several crucial analytical concepts: the notion of a linguistic teleology that is built into the cosmos at large; the reflexive or recursive modularity at work in the mind and in perception; the theme of intensification in relation to a preexisting reservoir of existential potential, such as one finds in mirrors; and, perhaps most critical, the breakdown in isomorphism or homology between the imagining subject and the world in which he or she is acting. These concepts may sound a little forbidding and abstract, but they can, I think, be simply stated. Together, they offer a distinctive characterization of our subject.

So let me say again: in a universe that is linguistic through and through, *any* use of language is a creative act that has elements of sheer musicality (first and foremost), intentionality (*vivakṣā*, possibly a secondary superimposition on the music), an urge to connect or to integrate disparate phenomena, and an emergence into form, whether or not visible to the external eye or ear. Naming is one mode of such creative linguistics; as far back as the *Upaniṣads*, reality is said to be susceptible to such transformations, classed as a "verbal handle, a name" (*vācârambhaṇam vikāro nāmadheyam*).[49] Eventually, in the medieval schools and among the poets and poeticians, this set of elements is defined as "imagination" (in the guise of *bhāvanā*). As such, it may well follow a Bhartṛharian trajectory from an initial, presemantic, inaudible buzz to an audible and meaningful word and then, if the process continues to its end, to a contoured and externalized object. In this sense, imagination as a form of language serves the standard vector of objectification; but like all other imaginative modes, it can also dissolve objects back into the undefined domain (before naming) from which they were drawn. Note that *bhāvanā* of this sort may not be dependent in any way on images, *stricto sensu,* though it *is* dependent on acoustic or subacoustic microprocesses as they impinge upon the mind. In a more general way, we could say that consciousness is moved from within to manifest itself to itself by turning back on itself, and that this movement back, the imaginative act par excellence, is full of potential objectivity.

Once the object exists—once the linguistic resonances have crystallized into some contoured form—the mind has a further role or set of roles to play. It will see or perceive the object, thereby altering it; better still, the perceptual act is itself creative and causal, an integral part of the imaginative generation, *bhāvanā,* that gives the object its name. *Bhāvanā,* situated somewhere within the perceiving mind, provides a micromodel of the generative and transformative forces at work within the cosmos at large. As the logicians have told us, *bhāvanā* is a causally effective feature of the self—specifically, the feature of the self that makes perception possible, including the perception that underlies memory (or replaces memory by calling up the buried original perception of the object) and feeds into attention and recognition. In the south Indian materials, however, this faculty—so intimate a part of our experience as to be immune to doubt—does much more than reproduce or recognize an impression that exists a priori. Specifically, it shapes, integrates, intensifies, penetrates, and perhaps transcends the perceived object or its impression, weaving a tensile amalgam of inner and outer residues into the perceptual act and imparting a powerful sense of reality that attaches to the object.

On the surface, the reality in question may appear paradoxical, an indissoluble marriage of real and unreal, the natural outcome of the figurative visualizing that affects every perceptual moment. Seeing is never free from figuration, and imaginative seeing—the heart of perception—is accordingly endowed with a truth-value, or a reality-claim, distinct from other such claims (for example, those of pure logical intellection). Figuration, always rich with potential reality, need not be paradoxical; it undermines the superficial givenness of the real and conscripts the unreal to the production of something that, by definition, is more than real. Such perceptual acts, heavily informed by imaginative *bhāvanā,* are nonrandom—they are profoundly linked to the evident externality of the object—but they are also continually new and fresh, and ultimately singular. When they penetrate deeply into the object, as in artistic production (a painting or narrative), and then emerge somewhere outside or beyond it, they effectively reenact the recursive aspect of creation itself, never an ex nihilo phenomenon but a reflex of existing materials in continuous recombinations. We saw how King Best is enticed into the mirror space of his beloved imagination and how Prabhāvatī penetrates through the surface of a painting in the course of reimagining her lover as a singular, living being. Stated more generally, the spectator is drawn into the frame of the artistic production; this frame then tends to dissolve, leaving the erstwhile spectator stranded within an imaginative world of undoubted integrity, fictive though it must be, where something novel and unexpected may begin to emerge. Here we have second-order *bhāvanā,* not reflexive in the Western sense of proliferating external frames, with a still-external spectator, but reflexive in the Indian mode of diving into the infinite space of the mirror. Such recursive acts, the stuff not merely of plays within plays but also of everyday perception, are causally effective precisely because they corrode their definitive, brittle, external, and probably unreal frame.

You need a mind capable of imaginative generation in order to touch a reality of such intensity. Figuration, whether in poetry or in normal perception, regularly intensifies (such is its raison d'être); it is no wonder that the Sanskrit poeticians speak of intensification as a primary feature of imaginative work and as one of the aesthetic ends such work intends. Here again we touch upon a causal node: if you intensify perception to the pitch we are speaking of, and if you allow for the imaginative reworking of the perceived in the course of perceiving it, you inevitably change the perceptual field as a whole. Indeed, you may change your whole world. Any increment in existential power has consequence.

This description does not lend itself to a crude materialism or, for that matter, to a stark body-mind division. It is not a question of animal spirits or their like; nor are we speaking of purely intrapsychic processes divorced from objectivity. The consequences of imagining in the south Indian style are mostly keyed to a realistic axiology. The world exists, as do the pieces of reality set loose in it by the imagining mind. Pure intellection has little to do with any of this. Imagination is not pure thought, *vikalpa,* and indeed not entirely limited to the mind, though it cannot dispense with the mind.

Nevertheless—to return to the sources of the sixteenth and seventeenth centuries—the imagining mind, though capable of modeling wider cosmic processes of generation, is capable of causal impact on the world precisely because it is no longer isomorphic with those processes. Here we have to reiterate a major historical theme. We began with Pūcalār and the temple he builds in his mind, and we then traced such themes back to the Vedic vision of 36,000 mentally generated fires and forward to the fully populated dramatic space produced in the Kerala theater. But there is a world of difference between effective acts of inner visualization, unspecified beyond being situated somewhere inside, and the imaginative perception of the self-defined, self-aware individual who knows himself or herself to be gifted in *bhāvanā* in the sense of activating a particular, central faculty of the mind to far-reaching effect. Both Pūcalār and the Vedic sacrificer appear to reproduce internally, and to fix in place by highly disciplined mental effort, processes that evolve externally in tight correspondence with these patterned inner visions. Not so the talented imaginers of Tenkasi and Senji. Continuous with the natural world, they have nonetheless broken away from it to the extent that their imagination is no longer homologous with God's; indeed, even God's own imagination is no longer homologous with his own interiority, as we saw in Śrīnivāsa Dīkṣita's play. The mind of the autonomous individual has jagged edges and dark pools. It cannot be derived from or reduced to some overriding principle or alien impulse. A substantial gap has opened up, an interactive and indeterminate space between the regular operations of the cosmos and the many ways the individual mind, implanted in that cosmos and partaking of its nature, imagines and thereby affects those operations. I repeat: such empty spaces are causally effective factors. A somewhat similar sense of dissonance between the human mind and the external world the mind perceives led, in Western Europe, to an opposite conclusion, namely, that the human imagination cannot, and should not, shape reality in its own images.

The language of objects may, however, distort the late medieval south Indian theories that have concerned us. Objects in the usual sense are, for our poets and essayists, probably the least of our imaginings. Normally, we apparently imagine some other person's or persons' imagining, in which we have a part or a stake—as we saw at several points in the texts we read. And even this way of stating things is surely too simple, too linear. One has to go through many imaginings-within-imaginings, many mutually configured, interactive imaginations, to reach and carry out even the simplest perceptual act. In Tamil, Telugu, and south Indian Sanskrit, it is this remarkable density and tangibility of mutually determined imaginative acts that is endowed with a "proverbial recalcitrance." Again, it is important to remember that we are speaking of causal sequence leading to effects that are not merely real but actually far more than real, their existential force continually and incrementally enhanced by ongoing compounded reimagining. In such a world, as we have seen, there is nothing that is not repeatedly imagined, including our own selves, but this description, far from unraveling self or world, is the best guarantee we have of any viable existence, especially our own. And yet: are some things really more real than others? After all that we have been through, it is strangely hard to say.

Notes

1. Mind-Born Worlds

1. With apologies to Kannada-speakers; sad to say, I have as yet no direct access to Kannada sources.
2. But on the latter see Chakrabarty 2000.
3. *Periya Purāṇam* 4175–4193.
4. Pulavar Aracu 1968: 351.
5. See Malamoud 1989 and section 1.2 of this book.
6. *Śatapatha Brāhmaṇa* 10.5.3.1–3.
7. Kuiper 1975.
8. Eggeling 1987: 4:375 opts for "substantial."
9. Later works have a term for this inner-outer correspondence: *sampad*, discussed at length in the Śaṅkara Advaita school of non-duality; see section 5.3.
10. See the excellent analysis in Tull 1989: 81–102.
11. Ibid., 101.
12. See section 5.2.
13. That is, the verses of the Vedas.
14. *Śatapatha Brāhmaṇa* 10.6.5.1–5. See discussion in Handelman and Shulman 1997: 190–193.
15. I owe the detailed synopsis of the *puṟappāṭu* to Heike Moser, following the tradition she was taught at the Keralakalamandalam by Kalamandalam Rama Chakyar, with some additions from my own experience of the closely related Muḻikkuḷam performance tradition. See also Śliwczyńska 2007 for a careful summary and study.
16. For a brief description of the individual segments (*cĕriyakku, valiyakku, kuṅkuṇam, bhramarī, cāri*, etc.) see Rajagopalan 2000: 51–54.
17. Śliwczyńska 2007: 360.
18. *brahmāvu ādi āyi tṛṇa-pippilikā-paryantam ellāvarkkum kūṭi ittam nṛttam cĕytu vandikkunnu.* Cited from the *āṭṭa-prakāram* texts in the Ammanūr tradition, with thanks to Heike Moser.

19. Or, according to Śliwczyńska 2007: 360, the actor receives *prasāda,* the god's gift of flowers or food, directly into his cupped hands, an honor usually reserved for Brahmins.
20. See Rajagopalan 2000: 48–54 for an attempt to specify the correspondences.
21. See discussion by Matilal 1986: 312–315, with comparative notes on imagination in Hume and Kant. The technical-philosophical usage of *vikalpa* is nicely stated as follows: "The verbal reports of our perceptual experience are *infused* or *soaked* with imagination in the sense of concept-application and object-identification." Ibid., 313.
22. E.g., *Pañcadaśī* 7.178.
23. See sections 5.1 and 5.3. *Kalpanā* gives us the standard Tamil word for imagination, *kar̲pan̲ai.*
24. Dasgupta 1975: 2:91. See Maṇḍanamiśra, *Brahmasiddhi* 1. Since the *jīvas* are the product of such imagination, they cannot be its source; but neither can *brahman* be its source, for axiomatic reasons. *Kalpanā* thus constitutes an ontic paradox.
25. See section 3.3.
26. Roughly belonging to the tenth to the twelfth centuries.
27. Śrīdhara (*Nyāya-kandalī* 119). Just as the *manas,* the thinking sense, can generate memory through *bhāvanā,* so the *manas* has the capacity to produce, with the help of this same *bhāvanā*-impression, the experience of direct perception *(pratyakṣânubhāva).* Śrīdhara thus distinguishes between objects that are called up from memory, *smṛty-upanīta,* which belong to the world of thought, and those that are called up by impression *(saṃskāropanīta),* which belong to actual sense perception. See also Shastri 1976: 461.
28. Gary Tubb, personal communication, 2004. Here there is a link to be made with some interpretations of Aristotle's notion of *phantasia;* see section 11.2 and Nussbaum 1978.
29. McCrea 2008: 64–65. McCrea's discussion of *bhāvanā* in Mīmāṃsā is by far the best introduction to this subject.
30. See Bhatta 2001: 1:23–24; Kauṇḍa Bhaṭṭa, *Vaiyākaraṇa-bhūṣaṇa-sāra, Dhātv-artha-nirṇaya,* 21.
31. Mazumdar 1977: 15 (italics in original).
32. See Shulman 2001: 207.
33. In Sureśvara we also find a link between memory and attention. See *Naiṣkarmya-siddhi,* chapter 2, and section 5.4 in this book.
34. My thanks to M. V. Krishnayya for discussion of this point.
35. See Shulman 2008b.
36. See Pollock's (2006) pathbreaking study of vernacularization; for a restatement of the role of Sanskrit in the late medieval south, see Bronner and Shulman 2006.

2. Poets, Playwrights, Painters

1. See Shulman 2001: 30–39. The poeticians made this praxis explicit; see Mammaṭa, *Kāvya-prakāśa* 1.1.
2. Most classical poets were men, although poetesses begin to leave their mark toward the end of the first millennium. On the question of visionary imagining, see Chapter 5. On the transition to a notion of the poet as a highly trained professional craftsman, for example in Rājaśekhara and Murâri, see Shulman forthcoming b; Granoff forthcoming.
3. *Raghu-vaṃśa* 5.22.
4. They also sometimes exemplify an acute failure of the imagination; see Shulman 2011.
5. The same theme, elaborately expanded, underlies the praxis of the still-living Sanskrit theater of Kerala, Kūḍiyāṭṭam; see Tammy Klein 2010 and section 1.3.
6. Cf. the *citrapada* of *Nāṭya-śāstra* 19.136; Bansat-Boudon 1992: 338–339.
7. *Abhijñāna-śākuntala* 6.142.
8. The Creator-god Brahmā has four heads.
9. As is still the case in Kūḍiyāṭṭam; see section 1.3.
10. On *tādātmya,* self-congruence, in Sanskrit plays, specifically those of Harṣadeva, see Shulman 2006: 25–29.
11. See sections 3.1 and 3.2.
12. As in Śiva's game of dice; see Handelman and Shulman 1998.
13. Including the complex and exquisite 3.13, beloved of the poeticians.
14. Doniger [*Ratnâvalī*] 2006: 45–46.
15. Shulman 2001: 285–288.
16. *atha tām eva priyatamāṃ hṛdaya-phalake saṅkalpa-tūlikayā likhitām iva: Vāsava-dattā* of Subandhu, 122, translated by Bronner 2010: 31.
17. Ibid.
18. See Chapter 8.
19. *Megha-dūta* 5.
20. New analyses of the messenger poems are forthcoming from Charles Hallisey and my student Sivan Goren.
21. *Kādambarī* 491–492; Layne 239–240.
22. *Chāndogya Upaniṣad* 8.2; see also section 5.1.
23. *Kādambarī* 493–494; Layne 240.
24. *Kādambarī* 489–491; Layne 238–239.
25. *Kādambarī* 498–499; Layne 242.
26. There is also an internal listener to the story, King Śūdraka, who happens to be a reincarnation of "that same Candrâpīḍa," though at this point he is still unaware of that fact.
27. Heesterman 1991.

28. *Śatapatha Brāhmaṇa* 1.1.1.4–6; *Vajasaneyi Saṃhitā* 1.5 and 2.28.
29. *atha saṃsthite visṛjate/ idam aham ya evâsmi so 'smīty.*
30. *Śatapatha Brāhmaṇa* 1.1.1.1, 4–6 (Eggeling's translation).
31. Thus Yohanan Grinshpon, forthcoming.
32. Velcheru Narayana Rao stressed this reading in a personal communication.
33. Amaru collection. Cf. the Tamil version of this verse, attributed to Antakakkavi, given in *Taṉippāṭar ṟiraṭṭu* 222.
34. Similarly—following much the same formula as Kādambarī's—with Sītā's nostalgic, painful statement in Bhavabhūti's *Uttara-rāma-carita* 3, prose after v. 21.
35. As in the case of Vyāsa in relation to his son, Śuka; see Shulman 1993: 108–132.
36. See Shulman 2001: 201–212.
37. Eviatar Shulman 2009; Chapter 5.
38. *Ṛg Veda* 1.161.11,13.

3. Singularity, Inexhaustibility, Insight

1. Bakhtin (1981) saw this as a diagnostic feature of the novel as a universal category.
2. Shulman 2001: 255–292; Bansat-Boudon 2000.
3. Thus H. V. Nagaraja Rao, to whom I am indebted for teaching this section of the *Kāśikā*.
4. See Sundar Kali 2006.
5. Thus Mammaṭa, *Kāvya-prakāśa* 1.1.
6. See section 5.1.
7. Tubb forthcoming a and b.
8. *Meghadūta* 18.
9. That is, the cloud, addressed throughout by the lovelorn *yakṣa*.
10. Thus the commentator Mallinātha: *āṣāḍhe vana-cūtāḥ phalanti pacyante ca megha-vātenety āśayaḥ*, "the wild mangos bear fruit and ripen in Āṣāḍha under the influence of clouds and wind."
11. An even more elaborate explication of the figure as *utprekṣā* is offered by the fourteenth-century Kerala commentator Pūrṇasarasvatī in his *Vidyul-latā:* "The force of the *utprekṣā* allows us to conclude that the mountain is also round and high. In the playful banter [*narma-saṃlāpaiḥ*] of couples flying in spaceships, the mountain assumes a particular, highly conspicuous loveliness, as if it were a breast, white as a piece of elephant's trunk, with a nipple black as the unfolding Nymphea, on the body of Earth, a young woman wearing the blue ocean as her sari, with her body painted with striking designs in the form of forests, kingdoms, mountains, and cities, and the Ganges flowing

like a set of necklaces around her neck." All this makes the mountain a domain of transcendent delight *(lokottara-camatkāra-gocaratvam)*—the implicit goal of all poetry. There is no doubt in Pūrṇasarasvatī's mind that the heavenly couples, drunk on love, are purposely *imagining* the earth as a young woman—that is, they project onto the visual trigger of mountain and cloud observed beneath them a fanciful, human identity that is entirely unreal.

12. See section 2.3.
13. As noted in section 2.3.
14. Tubb, forthcoming b, has discussed this problem in detail; I will not recapitulate his elegant argument here. Note that the Kashmiri poetician Rudraṭa (mid-ninth century) derives his typology of *utprekṣā* from two distinct logical matrices, one embodied in *upamā,* simile, and one active in *atiśayokti,* hyperbole. This distinction clearly reveals an awareness that simile alone cannot encompass or explain all types of *utprekṣā.*
15. Cf. the still earlier *Viṣṇudharmotta-purāṇa* 14.7 (Tubb forthcoming a).
16. Cf. the Tamil adaptation of Daṇḍin, *Taṇṭiyalaṅkāram* (twelfth century?): "*utprekṣā* [Tam. *taṟkuṟipp'eṟṟam,* literally a "raising up" or "projection"] is when instead of the natural mode [*tiṟam*] of either an animate or an inanimate substance, another [or: the other, *ayal ŏṉṟu*] mode is projected on to it."
17. The example is taken from *Taṇṭiyalaṅkāram* 2.12.
18. We also have *prastuta/aprastuta, prakṛta/aprakṛta,* etc. The terms *viṣaya* and *viṣayin* initially belong to the discussion of the figure *rūpaka.*
19. Yigal Bronner suggests as a possible translation of this term: "seeing *as.*"
20. Ruyyaka, *Alaṅkāra-sarvasva,* 67–68. I wish to thank Yigal Bronner and Gary Tubb for reading and commenting upon this text. See also Vidyācakravartin on this passage, particularly his clear statement that the subject of the comparison is "swallowed" by the object of the comparison, though in different degrees: only partially in *utprekṣā,* completely in hyperbole.
21. Referring to the face of a beautiful girl.
22. Both examples are from Vidyācakravartin's commentary on *Alaṅkāra-sarvasva of Ruyyaka,* 1965: 36. Hyperbole of this type thus removes all signs of the underlying comparison, leaving only the object of comparison in view.
23. Ibid., 67.
24. As the commentator Vallabha also concludes: see Tubb forthcoming b.
25. *viṣayasya nigaraṇaṃ svarūpataḥ pratītito vā. tatra svarūpa-nigaraṇam atiśayoktau. utprekṣāyām pratīti-nigaraṇam.* Samudrabandha on *Alaṅkāra-sarvasva* of Ruyyaka, 49.
26. Ibid., 50.
27. E.g., Mammaṭa 1.1.
28. Ruyyaka actually uses the term *sambhāvanam,* in the neuter.
29. Jayaratha, quoted by Janaki in her introduction to Ruyyaka 1965: 107.

30. In the beautiful example quoted by Mammaṭa 10.132; see also section 5.2.
31. *Sampradāya-prakāśinī* on *Kāvya-prakāśa* 10 (on *bhrāntimat*); see the excellent discussion by Janaki [on *Alaṅkāra-sarvasva* of Ruyyaka] 1965: 96, 107–109.
32. *viṣaya-viṣayiṇor anyatara-nigaraṇenâbheda-pratipattir adhyavasâyaḥ:* "Apprehension is the identity established when either the subject or the object of the comparison swallows the other." *Pratāpa-rudrīya,* 276.
33. The moon is the storehouse of *amṛta,* the sweet nectar of the gods.
34. *Ratnâpaṇa* of Kumārasvāmin on *Pratāparudrīya,* 276–277. Kumārasvāmin acknowledges his debt to the discussion by both Ruyyaka and Vidyācakravartin.
35. See text of *Abhinavabhāratī* as cited by Gnoli 1968: 3–21.
36. *Abhinavabhāratī* (Gnoli 1968: 5); *Locana* on *DhvĀ* 2.4.
37. See Pollock 2010: 145.
38. *tasmād dhetubhir vibhāvâkhyaiḥ kāryaiś cânubhāvâtmabhiḥ sahacāri-rūpaiś ca vyabhicāribhiḥ prayatnârjitatayā kṛtrimair api tathânabhimānyamānair anukartṛsthatvena liṅgabalataḥ pratīyamānaḥ sthāyī bhāvaḥ . . . anukaraṇa-rūpatvād eva ca nāmântareṇa vyapadiṣṭo rasaḥ/* Gnoli 1968: 4.
39. Ibid., 5.
40. That is, (the actor playing the part of) Rāma is happy in his love for Sītā: see Ingalls's note on the *Locana,* 1990: 229.
41. Mammaṭa, 4.28.
42. *Sampradāya-prakāśinī* on Mammaṭa 4.28.
43. See Shulman 2010.
44. Thus Abhinavagupta in Gnoli 1968: 7.
45. See the discussion of *bhāvanā* and its Mīmāṃsā background by McCrea 2008 and the brilliant reconstruction of Bhaṭṭa Nāyaka's innovation by Pollock 2010 ("production" is Pollock's translation of *bhāvakatva*).
46. See section 1.4.
47. Note that these details are generally classed as *artha-vāda,* that is, description, of various kinds, that is in itself extraneous to the actual injunction to performance. See Pollock 2010: 151; McCrea 2008: 68. I have borrowed the term "teleological" from McCrea 2008: 27.
48. See the verses cited by Mahima Bhaṭṭa, probably to be attributed to Bhaṭṭa Nāyaka: *Vyakti-viveka* 94; Gnoli 1968: 48.
49. See Dhanika on *Daśa-rūpaka* 4.43–45; Pollock 2010: 173.
50. Pollock 2010: 155.
51. See section 1.4.
52. Another translation of *sādhāraṇī-karaṇa* is "commonalization" (Pollock).
53. Dhanika 4.40–41; *Rasârṇava-sudhâkara,* 251.
54. See Pollock 2010.
55. See Bansat-Boudon 1992: 153.

56. Abhinavagupta, in Gnoli 1968: 14.
57. See Walton 1978: 5–27. My thanks to Maya Tevet Dayan for leading me to this essay and for insightful discussions of the theme.
58. On *ul-likh,* see Shulman forthcoming b.
59. Thus Abhinavagupta quotes the famous verse by Kālidāsa, *ramyāṇi vīkṣya,* from the opening of the fifth act of the *Abhijñāna-śākuntala,* immediately after defining the unobstructed awareness that is wonder (*sa câvighnā saṃvic camatkāraḥ;* Gnoli 1968: 14). See discussion in Shulman 2010. Elsewhere, Abhinavagupta ascribes the restless consciousness intimated by the Kālidāsa verse to "unobjectified desire," a constriction of the primordial fullness of awareness; see the note in Gholi 1968: 60–61.
60. Abhinavagupta (Gnoli 1968: 13); see Pollock 2010: 158 ("a surplus comprehension").
61. For *dhvanana,* see Abhinavagupta on *DhvĀ* 1.4.
62. "Just as the sounds of utterances (*dhvani* in the grammarian's sense) reveal the integral linguistic sign *(sphoṭa),* so also a good poem with its sound, as well as the literal sense, reveals, over and above the literal sense, a charming sense which has great aesthetic value." Kunjunni Raja 1969: 283, summarizing Ānandavardhana.
63. See Shulman 2005.
64. On Descartes' view of the imagination as only concrete and particular, see White 1990: 20–24.
65. Narayana Rao 1987: 159.
66. Gnoli 1968: 15.
67. *Dhvany-āloka, vṛtti* after 4.7.
68. See discussion in the introduction to Bronner, Shulman, and Tubb forthcoming.
69. *Dhvany-āloka* 4.13. The prose *vṛtti* following this verse explains: the mirror image is "empty of a factual body" *(tāttvika-śarīra-śūnya).*
70. In Ingalls's translation in 1990: 718 *(na hi śarīrī śarīriṇânyena sādṛśo 'py eka eveti śakyate vaktum).*
71. *ātmano 'nyasya sad-bhāve pūrva-sthity-anuyāyy api/ vastu bhātitarāṃ tanvyāḥ śaśi-cchāyam ivânanam.* 4.14. Translation in Bronner, Shulman, and Tubb forthcoming.
72. *Dhvanyāloka* 4.16–17, the concluding *kārikās* of the text.
73. See sections 5.2 and 5.3.
74. Ingalls, Masson, and Patwardhan 1990: 681.
75. See the discussion by Bronner and Tubb 2008, focusing in part on the same passage that will concern us.
76. From Kālidāsa's great play *Abhijñānaśākuntala,* which serves as a paradigm for drama at its best.

77. Literally, when the two *guṇas* of *rajas* and *tamas,* passion and darkness, have been swallowed up.
78. *Rasa-gaṅgādhara,* 28–29. Pollock 2010: 147 argues that this passage is "astonishingly wrong in every particular" insofar as it purports to represent Bhaṭṭa Nāyaka's view.
79. This view is in line with earlier analysis of the imagination by Nyāya logicians, who view it, essentially, as a mistake (a form of doubt in which one of the two positions is given greater weight). As we have seen, *bhāvanā,* with its implied imaginative component, is, for the early Nyāya, of a different order entirely.
80. *bhāvanā-viśeṣa-rūpasya doṣasya mahimnā kalpita-duṣyantatvâvacchādite svâtmany ajñānâvacchinne śuktikā-śakala iva rajata-khandaḥ samutpadyamāno 'nirvacanīyaḥ sâkṣibhāsya-śakuntalâdi-viṣayaka-ratyādir eva rasaḥ// Rasa-gaṅgādhara,* 30.
81. Following Mathurānātha Śāstri on this passage.
82. This is best stated by Bronner and Tubb 2008: "He [Jagannātha] first describes the reader's identification with the character as resting on a cognitive defect of an extraordinary nature—it cannot be described as real or unreal. Here too Jagannātha presses forward to a stricter and clearer vision, in which no mysterious status is allowed. The experience of the spectator or reader is simply a cognitive error, delightful though it may be. The reader is temporarily misled by the power of poetry, and the normal apparatus of epistemology is sufficient to explain this process."

4. Poetics 2

1. Thus Sreekantaiya 1980: 11 states categorically: "The exact equivalent of Imagination in Sanskrit poetics is *pratibhā* (also *pratibhāna*)." Similarly Tubb (n.d.) in his superb notes to *Rasagangādhara* 1. And see Raghavan 1973: 124–127; also Gnoli 1968: 49 (*pratibhā* as "intuition," including intuitive knowledge of future events).
2. *Vākyapadīya* 2.143: *viccheda-grahaṇe 'rthānāṃ pratibhânyaiva jāyate/ vākyārtha iti tām āhuḥ padârthair upapāditam.*
3. Ibid., 2.144: *idaṃ tad iti sânyeṣām anākhyeyā kathañ-cana/ pratyātma-vṛtti-siddhā sā kartrâpi na nirūpyate//*
4. Ibid., 2.146; see also *vṛtti* on 1.123. See section 1.4; see also discussion in Shulman 2001: 204–208. On *pratibhā* in Bhartṛhari, see Kunjunni Raja 1969: 225–226; Gopinatha Kaviraj 1924; Filliozat 1963 [*Pratāpa-rudrīya*]: xv–xix; Ben-Dor 1999; Sarangi 1995: 161–172.
5. *Vākyapadīya* 2.149–150. See Ben-Dor 1999.
6. *Vākyapadīya* 2.148. The analogy is probably not accidental. Ripeness or maturity may be necessary preconditions for the proper working of *pratibhā.*

7. Or, in the Ingalls et al. translation (120): "an intelligence capable of creating new things." See their note 6 (121).
8. Filliozat 1963: 294.
9. See note 1, and the note by Stchoupak and Renou 1946: 57.
10. See discussion by Pollock 2006.
11. See the penultimate verse of *Kāvya-mīmāṃsā* 4.
12. Translated by V. Narayana Rao 2002 as the epigraph of his book; reading *nyasyad* for *nyasyâvidagdha** at the beginning of *pāda c,* with Dalal and Sastry.
13. *Kāvayâlankāra-sūtra-vṛtti* 1.2.1–3; see discussion by Dalal and Sastry 1934: 153–154 and notes by Stchoupak and Renou on this passage.
14. But who, according to Vāmana, do have an ability to distinguish good from bad and can thus be trained to good taste.
15. But see Granoff 2000 for an insightful discussion of Rājaśekhara's theory of art (with reference to his *Viddha-śāla-bhañjikā*); also Granoff forthcoming on originality in Sanskrit theory and practice, again with reference to Rājaśekhara.
16. *Kāvya-mīmāṃsā* 4, p. 15.
17. McCrea 2008: 360–362.
18. On Kuntaka in general, see the fine study by McCrea 2008: 331–362.
19. This discussion is rooted in earlier debates, beginning with Daṇḍin and Bhāmaha, about the status of *svabhāvokti* in relation to ornamentation or, more specifically, to rival "modes of reference" available to poets (among others). See Bronner 2007: 93–94, 107.
20. *sâtiśayatva-śūnya-dharma-yuktasya vastuno vibhūṣitasyâpi piśācader iva tad-vid-āhlāda-kāritva-virahād anupâdeyatvam eva.*
21. Cf. Bhāmaha 1.12. Not writing poetry is no crime; it won't cause illness or lead to punishment; but writing bad poetry is a living death *(nâkavitvam adharmāya vyādhaye daṇḍanāya vā/ ku-kavitvaṃ punaḥ sakṣān-mṛtim āhuḥ manīṣiṇaḥ).*
22. On Mahima Bhaṭṭa and Kuntaka in relation to *svabhāvokti,* see Raghavan 1973: 122–129; Rajendran 1989.
23. See discussion immediately before the second *kārikā.*
24. *Nirmiti* here resumes *vakratā* from *kārikā* 1, as Kuntaka's gloss informs us.
25. *yan na varṇyamāna-svarūpāḥ padârthāḥ kavibhir abhūtāḥ santaḥ kriyante kevalaṃ sattā-mātreṇaiva parisphuratāṃ teṣāṃ tathā-vidhaḥ ko 'py atiśayaḥ punar ādhīyate yena kām-api sahṛdaya-hṛdaya-hāriṇīṃ ramaṇīyatām adhiropyante.*
26. The phrasing may be linked to Bhartṛhari's notions of "being" *(sattā)* and "second-order being" *(sattāyāḥ sattā): Kāla-samuddeśa* 79.
27. *Dhvanyāloka* 3.41–42. See also Narayana Rao and Shulman 1998: 103.

28. *Vikramorvaśīya* 1.8.
29. *tasmin sva-sattā-samanvayena svayam eva parisphuratāṃ padârthānāṃ tathā-vidha-parasparânvaya-lakṣaṇa-saṃbandhopanibandhanaṃ nāma navīnam atiśaya-mātram eva nirmiti-viṣayatāṃ nīyate, na punaḥ svarūpam.*
30. *Kāvyâlaṅkāra* 2.85 and 91. See section 3.2.
31. *yasmāt pratyakṣâdi-pramāṇopapatti-niścayâbhāvāt svābhāvikaṃ vastu dharmitayā vyavasthāpanaṃ na sahate, tasmād vidagdha-kavi-pratibhollikhitâlaṅ karaṇa-gocaratvenaiva sahṛdaya-hṛdayâhlādam ādadhāti.*
32. *nava-nava-pratibhāsânantya-vijṛmbhaṇād an-udghāṭita-prāya iva yo vākya-parispandaḥ sa jayati,* in this same passage commenting on 3.16.
33. *Kāvya-prakāśa* 1.3. This set of three goes back to *Kāvayâdarśa* 1.103.
34. Kumārasvāmin ad *Pratāpa-rudrīya* 1.1, quoting Mammaṭa: *śaktiḥ kavitva-bīja-rūpaḥ saṃskāra-viśeṣaḥ*. See notes by Filliozat 1963: 293–295.
35. Pollock 2005: 19–23 traces the debate back through Śrīvatsalāñchana (sixteenth century?), among others.
36. See Bronner and Tubb 2008.
37. Tubb's translation, n.d.: *lokottarâhlāda-janaka-jñāna-gocaratā.*
38. See, e.g., Viśvanātha Nyāya-pañcânana's *Bhāṣā-pariccheda (Kārikâvali)* with *Siddhânta-muktâvali* 158–164, on the *saṃskāra-guṇas;* see also section 1.4 of this book.
39. "Mull over" is Tubb's term.
40. *Rasa-gangādhara* 1, 5.
41. Ibid., 9. *Upasthiti,* "presence," "retention," can also mean "remembering."
42. Some apparently denied *jāti* status to *pratibhā,* seeing it as an *upādhi* (imposed property) of either the *akhaṇḍa* or *sakhaṇḍa* type. Tubb n.d., 12. reasonably suggests that Jagannātha's text is garbled at this point.
43. See Pollock 2005.
44. *na ca sator api vyutpatty-abhyāsayor yatra na pratibhotpattis tatrânvaya-vyabhicāra iti vācyam/ tatra tayos tādṛśa-vailakṣaṇye mānâbhāvena kāraṇatâvacchedakânavacchinnatvāt.* Technically, the absence of *pratibhā* even when both *vyutpatti* and *abhyāsa* are present does not impugn the workings of the causal sequence that has been posited—since we cannot show that either of thāe two was a necessary and defining feature of the projected effect. *Rasa-gaṅgādhara,* 11.
45. Pollock 2005: 33–34.
46. Such as the story of Nakkīrar/Natkīra at Madurai and Kalahasti; see Narayana Rao [*Kāḷahastîśvara-śatakamu*] 1987.
47. See the examples from Telugu in Narayana Rao and Shulman (*Prabhāvatī-pradyumnamu*) 2006: 91–97.
48. *sukhan ast ānkeh keh zīr tā bam azūst/ nah hamīn nāla khāmoshī ham azūst/ be takhayyul agar khiṭāb kunand/ az sukhan ṭaure intikhāb kunand/ var*

khamoshī ishāratī dārad/ sukhan ānjā 'ibāratī dārad/ (Faruqi 2004: 18). Pollock 2003: 96–97 has noted the possible link between Jagannātha and the Indo-Persian literary tradition.

49. In Tamil we have Cuntaramūrttināyaṉār, some of whose most beautiful *patikams* were composed while he was blind; the blind twin of the Iraṭṭaiyar, authors of *Tillaikkalampakam;* and the great seventeenth-century polymath-poet Antakakkavi, a contemporary of Jagannātha.
50. See Handelman 2006 on the haptic gaze.
51. See section 9.5.
52. Thus Śrīharṣa, *Naiṣadhīya-carita* 19.10; see Shulman 2007.
53. See section 7.2.
54. A good point of departure is the kind of syntactic mapping that Klein (2010) has produced for Vedic poetry. Classical Indian music, in both northern and southern variants, offers an even more inviting field for such analysis; see Shulman 2005.
55. A statistical majority of verses would probably fall within Ānanda-vardhana's third class of poems, *citra-kāvya,* "the pictureseque," lowest on his list. But there is no reason to consider his typology as adequate to the complexities of Sanskrit poetic production. See McCrea 2008: 241–246.
56. See the well-known but, in my view, far from satisfactory studies in Raghavan 1938; Raghavan 1973: 131–146; Gerow 1971: 220. For basic definitions, see Daṇḍin, *Kāvyâdarśa* 3.364–366; Bhāmaha, *Kāvyâlaṅkāra* 3.53–54; Ruyyaka, *Alaṅkāra-sarvasva,* 203–211.
57. Shulman 2011.
58. Both Mahima Bhaṭṭa and Ruyyaka offer detailed arguments to support this view.

5. Toward a Yoga of the Imagination

1. *Yoga-vāsiṣṭha* 3.101.4–29.
2. After the fashion of Chinese dolls, see Doniger 1984: 206–221.
3. See sections 1.2 and 1.4.
4. *bījāt kāraṇataḥ kāryam aṅkuraḥ kila jāyate/*
   na bījam api yatrâsti tatra syād aṅkuraḥ kutaḥ//
   kāraṇena vinā kāryaṃ na ca nāmopapadyate/
   kadā ka iva khe kena dṛṣṭo labdhaḥ sphuṭo drumaḥ//
   saṅkalpenâmbare yadvad dṛśyate viṭapâdikam/
   saṅkalpas tathābhūto na tatrâsti padârthatā// (*Yoga-vāsiṣṭha* 6.2).
5. According to the commentator of the *Vāsiṣṭha-candrikā,* the conches are actually planets and constellations in the sky, and the wheels are islands.

6. *snigdhā spaṣṭā mṛdu-sparśā mahā-vistāra-śālinī/*
nibiḍā nitya-nīrandhrā kva-cid asti mahā-śilā//
tasyântaḥ praphullāni padmāni su-bahūny api/
sarasyām iva ramyāṇi santy anantāni rāghava//
anyonya-prota-patrāṇi mitho vighāṭitāni ca/
mithaś copari rūḍhāni gūḍhāni prakaṭāni ca//
ūrdhva-mūlāny adho-mūlāny amūlānîtarāṇi ca//
teṣāṃ ca nikaṭe santi śaṅkhāḥ śata-saharaśaḥ/
cakraughāś ca mahākārāḥ padmavat saṃ-ni-veśinaḥ//
cic-chilaiṣā mayoktā te yasyām antar jagat-sthitiḥ/
ghanatvaikâtmakatvâdi-vaśād eṣā śilaiva cit//
apy atyanta-ghanâṅgāyāḥ su-nīrandhrâkṛter api/
vidyate 'ntar jagad-vṛndaṃ vyomnîva vipulo 'nilaḥ//
(*Laghu-yoga-vāsiṣṭha* 6.4.1–5, 7–8).

On this crafted and readable epitome of the *Yoga-vāsiṣṭha,* see Tubb forthcoming c. On rocks and awareness, see Handelman 1995b.

7. Tubb forthcoming c.
8. Eviatar Shulman 2009.
9. In something akin to the pliant mode that Daston and Galison (2007: 363–415) describe toward the end of their superb essay.
10. *Chāndogya Upaniṣad* 7.4.1–3; 8.1.5; and see, in particular, *Kauṣītaki Upaniṣad* 3.2. See also sections 1.2 and 1.4 in this book.
11. *sa yadi pitṛ-loka-kāmo bhavati, saṅkalpād evâsya pitaraḥ samuttiṣṭhanti, tena pitṛ-lokena sampanno mahīyate.* The formula varies in subsequent verses according to each subsequent wish.
12. Olivelle [Upaniṣads] 1996: 168.
13. See section 2.3.
14. *Naiṣadhīya-carita* 6.17.
15. Ibid., 6.14.
16. Recall that Nala had fallen in love with Damayantī after a goose described her to him, limb by limb.
17. *Naiṣadhamu* 3.88.
18. More precisely, *saṅkalpa-kalpanā,* the "active imagining/production of (many-faceted) imaginings."
19. *Bhāṣā-naiṣadha-campū* 1.23: *saṅkalpa-saṅgama-sukhânubhavasya nâham bhaṅgam karomi samaye samaye sametya/ sañcintya ānam iti tau sadayaṃ vihāya nidrā jagāma nipuṇeva sakhī sakāśāt//*
20. Cf. Bhavabhūti, *Uttara-rāma-carita* 3, prose following v. 14: Rāma tells us that his sorrow and confusion are rooted in his constant practice of imagining (the absent) Sītā *(saṅkalpâbhyāsa-pāṭavopâdāna eva rāmasya bhramaḥ).* The commentator Nārāyaṇa glosses *saṅkalpa* as *bhāvanā.*

21. *Tevāram* 2.3.1: *ke<u>l</u>a<u>r</u> pi<u>n</u> veṭa<u>n</u> ām/ pāvakaṅ kŏṭu ni<u>nr</u>atu polum.*
22. Cutler 1987.
23. Ibid., 37.
24. *Tevāram* of Cuntaramūrttināya<u>n</u>ār 59.10 (612).
25. *Tiruvācakam* 5.22.
26. Kuppuswami [*Saundarya-laharī*] 1991: vi. We see from this story that the graphic form of the text is endowed with a particular importance; in this Tantric world, oral syllables are meant to be seen.
27. Shulman 2007.
28. See Sanderson 2002: 1–3, especially n. 24, relating parts of the text to Kubjikā and the "Western Tradition."
29. The *Bhāvanā Upaniṣad* identifies meditative/imaginative praxis as the *antar-yāga,* the "interior sacrifice." Bhāskara-rāya quotes from the *Saundarya-laharī* (*sūtra* 30).
30. See Chapter 7. The sixteenth-century Orissan commentator Lakṣmī-dhara stresses this lack of intention, citing the saying, "Fire burns even when touched unintentionally."
31. See the *Ḍiṇḍima* commentary on this verse: the two parties to the transaction, the supreme goddess and the practioner, flow into each other, mingling beyond space and time, their consciousness "quivering" as one.
32. Cf. v. 95, *nibiḍayati:* the Creator compacts Time (the waning and waxing of the moon) for the sake of the goddess.
33. See section 3.4.
34. Mammaṭa, *Kāvya-prakāśa* 10.54.
35. See section 1.4.
36. *Bṛhad-āraṇyaka Upaniṣad* 3.1.9. The term *sampad(aḥ)* appears at 3.1.6. I wish to thank Lawrence McCrea and Yohanan Grinshpon for helpful discussions of *sampad.*
37. *Chāndogya Upaniṣad* 3.18.1.
38. Olivelle [Upaniṣads] 1996: 152: "That's how you are," following Brereton 1986.
39. *Brahma-sūtra-bhāṣya* 11.4 (77–78).
40. *Naiṣkarmya-siddhi* 2.53–54, 3.11, 27, 97.
41. See *Brahma-sūtra-bhāṣya* 3.3.50.
42. See section 1.2.
43. Tripathi 1978.
44. Ibid., 289.
45. Ibid., 298.
46. Jayaratha on *Tantrâloka* 29.148.
47. This statement is close to Abhinavagupta's remarks on *Nāṭya-śāstra* 1.107.
48. See, for example, Shulman 2007.
49. See Narayana Rao and Shulman 1998; Shulman 2010.
50. We return to this theme in Chapter 7.

51. *Haṃsa-sandeśa* 2.22; translated by Bronner and Shulman 2009.
52. *Dayā-śataka* 80; translated by Bronner and Shulman 2009.
53. See, e.g., *Vikramorvaśīya* 1.7.
54. Such forms of precise meditative absorption also characterize work such as the making of images for worship. See the description given by a contemporary Tamil *sthapati* or image-maker in Dalrymple 2009: 197.
55. Bronner and Shulman 2009.
56. See Eviatar Shulman 2010.
57. See section 1.4.
58. Bronner and Shulman 2009, verse 103.
59. E.g., Maṅkhaka, *Śrīkaṇṭha-carita* 25.140 *(etasmin sadasi prasiddha-vividhopâsīna-vidvad-vare);* in the following verse, this same assembly of attentive scholars is *śraddhânubandhâtithiḥ,* "fully focused."
60. See *Kumāra-saṃbhava* 5.82.
61. Hara 1963: 142.
62. This statement applies even to famous passages such as *Kaṭha Upaniṣad* 1.2, where Naciketas notices that there is something odd about his father's ritual performance.
63. See section 3.3.
64. See White 1964: 22–38.
65. *Kirātârjunīya* 4.33.
66. *Bhaṭṭi-kāvya* 2.7.
67. *Samādhi* is also the physical placement of an arrow on the bowstring; the distracted hunter may not even be able to perform this act.
68. Fallon 2009: 464.
69. On the question of introspection in relation to various forms of attention, see White 1964.
70. See the end of section 1.4.
71. White 1964: 44–59, distinguishing "realizing" from "noticing."
72. See section 3 of this chapter.
73. *Naiṣkarmya-siddhi* 2.2–3, 3.64, 125. A particular Piśāca who happened to overhear the conversation of Kṛṣṇa and Arjuna provides the paradigm.
74. *Āmukta-mālyada* 2.75–83.
75. Some forms of meditation, for example in Zen Buddhism, cultivate an unfocused awareness quite distinct from "concentration."
76. *Vākya-padīya* 1.44–47.
77. White 1964: 57.
78. *Raghu-vaṃśa* 2.27.
79. *Naiṣadhīya-carita* 3.95. Cf. 9.60, on Damayantī's combination of bored indifference to Nala's initial speech to her and the acute attention *(ādara)* that she pays to his mere presence before her.

6. Early Modern *Bhāvanā*

1. Annamayya 2:95, *cūce cūp' ŏkaṭi sūṭi guriy yŏkaṭi,* translated by Narayana Rao and Shulman 2005: 7.
2. Narayana Rao and Shulman 2005: 122–128.
3. See section 1.2; Symington forthcoming.
4. See section 5.2.
5. Annamayya 3:33; *nen' ŏkkaḍa lekuṇḍite nī kṛpaku pātram' edi,* translated by Narayana Rao and Shulman 2005: 27.
6. Annamayya 2:265, *ĕnta mātramunan ĕvvaru talacina;* translated by Narayana Rao and Shulman 2005: 37.
7. Narayana Rao, Shulman, and Subrahmanyam 1992, 2001.
8. "Tĕnnalrāma<u>n</u> katai," in *Katācintāmaṇi ĕ<u>n</u>ṟu vaḻaṅkukiṟa mariyātairāman katai:* 65–66. The story is amply documented in other Tamil and Telugu sources.
9. I first heard this version from Sistla Srinivas in Visakhapatnam.
10. Motzkin forthcoming, chapter 2.

7. Sīmantinī

1. For the family genealogy and an overview of the Tenkasi corpus, see Arunacalam 1977. There has been some discussion about the precise relationship between Ativīrarāma<u>n</u> and Varatuṅka<u>n</u>; see Gopinatha Rao 1910: 44. Arunacalam shows convincingly that Ativīrarāma<u>n</u> was adopted and brought up by his uncle Nĕlvelimāṟa<u>n</u>; hence he is sometimes said to have been Varatuṅka<u>n</u>'s cousin. The Tenkasi Pāṇṭiyas claimed to be descendants of the well-known medieval dynasty based in Maturai. See K. V. Sarma's introduction to his edition of the Sanskrit historical text, *Pāṇḍya-kulodaya* of Maṇḍala-kavi, itself probably a product of the Tenkasi "Renaissance."
2. Today included in printed versions of the so-called *Skanda-purāṇa, khaṇḍa* 3. Note change to **kāṇṭam* in the Tamil title. The Gokarṇam traditions were evidently widespread throughout the south; see, for example, the mid-sixteenth-century paintings of the Gokarṇam *ātma-liṅga* narrative at Lepâkṣi in southern Andhra.
3. *Piramottara-kāṇṭam* 9.
4. See Ratié 2010.
5. See Daston 2003; Huet 1993; and section 11.2 in this book.
6. See, e.g., *Pĕriya purāṇam* of Cekkiḻār 3360–3416 (Śiva mediates between Cuntaramūrttināyaṉār and Caṅkiliyār in their dreams); [Doniger] O'Flaherty 1984: 61–80; see also section 2.3 in this book.
7. This statement follows the Sanskrit prototype of our story: *Brahmottara-khaṇḍa* 9.43 *(sā tu vismṛta-puṃbhāvā).*

8. See section 1.4.
9. *tau ca vipra-sutau dṛṣṭvā prāptau kṛtaka-dampatī/ jñātvā kiṃ-cid vihasyâtha mene gaurī-maheśvarau// āvāhya dvija-mukhyeṣu deva-devaṃ sadā-śivam/ patnīṣv āvāhayām āsa sā devīṃ jagad-ambikām//* (9.33–34).
10. See section 5.3.
11. Symington forthcoming.
12. Ibid.
13. Ibid.
14. Ibid., acknowledging a debt to Vico.
15. Relevant to this discussion is Pandian's insightful discussion of externality and inner knowing in a modern Tamil anthropology: the external landscape is "folded in" to the interior of the person, thereby creating depth and a moral-reflective space. In effect, both interiors and exteriors are "involuted," perhaps through the operation of a principle of "sympathy" based on organic similarity. The external, "planted" in the inner space, can take root and grow there *(viḷai)*, like any seed, eventually ripening into thought. Pandian 2009: 211–214; 2010: 67–68, 74.
16. See section 1.4.
17. The Rĕḍḍi kings figure prominently in the local mythic tradition. Śrīnātha, in the late fourteenth century, mentions the site—Sarpapuram—along with the deity's name, Bhāva-nārāyaṇa, and the Nārada-kuṇḍikā in *Bhīmeśvara-purāṇamu* 2.65–66.
18. Sarpavaram also claims to be the site where Janamejaya's father, Parikṣit, was bitten by the snake Takṣaka and died.
19. Thus the story as told to me by Peddinti Venkatacaryulu, one of the temple priests, on February 13, 2010.
20. http://kakinadainfo.com/Sarpavaram.
21. *Sarpapura-kṣetra-māhātmya,* folio 19. Peddinti Venkatacaryulu says that Nārada performed *tapas* in order to achieve greater wholeness, since he was still half male and half female.
22. Rama Sastry 2008: 155–159; *Sarpapura-kṣetra-māhātmya;* oral version of the story narrated by Peddinti Venkatacaryulu. I wish to thank T. Sashi Sekhar and K. Ramachandra Reddy for taking me to Sarpavaram. The residual female hand is also a feature of Veṅkaṭeśvara at Tirupati.
23. See *Devī-bhāgavata-purāṇa* 6.28–29; [Doniger] O'Flaherty 1984: 81–89, with further sources listed there.
24. E.g., *Bhaṭṭi-kāvya* 12.69, 75; discussion in Shulman 2011.
25. Compare Kapferer 1997: 229–234.
26. Much as we saw in the *Tevāram* and the *Wave of Beauty* in section 5.2.

8. Nala in Tenkasi and the New Economy of Mind

1. Quite possibly it was to be read privately and not publicly recited, though we cannot be sure about this.
2. The *cāṭu* verse expressing this criticism is given in Arunacalam 1977: 32.
3. On the category opposition between the two types of poets, see Narayana Rao 1992.
4. Arunacalam 1977: 33.
5. She is credited with an elegant, elegiac verse improvised at the moment of her death; see Narayana Rao and Shulman 1998: 76–77. Others ascribe this verse to Varatuṅkarāman̲.
6. Arunacalam 1977: 44.
7. Ebeling 2010.
8. I want to thank Blake Wentworth for help in working through microfilm copies of nineteenth-century *Naiṭatams,* many with fine lithograph illustrations, in the Regenstein Library at the University of Chicago.
9. See *Naiṭatam* 3.8.
10. See discussion in Shulman 2001: 293–322.
11. Rajamani and Shulman 2010; also Handelman and Shulman 1998: 45–48.
12. See Trawick 1990: 133–134, 273–274; examples in Shulman 2001: 302–307.
13. See *Naiṭatam* 11.29, 31.
14. For *uḷḷam* in this or some closely related sense, see, e.g., 4.79; 11.8, 16, 18, 19, 32.
15. See Shulman 2001: 350–375.
16. *āṅk' atu keṭṭa vān̲ aracan̲ pŏr̲pin̲āl*
vīṅku toṇ māran̲ai vĕn̲r̲a nīy allāl
yāṅk' uḷar avan̲ r̲ŏṭutt' ĕyyum in̲ n̲ar̲āp
pūṅkaṇaiyāl varun tuyaram pokkuvār.
17. *kuru maṇi mekalaik kuvaḷaik kaṇ kŏlo*
pŏru matan̲ pakal̲iyo pŏymmai tīt' ĕn̲n̲un
tarumamo vuyir nilai taḷarntu vāṭum ĕn̲
marumam mīt' ūn̲r̲iya vāḷir̲ pol̲vate.
18. Nārāyaṇa on this verse.
19. See sections 3.1 and 3.2.
20. There is also *apahnuti,* "denial," "hiding" ("as if to heal their itching . . ."). The *Sāhitya-vidyādharī* says this verse is the riddle-like *samāsokti* + *apahnuti.*
21. These include metaphoric superimposition, *rūpaka* (the *kumil̲* flower = the woman's nose), which feeds into *atiśayokti,* hyperbole (the *kumil̲*-nose blocks the eyes' movement), an elliptical simile, *luptopamā* (the spear-like eyes), *svabhāvokti* (the eyes' uneven lateral movement), *vyatireka* mixed with *atiśayokti* (exiling the lotuses), *śleṣa* paronomasia (the lotuses have been exiled to the

vaṉam, forest/water), and another *atiśayokti,* perhaps with a tinge of *utprekṣā* (her eyes have taught Death how to kill).

22. I have attempted to capture something of the magical assonance: *suhṛdā / svahṛdā.* Note that in the original the true friend precedes the heart.
23. Cf. *Maṇimekalai* 27.9.
24. Thus 4.18, 4.20, etc.
25. Nārāyaṇa: *mitrasya prathama-grahaṇaṃ hṛdayâpekṣayā prādhānya-dyotanârtham.*
26. See section 7.2. Sīmantinī here assumes the role of the intimate, attuned friend and observer.
27. See Daston and Galison 2007; see also section 11.2 in this book.
28. Dayan 2008.
29. *Naiṣadhīya-carita* 6.14. See discussion of Śrīnātha's Telugu version of this verse in section 5.1 of this book.
30. *Naiṣadhīya-carita* 6.16–17.
31. *ambāṃ praṇatyopanatā natâṅgī nalena bhaimī pathi yogam āpa/*
 sa bhrānta-bhaimīṣu na tāṃ vvyavikta sā taṃ ca nâdṛśyatayā dadarśa//
 prasū-prasādâdhigatā prasūna-mālā nalasya bhrama-vīkṣitasya/
 kṣiptâpi kaṇṭhāya tayopakaṇṭhe sthitaṃ tam ālambata satyam eva//
 srag vāsanā-dṛṣṭa-jana-prasādaḥ satyeyam ity adbhutam āpa bhūpaḥ/
 kṣiptām adṛśyatvam itāṃ ca mālām ālokya tāṃ vismayate sma bālā//
 anyonyam anyatravad īkṣamāṇau parasparenâdhyuṣite 'pi deśe/
 ālingitâlīka-parasparântas tathyaṃ mithas tau pariṣasvajāte// (6.48–51).
32. Ibid., 6.52–53, 55–56.
33. See, e.g., *Naiṭatam* 4.84–93.
34. *Naiṣadhīya-carita* 13.34. See the fine discussion by Bronner 2010: 82–88. On the king as composed of the four deities of the cardinal directions, see Malamoud forthcoming.
35. The commentator glosses this as *sandeha.* In addition, *eḷḷuṟu* can mean "to be equated," in the way *śleṣa* equates or compares two discrete entities. Here it seems that the paronomastic pairing of Nala and each of the four gods, in turn, is seen at the end of the process as establishing a dubious but possible relation that is also slightly ridiculous, unlike the assertion of Nala's true, entirely human identity.
36. See Malamoud forthcoming; Dayan 2008.
37. *Katuvu* also means "to reflect."
38. See the sophisticated statement on the "paradoxical location of the imaginary object" by Abhinavagupta in Ratié 2010: 345n13).
39. Here the south Indian theories of the imagination part company with the northern Śaiva school of Recognition; Ratié 2010.

9. True Fiction

1. See the empirical list of genres in *Kādambarī, pūrva-bhāga,* 12–13.
2. See section 5.4.
3. On the shift from the inspired poet-bard who sees himself as a vehicle for the Muses to a professional literary craftsman, see Finkelberg 1998; Shulman forthcoming b. The full professionalization of the poet and the new aesthetic ideal that accompanies this process—*ullekhana,* "polishing"—seems to have taken place in India with the Kanauj poets of the ninth and tenth centuries. On the distinctive truth-value of poetry, see Mammaṭa's summary (following Abhinavagupta) of Śrīśaṅkuka's aesthetic ontology in *Kāvya-prakāśa* 4.28; see also section 3.3 in this book. I wish to record a debt to Fried 1980 for observations on absorption.
4. See Narayana Rao 1978: 50–56; Narayana Rao and Shulman (*Prabhāvatī-pradyumnamu*) 2006.
5. On Pĕddana see Satyanarayana 1967; also Shulman 2001: 322–350. I have benefited greatly from the remarkable commentary on the *Manu-caritramu* by Tanjanagaram Tevapperumallayya, published by R. Venkatesvar and Company (Madras, 1919), and kindly made available to me by Jithendra Babu.
6. Shulman 2001: 327–328.
7. See section 1.4.
8. *ā bhudeva-kumāruḍ' egina dadīyânūna-ramyâkṛtin*
   dā bhāvambuna nilpiy aṅga-bhava-kodaṇḍogra-maurvī-rava-
   kṣobâkampita-dhairyayaiy alatan acco' nilvak' accĕlva tad-
   bhū-bhṛṅ-mekhala-vĕṃṭa gānalabaḍin duḥkhâbdhi-nirmagnayai
   tiruguc u dharaṇī-suravaruḍ'
   arigina cŏpp' arasiy arasiy aṭa kānakay ā
   hariṇâṅka-mukhi sakhī-jana-
   parivṛtayai magiḍi vacci bhāvamulonan
9. Of being cursed by her if she discovered the truth.
10. The critical phrase, a powerful Sanskrit compound beautifully integrated into the Telugu verse, is: *apuḍu tat-pravara-deha-samiddha-śikhi-dīpti-śāmbarī-mahimace (saṅgrahiñcinaṭṭi-gandharva-mūrti-saukhyânubhūti/ calanam edina mānasâbjamuna niluva . . .). Manu-caritramu* 4.3.
11. Ramanujan 1970. There is some evidence that the guiding principles of classical Tamil poetry, including *uḷḷurai uvamam,* were well known to the major Telugu poets.
12. See section 3.1.
13. My thanks to M. C. Kanakaiah.

14. *uru-darī-kuhara-suptotthita-śārdūlamul jharavāri śoṇita-śaṅka drāva*
vana-kuñja-madhya-śādvala-caran-mṛga-paṅkti dāva-pāvaka-bhīti dallaḍillan
āśramântara-bhū-ruhâgramul muni-koṭi-baddha-kāṣāya-vibhrānti jūḍa
ghana-sānu-śṛṅga-śṛṅgāṭakambula kāñciy amarulu hemâdriy anucu vrāla
gāsĕ peśala-ruci kiṃśuka-pravāḷa-
ghusṛṇa-kisalaya-kaṅkeḷi-kusuma-guccha-
bandhujīva-japā-rāga-bāndhavambul'
an-nagambuna jaraṭhâruṇâtapamulu

15. See Shulman 2001: 340–342; see also the discussion of *bhrāntimat* in section 5.2 of this book.
16. The goddess Pārvatī, who took this form of the dark-skinned Kirātī hunter to accompany her husband, Śiva, similarly disguised as a Kirāta, to encounter the epic hero Arjuna. A variant reading, *kirātu**, focuses the simile on Śiva rather than Pārvatī.
17. Krsṇa is dark blue or black (this is the meaning of his name as well).
18. The Yamunā.
19. Añcanâcala.

20. *mṛganābhi-pankambu mĕyiniṇḍan aladina māyā-kirāti maicāya dĕgaḍi*
nava-piñcha-maya-bhūṣal' avadhariñci naṭiñcu paṅkajākṣuni-cĕlvu sunkam' aḍigi
kādamba-nikurumba-kalitayai pravahiñcu kāḷindi-garvambu gāku sesi
tāpiñcha-viṭapi-kāntāra-saṃvṛtamainay añjanācala-rekhan avaghaliñci
kavisĕ mariyunu gākola-kālakaṇṭha-
kaṇṭha-kalakaṇṭha-kari-ghaṭā-khañjarīṭa-
ghana-ghanāghana-saṅkāśa-gāḍha-kānti
gaṭika-cīkaṭi rodasī-gahvaramuna

21. The first half of the verse tells us explicitly that the nocturnal blackness goes far beyond any of the four first objects of comparison—so we also have here the figure of *vyatireka*, "surpassing."

22. *marunak' ŏsaṅga gālamu tamaś-chaṭa kāṭuka gā navodaya-*
sphurad-aruṇa-prabhā-pathika-śoṇita-sikta-sitoḍu-bhaktamun/
hari-haya-diṅ-nabhas-sthalamunan bali calli vaṭâṅkamun vasūt-
kara-bharitambunai vĕluga gāñci sudhā-nidhin ĕttĕn at-ta<u>r</u>in//

23. *inuḍ' astâdriki bova gŏllagŏni neḍ' etera dad-dīptin añ-*
jana-sambandha-ja-bāndhavambuna rati-śrāntâṅganā-netra-ko-
ṇa-nikāyambula ḍāci tad-dhavaḷiman dā būnĕno cŏppu mārp-
an anan vĕlvĕla-pā<u>r</u>ĕ dīpa-kaḷikā-vrātambu śātodarī

24. *Śatapatha-brāhmaṇa* 2.3.1–2.3.3.

25. See section 3.2.
26. One is reminded of the famous statement by Gorgias about tragedy as "a deceit in which the deceiver is more just than one who did not deceive, and the deceived is more wise than one who was not deceived." See Finkelberg 1998: 177.
27. Compare Bakhtin's view of Dostoyevsky's distinctiveness: "The author no longer illuminates the hero's reality but the hero's self-consciousness, as a reality of the second order." Bakhtin 1984: 49.
28. See section 2.3. One might argue that an embryonic framing of literary romance as fiction *is* present in Subandhu—though it lacks certain of the systemic features we have seen in Pĕddana.
29. *Prabhāvatī-pradyumnamu* 11.125–126; Narayana Rao and Shulman (*Prabhāvatī-pradyumnamu*) 2006: 16.
30. Ibid., 85–109.
31. The *Vasu-caritramu* was thus composed almost exactly at the time Ativīrarāma Pāṇṭiyaṉ was writing the *Naiṭatam* in Tenkasi, further south.
32. But in Kampaṉ's Tamil version (1.540), Ahalyā's return to human form is compared to "a person cutting loose from the confusion inside him and taking on form with true knowledge [*mĕy uṇarvu*] as he reaches the feet of the Lord"—an epistemic shift that models the existential one. A modicum of agency attaches to Ahalyā, who has, no doubt, been a suffering, silent witness to the life going on around her.
33. I thank Yigal Bronner for formulating this point.

10. The Marriage of Bhāvanā and Best

1. His descendants, some living today in Chennai/Madras, pride themselves on their lineage. In particular, I would like to thank Tiru K. Jayaramachandran, who has devoted much of his life to documenting the literary career of Śrīnivāsa Dīkṣita, for sharing with me some of the rich material he has collected.
2. See Srinivasachari 1943: 78. The poet was also granted land rights in the village of Kotlāmpākkam, near Panrutti.
3. See Bronner 2010.
4. On Sanskrit allegories, see Tieken 2010; on the *Prabodha-candrodaya,* see Kapstein's introduction to his translation of the text (2009).
5. *Abhijñanaśākuntala* 1.9; cf. *Vikramorvaśīya* 1.4. On the programmatic burden of such verses, see Shulman 2001: 187–189.
6. Note that this question by Best to himself, or to the Clown, is almost the same one that Imagination's father is constantly asking himself (who is that Lord of the World?).

7. *puruṣottama eva mama vallabha iti su-dṛḍhaś câdhyavasāyaḥ*. On "determination" or "apprehension" *(adhyavasāya),* see section 3.2 and Ratié 2010: 343–344.
8. This statement is an almost exact replica of Daṇḍin's example of the figure *paryāyokta; Kāvyâdarśa* 2.295–296.
9. This closing verse (42) is closely modeled on *Abhibjñāna-śākuntala* 1.3.
10. See section 7.2.
11. See section 8.5.
12. Recall Sāmavān who undergoes the opposite gender transformation under the influence of Sīmantinī's imagination (section 7.2), and note again the dependable linkage between this theme and the contemporaneous discourse on mind.
13. See section 8.4.
14. *Abhijñāna-śākuntala* 5.2.
15. See section 2.3.
16. Renumbering (38, again, in the printed text). This may be the place to note that the Sarasvati Mahal edition, which is all we have, is so full of misprints and misreadings that we would almost certainly be better off with the original, barely legible manuscripts.
17. This verse quotes *Abhijñāna-śākuntala* 1.9 and also includes a somewhat arcane grammatical reference (*Aṣṭâdhyāyī* 5.2.16).
18. Compare Harṣadeva's articulation of this same problem; see section 2.2.
19. See section 8.4; Dayan 2008.
20. But see section 9.5.
21. That is, two official wives of Viṣṇu's.
22. For example, in the *Vāsava-dattā,* a pivotal text in the history both of classical Indian dream theory and of *kāvya*-based models of the mind; see Bronner 2010: 28–29. On the shared dream, see Doniger [O'Flaherty] 1984: 65–71.
23. See Handelman and Shulman forthcoming.
24. My thanks to Lorraine Daston for this suggestion.
25. This point was made by Jan Assmann in conversation.
26. Note the crucial role of writing in this moment of decision.
27. *Tiruvaruṭpayan̲* 6.8.

11. Toward Conclusion

1. Cerulli 2009; Zimmer 1948.
2. See Narayana Rao, Shulman, and Subrahmanyam 2001.
3. Kapil Raj 2010.
4. See the Tamil and other vernacular extensions of the classical textbook on botany, *Vṛkṣâyur-veda.*

5. See section 9.5.
6. As in the Kashmiri materials linked by Ratié 2010 to a theory of the imagination.
7. Cited in section 3.3; Ingalls, Masson, and Patwardhan [*Dhvany-āloka*] 1990: 681.
8. Aristotle, *De Anima* 3.3 (428a11).
9. In India, as we have seen, there is a strong presumption that awareness, when most free and whole, may be devoid of objects/contents.
10. Hamlyn 1978: 131. Similarly Nussbaum 1978: 231: "The most fruitful approach in determining what is meant in any given context [by *phantasia* and *phantasma*] is always to remain aware of the connection with the verb *phainesthai* [to appear]."
11. *De Anima* 3.3 429a: *phantasia* is said to be derived from *phaos,* "light, without which one cannot see."
12. Nussbaum 1978: 245.
13. Ibid., 268. This reading of *phantasia* may, however, be rather idiosyncratic.
14. Vernant 1991: 168, citing *Sophist* 240b11.
15. Vernant 1991: 173.
16. Ibid., 181.
17. See section 1.3.
18. See discussion in Vernant 1991: 167–168, 186–192.
19. See White 1990.
20. *Metaphysics* 12.7 1072b26 ff. See Nussbaum 1978: 267: "God would not require *phantasia.*" Glenn Most has rightly pointed out, in private communication, that a more satisfying theory of the imagination in ancient Greece might prefer popular sources on magic, religion, and emotion to the philosophers' discussions.
21. Philostratus Vit. Ap. Tyran. 6.19; Vernant 1991: 185.
22. Hadot 2006: 60.
23. Ibid., 65–66.
24. Also *wahm,* but the latter tends to be specified as "illusion," "unreal phantasy": see, e.g., Chittick 1989: 122.
25. Chittick 1989: 16. On Ibn al-ʿArabī's thought in general, see Chodkiewicz 2005; Corbin 1969; Izutsu 1983.
26. "Imagination is the widest thing known." Cited in Chittick 1989: 122.
27. Following Sviri 2008. I am grateful to Sara Sviri for discussions of Ibn al-ʿArabī and for commenting on this section.
28. See diagram in Chittick 1989: 16.
29. Corbin 1969; see also sections 3.2, 3.3, and 5.3 in this book.
30. *Wa-ay quwwa a'zam quwattan miman yulḥiqu al-muḥāl al-wujūd bi'l-wujūd al-maḥsūsi ḥatta tarāhu al-abṣār ka-wujūd al-jism fi makānain.* The author

continues by asserting that nothing is easier than combining the impossible with the possible, and nothing more difficult than combining the possible with the impossible.

31. Ibn al-ʿArabī, *Al-Futūḥāt al-Makkiya,* Chapter 558; translation by Chittick 1989: 124.
32. Cited in Chittick 1989: 116.
33. *Fuṣūṣ al-ḥikam* 9, translated by Dagli 2004: 101.
34. Like the dream within a dream; Sviri 2008: 532.
35. See sections 5.1–3. It is also of interest that Ibn al-ʿArabī cites a story precisely parallel to the famous Lavaṇa episode from the *Yoga-vāsiṣṭha:* this is the story of Jawhari, who looked into the water of the Nile and "saw himself in the way a dreamer sees things, as though he were in Baghdad." In his dream-like Baghdadi existence, Jawhari was married and had several children. Still standing in the Nile, he came back to himself and went home; several months later, however, his Baghdadi wife and children turned up in Cairo, and he recognized them at once. "Thus what happened in the Imagination emerged [concretely] in sense-perception." *Al-Futūḥāt al-Makkīya,* chapter 73; Chodkiewicz 2005: 113–114. See Doniger [O'Flaherty] 1984: 132–143.
36. Cited in Chittick 1989: 116.
37. Daston 2003.
38. Even a very modern thinker such as Bergson thinks of the *sensus communis,* which he calls *bon sens,* as synonymous with attention; A. Assmann, in press.
39. Ibid.
40. Ibid.
41. Daston 2003.
42. Ibid.
43. Daston 2011.
44. Condillac 1924: 24–37; Daston and Galison 2007: 223–225.
45. Cited from the *Encyclopédie,* Daston and Galison 2007: 225.
46. Daston and Galison 2007: 224.
47. Daston 2011.
48. *Rāmāyaṇa* 1.4.36: *sa câpi rāmaḥ pariṣad-gataḥ śanair bubhūṣayā saktamanā babhūva ha.*
49. In Olivelle's apt translation [Upaniṣads]: 148.

Bibliography

Primary Sources in Sanskrit, Telugu, Tamil, and Malayalam

Abhijñāna-śākuntala of Kālidāsa. Varanasi: Chowkhamba Sanskrit Series, 1976.

Adhyātma-saṅkīrtanalu of Annamayya. Vols. 2 and 3. Ed. Gauripeddi Ramasubba Sarma. Tirupati: Tirumala tirupati devasthanamulu, 1998.

Aiṅkuṟunūṟu. With the commentary of Pŏ. Ve. Comacuntaraṉār. Tirunelveli: South India Saiva Siddhanta Works Publishing Society, 1972.

Alaṅkāra-sarvasva of Ruyyaka. With *Sañjīvanī* commentary of Vidyācakravartin. Ed. S. S. Janaki. Delhi: Meharchand Lachhmandas, 1965.

———. With commentary by Samudrabandha. Trivandrum: University of Kerala, 1926.

Āmukta-mālyada of Kṛṣṇa-deva-rāya. Ed. Vedam Venkataraya Sastri. Madras: Vedam Venkataraya Sastri and Brothers, 1964.

Aṣṭâdhyāyī of Pāṇini, with *Kāśikā-vṛtti*. Delhi: Caukhamba Samskrta Pratishana, 2005.

Bhaiṣmī-pariṇaya-campū of Ratna-kheṭa Śrīnivāsa Dīkṣita. Tirupati: Venkatesvara Oriental Series, 1991.

Bhāmatī of Vācaspati Miśra on the *Brahma-sūtra-bhāṣya* of Śaṅkara. Ed. with English trans. by S. S. Suryanarayana Sastri and C. Kunhan Raja. Madras: Adyar Library and Research Center, 1992.

Bhāṣā-naiṣadha-campū of Maḻamaṅgalam. Kottayam: National Book Stall, 1985.

Bhāṣā-pariccheda with *Siddhânta-mukhâvali* of Viśvanātha Nyāya-pañcânana. Calcutta: Advaita Ashram, 1940.

Bhaṭṭi-kāvya. Ed. Maheswar Anant Karandikar and Shailaja Karandikar. Delhi: Motilal Banarsidass, 1982.

———. Trans. Oliver Fallon. *Bhaṭṭi's Poem. The Death of Rāvaṇa*. New York: New York University Press, 2009.

Bhāvanā-puruṣottama of Ratna-kheṭa Śrīnivāsa Dīkṣita. Ed. S. Swaminatha Sastri. Tanjavur: Sarasvati Mahal Library, 1979.

Bhāvanā Upaniṣad. With commentary of Bhāskarāya. Madras: Ganesh, 1976.

Brahma-siddhi of Maṇḍana Miśra. Ed. Kuppuswami Sastri. Delhi: Satguru Publications, 1984.

Brahma-sūtra-bhāṣya of Śaṅkarâcārya. Bombay: Nirnaya Sagar Press, 1934.

Daśa-rūpaka of Dhanañjaya, with the *Avaloka* commentary of Dhanika. Ed. T. Venkatacharya. Adyar: Adyar Library and Research Centre, 1969.

Dayā-śataka of Vedânta Deśika. Tirupati: Tirupati Tirumala Devasthanam, 1982.

———. Trans. Yigal Bronner and David Shulman. *"Self-surrender," "Peace," "Compassion" and "The Mission of the Goose."* New York: New York University Press, 2009.

Devī-bhāgavata-purāṇa. Delhi: Bharatiya Vidya Prakashana, 2001.

Dhvany-āloka of Ānanda-vardhana. Ed. Pullela Sri Ramacandrudu. Hyderabad: Sri Jayalakshmi Publications, 1998.

———. Trans. Daniel H. H. Ingalls, Jeffrey Moussaieff Masson, and M. V. Patwardhan. *The Dhvanyāloka of Ānandavardhana with the Locana of Abhinavagupta*. Cambridge, Mass.: Harvard University Press, 1990.

Haṃsa-sandeśa of Vedânta Deśika, with commentary by Ranga Chariar. Madras: Vedanta Desika Research Society, 1983.

———. Trans. Yigal Bronner and David Shulman. See *Dayā-śataka*.

Irāmâvatāram of Kampaṉ. Tiruvanmiyur: U. Ve. Cāminātaiyar Nūl Nilaiyam, 1967.

Kādambarī of Bāṇa. Ed. Kasinath Pandurang Parab and Wasudeva Laxmana Shastri Pansikar. Delhi: Nag Publishers, 1985.

———. Trans. Gwendolyn Lane. *Kādambarī. A Classic Sanskrit Story of Magical Transformations*. New York: Garland Publishing, 1991.

Kāḷahastîśvara-śatakamu of Dhūrjaṭi. Ed. Nidadavolu Venkata Rao. Hyderabad: Andhra Pradesh Sahitya Akademi, 1966.

———. Trans. V. Narayana Rao and H. Heifetz. *For the Lord of the Animals: Poems from the Telugu. The Kāḷahastīśvara Śatakamu of Dhūrjaṭi*. Berkeley: University of California Press, 1987.

Kaḷā-pūrṇodayamu of Piṅgaḷi Sūranna. Madras: Vavilla Ramaswamy Sastrulu and Sons, 1968.

———. Trans. Velcheru Narayana Rao and David Shulman. *The Sound of the Kiss, or the Story That Must Never be Told*. New York: Columbia University Press, 2002.

Karṇāṭaka rājākkaḷ cavistāra carittiram of Cĕñci Nārāyaṇaṉ. Madras: Madras Government Oriental Series, 1952.

Kāśikā-vṛtti. Ed. A. Sharma and K. Deshpande. Hyderabad: Osmania University, 1969–1970.

Katācintāmaṇi ĕṉṟu vaḷaṅkukiṟa mariyātairāmaṉ katai. Madras: R. J. Pati Company, 1975.

Kāvyâdarśa of Daṇḍin. Edited by O. Boehtlingk. Leipzig: H. Haessel, 1890.
Kāvyâlaṅkāra of Bhāmaha. Ed. P. V. Naganatha Sastry. Delhi: Motilal Banarsidass, 1970.
Kāvyâlaṅkāra-sūtra-vṛtti of Vāmana. Poona: Oriental Book Agency, 1927.
Kāvya-mīmāṃsā of Rājaśekhara. Ed. C. D. Dalal and R. A. Sastry. Baroda: Oriental Institute, 1934.
———. Trans. Nadine Stchoupak and Louis Renou. *La Kāvyamīmāṃsā de Rājaśekhara*. Paris: Imprimerie Nationale, 1946.
Kāvya-prakāśa of Mammaṭa. Ed. Ganganatha Jha. Delhi: Bharatiya Vidya Prakashan, 1985.
Kirātârjunīya of Bhāravi. Bombay: Nirnaya Sagar Press, 1954.
Kumāra-saṃbhava of Kālidāsa. Ed. M. R. Kale. Delhi: Motilal Banarsidass, 1967.
Kuṟuntŏkai. Ed. U. Ve. Cāminātaiyar. Madras: Kabir Press, 1947.
Laghu-yoga-vāsiṣṭha of Abhinanda. Delhi: Motilal Banarsidass, 1985.
Mahā-bhārata, with the commentary of Nīlakaṇṭha. Ed. Ramchandrashastri Kinjawadekar. New Delhi: Oriental Books Reprint Corporation, 1850.
Mahā-bhāṣya of Patañjali, with *Pradīpa* commentary. Ed. M S. Narasimhacharya. Pondichéry: Institut Français d'Indologie, 1973–1983.
Maṇimekalai of Cīttalaiccāttaṉār, with commentary by Po. Ve. Comacuntaranar. Madras: Saiva Siddhanta Works Publishing Society, 1971.
Manu-caritramu of Pĕddana. Madras: R. Venkatesvar and Company, 1919.
Megha-sandeśa of Kālidāsa. Ed. N. P. Unni, with commentaries by Dakṣiṇāvartanātha, Pūrṇasarasvatī, and Parameśvara. Delhi: Bharatiya Vidya Prakashan, 1987.
Naiṣadhīya-carita of Śrīharṣa. With commentary by Nārāyaṇa. Delhi: Meharchand Lacchmandas Publications, 1986.
Naiṣkarmya-siddhi of Sureśvara. Ed. and trans. A. J. Alston. London: Shanti Sadan, 1959.
Naiṭatam of Ativīrarāma Pāṇṭiyaṉ. Madras: n.p., c. 1907.
Nāṭya-śāstra of Bharata, with the *Abhinavabhāratī* of Abhinavagupta. Vol. 1, ed. K. Krishnamoorthy. Baroda: Oriental Institute, 1992. Vol. 2, ed. V. N. Kulkarni and Tapasvi Nandi. Baroda: Oriental Institute, 2001.
Niraṅkuśopâkhyānamu of Rudrakavi. Kadapa: Akasavani, 1976.
Nyāya-kandalī of Śrīdhara, with *Praśasta-pāda-bhāṣya*. Banaras: 1895.
Nyāya-kosa of Bhimacharya Jhalkikar. 4th ed. Poona: Bhandarkar Oriental Research Institute, 1978.
Pañcadaśī of Vidyâraṇya. Madras: Sri Ramakrishna Mutt, 1975.
Pāṇḍya-kulodaya of Maṇḍala-kavi. Ed. K. V. Sarma. Hoshiarpur: Vishveshvaranand Vishva Bandhu Institute of Sanskrit and Indological Studies, 1981.
Pĕriya Purāṇam of Cekkiḻār. Tirunelveli: South India Saiva Siddhanta Works Publishing Company, 1970.

Piramottara-kāṇṭam of Varatuṅkarāma Pāṇṭiyar. Tiruvitaimarutur: Makāliṅkacuvāmi Devasthānam, 1974).

Prabhāvatī-pradyumnamu of Piṅgaḷi Sūranna. Ed. Bommakanti Venkata Singaracarya and Balantrapu Nalinikanta Ravu. Vijayavada: M. Sesacalam and Company, 1970; reprinted 1990.

———. Trans. V. Narayana Rao and David Shulman. *The Demon's Daughter: A Love Story from South India.* Albany: State University of New York Press, 2006.

Prabodha-candrodaya of Krsṇa Miśra. Ed. Sita Krishna Nambiar. Delhi: Motilal Banarsidass, 1971.

———. Trans. with an introduction by Matthew Kapstein. *The Rise of Wisdom Moon.* Clay Sanskrit Library. New York: New York University Press, 2009.

Pratāpa-rudrīya of Vidyānātha, with the *Ratnâpaṇa* of Kumārasvāmin. Ed. Dr. V. Raghavan. Madras: Samskrit Education Society, 1979.

———. Trans. with an introduction and notes by Pierre-Sylvain Filliozat. *Le Pratāparudrīya de Vidyānātha.* Pondichéry: Institut Français d'Indologie, 1963.

Priya-darśikā of Harṣavardhana. Ed. with commentary by R. V. Krishnamachariar. Srirangam: Sri Vani Vilas Press, 1906.

Raghu-vaṃśa of Kālidāsa. Ed. Gopal Raghunath Nandargikar. Delhi: Motilal Banarsidass, 1982.

Rāmāyaṇa of Vālmīki. Ed. K. Chinnaswami Sastrigal and V. H. Subrahmanya Sastri. Madras: N. Ramaratnam, 1958.

Rasa-gaṅgādhara of Jagannātha Paṇditarāja, with commentary by Mathurānātha Śāstri. Delhi: Motilal Banarsidass, 1983.

Rasârṇava-sudhâkara of Siṃhabhūpāla. Ed. T. Venkatacharya. Madras: Adyar Library and Research Centre, 1979.

Ratnâvalī of Harṣadeva. Ed. M. R. Kale. Delhi: Motilal Banarsidass, 1984.

———. Trans. Wendy Doniger. *The Lady of the Jewel Necklace and The Lady Who Shows Her Love.* Clay Sanskrit Library. New York: New York University Press, 2006.

Rāvaṇolbhavam (from the Bhāṣā-rāmāyaṇa-campu) of Punam. Trissur: Kerala Sahitya Akademy, 1996.

Ṛg Veda. Bombay: Svadhyaya Mandal, 1957.

Sarasvatī-kaṇṭhâbharaṇa of Bhojadeva. Ed. Kedara Natha Sarma and Vasudeva Sarma. Varanasi: Chaukhamba Orientalia, 1987.

Sarpapura-kṣetra-māhātmya. British Library, IOL 4843/IO 2842d (EGG 3666) [*Piṭhāpuram tālūkālona sarpavaram kṣetra-māhātmyam*]. MacKenzie Collection. 1825.

Śatapatha-brāhmaṇa (Mādhyandina Recension). Delhi: Nag Publishers, 1990.

———. Trans. Julius Eggeling. Delhi: Motilal Banarsidass, 1963; reprinted 1987.

Saundarya-laharī. Ed. with a series of Sanskrit commentaries by A. Kuppuswami. Delhi: Nag Publishers, 1991.

Śiśupāla-vadha of Māgha. Varanasi: Chaukhambha, 2000.

Śrīkaṇṭha-carita of Maṅkhaka. Delhi: Motilal Banarsidass, 1983.

Taṉippāṭar̲ṟiraṭṭu. Ed. M. Vīraveṟ Piḷḷai. Madras: Tiruvaḷḷuvar puttaka nilaiyam, 1940.

Taṇṭiyalaṅkāram. Madras: South Indian Saiva Siddhanta Works Publishing Company, 1984.

Tantrâloka of Abhinavagupta, with commentary of Jayaratha. Allahabad: Indian Press, 1918.

Tarka-saṅgraha, with the *Dīpaka* of Annambhaṭṭa. Ed. Yashwant Vasudev Athalye. Poona: Bhandarkar Oriental Research Institute, 1988.

Tevāram of Cuntaramūrttināyaṉār. Tarumapuram: Tarumaiyātīṉam, 1964.

———. Trans. D. Shulman. *Songs of the Harsh Devotee.* Philadelphia: Department of South Asia Regional Studies, University of Pennsylvania, 1990.

Tevāram of Tiruñāṉacampantar. Tarumapuram: Tarumaiyātīṉam, 1954.

Tiruvācakam of Māṇikkavācakar. Ed. G. U. Pope. Oxford: Clarendon Press, 1900.

Tiruvaruṭpayaṉ of Kŏṟṟavaṉkuṭi Umāpati Tevanāyaṉār. Madras: Velur Devastāṉa Iṟaipaṇi Maṉṟam, 1958.

Upaniṣads. *Aṣṭādaśa upaniṣadaḥ.* Poona: 1958.

———. Trans. Patrick Olivelle. *Upaniṣads.* New York: Oxford University Press, 1996.

Uttara-rāma-carita of Bhavabhūti. Ed. P. V. Kane and C. N. Joshi. Delhi: Motilal Banarsidass, 1971.

———. Ed. Sankara Rama Sastri, with commentary of Nārāyaṇa. Mylapore: Sri Balamanorama Press, 1932.

Vaiyākaraṇa-bhūṣaṇa-sāra of Kauṇḍa Bhaṭṭa. Ed. Balakrsna Pancholi. Varanasi: Chawkhamba Sanskrit Samsthan, 2006.

Vājasaneyi-saṃhitā of the *Mādhyandina-śukla-yajur-veda.* Delhi: Motilal Banarsidass, 1971.

Vakrokti-jīvita of Kuntaka. Ed. K. Krishnamoorthy. Dharwad: Karnatak University, 1977.

Vākya-padīya of Bhartrhari. Ed. K. Raghavan Pillai. Delhi: Motilal Banarsidass, 1971.

Vāsava-dattā of Subandhu. Srirangam: Vani Vilas Press, 1906.

Vikramorvaśīya of Kālidāsa. Ed. H. D. Velankar. Delhi: Sahitya Akademi, 1961.

———. Trans. Velcheru Narayana Rao and David Shulman. *How Urvaśī Was Won.* New York: Clay Sanskrit Library, 2009.

Vṛkṣâyur-veda of Parāśara. *A Treatise on Plant Science.* Ed. N. N. Sircar and Roma Sarkar. Delhi: Sri Satguru Publishers, 1996.

Vyakti-viveka of Rājānaka Mahima Bhaṭṭa. With commentary by Rājānaka Ruyyaka. Ed. T. Ganapati Sastri. Trivandrum: Travancore Government Press, 1909.

Yoga-vāsiṣṭha-mahā-rāmāyaṇa. Kasi: Acyuta-grantha-mala, Saṃvat 2004.

Secondary Literature

Aristotle. 1980. *De Anima*. Ed. A. Jannone. Paris: Société d'édition "Les Belles Lettres."

Arunacalam, Mu. 1977. *Tĕṉkācip pāṇṭiyar*. Tirucirrampalam, Māyūram District: Kānti Vittiyâlayam.

Assmann, Aleida. Forthcoming. "The Tri-cameral Mind and the Separation of Scientific Cultures."

Assmann, Jan. 1992. "Akhanyati's Theology of Light and Time." *Proceedings of the Israel Academy of Sciences and Humanities* 7, no. 4: 143–176.

Babel, Isaac. 1991. *Detstvo i drugiye rasskazi*. Jerusalem: Biblioteka Alia.

Bakhtin, M. M. 1981. *The Dialogic Imagination: Four Essays*. Ed. Michael Holquist, trans. Caryl Emerson and Michael Holquist. Austin: University of Texas Press.

———. 1984. *Problems in Dostoyevsky's Poetics*. Ed. and trans. Caryl Emerson. Minneapolis: University of Minnesota Press.

Bansat-Boudon, Lyne. 1992. *Poétique du théâtre indien: Lectures du Nāṭyaśāstra*. Paris: École française d'Extrême-Orient.

———. 2000. "L'Épopée mise en scène: L'Example de l'Uttararāmacarita." *Journal Asiatique* 288: 83–111.

Becker, A. L. 1995. *Beyond Translation: Essays toward a Modern Philology*. Ann Arbor: University of Michigan Press.

Ben-Dor, Sharon. 1999. "The Term *Pratibhā* According to Bhartṛhari" (Hebrew). MA thesis, Hebrew University.

Bhatta, V. P. 2001. *Navya-Nyāya Theory of Verbal Cognition: Critical Study of Gadādhara's Vyutpattivāda*. Delhi: Eastern Book Linkers.

Brereton, Joel. 1986. "*Tat tvam asi* in Context." *ZDMG* 136: 98–109.

Bronner, Yigal. 2007. "This Is No Lotus, It Is a Face: Poetics as Grammar in Daṇḍin's Investigation of the Simile." In Sergio La Porta and David Shulman, eds., *The Poetics of Grammar and the Metaphysics of Sound and Sign*. Leiden: Brill, 91–108.

———. 2009. *Extreme Poetry: The South Asian Movement of Simultaneous Narration*. New York: Columbia University Press.

———. 2010. "Arriving at a Definition: Appayya Dīkṣita's Meditation on the Simile and the Onset of New Poetics." In D. Shulman, ed., *Language, Myth and Ritual in Ancient India and Iran*. Jerusalem: Israel Academy of Sciences and Humanities, 195–230.

Bronner, Yigal, and David Shulman. 2006. "A Cloud Turned Goose: Sanskrit in the Vernacular Millennium." *Indian Economic and Social History Review* 43: 1–30.

Bronner, Yigal, David Shulman, and Gary Tubb, eds. Forthcoming. *Sanskrit Kāvya: Innovations and Turning Points.*

Bronner, Yigal, and Gary Tubb. 2008. "*Vastutas tu:* Methodology and the New School of Sanskrit Poetics." *Journal of Indian Philosophy* 36: 619–632.

Cerulli, Anthony. 2009. "Narrative Wellbeing: Ānandarāyamakhin's 'The Joy of Life' *(Jīvānandanam)*." *Indian Journal of History of Science* 44, no. 2: 222–235.

Chakrabarty, Dipesh. 2000. *Provincializing Europe: Postcolonial Thought and Historical Difference.* Princeton: Princeton University Press.

Chatterjee, Kamala. 1978. "Brahman as Ignorant." *Journal of the Indian Academy of Philosophy* 17: 1–16.

Chittick, William C. 1989. *The Sufi Path of Knowledge: Ibn al-ʿArabī's Metaphysics of Imagination.* Albany: State University of New York Press.

Chodkiewicz, Michel, ed. 2005. *Ibn al-ʿArabī, the Meccan Revelations.* Trans. Willian C. Chittick and James W. Morris. New York: Pir Press.

Cina Sitaramasvamisastrulu, Vajjhala. 1965. *Vasu-caritra-vimarśanamu.* Madras: Vavilla Ramasvamisastrulu and Sons.

Condillac, Étienne Bonnot de. 1924. *Essai sur l'origine des connaissances humaines.* Paris: Librairie Armand Colin.

Corbin, H. 1969. *Creative Imagination in the Sufism of Ibn ʿArabi.* Trans. Ralph Manheim. Princeton: Princeton University Press.

Cutler, Norman. 1987. *Songs of Experience: The Poetics of Tamil Devotion.* Bloomington: University of Indiana Press.

Dagli, Caner K. *See* Ibn al-ʿArabī.

Dalal, C. D., and R. A. Sastry. *See* Rājaśekhara.

Dalrymple, William. 2009. *Nine Lives: In Search of the Sacred in Modern India.* London: Bloomsbury.

Dasgupta, Surendranath. 1975. *A History of Indian Philosophy.* 5 vols. Delhi: Motilal Banarsidass.

Daston, Lorraine. 2003. "The Material Powers of the Imagination and the Boundaries of the Self in Early Modern Europe." Conference on "Inner Temptations: The Early Modern Imagination," Northwestern University, December.

———. 2011. "Projection and Perfect Passivity." In Natascha Adamowsky, Robert Felfe, Marco Formisano, George Toepfer, and Kirsten Wagner, eds., *Affektive Dinge: Objektberührungen in Wissenschaft und Kunst.* Göttingen: Wallstein.

Daston, Lorraine, and Peter Galison. 2007. *Objectivity.* New York: Zone Books.

Dayan, Maya Tevet. 2008. "The Unseen Man Who Saw Himself in Mirrors: Metaphysics of Reflections in the *Naiṣadhīyacarita*." In Shalva Weil and

David Shulman, eds., *Karmic Passages: Israeli Scholarship on India*. Delhi: Oxford University Press, 104–120.

Dhanika. See *Daśa-rūpaka*.

Doniger, Wendy. 1976. *The Origins of Evil in Hindu Mythology*. Berkeley: University of California Press.

———. 1984. *Dreams, Illusion, and Other Realities*. Chicago: University of Chicago Press.

———. See *Ratnâvalī*.

Ebeling, Sascha. 2010. *Colonizing the Realm of Words: The Transformation of Tamil Literature in Nineteenth-century South India*. Albany: State University of New York Press.

Eggeling, Julius. See *Śatapatha Brāhmaṇa*.

Ezrahi, Yaron. Forthcoming. *Imagining Democracy from the Modern to the Postmodern Era*. Cambridge: Cambridge University Press.

Fallon, Oliver. See *Bhaṭṭi-kāvya*.

Faruqi, Shamsur Rahman. 2004. "A Stranger in the City: The Poetics of *Sabk-i Hindi*." *Annual of Urdu Studies* 19: 1–93.

Finkelberg, Margalit. 1998. *The Birth of Literary Fiction in Ancient Greece*. Oxford: Oxford University Press.

Freeman, Rich. 2003. "Genre and Society: The Literary Culture of Premodern Kerala." In Sheldon Pollock, ed., *Literary Cultures in History: Reconstructions from South Asia*. Berkeley: University of California Press, 437–500.

Fried, Michael. 1980. *Absorption and Theatricality: Painting and Beholder in the Age of Diderot*. Berkeley: University of California Press.

Galison, Peter. *See* Daston, Lorraine.

Gerow, Edwin. 1971. *A Glossary of Indian Figures of Speech*. The Hague: Mouton.

Gnoli, Raniero. 1968. *The Aesthetic Experience According to Abhinavagupta*. 2nd ed. Varanasi: Chowkhamba Sanskrit Series.

Gold, Ann Grodzins, and Bhoju Ram Gujar. 2002. *In the Time of Trees and Sorrows: Nature, Power, and Memory in Rajasthan*. Durham, N.C.: Duke University Press.

Gopinatha Kaviraj. 1924. "The Doctrine of *Pratibhā* in Indian Philosophy." *Annals of the Bhandarkar Oriental Research Institute* 6: 1–18, 113–132. Reprinted in Gopinatha Kaviraj, *Aspects of Indian Thought*. Calcutta: University of Burdwan, 1966, 1–44.

Gopinatha Rao, T. A. 1910. *Travancore Archaeology Series*, vol. 1. Madras: Methodist Publishing House.

Granoff, Phyllis. 2000. "Portraits, Likenesses, and Looking Glasses: Some Literary and Philosophical Reflections on Representation and Art in Medieval India." In Jan Assmann and Albert Baumgarten, eds., *Representation in Religion: Studies in Honor of Moshe Barasch*. Leiden: E. J. Brill, 63–107.

———. Forthcoming. "Putting the Polish on the Poet's Efforts: Reading the *Karṇasundarī* as a Reflection on Poetic Creativity." In Yigal Bronner, David Shulman, and Gary Tubb, eds., *Sanskrit Kāvya: Innovations and Turning Points.*

Grinshpon, Yohanan. Forthcoming. "Inference and Self: A Note on Sankara's Cogito."

Gwynn, J. P. L. 1991. *A Telugu-English Dictionary.* Delhi: Oxford University Press.

Hadot, Pierre. 2006. *The Veil of Isis: An Essay on the History of the Idea of Nature.* Trans. Michael Chase. Cambridge, Mass.: Harvard University Press.

Hamlyn, D. W. 1978. *Aristotle's De Anima, Books II, III.* Oxford: Clarendon Press.

Handelman, Don. 1995a. "Cultural Taxonomy and Bureaucracy in Ancient China: *The Book of Lord Shang.*" *International Journal of Politics, Culture, and Society* 9: 263–293.

———. 1995b. "The Guises of the Goddess and the Transformation of the Male: Gangamma's Visit to Tirupati and the Continuum of Gender." In D. Shulman, ed., *Syllables of Sky: Studies in South Indian Civilization in Honor of Velcheru Narayana Rao.* Delhi: Oxford University Press, 281–335.

———. 2006. "Postlude: Toward a Braiding of Frame." In D. Shulman and Deborah Thiagarajan, eds., *Masked Ritual and Performance in South India: Dance, Healing, and Possession.* Ann Arbor: Centers for South and Southeast Asian Studies, University of Michigan, 246–242.

Handelman, Don, and David Shulman. 1997. *God Inside Out: Śiva's Game of Dice.* New York: Oxford University Press.

———. 1998. *Śiva in the Forest of Pines: An Essay on Sorcery and Self-Knowledge.* Delhi: Oxford University Press,

———. Forthcoming. "*The Chess Players:* Royal Rituals of Destruction."

Hara, Minoru. 1963. "Note on Two Sanskrit Religious Terms: *Bhakti* and *Śraddhā.*" *Indo-Iranian Journal* 7: 124–145.

Hartman, Geofrrey. 1966. *The Unmediated Vision: An Interpretation of Wordsworth, Hopkins, Rilke, and Valery.* New York: Harcourt, Brace, and World.

Heesterman, Jan. 1991. "'I Am Who I Am': Truth and Identity in Vedic Ritual." In Gerhard Oberhammer, ed., *Beiträge zur Hermeneutik indischer und abendländischer Religionstraditionen.* Vienna: Der Österreichischen Akademie der Wissenschaften.

Huet, Marie-Hélène. 1993. *Monstrous Imagination.* Cambridge, Mass.: Harvard University Press.

Ibn al-ʿArabī. 2002. *Al-Futūḥāt al-Makkiyya.* Beirut: Dar al-Fikr.

———. 2004. *Futūḥ al-ḥikam* [The ringstones of wisdom]. Trans. Caner K. Dagli. Chicago: Great Books of the Islamic World.

———. *See* Chodkiewicz, Michel.

Izutsu, Toshihiko. 1983. *Sufism and Taoism*. Berkeley: University of California Press.

Kapferer, Bruce. 1997. *The Feast of the Sorcerer: Practices of Consciousness and Power*. Chicago: University of Chicago Press.

Kapil Raj. 2010. *Relocating Modern Science: Circulation and the Construction of Knowledge in South Asia and Europe, 1650–1900*. London: Palgrave Macmillan.

Kapstein, Matthew. See *Prabodha-candrodaya*.

Klein, Jared. 2010. "Categories and Types of Stylistic Repetition in the *Ṛg-Veda*." In David Shulman, ed., *Language, Ritual and Poetics in Ancient India and Iran: Studies in Honor of Shaul Migron*. Jerusalem: Israel Academy of Sciences and Humanities, 16–38.

Klein, Tammy. 2009. "When Imagination and Sign Meet: The Birth of a New Poetics in Kudiyattam. A Study of *Tapatī-saṃvaraṇam*" (Hebrew). MA thesis, Hebrew University.

Kuiper, F. B. J. 1975. "The Basic Concept of Vedic Religion." *History of Religions* 15: 107–120.

Kunjunni Raja, K. 1969. *Indian Theories of Meaning*. 2nd ed. Madras: Adyar Library and Research Centre.

Malamoud, Charles. 1989. *Cuire le monde. Rite et pensée dans l'Inde ancienne*. Paris: Editions La Découverte.

———. Forthcoming. "Shadows in the *Naiṣadhacarita*." In Yigal Bronner, David Shulman, and Gary Tubb, eds., *Sanskrit Kāvya: Innovations and Turning Points*.

Matilal, Bimal Krishna. 1977. *Nyāya-Vaiśeṣika* [A history of Indian literature]. Wiesbaden: Otto Harrasowitz.

———. 1986. *Perception: An Essay on Classical Indian Theories of Knowledge*. Oxford: Clarendon Press.

Mazumdar, Pradip Kumar. 1977. *The Philosophy of Language in the Light of Paninian and the Mimamsaka Schools of Indian Philosophy*. Calcutta: Sanskrit Pustak Bhandar.

McCrea, Lawrence J. 2008. *The Teleology of Poetics in Medieval Kashmir*. Cambridge, Mass.: Harvard University Press.

———. 2010. "Poetry in Chains: Commentary and Control in the Sanskrit Poetic Tradition." In D. Shulman, ed., *Language, Ritual and Poetics in India and Iran: Studies in honor of Shaul Migron*. Jerusalem: Israel Academy of Sciences and Humanities, 231–248.

Minkowski, C. 2008. "The Study of Jyotiḥśāstra and the Uses of Philosophy of Science." *Journal of Indian Philosophy* 36: 587–597.

Montaigne, Michel de. 1685—1686. *Essays of Michael, Seigneur de Montaigne*. Trans. Charles Cotton, Esq. London: T. Basset et al.

Motzkin, Gabriel. Forthcoming. *The Door to Times Past: A Cognitive Philosophy of History.*

Narayana Rao, Velcheru. 1978. *Tĕlugulo kavitā viplavāla svarūpam.* Vijayavada: Visalandhra pracuranalayam.

———. 1992."Kings, Gods, and Poets: Ideologies of Patronage in Medieval Andhra." In Barbara Stoler Miller, ed., *The Powers of Art: Patronage in Indian Culture.* Delhi: Oxford University Press, 142–159.

———. 2002. *Twentieth Century Telugu Poetry: An Anthology.* Delhi: Oxford University Press.

———. See *Kāḷahastīśvara-śatakamu.*

Narayana Rao, Velcheru, and David Shulman. 1998. *A Poem at the Right Moment: Remembered Verses from Pre-Modern South India.* Berkeley: University of California Press.

———. 2005. *God on the Hill: Temple Poems from Tirupati.* New York: Oxford University Press.

———. 2012. *Śrīnātha: The Poet Who Made Gods and Kings.* New York: Oxford University Press.

———. See *Kaḷā-pūrṇodayamu.*

———. See *Prabhāvatī-pradyumnamu.*

———. See *Vikramorvaśīya.*

Narayana Rao, Velcheru, David Shulman, and Sanjay Subrahmanyam. 1992. *Symbols of Substance: Court and State in Nāyaka-Period Tamil Nadu.* Delhi: Oxford University Press.

———. 2001. *Textures of Time: Writing History in South India 1600–1800.* Delhi: Permanent Black.

Nussbaum, Martha. 1978. *Aristotle's De motu animalium.* Princeton: Princeton University Press.

O'Flaherty, Wendy Doniger. *See* Doniger, Wendy.

Pandian, Anand. 2009. *Crooked Stalks: Cultivating Virtue in South India.* Durham, N.C.: Duke University Press.

———. 2010. "Interior Horizons: An Ethical Space of Selfhood in South India." *Journal of the Royal Anthropological Institute* 16: 64–83.

Pollock, Sheldon. 2003. "Sanskrit Literary Culture from the Inside Out." In Sheldon Pollock, ed., *Literary Cultures in History: Reconstructions from South Asia.* Berkeley: University of California Press, 39–130.

———. 2005. *The Ends of Man at the End of Premodernity.* Amsterdam: Royal Netherlands Academy of Arts and Sciences.

———. 2006. *The Language of the Gods in the World of Men.* Berkeley: University of California Press.

———. 2008. "Theory and Method in Indian Intellectual History." *Journal of Indian Philosophy* 36 (special issue).

———. 2010. "What Was Bhaṭṭa Nāyaka Saying? The Hermeneutical Transformation of Indian Aesthetics." In Sheldon Pollock, ed., *Epic and Argument in Sanskrit Literary History: Essays in Honor of Robert P. Goldman*. Delhi: Manohar, 143–184.

Pulavar Aracu. 1968. *Pĕriya purāṇa vacaṉam*. Chennai: Kaḻakam.

Raghavan, V. 1938. "The History of *Bhāvika* in Sanskrit Poetics." *Indian Historical Quarterly* 14: 787–798.

———. 1973. *Studies on Some Concepts of the Alaṃkāra Śāstra*. Madras: Adyar Library and Research Centre.

———. 1978. *Bhoja's Śṛṅgāra Prakāśa*. Madras: Punarvasu.

Rajagopalan, L. S. 2000. *Kudiyattam: Preliminaries and Performance*. Chennai: The Kuppuswami Sastri Research Institute.

Rajamani, V. K., and David Shulman. 2010. *The Mucukunda Murals in the Tyāgarājasvāmi Temple, Tiruvārūr*. Chennai: Prakriti Foundation.

Rajendran, C. 1989. "Mahimabhaṭṭa and Kuntaka." *Pūrṇatrayī. Ravi Varma Samskrta Granthavali Journal* [Tripunithura, Government Sanskrit College] 16, no. 2: 31–40.

Ramanujan, A. K. 1970. *The Interior Landscape*. London: Peter Owen.

Rama Sastry, Janaki, ed. 2008. *East Godavari*. Visakhapatnam: Verve Books.

Ramaswamy, Sundara. 1966. *Ŏru puḷiya marattiṉ katai*. Madras: Cre-A.

Ratié, Isabelle. 2010. "'A Five-Trunked, Four-Tusked Elephant Is Running in the Sky': How Free Is Imagination According to Utpaladeva and Abhinavagupta?" *Asiatische Studien/Études Asiatiques* 64, no. 2: 341–385.

Sanderson, Alexis. 2002. "Remarks on the Text of the *Kubjikāmatatantra*." *Indo-Iranian Journal* 45: 1–24.

Sarangi, A. C. 1995. *Gleanings in the Sanskrit Grammatical Tradition*. Delhi: Eastern Book Linkers.

Satyanarayana, Viswanatha. 1967. *Allasānivāni allikajigibigi*. Viyavada: V. S. N. and Sons.

Shastri, Dharmendra Natha. 1976. *The Philosophy of Nyāya-Vaiśeṣika and Its Conflict with the Buddhist Dignāga School*. Delhi: Bharatiya Vidya Prakashan.

Shulman, David. 1987. "The Anthropology of the Avatar in Kampaṉ's Irāmâvatāram." In Shaul Shaked, David Shulman, and Guy Stroumsa, eds., *Gilgul: Essays in Transformation, Revolution and Permanence in the History of Religions (Festschrift R. J. Zwi Werblowsky)*. Leiden: E. J. Brill, 270–287.

———. 1993. *The Hungry God: Hindu Tales of Filicide and Devotion*. Chicago: University of Chicago Press.

———. 2001. *The Wisdom of Poets: Studies in Tamil, Telugu, and Sanskrit*. Delhi: Oxford University Press.

———. 2005. "The Buzz of God and the Click of Delight." In Angela Hobart and Bruce Kapferer, eds., *Aesthetics in Performance: Formations of Symbolic Construction and Experience*. New York: Berghahn Books, 43–63.

———. 2006. "Toward a New Theory of Masks." In D. Shulman and D. Thiagarajan, eds., *Masked Ritual and Performance in South India: Dance, Healing, and Possession*. Ann Arbor: Centers for South and Southeast Asian Studies, University of Michigan, 17–58.

———. 2007. "How to Bring a Goddess into Being through Visible Sound." In Sergio La Porta and David Shulman, eds., *The Poetics of Grammar and the Metaphysics of Sound and Sign*. Leiden: Brill, 305–341.

———. 2008a. "Illumination, Imagination, Creativity: Rājaśekhara, Kuntaka, and Jagannātha on *Pratibhā*." *Journal of Indian Philosophy* 36: 481–505.

———. 2008b. "Une théorie hindoue de la conscience et de ses niveaux." In Association Franco-Israélienne pour la Récherche en Neurosciences, *Le cerveau: l'inconscient, le conscient et la créativité*. Paris: Le Manuscrit, 170–184.

———. 2010. "Notes on *Camatkāra*." In David Shulman, ed., *Language, Ritual and Poetics in Ancient India and Iran: Studies in Honor of Shaul Migron*. Jerusalem: Israel Academy of Sciences and Humanities, 257–284.

———. 2011. "Notes on *Bhāvikâlaṅkāra*." In P. Schalk and Ruth van Nahl, eds., *The Tamils: From the Past to the Present: Celebratory Volume in Honour of Professor Alvapillai Veluppillai*. Colombo: Kumaran Book House, 215–230.

———. Forthcoming a. "Waking Aja." In Yigal Bronner, David Shulman, and Gary Tubb, eds., *Sanskrit Kāvya: Innovations and Turning Points*.

———. Forthcoming b. "Murâri's Depths." In Yigal Bronner, David Shulman, and Gary Tubb, eds., *Sanskrit Kāvya: Innovations and Turning Points*.

Shulman, Eviatar. 2009. "Creative Ignorance: Nāgārjuna on the Ontological Significance of Consciousness." *Journal of the International Association of Buddhist Studies* 30, nos. 1–2: 139–173.

———. 2010. "Mindful Wisdom: The *Sati-paṭṭhāna-sutta* on Mindfulness, Memory and Liberation." *History of Religions* 49, no. 4: 393–420.

Śliwczyńska, Bożena. 2007. "The Ritual of Beginning: The *Puṟappāṭu* Segment of the Kūṭiyāṭṭam Theatre Tradition." In M. Nowakowska and J. Woźniak, eds., *Theatrum Mirabiliorum Indiae Orientalis* (A Volume to Celebrate the 70th Birthday of Professor Maria Krzysztof Byrski). Warsaw: Elipsa, 357–361.

Sreekantaiya, T. N. 1980. *Imagination in Indian Poetics and Other Literary Studies*. Mysore: Geetha Book House.

Srinivasachari, C. S. 1943. *A History of Gingee and Its Rulers*. Annamalainagar: Annamalai University.

Sundar Kali. 2006. "Masquerading Death: Aspects of Ritual Masking in the Community Theaters of Tanjavur." In D. Shulman and D. Thiagarajan, eds., *Masked Ritual and Performance in South India: Dance, Healing, and Possession*. Ann Arbor: Centers for South and Southeast Asian Studies, University of Michigan, 89–106.

Sviri, Sara. 2008. *Hasufim: Antologia*. Tel Aviv: University of Tel Aviv Press.

Symington, Neville. Forthcoming. *The Psychology of the Person.*

Tevet, Maya. *See* Dayan, Maya Tevet.

Tieken, Herman. 2010. "Aśvaghoṣa and the History of Allegorical Literature in India." In Eli Franco and Monika Zin, eds., *From Turfan to Ajanta: Festschrift for Dieter Schlingloff on the Occasion of His Eightieth Birthday.* Bhairahawa: Lumbini International Research Institute, 993–997.

Trawick, Margaret. 1990. *Notes on Love in a Tamil Family.* Berkeley: University of California Press.

Tripathi, Gayan Charan. 1978. "The Daily Pūjā Ceremony of the Jagannātha Temple and its Special Features." In Anncharlott Eschmann, Hermann Kulke, and Gaya Charan Tripathi, eds., *The Cult of Jagannath and the Regional Tradition of Orissa.* Delhi: Manohar, 285–308.

Tubb, Gary. Forthcoming a. "*Aupamyotprekṣā:* Poetic Fancy Based on Similitude."

———. Forthcoming b. "Theories of Semantics and the Analysis of Poetic Fancy in the Sanskrit Tradition."

———. Forthcoming c. "The *Laghu Yogavāsiṣṭha* and its Relation to the *Yogavāsiṣṭha.*

———. n.d. Notes on *Rasa-gaṅgādhara* 1.

Tull, Herman W. 1989. *The Vedic Origins of Karma: Cosmos as Man in Ancient Indian Myth and Ritual.* Albany: State University of New York Press.

Varadarajan, M. 1969. *The Treatment of Nature in Sangam Literature.* Tirunelveli: South Indian Saiva Siddhanta Works Publishing Company.

Vernant, Jean-Pierre. 1991. *Mortals and Immortals: Collected Essays.* Ed. Froma I. Zeitlin. Princeton: Princeton University Press.

Vimala, Katikaneni, and David Shulman. 2008. "The Girl in the Rock: A Telangana Tale and Vasiṣṭha's Retelling." *Indian Folklore Research Journal* 5: 1–26.

Walton, K. K. 1978. "Fearing Fictions." *Journal of Philosophy* 75, no. 1.

Weiskell, Thomas. 1976. *The Romantic Sublime: Studies in the Structure and Psychology of Transcendence.* Baltimore: Johns Hopkins University Press.

White, Alan R. 1964. *Attention.* Oxford: Basil Blackwell.

———. 1990. *The Language of Imagination.* London: Basil Blackwell.

Zimmer, Heinrich. 1948. *Hindu Medicine.* Baltimore: Johns Hopkins University Press.

Zimmerman, Francis. 1987. *The Jungle and the Aroma of Meats: An Ecological Theme in Hindu Medicine.* Berkeley: University of California Press.

Index